BRITISH GLASS

1800-1914

Frontispiece. The Flint Glass Makers' Friendly Society Certificate, presented to Edward Millinchamp on 5 November 1864. (See page 8 for key.)

BRITISH GLASS

1800-1914

by Charles R. Hajdamach

Antique Collectors' Club

British Library Cataloguing-in-Publication Data
A catalogue record for this book is available from the British Library

Printed in England on Consort Royal Satin from Donside Mills, Aberdeen,
by the Antique Collectors' Club Ltd., Woodbridge, Suffolk IP12 1DS

Antique Collectors' Club

The Antique Collectors' Club was formed in 1966 and now has a five figure membership spread throughout the world. It publishes the only independently run monthly antiques magazine, *Antique Collecting*, which caters for those collectors who are interested in widening their knowledge of antiques, both by greater awareness of quality and by discussion of the factors which influence the price that is likely to be asked. The Antique Collectors' Club pioneered the provision of information on prices for collectors and the magazine still leads in the provision of detailed articles on a variety of subjects.

It was in response to the enormous demand for information on 'what to pay' that the price guide series was introduced in 1968 with the first edition of *The Price Guide to Antique Furniture* (completely revised 1978 and 1989), a book which broke new ground by illustrating the more common types of antique furniture, the sort that collectors could buy in shops and at auctions rather than the rare museum pieces which had previously been used (and still to a large extent are used) to make up the limited amount of illustrations in books published by commercial publishers. Many other price guides have followed, all copiously illustrated, and greatly appreciated by collectors for the valuable information they contain, quite apart from prices. The Antique Collectors' Club also publishes other books on antiques (including horology and art), garden history and architecture, and a full book list is available.

Club membership, open to all collectors, costs little. Members receive free of charge *Antique Collecting*, the Club's magazine (published ten times a year), which contains well-illustrated articles dealing with the practical aspects of collecting not normally dealt with by magazines. Prices, features of value, investment potential, fakes and forgeries are all given prominence in the magazine.

Among other facilities available to members are private buying and selling facilities, the longest list of 'For Sales' of any antiques magazine, an annual ceramics conference and the opportunity to meet other collectors at their local antique collectors' clubs. There are over eighty in Britain and more than a dozen overseas. Members may also buy the Club's publications at special pre-publication prices.

As its motto implies, the Club is an organisation designed to help collectors get the most out of their hobby: it is informal and friendly and gives enormous enjoyment to all concerned.

For Collectors — By Collectors — About Collecting

The Antique Collectors' Club, 5 Church Street, Woodbridge, Suffolk IP12 1DS

For Jonathan and Richard

Contents

Key to Glass Maker's Emblem (see Frontispiece)

Nos. 1 & 5. Illustrations of Aesop's Fable of the Bundle of sticks, showing that Union is Strength.

2. Justice with the Sword & Scales.

3. The Goddess of Fame crowning the Designer (a) & the Workman (b) with a wreath of Laurel showing the Alliance of Art with Manufacture.

4. Truth with a Mirror & Olive branch, the Cornucopiae or Horn of plenty being at Her feet.

6. Exterior of a Glass-House & Premises.

7. Interior of a Glass-House showing the Furnace &c, and men at work in the Press, Bottle, General blowing and Table Glass Departments.

8. Interior of a Show-Room exhibiting the finished work.

9. The Rose, Shamrock and Thistle, emblematic of the three Countries, England, Ireland & Scotland.

10. The Oak, Laurel & Olive representing Strength, Honour and Peace.

The design of the certificate may date from September 1849 when the Society was reorganised on the lines of the 'New Model' unions. A black and white version presented to Richard Pugh in Ireland in 1855 credits Benjamin Richardson I as the designer of the certificate. The statement by John Northwood II in his book about his father that John Northwood I designed the emblem in about 1858 would seem to be erroneous. Height 22½ in. (57cm), width 19⅝ in. (50cm).

Acknowledgements

Whether glassmaker, dealer or collector, the people in the glass trade are some of the friendliest it has been my good fortune to meet. Many have made the writing of this book a much easier task to undertake and I express my heartfelt thanks to them.

To Michael Parkington, for unlimited use of his collection and not least for his taste, integrity and flair; his wife, Peggy Parkington; Graham and John Knowles of the Hulbert of Dudley Group of Companies for their generous sponsorship of Broadfield House Glass Museum; Jack and Penny Pacifico; Dill and Pat Hier; Stan Eveson, the former Technical Director at Thomas Webb and Sons who has unselfishly supplied important facts about the history of the company; C. David Smith, whose lifelong experience at Webb Corbett and love of the glass industry helped me to appreciate many of the subtle skills which otherwise would have gone unnoticed; Mr and Mrs Stuart Gittins for information on Joshua Hodgetts; Malcolm Andrews, John Davies and Chris Greenaway at the International Glass Centre, Brierley Hill; and the Leisure Services Committee of Dudley Metropolitan Borough Council for allowing me to write this book and to use the collections and resources at Broadfield House Glass Museum (see page 11). Glasses, pattern books and any items illustrated with no acknowledgement are in the collection of Broadfield House Glass Museum.

To Cyril Manley; Mrs M.Duckhouse; Neil Wilkin; Mrs Laura Seddon; Mrs Jane Roberts; Brian Murray, Cannon Hall Museum, Barnsley; Glennys Wild, Birmingham Museum and Art Gallery; Nick Dolan, Sunderland Museum and Art Gallery; Karen Walton, Bristol City Museum and Art Gallery; Mrs J. Perry; Mrs Jo Marshall of Phillips; Miss Rachel Russell of Christie's; Perran Wood of Sotheby's; Jane Holdsworth, formerly of Asprey's; John Smith of Mallett's; David Radmore for information on Dudley glassworks; Giles Haywood; Roger Dodsworth; Hilary Atkins; Eleanor Matchett; Mark Stubbs; Jeanette Hayhurst; Rosalie Davies; Sam Thompson of Royal Brierley Crystal; Herbert W. Woodward; Christine Golledge, Curator of the Stuart Crystal Museum; Ian Wolfenden; Katy Holford; Richard Dennis; Janet Flack of Essex for information on her ancestor Charles Aubin; Judy Rudoe at the British Museum for information about P.R.F. D'Humy; Brian Cook, Keeper at the British Museum for bringing the information about John Henning to my notice; H.J. Haden; Bob and Yvonne Wilkes; Tony and Bernice Waugh; Mr and Mrs Evans; Sister Ann Patricia for information about Daniel and Lionel Pearce; Miss D. Pearce; Jon One Enterprises; Bristol and Avon Family History Society; Michael and Roger Hickman; Mr S. Hill and Mrs J. Bailey; Mr and Mrs Southall; Mrs Hill and Mr M. Hill; Robin Hamlyn at the Tate Gallery for information about Thomas

9

Stothard; Peter Glews; Mrs Oakley, Manchester; Mrs Mary Boydell; Jennifer Opie at the Victoria and Albert Museum; Alan Leach; Ray Notley; Mr Goodchild, Archivist at Wakefield Libraries; Mr Craig, Amblecote; Mr and Mrs R. Worrall; Mr and Mrs Wolf, Droitwich; David and Rosemary Watts; Dr Harwood Stevenson; Mr and Mrs Malpass; Mrs Florence West; Mrs Betty Rhodes; Philip and Patricia Chapman; and to Horace for his birth certificate.

To Neil Jordan, the Patents Librarian at Manchester City Library for providing endless photocopies from the Patents Abridgments; Dudley Fowkes, the County Archivist at Staffordshire County Record Office for permission to reproduce the map of the Dial Glasshouse in Plate 3, ref. no. D648/3/2.

All items from the *Pottery Gazette and Glass Trades Review* are reproduced by kind permission of Tableware International, by courtesy of Antony Pike, the Director of International Trade Publications Ltd. responsible for publishing *Tableware International.*

In the United States and Canada: Mrs Juliette K. Rakow; Billy Hitt; Mrs Elizabeth Shute, Ottawa; Olive Jones, Parks Canada; Donald M. Smith; Jane Shadel Spillman at the Corning Museum of Glass; Janie Chester Young of the New Bedford Glass Museum which sadly has been forced to close; Dorothy-Lee Jones and Lauriston Ward Jnr. of the Jones Museum, Maine; Lloyd and Jane McDowell, Fremont, Ohio; Ruth Might, Fremont, Ohio; Frank Fenton of the Fenton Glass Company; Viking Glass Company, West Virginia; Louise Luther of Skinner Inc., Boston; Estelle F. Sinclair.

In Australia: the National Gallery of Victoria, Melbourne.

Posthumously to Colin Gill, Cyril Kimberley, Horace Richardson, Mr and Mrs J. Hickman, and to D.R. Guttery, who, I discovered by chance, wrote his book *From Broad Glass to Cut Crystal* opposite the house where most of the present book was completed.

For the photography I am indebted to Frank Power of Dudley for the majority of the black and white photographs and to Trevor Frost of Peter Moss Photography, Halesowen, who composed and took the wonderful colour photographs, with the exception of the Corning plate of the Northwood cameos. I am also grateful to Christine Hajdamach for black and white photography and to Alison Meads who provided the excellent line drawings.

To John Steel and the Antique Collectors' Club for commissioning the manuscript, for their patience and for the generosity of fifty colour plates and particularly to Primrose Elliott for her excellent work on editing the text. To my wife, Ann Smith-Hajdamach, for proof-reading the manuscript with exacting attention to detail.

To my mother for her encouragement, and to my father who did not live to see the publication of my efforts.

Finally I would like to acknowledge all the great glassmakers and decorators of the nineteenth century, some who are mentioned by name, others who remain anonymous and unknown. Their unique skills will live on through their glass.

Broadfield House Glass Museum

Throughout this book the reader will find references to Broadfield House Glass Museum and indeed the majority of glasses illustrated in the following pages are drawn from the permanent and loan collections at the museum. This short note on the history of Broadfield House and its collections explains the relevance of the museum to nineteenth century glass.

Although Broadfield House Glass Museum only opened in 1980 the idea for a glass museum in Stourbridge was already well established in 1892 when the following comment was written:

> It is a matter of much regret that, unlike Birmingham, Stourbridge should still be without an art gallery or Museum, in which might be shown specimens of the beautiful glass made in the town, and which have given the district a more than European reputation. Some of the showrooms at the manufactories are in themselves art museums, but in too many cases the treasures they contain are only seen by customers of the firms. What is sadly wanted is a public museum, in which may be exhibited to the public at large samples of the best qualities of glass which are from time to time produced at the works of the neighbourhood. Such a collection could not fail to be of advantage in many ways. It would tend to foster a love of the beautiful on the part of the residents, and would give strangers a better idea of the class of work made in the town, examples of which are too frequently only seen in the leading shops in London and other cities.

Sir Philip Cunliffe Owen, the Director of the South Kensington Museum, strongly advocated the setting up of a local museum when he attended the prize-giving at Stourbridge School of Art in 1885. Other commentators echoed the idea and suggested that the museum should be closely allied to the School of Art. But it was only some fifty years later, in the 1930s, that the first public collection was formed, not at Stourbridge, but at Brierley Hill, when a local man, W. Skidmore Westwood, gave a collection of two hundred glasses. Notable additions consisted of a gift of Stevens and Williams glass by the firm, and four impressive cameo vases by Lechevrel and Woodall given by members of the Richardson family.

In a mood of friendly rivalry to the Brierley Hill Glass Collection, Stourbridge decided to establish its own glass museum following an exhibition of local glass as part of the Festival of Great Britain celebrations. Two exceptional collections, from Benjamin Richardson III and John Northwood II, formed the basis of the museum and emphasised the local aspect which complemented the more international flavour of the neighbouring museum.

After local government reorganisation, plans were made in 1976 by Dudley Metropolitan Borough Council to amalgamate the two collections at Broadfield House, a fine early nineteenth century building in Kingswinford, near Stourbridge. The house and estate is first recorded on a map of the area in 1820 when it was lived in by Diana Briscoe, referred to in the local directories as a 'gentle-woman'. The house continued as a private residence until, in the middle years of the Second World War, it was purchased by Mr McMaster, a local industrialist, and eventually became a home, first for young mothers and babies and then senior citizens. It was vacated in the mid-1970s and in 1979 work began to transform it into a museum.

When Princess Michael of Kent opened Broadfield House Glass Museum on 2 April 1980 a hundred year old dream was realised. For the first time in the history of one of the most famous glass areas in the world, local residents and visitors could appreciate the full glories of Stourbridge glassmaking. Nowhere else were they able to admire such a wide selection of high quality nineteenth and twentieth century Stourbridge and English glass complemented by European and American examples.

Following the 1981 national award for 'Best Small Museum', a number of important gifts and loans consolidated the museum's standing. Generous sponsorship by Graham and John Knowles of The Hulbert Group of Companies in Dudley has enabled examples of Midlands glassware to be saved for the district. The outstanding private collection on loan from Michael Parkington has widened the scope of the collections even further and has been enhanced by gifts and loans, both large and small, from many individuals. A vigorous purchasing policy continues to expand the scope of the museum.

With a fine archive and library to complement the glass collections, a regular programme of temporary exhibitions and a working glass studio, Broadfield House Glass Museum is an internationally recognised centre for the study and enjoyment of glass, and a fitting memorial to the glassmakers of the Stourbridge district.

* * * * *

Broadfield House Glass Museum is situated close to the centre of Kingswinford on the A491 route between Stourbridge and Wolverhampton. The museum is open throughout the year from Tuesday to Sunday from 2 p.m. to 5 p.m., also on Saturday morning from 10 a.m. to 1 p.m. and Bank Holiday Mondays from 2 p.m. to 5 p.m. It is closed on Mondays and Christmas Day, Boxing Day and New Year's Day. Groups and parties can visit the museum outside normal opening hours by prior appointment. Further enquiries should be addressed to the Museum at Barnett Lane, Kingswinford, West Midlands DY6 9QA, or by telephoning 0384 273011 (facsimile number 0384 453576).

Introduction

The nineteenth century can justifiably be called the Golden Age of British Glass. In 1800 the application of steam power to glass cutting allowed England to become the foremost exponent of exquisite cut glass. At the end of the century the production of Art glass carried the germ of developments found in glass of the twentieth century. In the intervening one hundred years British glassmakers created a kaleidoscope of shapes, colours and decorative techniques which far outstripped any other country for the sheer genius of their technical virtuosity and aesthetic sensibility. No other nation could compete with the glassmakers of Stourbridge, of Birmingham, of Manchester, of Bristol, of London, of the North-East and of Scotland. Perhaps the only other period in which one could find cameo, rock crystal, engraving, cutting of every description, furnace applied decoration and moulded glass was during the Roman Empire.

But, whereas the Roman achievements were spread over four centuries, in England and especially in the Stourbridge district the flowering of those techniques came together during a mere one hundred years.

The multitude of contrasting styles and eclectic influences in British nineteenth century glass has often led to the accusation that the period is a jumble of unconnected threads. If that criticism needs any response perhaps we should remember Hogarth's dictum that 'exuberance is beauty' and revel in the sheer brilliance and expertise, the flair, the humour and the certainty of perfection to be found in the glass of the last century.

That glorious legacy, left to us by the finest glassmakers in the world, is celebrated in these pages.

Charles R. Hajdamach

Glasshouses

Despite working in factories and workshops which were badly lit and poorly ventilated, nineteenth century glassmakers and decorators produced exquisite objects ranging from the delicate and sophisticated to the brash and exuberant. The layout and operations of those glass factories varied enormously. Whereas the window, bottle and pressed glass factories operated large premises built specially to suit the needs of mass-production, the traditional handmade blown glass industry remained housed largely in the cones and adjacent outhouses built in the eighteenth century. The appearance of glass cones throughout the country, especially in the last quarter of the eighteenth century, created an industrial heritage which was to last for the next hundred years but which today has almost completely disappeared.

THE GLASS CONE

The English glass cone is unique. In the French encyclopedia by Diderot and D'Alembert (1751-71) the characteristic cone shape is described as 'Verrerie Angloise'. Developed from the need to produce a greater draught in order to

Plate 1. View of Wordsley in about 1900 showing glass cones. From a postcard in the collection of H.J. Haden.

Plate 2. The Red House glass cone in 1902, now the site of Stuart Crystal. Photograph courtesy Stuart Crystal.

maximise the heat from the coal which was introduced as a fuel from 1615, the cones, some standing as high as 150ft. (45.75m), became an impressive sight in glassmaking areas. Grouped together as at Wordsley in the West Midlands (Plate 1), or set singly in the landscape, the glass cone dominated every other building whether mill or church or castle ruins. Some continued to operate without a break for 150 years. The Red House cone, for example, still standing on the site of the modern Stuart Crystal works in Wordsley, was built to a height of 100ft. (30.5m) some time in the late 1780s and was still in operation in 1939 (Plate 2).

Although the cone was the focal point of the site, the layout of the ancillary

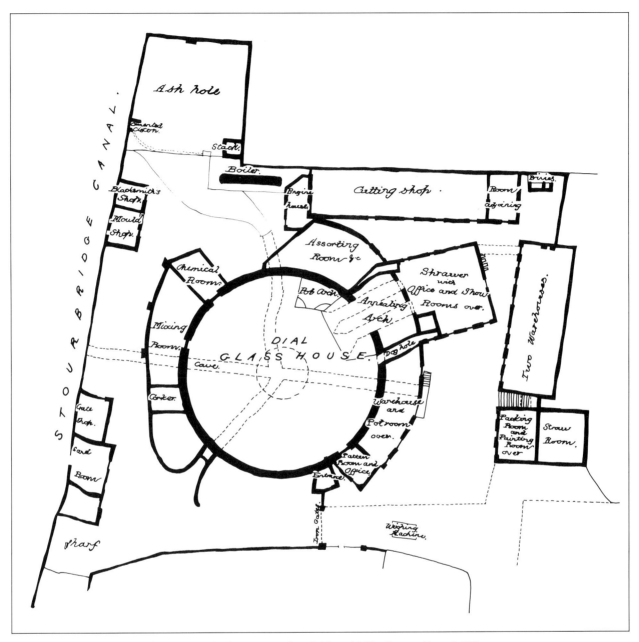

Plate 3. Plan of the Dial Glasshouse, Audnam, near Stourbridge, 1866. County Record Office, Stafford.

services of mixing rooms, mould stores, cutting shops, packing rooms, warehouses and offices was dependent on a number of factors ranging from initial investment to the size of the site itself. A plan of the Dial Glasshouse, drawn up in 1866, shows a single cone with virtually all the extra services butted on to the cone (Plate 3). The plan clearly shows the four passages or air tunnels under the cone, described as 'caves', which gave the draught through the furnace. Later in the century they were used to bring in coal to the base of the furnace. A plan of the larger Wordsley glassworks run by the Richardson family shows a single cone adjacent to a single storey glasshouse but with larger facilities for workshops and

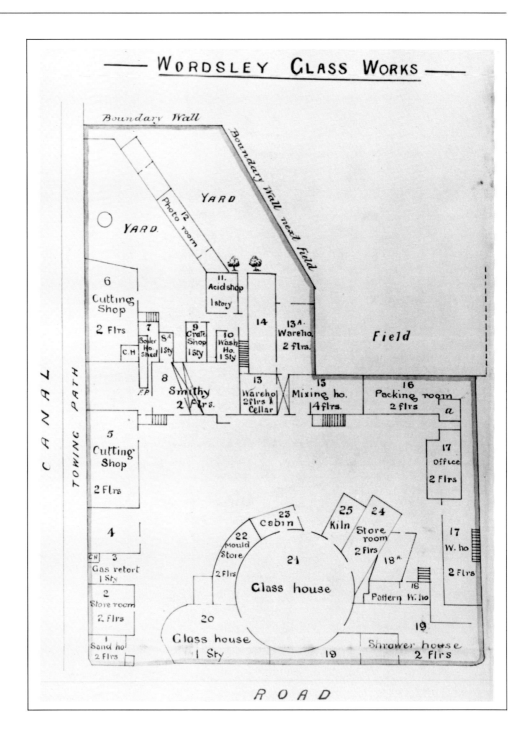

Plate 4. Plan of the Richardson glassworks, 1865-71.

warehouses situated around the main courtyard (Plate 4). Built in the 1820s, the Wordsley site, like its earlier neighbour the Dial, capitalised on the new canal system which allowed coal and raw materials to be shipped into the very heart of the factory and finished products to be dispatched equally quickly to the various markets. An engraving from a Richardson letterhead of 1900 shows the same site with the addition of a second chimney and demonstrates the benefits of a corner site between road and canal (Plate 5). The engraving suffers from the

Colour Plate 1. Pot changing at Stuart Crystal on a Friday afternoon, October 1984. The men involved in the pot changing are usually the gaffers of their particular chairs and will have completed a full day's work of skilled glassmaking before embarking on the pot change in the afternoon. After observing this operation, which is a combination of sheer strength and delicate manoeuvring, one comes away with the greatest admiration for the skill, dedication, and great sense of humour of these glassmakers. The operation no longer takes place at the factory due to the removal of the two pot furnaces to make room for the installation of a continuous feed tank furnace, the first of its kind in the crystal glass industry in this country.

characteristic nineteenth century artistic licence which gives the false impression of a huge factory complex but the site and some of the buildings can still be identified today, across the canal from the Stuart Crystal works. A unique nineteenth century view of a Stourbridge factory at work is depicted in a scene of the Richardson interior said to have been painted by Emily Hodgetts during the 1830s (Plate 6). The furnace is unusual with its large metal covers hoisted during working hours to allow access to the pots and lowered at the end of the shift to conserve the heat inside the furnace. The stoke hole for the furnace can be seen to the left of centre. Also unusual are the strange hats worn by the glassmakers, a detail not illustrated or recorded elsewhere. Less unusual is the assistant on the left carrying in two foaming tankards of beer. Today the workmen have to make do with cold tea drunk from milk bottles.

Plate 5. View of the Richardson glassworks, taken from a company letterhead of about 1900.

Plate 6. Interior of the Richardson glasshouse, about 1830-40, said to have been painted by Emily Hodgetts, a member of the Richardson family. Oil on panel, 12in. x 19½in. (30.3cm x 49.5cm).

Plate 7. The Coalbournhill Glassworks, about 1844. Now the main office of Webb Corbett, part of the Royal Doulton group, the building to the left known as Harlestones can still be seen on the main Stourbridge to Kingswinford road.

Plate 8. Interior of the London glassworks of Apsley Pellatt. Engraving, 4½in. x 6in. (10.7cm x 15cm), inscribed 'For Brayley's History of Surrey, Falcon Glasshouse, Holland Street, Blackfriars. Mr. Apsley Pellatt Proprietor By whom this Plate was presented. Published by & for R.B. Ede May 1842'.

THE END OF THE GLASS CONE

By the end of the eighteenth century there was a move towards glasshouses with two or more furnaces when glasshouse owners realised the restrictions of a single furnace. Larger working areas and more furnaces allowed greater production and, more importantly, a second furnace would guarantee that orders could be met if one furnace had to be temporarily extinguished. The new glasshouses consisted of circular or rectangular buildings with a large central chimney. A view of the Coalbournhill Glassworks of about 1844 shows the new type adjacent to the older cone (Plate 7). The improved arrangement inside can be seen clearly in an engraving of about 1842 of the Falcon Glasshouse in London, run by Apsley Pellatt, one of the pioneers of glass techniques and processes in the nineteenth century (Plate 8). Two large furnaces and a smaller single pot furnace or glory-hole are connected by flues to the chimney stack. Another later variation was to place the furnace and pots in the base of the chimney stack itself. The Harbridge Crystal works in Stourbridge used this arrangement in the 1920s and 1930s, as did some of the smaller American pressed glass companies. The set-up can still be seen today at the reconstructed Wheaton glassworks in Wheaton Village, New Jersey.

At the other end of the scale from the single or double furnace factories were the large industrial complexes of the bottle and window glass companies. The sites of the Chance Brothers glassworks in Birmingham and the Hartley glassworks in Sunderland were virtually self-contained communities with housing and other facilities for the workers provided adjacent to the main works. Consequently the end of the nineteenth century saw the majority of glasshouses become indistinguishable from the general mass of factory buildings. Although a few glass cones continued in use into the twentieth century most fell into disrepair and were demolished or collapsed under their own weight.

Today only four glass cones survive. They stand at Alloa in Scotland on the site of United Glass, at Lemington near Newcastle upon Tyne as part of Glass Tubes, at Wordsley near Stourbridge on the Stuart Crystal site, and, the oldest surviving cone, built about 1740 and now an empty shell surrounded by incongruous flower beds, at Catcliffe near Sheffield. A handful of others have been reduced in size, sometimes roofed over and used as factory space or, in one instance at Bristol, as a restaurant.

POTS AND POT MAKERS

The pot maker was, and still is, the unsung hero of the glassworks. His skills were legendary but were kept a closely guarded secret. Stories abound in the glassmaking districts of pot makers downing their tools and enjoying a pipe of tobacco on the appearance of visitors to the pot shop. Work did not begin again until the 'stranger' left.

The success of the glasshouse depended entirely on the pot maker's ability to build pots which would withstand many weeks or months of constant high temperatures and re-filling with the raw materials. If the pot had imperfections within its internal structure these would quickly show up as cracks once the pot was set inside the furnace and the molten contents, representing a substantial financial investment, would escape and run out on to the floor of the furnace. Likewise, if the pots were made too small this would result in the glass being worked out before the end of the working day resulting in less glass being made, smaller wages for the glassmakers and less profit for the owner.

A writer in the *Pottery Gazette and Glass Trades Review* (hereafter referred to as the *Pottery Gazette*) in August 1898 described the crucial part played by the pot maker:

Most of the pots used in the English glasshouse are made of the best Stourbridge fireclay, carefully ground and mixed with a certain quantity of old broken pots or potsherds, as they are called, which are also ground up, and when mixed with the new clay, strengthen it very considerably, so that when the pots are made they are not liable to crack when subjected to great heat. As the largest of these pots have to hold from 15 to 18cwt. [762-914kg] of metal, my readers will see the importance of having them strong enough to bear this heavy pressure, as should one of the large pots happen to crack whilst in the furnace and filled with metal, it might mean a considerable loss to the glass manufacturer, especially if it has gone so far that it cannot be repaired immediately; for not only does he run the risk of losing his metal by its running into the furnace, but the cost of the pot also, which, with the expenses incurred of getting it ready and placing it in the furnace amounts to £10 or more, not reckoning for any inconvenience to which he might be put by not being able to execute his orders according to promise.

The pot shop consisted of mixing rooms, storage areas for the prepared clay and two or three main rooms for making the pots. A typical scene inside a pot shop was recorded at the turn of the century at Thomas Barron's glass bottle works at Mexborough in South Yorkshire (Plate 9). It portrays every stage of pot making from the rolls of clay on the bench to the completed pots at the back of the room. Once the fireclay was mixed with water and trodden with bare feet to remove any air bubbles it was formed into sausage shaped lumps by the

Plate 9. The pot shop at Thomas Barron's bottle works, Mexborough, South Yorkshire. Original in collection of Wakefield Libraries.

apprentice in readiness for the pot maker. The base of the pot was usually formed in a circular tray and tipped out on to the wooden slab. From here the pot maker gradually built up the 3in. (7.5cm) thick wall of the pot using the pottery coiling method. After raising the wall by two or three coils he would move on to the next pot, allowing the previous pot to rest and settle under strips of wet sacking. It was normal to work as many as twenty-four pots in sequence. Some pot makers would place a loose fitting, circular, fireclay gathering ring inside the pot before it was finished otherwise the ring would not fit through the normal arch opening. Once the pot was filled and the glass melted, the ring would float on the surface of the glass and the glassmaker would take his gather from inside the ring where the best quality glass was available. Today the fireclay ring is made in two semi-circular parts fitted together with jigsaw style lugs and placed inside the pot once the glass is molten. An awkward part of the making involved finishing the dome of the pot without it collapsing because at this stage there was no access to the inside. One trick of the trade was to blow air into the interior through a straw or pipe, thereby increasing the air pressure just enough to assist in holding up the dome. Once the dome of the pot was completed the pot maker worked on the characteristic arch shape opening using a wooden former which was attached to the side of the pot. After building up the arch the hole was cut giving access once again to the interior of the pot. All that remained to be done was to stamp the pot maker's name on to the bottom ledge plus a date and reference number.

After the pots were finished they remained in the room in which they were made to dry out gradually. In a modern pot shop the drying process will take from eight to ten weeks with humidity levels reaching 80%. While the pots were drying out the pot maker would move to the next work-room to begin the same process again.

Today, at Stuart Crystal, one of the last Stourbridge firms to make glasshouse pots, the pot maker uses clay from Germany. Other companies in the district buy their pots which are made from fireclay deposits in Yorkshire. The re-cycling of a certain proportion of ground-up old pots is no longer carried out. The use of Stourbridge fireclay, one of the reasons why the industry settled in the area, was discontinued after the Second World War.

SETTING THE POTS

Before the finished pot could be used inside the furnace it had to be kept inside a pot arch or annealing oven to bring it up to the temperature of the main furnace. At this stage the task of pot changing or pot setting could begin. Pot changing was always carried out on Friday afternoons to cause the least possible disruption and to allow a continuous supply of molten glass for the glass blowers. At the Stuart Crystal factory, before the introduction of a continuous feed tank furnace which replaced the traditional pot furnace, the team of men setting the pots consisted of the gaffers of their particular chairs who had completed a full day of glassmaking before embarking on the pot setting. During the operation the team was subjected to temperatures reaching as high as 1,000° Centigrade

(2,012°Fahrenheit). Pot changing is one of the most spectacular and awe-inspiring sights within a glassworks (Colour Plate 1). Something of that excitement was captured by the author of *The Manufacture of Glass* in 1845.

The reader will suppose that 'setting a new pot' is one of the most tremendous operations of the glasshouse. Through the kindness of Mr. Pellatt the writer was present during one of these operations. The first part of the process was to get out the old pot, which had done duty for seven months, but was now rendered worthless from having 'sprung a leak'... the wall of one of the arches was to be taken down, exposing the men to the naked heat of a huge furnace. The men were about 24 in number, two or three of whom worked at a time, and were frequently relieved. The difficulty of getting out the old pot was very great: it was in fact cemented to the floor by the glass which escaped from the crack. The men therefore had to work at the bottom of the crucible with huge crow-bars, resting upon a little roller, supported upon an iron frame, placed at the mouth of the opening. The blows of the crow-bars brought away large pieces of glass, soiled and blackened by the ashes of the furnace, fire bricks, masses of clay, and sometimes pieces of the pot itself. The crow bar was held by two or three men, who gave a few blows, and then retreated from the fierce heat, to be succeeded by two or three others, who performed their minute's work, and retreated to the shelter furnished by the massive wall of the furnace.

At length the pot being loosened all round...a low iron truck on two wheels was thrust under it; and thus it was withdrawn and thrown aside at some distance. The floods of heat which now radiated from the opening were terrible...there was no shield — no defence. And here was, perhaps, the most arduous part of the operation; the floor of the furnace had to be prepared to receive the new pot: for this purpose the most fire-proof workman was selected; he was furnished with a kind of shovel, with a handle fourteen or fifteen feet long [4.5m], resting on the roller. A number of men stood by, each holding a large kneaded piece of fire-clay — one of them, as he was directed, went up to the mouth of the opening, and placing his piece of clay on the shovel, quickly retreated. The clay was then deposited on the bed of the furnace, and worked quickly with the spade. [In a modern factory the clay has been replaced by a few shovels of sand to create a flat and level bed for the pot.]

Another party of men then went with the iron truck to the annealing oven; its folding doors being thrown open, revealed the pots, now mounted at about a yard from the floor, glowing at a bright red heat. To thrust in the truck under one of them and bring it out, was the work of a moment; it was quickly wheeled to the furnace; deposited in its place, and being held by crow-bars, the truck was drawn out from under it; the whole being accomplished with a dexterous celerity which pleased and satisfied the onlooker.

The next part of the operation was to close up the opening, for which purpose two heated masks of fire-clay were brought on shovels; these rose from the ground about a yard high; upon them were placed bricks and fire-clay. The mouth of the pot being closed with a temporary screen of clay, the rest of the opening was closed up with great despatch by a number of men, each bearing a portion of clay or a brick, which he knew precisely where to deposit.

The final job of the pot setting was to give the newly bricked wall of the furnace

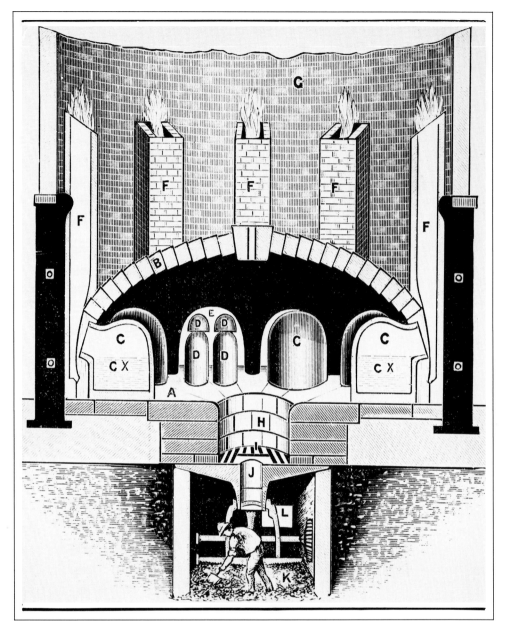

Plate 10. Cross-section of a ten-pot furnace. From the Pottery Gazette, *August 1898.*

a layer of fireclay to cover any small gaps and holes. By Saturday morning this had settled and any cracks that had appeared were covered over with more fireclay. Following a final check on Sunday morning the pot was 'charged' or filled with the raw ingredients which would melt and be ready for working on Monday or Tuesday.

THE FURNACE

A view of a cross-section of a ten-pot furnace was illustrated in the *Pottery Gazette* of August 1898 (Plate 10). The key describes the setting in detail:

A. The siege on which the pots rest inside the furnace; some of the large firebricks with which this is built weigh several hundredweight each.
B. The crown or dome of the furnace.
C. The large round pots which hold the crystal glass.
Cx. The metal in the pot.
D. The oval pots and dandies which hold the coloured metals. It will be noticed that the sizes of these pots are so arranged that when two ovals are placed side by side, with a dandy on top of each, the four take up the same amount of room in the arch under which they are placed as one of the large round pots.
E. The arches round the furnace, under each of which a pot is placed, and when in position the front of the arch is built up with firebricks, leaving only the mouth of the pot exposed, so that the men can gather out the metal as required.
F. The flues.
G. The chimney or stack up which the smoke from the furnace passes.
H. The eye or firehole which holds the fuel.
I. The bars forming the grate at the bottom of the firehole through which the ashes and cinders fall (and sometimes the molten glass when a pot breaks). It is a fine sight (although not very profitable to the manufacturer) when a pot does happen to break, to see the shower of molten glass running out of the furnace through the bars into the cave below, and vividly calls to mind the showers of burning lava during a volcanic eruption.
J. A patent feeder in the centre of the grate, by which the furnace is fed with fuel pushed up from underneath by a hopper worked by machinery. Some of the old furnaces in work at the present time which have not the patent feeder, are fed from the inside of the glasshouse, the fuel being pushed down a narrow tunnel into the firehole. [The latter can be seen in Plate 6, the interior of the Richardson glasshouse.]
K. The cave, or passage, which runs underneath the furnace, and is connected with the open-air at each end entrance, which creates an underdraught, and supplies the necessary amount of oxygen for the combustion of the fuel.
    The size of a ten-pot furnace is 19 feet [5.79m] outside diameter of siege, 4 feet 6 inches [1.37m] in height from the siege to the inside centre of dome, and the arches under which the pots rest are 3 feet 1 inch wide by 3 feet 3½ inches high [.94 by 1m].
L. The entrance to the cave.

The most fascinating detail of the illustration is the figure, known as the teazer, loading the coal in the tunnel under the furnace. The furnaces were attended by two sets of teazers, with two men in each set. One set relieved the other every eight or twelve hours around the clock. Their job was to wheel out the ashes and work the patent feeder ensuring that the furnace was well supplied with coal. The teazer was also probably responsible for maintaining the fire at the head of the annealing tunnel, known as the lehr. The finished glassware was placed on to steel pans or trays at the beginning of the lehr where the heat was greatest. As

Plate 11. The mouth of the annealing lehr at Stuart's in 1902. Photograph courtesy Stuart Crystal.

it passed down the arched chamber it gradually cooled until it arrived at the shrawer or discharge end where the glass was checked for cracks or damage and washed to remove the soot and grime picked up inside the lehr. A photograph taken inside the Stuart cone shows the piles of coal stacked around the entrance to the lehr (Plate 11).

WORKING CONDITIONS, HOURS, WAGES AND BOY LABOUR

Throughout the nineteenth century the scene inside the Richardson factory (Plate 6) could have been found in every glassworks in the country where hand-blown glass was made. When the *Gentleman's Journal* featured the Stuart factory in 1902 the glassmakers were still working directly in front of the furnaces inside the glass cone, surrounded by soot and grime (Plates 12 and 13). Glassmakers in the flint glass trade worked in teams of four known as a 'chair', consisting of the workman or gaffer, the servitor, the footmaker and the taker-in. The workman performed all the most difficult work while the servitor gathered the glass and blew the initial shape. The footmaker brought extra gathers for the workman to shape the stem and feet. The taker-in, usually a young boy, would place the finished article into the annealing oven. Each chair would specialise in one type of article and would normally work from two pots in the furnace.

Glassmaking started on a Monday or Tuesday morning and the glassmakers then worked six hours on and six hours off throughout the day and night until

Plate 12. Glassmaking at Stuart and Sons inside the Red House cone, 1902. Photograph courtesy Stuart Crystal.

Plate 13. Glassmaker at Stuart and Sons, 1902. Photograph courtesy Stuart Crystal.

Thursday night or Friday morning when all the glass was worked out of the pots. If a glassmaker did not turn up for work at the changeover period one of his workmates would have to continue into the next shift. Variations would occur depending on the employer or on special circumstances in the glasshouse when the shift could be of nine hours in the day and three at night, or eight and four, or seven and five.

Wages were calculated in a complex manner whereby the number of items made on piece-work were transferred into a time wage. A six hour shift was called a 'turn' and consisted of two 'moves' with a nominal week made of up eleven moves. The employers and the union would agree on a figure for the amount of glass to be produced per move, depending on size and difficulty of manufacture. Any items over the agreed figure were paid as over-work although they were made in the normal working time and not in the accepted sense of overtime in other trades. One example, taken from the wages books at Stevens and Williams in 1861, shows the idea in practice:

Number produced	Moves	Nominal weekly wages, 11 moves	Over-work per move	Wages paid
1,560	15½ (i.e. 100 per move)	40s.	3s.6d.	55s.9d.

A weekly wage depended on a variety of circumstances and therefore it is impossible to give a general figure for all glassmakers. However, to give some idea of earnings, in 1848 a blower received 25s. a week upwards, rising in 1858 to 56s. a week, although this dropped in 1866 to 48s.6d. Gatherers earned on average 20s. a week in 1848 rising to 29s. a week by 1858. Children and young persons earned from 3s. per week up to a maximum of 10s. with the average being in the region of 4s. to 5s.

The question of boy labour in the glassworks was discussed and argued about throughout the century. The *Enquiry into the Employment of Children* veered towards the side of the glasshouse owners when it published its findings in 1843:

> The nature of the employment of boys in glass-making is only to attend at the side or behind the chairs of the men who are seated at work in front of the furnaces. The endurance of the heat does not appear to injure the health of the boys, the ventilations being so well and amply provided. Viewing this circumstance, in addition to those of the regular relays of hands, to the night-set alternating with the day-set, to the week's work being commonly limited to four days, and to the fact of scarcely any children ever being employed at glass-making until they are twelve years of age, I venture to submit that, in the event of legislative interference on the employment of children and young persons, these circumstances should all receive a due consideration.

In reality the full range of jobs undertaken by the boys included cleaning the blowing-irons, holding moulds for the glassmaker to blow into, carrying finished glass into the annealing ovens, occasionally gathering molten glass from the pots and generally waiting on the glassmakers in their particular team. Faced with intransigent opposition from the establishment little progress was made by the campaigners until the 1890s when the pages of the *Pottery Gazette* were filled with points for and against. In 1895 the Government set the minimum age for night employment of boys at fourteen years old, but the issue was raised once more in the early part of the twentieth century when glasshouse owners yet again forecast bankruptcy and closure, raising of prices, lessening of efficiency and reduction in the quality of the glass if the minimum age was to be raised to fifteen or sixteen.

The incidence of accidents and fatalities was low considering the constant working with furnaces, hot glass, heavy machinery and noxious materials such as red lead and putty powder. Reports of accidents tended to concentrate on the more tragic events. The steam-powered machinery for driving the cutting wheels proved to be one of the most dangerous pieces of equipment as men and boys could be caught in the straps which connected the main shaft to the benches. Glasshouse chimneys were another potential source of danger. In 1850, for example, two glass cutters were killed when a 50ft. (15.25m) chimney collapsed on to the cutting shop at the Durham works of Joseph Price. One particularly horrifying accident happened in 1893 at the glass bottle works of Messrs Wright and Co. in Brierley Hill. Three men had gone underneath the large Siemens tank furnace to investigate a small leakage of glass when one of the fireclay slabs forming the base of the tank collapsed into the tunnel, releasing a flood of molten glass which engulfed two of the men. One accident on 12 September 1894 occurred at the Richardson glassworks when two men were severely burnt because one of their workmates dipped a wet ladle into molten glass which resulted in hot glass flying in all directions. Accidents with molten glass were less common than one might have expected for, just as today, the glassblowers had a sixth sense of the movements and positions of their team-mates so that injuries through burns were kept to a minimum. Less easily documented and therefore more easily ignored were the cumulative effects of inhalation of the harmful chemicals employed in certain parts of the industry. Red lead in the mixing room prior to filling the pots, fumes from the warm hydrofluoric acid during the etching process and the lead-based putty powder used for polishing cut glass were some of the more noxious hazards in a glass factory.

The Glassmaker's Tools

The equipment and tools of the glassmaker have remained unaltered, except for the occasional refinement, for centuries. The main glassmaking tools, excluding the blowing-iron and pontil rod, illustrated in the *Pottery Gazette* in August 1899 (Plate 14), consisted of:

1. Steel scissors for cutting hot glass.
2. Parrot-nose shears for cutting a rod of glass without destroying its roundness.

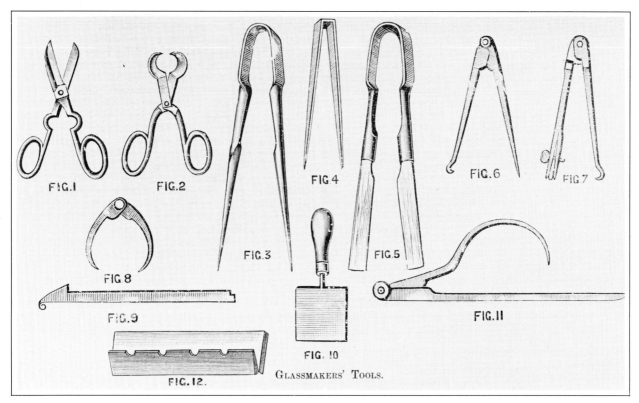

GLASSMAKERS' TOOLS.

Plate 14. Glassmakers' tools. From Pottery Gazette, *August 1899.*

3. Pucellas, the principal tools of the glassmaker. The prongs have a certain amount of spring allowing a wide variety of operations.
4. Steel pincers for taking hold of pieces of hot glass which may have to be attached to the body of an article, for example handles of jugs.
5. Wooden tools resembling pucellas, but fitted with wooden prongs, used for shaping hollow glasses and kept wet to reduce the amount of burning on contact with the hot glass.
6. Compasses for measuring length or depth (i.e. the bowl of a wineglass), the small hook on one end being to hook on the rim and prevent slipping.
7. Compasses with chalk at one end to mark hot glass, i.e. a line round the top of the glass to guide the shearing-off or marking position of lip or handle.
8. Callipers for measuring diameter or thickness.
9. The measure stick, 12in. (30.5cm) steel, marked with chalk to check size of article.
10. Palette for flattening glass.
11. Iron compasses for measuring the depth of large bowls.
12. Footboards for forming the feet of wineglasses etc. formed of two strips of wood hinged with leather.

The footboard was a nineteenth century addition to the range of tools. By squeezing the molten glass a smooth, thin and regular foot was produced without the striations and ridges of eighteenth century feet produced with the pucellas.

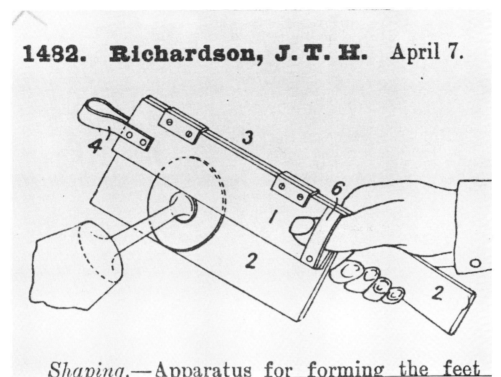

1482. Richardson, J. T. H. April 7.

Shaping.—Apparatus for forming the feet

Plate 15. Patent design for footboard by J.T.H. Richardson, 1876.

In April 1876 J.T.H. Richardson of the Tutbury Glassworks patented a handled and springed footboard to allow greater control (Plate 15). The summary of the patent described the board as 'Apparatus for forming the feet of wineglasses, goblets, and other similar articles, is composed of two wood, metal, etc. boards or slabs, 1,2 hinged together at 3 and held apart by a spring 4. The board 2 is provided with a handle which is held, as shown, the front and narrower board 1 having a loop 6 engaged by the thumb for manipulating it.'

Well-made glass tools were prized possessions and would be handed down from father to son or passed between skilled glassmakers. One of the famous Victorian manufacturers of glassmakers' tools was Joseph Rann of Woodside, near Dudley in the West Midlands. In 1905 the *Black Country and its Industries* described him as:

> one of our local manufacturers whose name is familiar throughout the world where glass-making is known as an industry. This firm has been established very long ago and is one of the very few in this country who apply themselves exclusively to this special branch of toolmaking. It will be readily understood by our readers that Mr. Rann must not only have studied closely the way to produce these tools, but must also have a comprehensive knowledge of the work for which they are required, which makes the work much more complicated. At his works at Woodside he manufactures all the different kinds of moulders' and glassblowers' tools, crate-bits etc., all of the finest quality and properly finished. This maker's goods are also noted for their workmanship and design.

One pair of Rann's shears was still in use by the late Colin Gill in the early 1980s, testifying to 'their workmanship and design'. The current expert for glass tools is Ivan Smith of Cutnall Green, Hereford, who continues the great tradition set by the Rann family.

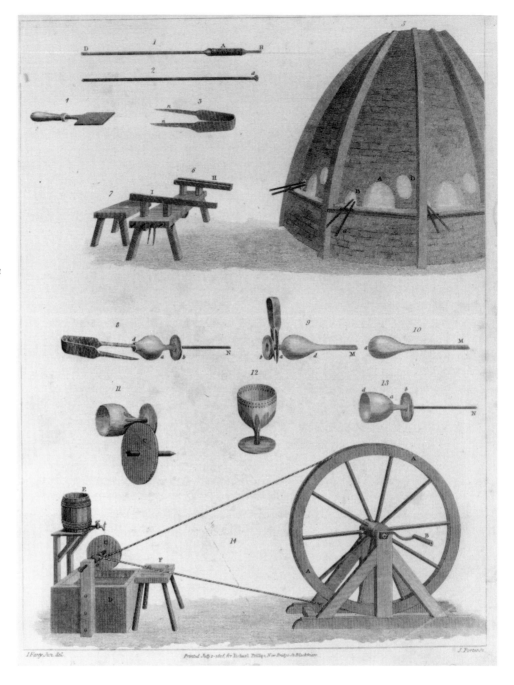

Plate 16. Print of 1806 showing a glassmaker's chair, stages in blowing a goblet, and a hand powered cutting wheel. The sequence of blowing and cutting the goblet is wrongly numbered; the correct order is 10, 9, 8, 13, 11 and 12.

GLASSBLOWING AND THE PONTIL MARK

All glass made on the blowing-iron follows the same basic process. The sequence of making a wineglass, for example, illustrated in a print of 1806 (Plate 16), began with the hot gather of molten glass picked up on the tip of the blowing-iron, rolled on the marver and blown into a bubble. When the shape of the bowl was formed another gather of glass was brought and applied to the base of the bowl and shaped into the stem. Another gather was cast on to the end of the newly made stem (hence the name cast foot) and squeezed into the circular shape of the foot using the footboards. Blown feet required a bubble to be blown and attached

Plate 17. Two gadgets, one holding a wineglass which bears the ghost impression of the jaws.

to the base of the stem, cracked off the blowing-iron and opened out with the pincers to form the foot. If a folded foot was required it was a simple matter to turn over the rim either upwards or under. The wineglass was then transferred on to a solid iron, known as the pontil rod, using a small gather of molten glass on the tip to attach the pontil rod to the foot. The glass was then cracked off the blowing-iron and the rim of the glass was re-heated, sheared and given its final shape. Any other features such as handles or pouring lips for jugs, bowls and decanters were added at this point. The glass was broken off the pontil rod by sawing a slight nick into the join, dribbling cold water on to the crack and knocking it off with a sharp tap to the pontil rod. Placed into the annealing lehr, the glass cooled gradually, usually overnight, until it was ready the next day for any further decoration, i.e. cutting, enamelling or engraving. The same process, including the use of the pontil rod, can still be seen in many glass factories ranging from the major cut glass companies to the smaller studio glassworks. The appearance of a pontil mark or scar should therefore not be taken as a sign of age. Likewise the absence of a pontil mark does not mean that the piece is modern. Much Roman glass, for example, bears no evidence of a pontil.

   In the nineteenth century a piece of equipment known as the gadget was introduced to replace the pontil rod (Plate 17). The gadget consisted of a hollow tube containing a spring-loaded rod leading to a set of jaws which opened when the plunger was operated. The foot of the hot wineglass was slid into the jaws, the spring was released and the foot was clamped firmly while the rim of the glass

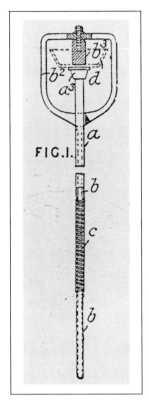

FIG.1.

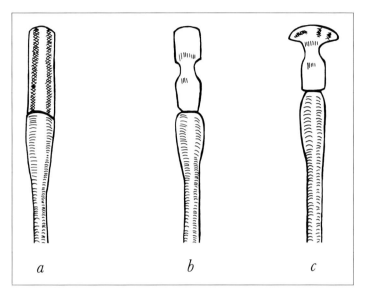

Plate 19. Stages in making a decanter stopper.

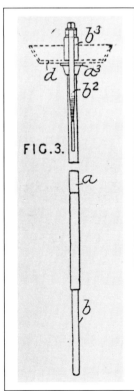

FIG.3.

Plate 18. Patent design for a gadget by Edward Moore, 1898.

was finished. The metal jaws were covered with a binding of asbestos string but the pressure would still leave a ghost impression on the top surface of the foot. The mark left on the underside would resemble a letter 'T' or 'Y'. Other items such as bowls would be held from the inside on gadgets with different shaped jaws or arms (Plate 17, left).

Although it has been suggested by Harold Newman in his *Illustrated Dictionary of Glass* that the gadget was introduced some time between 1760 and 1800, the glasses which have been seen with the ghost impression on their feet have all dated from the mid-nineteenth century onwards. With the large number of registered patents for equipment from the 1860s onwards it may be that the gadget was introduced during this period. In February 1898 Edward Moore patented a variation on the gadget (Plate 18). It consisted of:

> a spring punty for use in 'sticking up' articles of glass without a central stem or foot, such as dishes, tumblers, etc. The punty rod b passes through a tube a and carries at its end a stirrup-shaped frame b2 carrying a stud b3. The dish etc. d is gripped between the stud b3 and the base plate a3 which forms the end of the tube a, by the tension of the spring c, which urges the punty rod downwards within the tube. To release the finished article the projecting end of the punty rod has only to be pressed upon the ground.

This variation of the gadget may have been used either for fire polishing pressed glass or altering the shape of the article. The central stud inside the glass would have obstructed other work such as shearing the rim.

STOPPERS AND STOPPERING

A little appreciated aspect of the glasshouse was the making and fitting of stoppers into decanters. To make a stopper a gather of glass was picked up on the iron and marvered into shape (Plate 19a). The neck was cut in with the pincers, as was the peg which fitted into the decanter (Plate 19b). The head of the stopper was the last part to be shaped. For a mushroom stopper (Plate 19c) the workman used the outer end of his pincers while turning the iron on the arms of the chair. All that remained was to crack the stopper off the blowing-iron and place it in the annealing oven. Hollow stoppers were blown first to the required shape, the glass squeezed together to seal the bubble, cut in to form the peg and cracked off the iron.

The process of stoppering the decanter was a distinct, separate trade performed by the stopperer who worked at his lathe, usually in the cutting shop where the decanters and stoppers could be passed directly to him after they had been decorated. The job was performed in two stages: firstly the inside of the neck was ground and then the stopper was ground to match the neck.

The inside of the neck needed to be perfectly round in order to take the stopper and ensure an exact fit. To do the grinding, the stopperer used a wooden plug, about 6in. (15.25cm) long, fixed into the stoppering lathe and fitted with a tapered tin ferrule which corresponded to the required diameter of the neck. A mixture of water and emery powder was dribbled on to the revolving plug as the stopperer held the decanter with the inside of the neck pressing against the plug until it was ground to the correct size.

The next stage was to grind the peg of the stopper to match the neck. The pegs were made slightly thicker than required to allow the stopperer a little lee-way in the fitting stages. On a lathe similar to those used by the glasscutters the stopperer ground the peg to a size just a little thicker than would allow it to fit properly. The final stage was to grind the stopper directly into the neck. The head of the stopper was fixed into a wooden chuck and fixed into the same lathe which had held the wooden plug. The stopper spun in the lathe and the water and emery mixture was used again as the grinding agent while the decanter was pressed against the peg. The glass to glass grinding ensured an absolutely perfect fit.

At this point the stopperer had two choices for the final finish of the stopper, depending on the price of the article. On cheaper items the neck and the stopper were left rough, in which case the only job remaining was to smooth the pontil mark left on the end of the peg. In the best work the neck and stopper were 'polished bright'. The peg was polished in the same way as cut glass, i.e. firstly on a wood wheel with pumice and water and finally on a brush wheel with putty powder. The inside of the neck was polished by holding it on a revolving wooden plug fed with pumice and water. The final polish was achieved with putty powder. When a large batch was processed, each decanter and stopper was scratched with a corresponding number, to prevent the wrong stoppers being placed in decanters when they were passed to the warehouse to be cleaned before being sent off for sale. Although it is not an infallible rule, when they are marked the number on the decanter will be found on the inside lip of the rim where the stopper fits in. On the stopper it can be found either on the ground pontil or on the side of the peg.

An extra job performed by the stopperer was to finish off napkin rings. At Stevens and Williams in 1883 napkin rings, in clear glass cased with pink, were 'opened by stopperer, flatted top and bottom'.

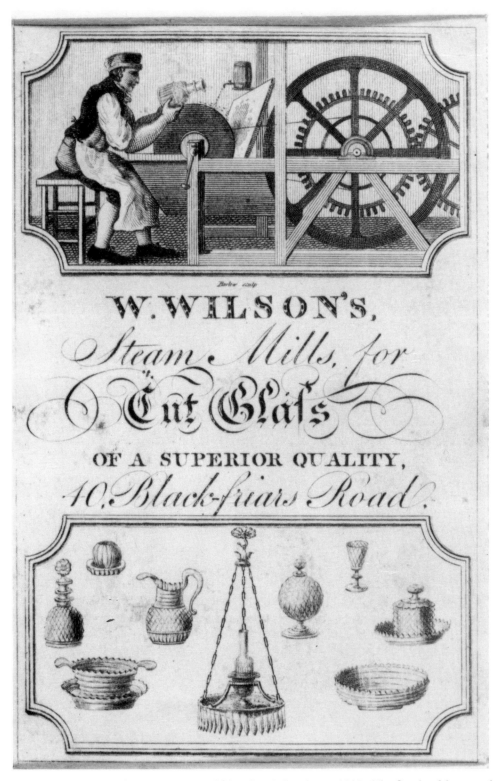

Plate 20. Trade card of W. Wilson, Blackfriars Road, London, c.1807. The Corning Museum of Glass.

CHAPTER TWO

Regency Cut Glass

Regency cut glass was the perfect embodiment of the extravagance and splendour of the Empire style. From 1800 until the 1820s it became the model for every glass producing country to imitate and some European factories were even established specifically to compete with the British innovation. The importance of cut glass from the Regency period was first recognised and acknowledged by the late Hugh Wakefield in his book *Nineteenth Century British Glass*. He compared the glass in stature to the great traditions of sixteenth century Venice with its hot manipulation of glass, and seventeenth and eighteenth century Central Europe with its magnificent engraved glass. With the cut glasses of the 1830s and 1840s, Regency glass established the tradition for cut glass for which England is renowned to the present day.

The repertoire of deep cutting on Regency cut glass was made possible by the technological revolution which brought in steam power to drive the cutting lathes. Until the end of the eighteenth century all cut glass was decorated on lathes which were driven either by hand or, very occasionally, by water. The hand operated set-up with the large fly-wheel, usually worked by women or young boys, was illustrated in a print dated 1806 (Plate 16). The traditional credit for the introduction of steam power is given to James Dovey of Stourbridge and John Benson of Dudley around 1790. The upper panel of a trade card of 1807 from a London firm supplying 'steam mills for cut glass' shows the new drive mechanism while the lower panel proves the advantages of the new machinery by showing a range of diamond cut tableware and a light fitting with cut drops (Plate 20). The speed and power of the steam driven equipment saw the end of the shallow cutting of the eighteenth century. The cut glass factories could now cut deep prisms, strawberry diamonds, hobnails, fans and splits, and create a vast output in a shorter time. With the ready availability of large suites of glass it is no wonder that the style became so popular. Even the caddy spoon was transformed into an ostentatious work of art (Plate 21).

The new fashion was nowhere more apparent than in the glittering table services which must have been an awe inspiring sight when laid out on a dining table. One of the most lavish of these early services (Plate 22) originated in a glassmaking area which in the past would not have been considered as possessing the expertise for that standard of work, let alone at such an early date. Until its accurate identification by Cherry and Richard Gray in 1987, the Warrington service made for the Prince of Wales between 1806 and 1810 was usually attributed to the workshop of John Blades in London, presumably on the grounds that a provincial factory was incapable of such quality. The service was also thought to be at least ten or twenty years later.

Plate 21. Tea caddy spoons, c.1810-25. Length of the longest (bottom left) 3¾ in. (9.5cm). Michael Parkington Collection.

In 1806 the Prince of Wales spent the autumn on Merseyside and was the guest at a lavish dinner organised by the Liverpool Corporation on 18 September. The ornate cut glass service, engraved with the Liver Bird crest of Liverpool, was provided for the occasion by the local firm of Perrin Geddes and Co. It created such an impression upon the Prince that he 'requested the Mayor to order him a few dozen glasses of the same sort'. The original order given by the Council to Perrin Geddes and Co. at the Bank Quay Glass Works, Warrington, consisted of twelve decanters, thirty-six coolers, six carafes or water jugs, six dozen claret glasses and six dozen port glasses but this was felt to be too small a number for the Prince's table and a further order was placed for twelve decanters, four dozen wines, four dozen claret glasses and three dozen goblets. The suite was engraved with the Prince of Wales' feathers in place of the Liverpool crest. An extra four dozen decanters and wine glasses in the same style were presented to each of two of the dignitaries and engraved with their own crests. The majority of the Prince of Wales service is held at Windsor Castle with some examples still in the possession of descendants of the original owners of the glass company while other pieces have found their way into private collections. As one would expect for a royal gift, the quality of the cutting and engraving is superb and was rarely surpassed in the following decades.

Plate 22. Wineglass cooler and claret or port glass, engraved with the Prince of Wales' feathers, by Perrin Geddes and Co., Warrington, c.1806-10. Height of glass 4¾ in. (12cm). Michael Parkington Collection.

If the identity of the service has at last been solved, at least two other questions have arisen about glasses which are similar to the Warrington examples. One concerns a number of wineglasses with identical cutting but made in green glass and engraved with the initials J.A.M. The other concerns an identical pattern to the Prince of Wales service which appears in the Thomas Webb pattern books in designs numbered 29086 and 29363 which can be dated to 1906. A pencil inscription with pattern 29086 states it was supplied to Thomas Goode and Co. Examples of the Webb glasses, engraved with crests, are in the collections at the Corning Museum of Glass. The full story behind the appearance of identical patterns a hundred years after the originals is still to be researched.

The next landmark in the history of Regency cut glass came in 1824 with the Londonderry service made at another relatively unknown factory, that of the Wear Flint Glass Company at Deptford in Sunderland. On 6 November 1824 the *Newcastle Courant* informed its readers that:

> A table service of glass — value nearly 2000 guineas — has been manufactured by the Wear Flint Glass Company for the Marquess of Londonderry and on Saturday last the Marquess and Marchioness, General Aylmer, Colonel Brown and other persons of distinction visited the manufactory for the purpose of inspecting it and expressed the highest approbation.

Plate 23. Four items from the Londonderry table service, by the Wear Flint Glass Company, Sunderland, c.1824. With the exception of the oval bowl, the pieces are engraved with the Londonderry coat of arms. Height of goblet 4¾in. (12cm). On loan to Sunderland Museums.

The two hundred piece service consisted of decanters, claret and water jugs, goblets, tumblers, honey jars, finger bowls, ice buckets, butter jars, almond dishes, plates and bowls which formed a dessert suite and a separate wine service (Plate 23). Unlike the Warrington service the Sunderland pieces vary in the cut pattern on some of the bowls, jugs, decanters and goblets. The service seems to have been ordered and made between 1823 and 1824 at the instigation of the Marchioness of Londonderry to celebrate her husband's titles of Third Marquess in 1822 and Earl Vane in 1823. The service has remained intact at the family home at Wynyard Hall.

The Warrington and Londonderry services show the wide variety of styles which are found on Regency cut glass. Many of the features are peculiar to the period providing an invaluable set of guidelines to assist with recognition. The most common feature is the band of cut diamonds framed between lines of step cutting at the top and bottom (Plate 24). A bowl, possibly made for a royal service, demonstrates the preference for setting the panels in horizontal formations but has the added feature of a row of ten, almost three-dimensional crowns around the rim (Plate 25). Feet were cut on the underside with a star, the points taken to the very edge of the glass, while the characteristic step cutting featured prominently on the necks and shoulders of decanters, jugs and celery vases. Handles were cut flat on either side with a notch or two at the highest point

Plate 24. Cream jug with step cutting and panel of cut diamonds, English, first quarter 19th century. Height 5 ¼ in. (13.4cm). Michael Parkington Collection.

Plate 25. Oval bowl cut with ten crowns, English, first quarter of 19th century. Length 10in. (25.5cm). Michael Parkington Collection.

43

Plate 26. Jug, with diamond, step and pillar cutting, English, first quarter of 19th century. Height 9⅝in. (24.5cm). Michael Parkington Collection.

of the loop to provide a thumb grip. The very best quality handles were cut with a serrated pattern (Plate 26). A variation of the close diamond cutting was the strawberry diamond pattern consisting of very fine criss-cross cuts on the flat top of the diamonds (Plate 27). Both types are seen side by side in the loose leaf pages of designs which are connected with William Haden Richardson (Plates 28 and 29).

The designs appear in a sketchbook and related loose sheets which contain just over 250 individual drawings for cut glass vessels plus sixteen sheets of lighting equipment. The archive has been described as 'the WHR drawings' due to the initials found next to a design of a sugar bowl. The initials match those of William

Plate 27. Bowl and cover cut with strawberry diamonds, English, c.1810s-20s. Height 6⅜ in. (16.3cm). Hulbert of Dudley Collection.

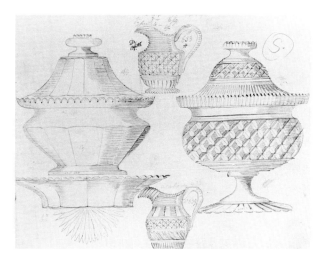

Plate 28. Page from the 'WHR' designs, c.1810-28. The stemmed bowl and cover cut with strawberry diamonds is a sugar basin. The bowl, cover and stand on the left was used as a butter dish.

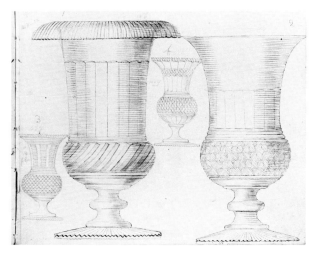

Plate 29. Page from the 'WHR' designs, c.1810-28, showing celery vases.

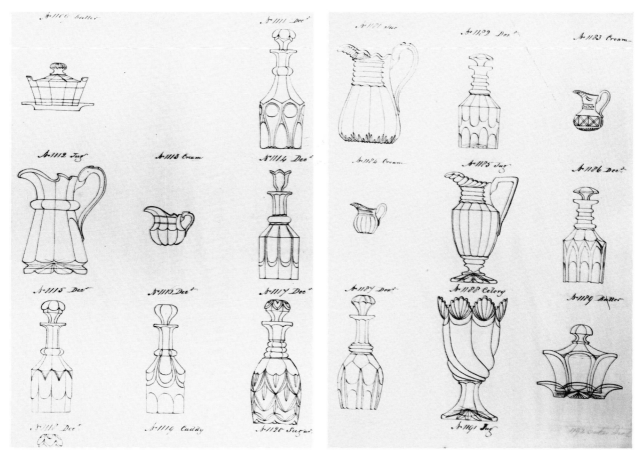

Plate 30. Page of cut designs from the Webb Richardson factory, c.1830s.

Plate 31. Page of cut designs from the Webb Richardson factory, c.1830s.

Haden Richardson found on documented Richardson patterns (Plate 57). The Regency style of the designs in the drawings can be dated from the mid-1810s to the late 1820s, which matches the 1814, 1824 and 1825 dates found in the watermarks. It is known that William Haden Richardson worked for the Hawkes factory from 1810 until 1828 and therefore the patterns should be attributed initially to the Dudley factory. In view of the scant evidence that currently exists for the Hawkes factory, the designs, even with a tentative attribution, are of vital importance in the quest to unravel the Hawkes legend.

The WHR drawings are the fourth known group of designs which help to define the transition from the diamond and step cut patterns to the broad flute style of cutting. On the evidence of William Haden Richardson's awareness of the latest fashions, as proved by the products of the Richardson factory, it seems fair to take the WHR drawings as representative of the current styles employed by the cutting shops in Dudley, Stourbridge, Birmingham and London. The broad flute style outgrew its beginnings in the Regency period to become the major feature of cut glass in the 1830s. In 1834, when John Gold of Birmingham took out his patent for a machine to cut broad flutes, it must have been to capitalise on the new trend.

The other three sets of published drawings are from the Waterloo Glass

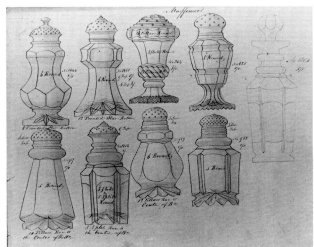

Plate 32. Page of wineglass designs from the Webb Richardson factory, c.1830s.

Plate 33. Page of designs for cut 'Muffineers' from the Webb Richardson factory, c.1830s.

Company and the Waterford factory in Ireland, and the Holyrood Glass Works in Edinburgh. The WHR drawings therefore become of paramount importance because they are the first English designs for Regency cut glass to be identified. With the Warrington and Sunderland glass services, they begin to question the long accepted term 'Anglo-Irish' as an accurate description of cut glass from the first decades of the nineteenth century. For example, the appearance of the turnover rim in the WHR designs no longer guarantees this feature a purely Irish origin (Plate 29). Further evidence for the reassessment of the origins of early nineteenth century cut glass comes from the surviving pattern books which were kept by the new partnership of William and Benjamin Richardson and Thomas Webb in 1829.

The designs were recorded in two sets of books, one in a numerical order as the glass was made and another organised by type of object. The pattern numbers must date presumably from 1829, the start of the partnership, until the middle years of the 1830s. Four pages, two from each set of books, show the predominance of the broad fluted style, available on every type of glass, ranging from decanters and wineglasses, cream jugs, butter dishes, to celery vases and muffineers (Plates 30 to 33). Of special interest are the straight or swirling

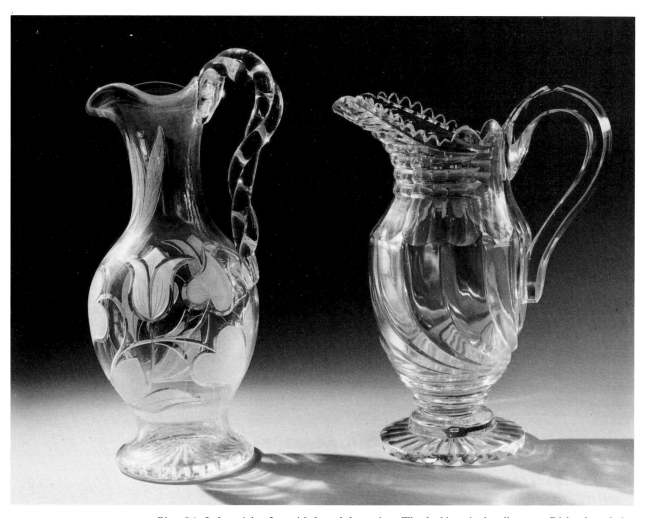

Plate 34. Left to right. Jug with frosted decoration. The double twist handle was a Richardson design from the early 1850s. Height 11½ in. (29.2cm). Jug with pillar cutting which matches a design in the Webb Richardson books, c.1830s. Height 10⅛ in. (25.7cm).

pillared cuts which reappear in rock crystal glass (Plate 31, bottom centre, and 34 right). Some objects were available in different colour combinations with prices to match. The flower vase in pattern number 2105 sold for 6s. if it was 'Frosted and Embossed' (Plate 35). In this technique the stylised leaf pattern was cut into the glass while the surrounding panel was frosted. The 9in. (23cm) vase was also available in clear glass (7s.6d.), in stained (12s.), cased with blue (13s.), ruby (14s.6d.) and in 'blue and cut 7 flutes all down' (10s.6d.). Smaller versions in ruby or blue sold for 13s.6d. and 12s.6d. The bowls of the 'Hasting Goblets' were given the same frosted treatment (Plate 36). The technique continued in production into the early 1850s (Plate 34, left).

The patterns clarify some of the confusion centred around the use to which certain shapes were put (Plates 37 to 40). Sugar basins were no longer covered

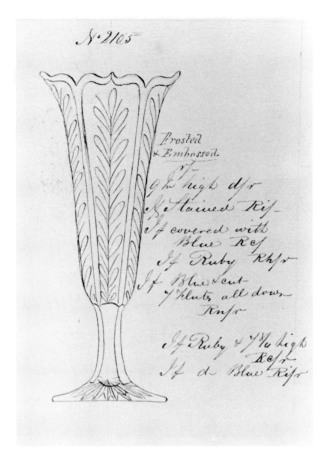

Plate 35. Design for a 'Frosted and Embossed' vase from the Webb Richardson factory, c.1830s.

Plate 37. A detail of a page from the Webb Richardson pattern books for 'Sugars', c.1830s. Of the 192 designs spread over eight pages, only twenty-nine have a cover. In comparison, of the 108 designs for 'Butters', only nine are without covers, but all have stands. Size of page 17⅛ in. x 10⅞ in. (43.5cm x 27.5cm).

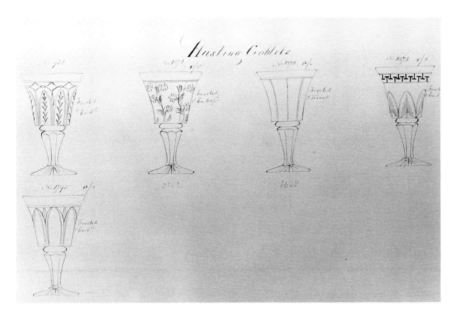

Plate 36. Page of designs for 'Hasting Goblets' from the Webb Richardson factory, c.1830s. The reason for the name Hasting is not clear.

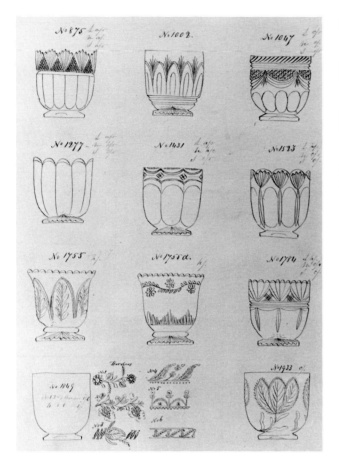

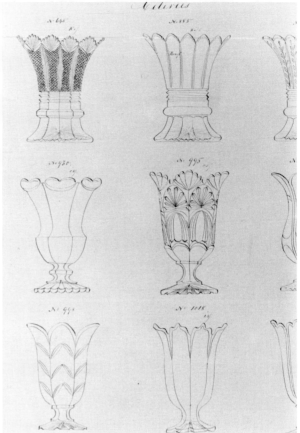

Plate 38. A detail of a page of twenty-four designs for 'Caddies' from the Webb Richardson books, c.1830s. One other page shows three more designs. Size of page as Plate 37.

Plate 39. A selection of 'Celeries' from a total of forty-four designs from the Webb Richardson books, c.1830s. The celery vase matching the top left design is illustrated in Colour Plate 45. Size of page as Plate 37.

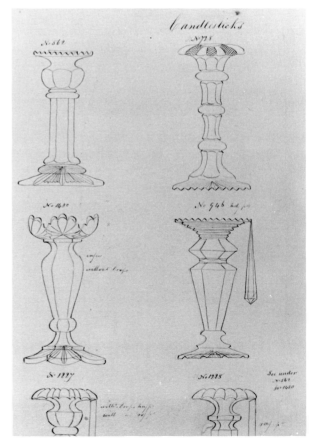

Plate 40. A selection of 'Candlesticks' from the Webb Richardson books, c.1830. Of the thirty-six designs, spread over three pages, six are shown with droppers although the notes beside some of the patterns imply that each design could be fitted with droppers if required. Size of page as Plate 37.

Drop Pinching.

Plate 41. Illustration from Apsley Pellatt's Curiosities of Glassmaking *showing a glassmaker pressing glass drops for candelabra and chandeliers.*

like their Regency predecessors. Stemmed and footed versions were more popular than the bowl forms. Caddies, on the other hand, appear in one standard shape but could be had in large, medium or small sizes. The designs would seem to be final proof that this shape of bowl was used in a tea caddy for blending teas and not as a sugar bowl which some evidence has suggested. The ubiquitous celery vase was offered in the more usual stemmed variety and in a less well-known shape of a waisted vase. On the example with pattern number 645 (Plate 39) the panels of Regency diamonds are still in use but have been turned through ninety degrees in keeping with the latest style. The pattern was identified on a vase in

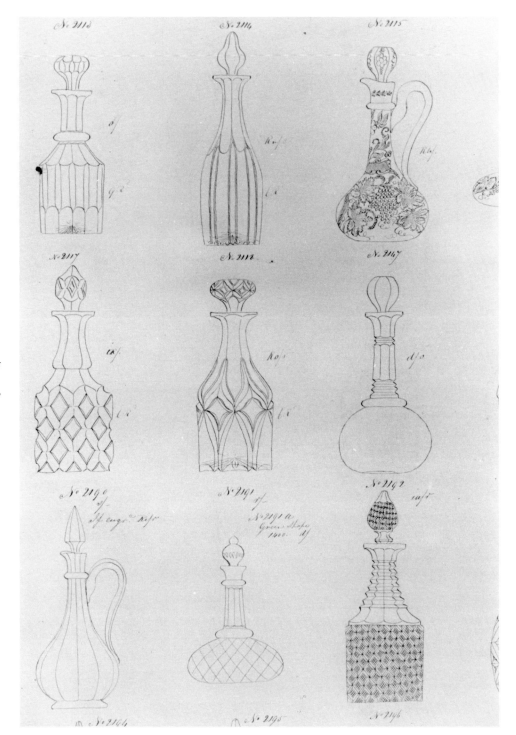

Plate 42. Page of designs for decanters from the Webb Richardson factory, c.1830s.

the Broadfield House Glass Museum collections (Colour Plate 45). Without the benefit of the design the style of cutting on the celery could be confused with the later vertical cutting practised during the 'Brilliant' period. A jug from the Stevens and Williams factory executed fifty years later carries the same pattern. The designs for candlesticks provide valuable proof for the early stages in the development of lustres. The optional addition of drops to the candlestick would

Colour Plate 2. Decanters and glasses in various shades of the characteristic apple green colour which was popular during the 1830s and 1840s. The two decanters on the left have been identified in the Richardson pattern books while the circular cut hollows on the third decanter match the pattern on one of the handled decanters in Colour Plate 3. The two wineglasses also resemble designs in the Richardson pattern books. Heights, left to right: 14in. (35.5cm), 5¼ in. (13.5cm), 10¼ in. (26cm), 5in. (12.5cm), 13⅜ in. (34cm). The two decanters on the left Hulbert of Dudley Collection.

increase the price by more than half, from 40s. to 68s. per pair. Drops and spangles were formed by drop pinching using a brass mould operated by hand (Plate 41). Chandelier arms required a more powerful lever press. The rough surface of the drops and arms was sharpened by polishing in the cutting shop. According to Pellatt, 'a considerable number of the Glass drops used for chandeliers, girandoles, and candlesticks, in England, are pinched from thick tumbler bottoms, or waste glass, causing a variety of tint, and inferior refraction.'

Among the broad flute designs the occasional pattern reveals the infiltration of the next generation of fashionable styles (Plate 42). Architectural motifs of pointed arches and quatrefoil windows were translated into cut glass traceries to resemble the Gothic style so passionately advocated by A.W.N. Pugin. When cased glass was introduced it offered an ideal medium to imitate the medieval patterns of genuine Gothic fragments which were published in such books as

Plate 43. View of Mr Blades' Upper Showroom, London. 'No. 4 of Ackermann's Repository of Arts &c Pub. April 1 1823'. 4¾in. x 7¾in. (12cm x 19.7cm).

Pugin's *Floriated Ornament* of 1849 (Colour Plate 5). The obvious comparison with church plate afforded by the silvered glass of Varnish and Hale Thompson provided the all-important religious connection that was inherent in the Gothic Revival (Colour Plate 25).

Some of the Richardson designs were available in an attractive apple green colour which is only found at this date (Colour Plate 2). A number of existing green pieces can be matched to patterns in the Richardson books but, fortunately for the collector, there are many further discoveries yet to be made (Colour Plate 3). Judging by the existence of relatively large numbers of glasses in this colour it would appear to have been preferred to amethyst or amber (Colour Plate 4). The gradual discovery of early nineteenth century English coloured glasses and the circumstantial evidence surrounding them, as in the case of the stained amber vase (Plate 60), suggests that experiments with colour technology were carried out simultaneously in England, France and Bohemia rather than, as has been accepted before, that England lagged behind its competitors. Stunning proof which underlines this theory is found in a set of finger bowls in yellow glass comparable to the 'Annagrun' or yellow-green colour, achieved with uranium, which had been discovered by Josef Riedel in Bohemia in the 1830s. The finger bowls and matching plates in clear glass, partly frosted and engraved, were used at a banquet in the Guildhall for Queen Victoria in 1837 to celebrate her first official visit to the City of London (Colour Plate 4).

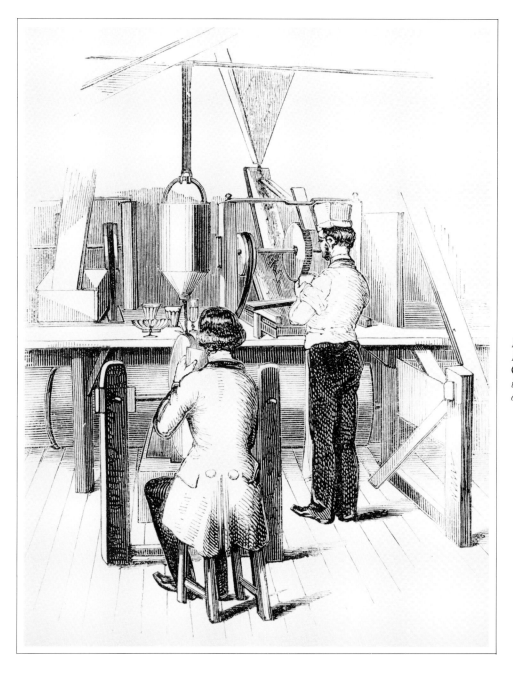

Plate 44. Illustration from Pellatt's Curiosities of Glassmaking *showing the two methods of overhand and underhand cutting.*

In the four decades after the Liverpool Corporation commissioned the dazzling service for the Prince of Wales, cut glass reached its pinnacle as a symbol of power, wealth and status. Nowhere was the opulence and sheer grandeur more apparent than in the magnificent surroundings of the London cut glass showrooms (Plate 43).

THE TECHNIQUES OF CUTTING

In the transition from hand to steam driven cutting lathes the position of the drive belt remained unaltered. As late as 1849 Apsley Pellatt illustrated cutting machinery driven by a large drum placed at ground level (Plate 44). It is not

Colour Plate 3. Designs for handled decanters from the pattern books of W.H., B. and J. Richardson, Wordsley, c.1840. The price note by the side of the right-hand decanter states 'Claret ie/- [23/-] Dec[anter] Rd/- [17/-] Flint Rr/- [16/-] Claret ii/- [22/-]'. The last two prices are for clear versions selling at 1s. less than the green. Page size 16¾ in. x 10¾ in. (42.5 x 27.5cm).

known how widespread this layout was but the presence of a large driving shaft along the floor must have been somewhat inconvenient. Even by the time Pellatt had published his book, the more typical layout of a cutting shop had been recorded in Wordsley, in a painting which probably shows the Richardson shop (Plate 45). The drive shaft was moved to a central position in the ceiling to allow more working space on the floor of the shop. The boiler plant and engine house were located in a shed at the end of the cutting shop, seen clearly in the plan of the Dial Glasshouse (Plate 3).

In the Wordsley shop all the cutters are working with the glass held on top of the lathes. The Pellatt drawing shows an alternative method, referred to regularly in advertisements for jobs which specified either an overhand or underhand cutter. The difference between the two, apart from the position of the glass on the wheel, may have been a standing or sitting position for the cutter himself. A glass model of a cutter's lathe closely resembles the Pellatt drawing apart from

Colour Plate 4. Influenced by European developments, English coloured and cut glass continued to be made for a wealthy market throughout the first half of the century, despite the handicaps imposed by the Glass Excise. The amber scent bottle, normally attributed to England, shows the problems that can be encountered in distinguishing between English and contemporary European glasses. For example, stoppers in the shape of cornucopias are found on glasses from the Saint Louis factory in about 1848. However, the deeply cut, thick foot is more reminiscent of Bohemian glass, seen to good effect on the vase on the extreme left of Colour Plate 8.

Scent bottle, amethyst glass cut with flutes and strawberry diamonds, English, c.1835, height 11in. (28cm). Scent bottle, amber glass cut with flutes, probably French, c.1840s, height 9¾ in. (25cm). Finger bowl and plate, the bowl in yellow glass, engraved with roses, thistles and shamrock; the plate engraved with a border of roses and leaves. Both pieces bear the royal cipher with the initials VR and the arms of the City of London, and were part of a suite of glass used by Queen Victoria at her first banquet in the City of London. English, c.1837. Diameter of plate 7½ in. (19cm), height of bowl 3¾ in. (9.5cm). Michael Parkington Collection.

the one crucial element of the driving mechanism (Plate 46). In the model the treadle mechanism is more akin to the glass engraver's lathe. The accuracy of the model, underlined by the Pellatt drawing, raises the question of where this type of lathe may have been used. The most likely user would be the free-lance cutter working from home. The small cutting shops employing a few men and boys already had access to steam power and their workshops must have been similar to the layout illustrated by Pellatt or the Wordsley painting. In the 1851 Exhibition, C. Sinclair of 69 Old Street, St. Lukes, showed a 'model, in glass, of a glasscutter's cutting tool', but no other details were given. A unique record of cutting lathes was noted in the back of one of the Richardson pattern books and gives more information on prices and materials:

Plate 45. Oil painting of Wordsley cutting shop, probably Richardson's, c.1830s. The artist is not known although it has been suggested it was painted by one of the ladies in the Richardson family, probably the artist of Plate 6. 9¾in. x 15in. (24.75cm x 38cm).

Plate 46. Glass model of foot-operated cutting lathe, possibly 19th century. Height 7⅞in. (20cm).

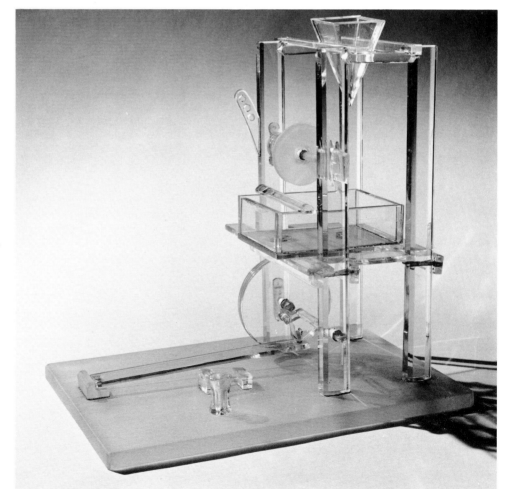

Plate 47. Stuart and Sons cutting shop, c.1902. Photograph courtesy Stuart Crystal.

Joseph Corbett Saw Mills Chaddesley Corbett near Kidderminster
August 12 1859
Glass Cutters troughs in either Elm or Red Deal Wood
1¼ in. [3.175cm] thick and Iron Clipd at the Corner and bottom 11/6 ea.
ditto if 1½ in. [3.81cm] thick and Iron clips at the Corner and bottom 13/- ea
Oak Glass Cutters frames Screwd each together and Iron Clipd at top of the Pad
22/- each
all delivered free here

The layout of the Wordsley cutting shop remained the standard set-up throughout the nineteenth century. Virtually the same scene was photographed by the *Gentleman's Journal* for a feature on the Stuart works in 1902 (Plate 47). As late as 1957 the same mode of practice was to be found in the Thomas Webb factory (Plate 48).

Until the introduction of the diamond cutting wheel in the 1970s, all cutting required three main operations of roughing, smoothing and polishing. In the roughing process, iron wheels were fed with a steady trickle of water and sand,

Plate 48. Glass cutter at Thomas Webb's, c.1950. Photograph courtesy Stan Eveson.

from a conical container suspended above the wheel, to provide the abrasive action. At this stage the cuts did not meet exactly, allowing the smoothing wheels to make the final precise pattern. Smoothing wheels consisted of fine grain stones fed only with water. In the same way as a copper wheel engraver would have a huge selection of different sizes and thicknesses of wheels, the cutter would use wheels of different sizes and different compositions for separate parts of decanters or wineglasses. Even the notches or nicks on the stem of a wineglass would require a specific wheel. One authority on brilliant cutting, writing in 1908 in the *Pottery Gazette,* stated that 'the stone used for cutting is a carboniferous sandstone, obtained from the Craigleith Quarry near Edinburgh, no other seeming to give the necessary combination of qualities'. Wheels would be changed on the lathe as required and would regularly need sharpening to maintain the correct profile. A flysheet by John Crowther of Sheffield, who is recorded in the trade directories from 1864 to 1871, lists the full range of wheels:

SCALE OF PRICES OF
STONE FOR GLASS CUTTERS AND DENTISTS

And all kinds of FANCY GRINDING, for Cash, Delivered at the Canal Wharf, or any of the Sheffield Railway Stations, Manufactured by

JOHN CROWTHER, STONE MERCHANT
PARK STONE & MARBLE SAW MILLS SHEFFIELD

MITRE STONE, per Inch Diameter

	d.
From 3 inch to 6 inch diameter, and from ¼ to 1 inch thick	2
From 6 inch to 9 inch diameter, and from ½ to 1 inch thick	2½
From 9 inch to 12 inch diameter, and from ¾ to 1 inch thick	2¾
From 12 inch to 18 inch diameter, and from ¾ to 1 inch thick	3
From 18 inch to 24 inch diameter, and from ¾ to 1 inch thick	3½

Neck, Flute & Edge Stones per In. Diameter

From 6 inch to 12 inch diameter, and from 1 to 1½ inch thick	2
From 12 inch to 24 inch diameter, and from 1 to 1½ inch thick	2½
From 24 inch to 30 inch diameter, and from 1 to 1½ inch thick	3

SIDE STONE, per Inch Diameter

From 12 inch to 24 inch diameter, and from 1 to 1½ inch thick	2½
From 12 inch to 24 inch diameter, and from 1½ to 2 inch thick	3

Up-right & Prism Stones, per In. Diameter

From 10 inch to 20 inch diameter, and from 1½ to 2in. thick	3
From 10 inch to 20 inch diameter, and from 2 to 2½in. thick	3½
From 10 inch to 20 inch diameter, and from 2½ to 3in. thick	4

PUNTEY STONES, per Inch Diameter.

From 3 inch to 6 inch diameter, and from 1 to 1½in. thick Best quality	1½
From 3 inch to 6 inch diameter, and from 1 to 1½in. thick Second quality	1¼

Stones for Drop Cutting, per Inch Diameter

From 9 inch to 12 inch diameter, and from 1½ to 2in. thick	2
From 12 inch to 18in. diameter, and from 1½ to 2in. thick	2½

J. Crowther, having for some years directed his attention to the selecting of stone for the different purposes in the businesses, flatters himself that he can sell any article rarely to be met with. A trial will be the best proof.

REFERENCES:— Messrs. Wood and Perkes, Glass Works, Worsbro' Dale; and the following Sheffield Glass Cutters; Mr. Jefrey, Castle Mills; Mr. Blunn, Coulston Crofts; Mr. Bate, Nursery Steam Grinding Wheel, and Mrs. Jackson, Pear Street.

N.B. — J. Crowther continues to supply his friends and the public with his improved Self-acting Natural Stone Water Filters.
ALL WARRANTED AT 20s. & UPWARDS

Polishing the matt surface left by the cutting wheels was a lengthy three part process, prior to the invention of acid polishing. The first stage involved the use of wooden wheels of willow, cherry or poplar fed with a slurry of wet pumice; the next stage involved a brush wheel fed with pumice or putty powder; the final stage used wood or cork wheels and putty powder which was a poisonous substance obtained from molten lead. An apprentice would have the task of 'feeding up' the wet mix of putty powder on to the rotating wheels for the polisher. Without adequate safety precautions, the noxious powder contaminated the working atmosphere and would be inhaled and swallowed by the polishers and the apprentices throughout the day and at meal times. Constant absorption produced a disease of the nervous system known in the trade as 'dropped hands'. *The Enquiry into the Employment of Children* examined the working conditions in the cutting shop and touched upon the effects of polishing with putty powder (Appendix 2). Despite constant enquiries into the use of lead in the cutting shops, the process was not to disappear until the twentieth century.

Acid polishing of glass began to appear in the 1880s. At Thomas Webb's a note by the side of pattern number 17723 in 1889 states 'first large piece polished by acid'. At Stevens and Williams a design for a decanter, pattern number 18666 dated 10 July 1893, is described as 'Early Victorian Acid Polished'. When acid polishing was introduced, glasses were given individual treatment to ensure a crisp definition of the cut patterns which could still show the grain marks of the cutting wheels. Modern glasses are given a set time in the acid bath which can lead to a very rounded edge on the cuts.

---------- CHAPTER THREE ----------

The Dudley Glass Industry

Since the beginning of the twentieth century the history of the Dudley glass-works has been forgotten or underrated. The main reason for this neglect is the almost complete lack of identifiable glass made in the town, while the absence of pattern books and detailed documentary evidence about the products also prevents any objective assessment. At a time when the ownership of a glassworks was a perilous undertaking which could lead quickly to bankruptcy, most glass proprietors were intent on survival rather than producing publicity material which might have been saved for posterity. Trade magazines were non-existent during the heyday of the Dudley glass industry and the earliest local newspaper, the *Wolverhampton Chronicle,* began publication only in 1830 when most Dudley works were already complaining of financial problems due to the Glass Excise, which seems eventually to have forced the closure of the most important of the factories.

Ironically the statistics presented in the *Thirteenth Report of the Commission of Inquiry into the Glass Excise* in 1835 provide the main evidence for restoring the forgotten reputation of the Dudley glassmakers. Five factories from the town are listed with the payments made in 1833:

Thomas Hawkes of the Dudley Flint Glassworks	(£5,593.1s.6d.)
Thomas Badger & Co. of the Phoenix Glassworks	(£4,870.7s.3d.)
Joseph Guest & Co. of the Castle Foot Glassworks	(£4,008.12s.9d.)
Thomas Davis & Co. at Dixons Green	(£3,460.14s.3d.)
Joseph Stevens & Co. at Holly Hall	(£2,938.14s.3d.)

Only the works of Webb and Richardson at Wordsley paid more than the Hawkes, Badger and Guest factories. The prodigious output suggested by these figures confirms the Hawkes factory as the most important of the five Dudley works at that date.

THE DUDLEY FLINT GLASSWORKS

Situated at the corner of Priory Street and Stone Street in the centre of Dudley, the Dudley Flint Glassworks had been established by the early 1770s by Abiathar Hawkes who subscribed to the cutting of the Stourbridge-Dudley canal in 1776. His four sons, George, Roger, Abiathar and Thomas, ran the glassworks in various partnerships with each other, but it was under Thomas' guidance, with the assistance of the Richardson brothers, that the firm became famous. His respected position in local society must have helped him enormously in his glass business. In 1834 the Dudley Tories selected him to oppose Sir John Campbell as Member of Parliament. He duly succeeded in winning the seat and held it for

Plate 49. Celery vase with the coat of arms of the Earls of Dudley, c.1825-33. Height 10½ in. (26.5cm). It is unusual in that the main cylindrical body lifts out of the oval base.

a further ten years with increasing majorities, but the *Daily News* of 1849 was less than kind to him when it stated that:

> Mr. Hawkes was an amiable man whose family had made their property in Dudley, and who had himself been engaged in the glass trade of the district. He was a man of some ambition, and had aimed for a long time at high society and a seat in Parliament, without having either the means sufficient for the one, or the ability desirable for the other. However, the Dudley Tories were disposed to gratify him, the more so as he was a man very likely to succeed at an election from his general popularity, and the more so from his residence being next door to Himley Hall (the seat of the Earls of Dudley). Mr. Hawkes probably acquired some additional influence in consequence of the marriage of one of his daughters with the brother and heir presumptive of Lord Ward. The peer himself was for a long time

Plate 50. The Smoke Room of the Dudley Arms Hotel by W. Pringle, 1829. Oil, 21 ¼ in. x 29 ¼ in. (54cm x 74.25cm). The characters include Thomas Badger, standing centre and speaking, with to his right his brother, Isaac, and to Thomas' left Major Thomas Hawkes, the owner of one of the Dudley glasshouses. On the two tables, amongst the rummers, jugs and clay pipes, are glass sugar crushers which were used to break up and stir the sugar in the hot toddy. Slices of lemon can be seen in some of the glasses. The hotel was situated in the market-place in Dudley, close to the present fountain which was shown at the 1878 Paris Exhibition.

understood to be the lady's suitor, but the younger brother ultimately obtained her hand. Mr. Hawkes might have continued, under these circumstances, to represent the town, but unfortunately the pressure of pecuniary embarrassments obliged him, in 1844, to go abroad, with a view to repair his fortunes. He accordingly relinquished his seat.

Further proof of Hawkes' social and financial connections is illustrated in a map of 1808 which shows the Dixons Green glasshouse with adjacent plots of land owned by Lord Dudley and Thomas Hawkes. Such close connections suggest that the celery vase, engraved with the coat of arms of either William, the third Viscount who died in 1823, or his son John William, the fourth Viscount who died in 1833 when the viscountcy and earldom became extinct, was made, cut and engraved at the Hawkes' works (Plate 49). The firm is supposed to have been one of the earliest users of steam power for cutting which was certainly needed to achieve the deep and regular diamond cuts on the celery vase, impossible under the former method of driving the cutting wheels. In 'Trade Reminiscences' about Hawkes, the *Pottery Gazette* in July 1888 wrote:

> in this early period of glass manufacture, when the steam engine was first applied to glass cutting, and when the diamond cut work was not only fashionable, but a necessary adjunct to every good family, Thomas Hawkes made his mark.

His other social duties included Justice of the Peace, Captain of the Yeomanry and Chairman of the Glassmasters' Association, in which role he is seen in the company of other glassmakers and industrialists in the Smoke Room of the Dudley Arms Hotel (Plate 50).

In 1794 the *Prices of Flint Glass by Thomas and George Hawkes* listed one hundred items although many were issued in different shapes and sizes or with alternate choices of cutting. Some of the more fascinating entries include 'cyders purled or twisted, chimneys for lamps, eye glasses, egg cups, fountains, Flower of Benjamin, Godfreys, inks for excise men, lacemakers' lights, muffineers, Oppodeldocks, toys, urinals and watch balls' as well as the more usual range of wines, rummers, tumblers and decanters. Examples are impossible to identify, but there seems no doubt that they were of the highest quality judging by the report in Bentley's *Worcestershire Directory* of 1840, which described the works as:

> having been conducted to the present day, with unabated vigour, skill and success; producing some of the finest specimens of glass work to be found in any part of the world; their articles in opal turquoy, and gold enamel, being universal allowed to stand unrivalled. The last mentioned inimitable article was first brought to perfection here in 1834, and this is still the only house who succeed in bringing it to perfection. The splendid gold enamel dessert service, furnished to the Corporation of London on her Majesty's first visit to the Guildhall on the 9th November, 1837, was manufactured here.

This statement has led to much speculation about the style and technique of the gold enamel service, which may have been a conscious attempt to copy and surpass the Bohemian and German technique of *zwischengoldglas*. A plate in the Victoria and Albert Museum, decorated on the underside with gilding and enamelling, and sealed with a layer of metal foil, is usually attributed to the firm. A similar plate but with the royal coat of arms of George III, made between 1801 and 1816 and attributed to John Grahl of Dublin, is in the Pilkington Glass Museum. A third plate, with gilt and enamelled roses and buds, has the underside and the rim enclosed with a silver plated mount complete with a swivel handle (Plate 51). A variation of the technique, in the form of a double-walled vase and cover in the Victoria and Albert collection, is also attributed to Hawkes. The making of these vessels consists of blowing two similar pieces, one slightly larger than the other. The larger piece is decorated on the interior and the smaller one on the exterior, and then the two are fitted together to form a single heavy shape with the decoration sandwiched in the middle. It is quite common to find the decoration peeling away from the glass where air has entered the interior space. Enamelling seems to have been part of the Hawkes factory repertoire for the 1794 price-list mentions enamelled blue glass sugar basins, cream jugs, jars and beakers but it does not give any details of shape or subject matter. Nor do any of the contemporary reports mention the double-walled technique which seems a strange omission in view of its elaborate nature. Until more definite information is discovered, the problems of identifying the Hawkes service and similar products must remain unsolved.

Although nothing is known of the 'opal turquoy' mentioned in the 1840 directory, a look at some of the glass from the Continent suggests possible

Plate 51. Plate enamelled and gilt on the underside, possibly the 'gold enamel' service made by Thomas Hawkes, mid-1830s. Diameter 9in. (23cm).

influences and comparisons. A private French journal of 1824 mentions 'opaque white glass called opal; pink called hortensia; blue called turquoise, and green called emerald', and it may have been these French products which Hawkes imitated in an effort to compete with foreign products through his flourishing export trade. Two price-lists of 'Flint Glass for Exportation', dated 12 April 1815 when the factory was run by Thomas and George Hawkes, are in the library at the Henry Ford Museum and Greenfield Village at Dearborn, Michigan. One list is for Druggists' Furniture, i.e. phials, measures, salt and smelling bottles, cupping glasses, funnels, rounds and stoppers, etc. The Flint Glass list contains some of the items from the Druggists' section but it mentions some tantalising items including 'cans, lemonade, common or double flint; cruets; custard cups; finger cups, white, blue, green or purple; water bottles; hock glasses; mustards; muffineers; pattypans; root glasses; syllabubs; salts, sweetmeat shells'; and dessert and table services 'from 40 to 500 guineas and upwards'. Both lists mention Slater & Co. as the Philadelphia agents.

Most of the other information about Hawkes' glassware comes from the

Plate 52. Claret jug and stopper from the Hawkes factory, engraved by William Herbert with a scene of 'The Road' showing 'The Wonder' stagecoach which operated between Birmingham, Stourbridge and London. Signed and dated 1833. Height 11 ⅝ in. (29.5cm). Private collection on loan to the Victoria and Albert Museum.

Plate 52A. Detail of the engraving on the claret jug in Plate 52.

reminiscences about Dudley which formed a nostalgic feature of the *Pottery Gazette* in the 1880s and 1890s. An article in the January 1882 issue states that:

> as early as 1830 etching on glass was rendered commercially useful by Thos. Hawkes and Co. of Dudley, where gold enamelled plates were made and ornamented by the etched process by a Mr. Wainwright and others. In 1835 the firm produced a plateau presented to the Hon. Spring Rice, afterwards Lord Monteagle. This was engraved by William Herbert, and etched by the same artist.

A man named Denby is also mentioned as having 'brought etching onto glass into practical use'. Joseph Cowdey, an acid maker of Castle Street, mentioned in 1820, may have been a supplier for the glassworks. One cannot be sure of the accuracy of these statements written fifty years after the events, but they are made with some authority and there is no doubt about the importance of the Hawkes factory at this date.

In July 1884 a report mentioned that:

> Hawkes brothers first made flint-moulded bottles in open and shut moulds, early this century. This was a remarkable firm, and perhaps made a greater variety of glass than any other house, past or present. It was the custom for glass manufactures in the past to make nearly everything. Hawkes made bottles in moulds, cut glass, muffs for windows, spread glass, coloured glass, phials for surgeons, patent medicine bottles — (perhaps the earliest pressed glass was made in Dudley) — chandelier drops and spangles. The Highbury Barn London chandeliers were made here, wonderful examples at that period, about 1836. Hawkes cut glass when glass-cutting was done by hand; and up to the end of his day, about 1842, he worked the 'Sun and Planet' engine, exactly like the one in South Kensington. They made epergne glass when it was a novelty, in this country. Here the early diamond cut glass was largely designed and executed; and Hawkes' showroom, as I remember it, was a marvel for this class of goods.

Other reports of 1890, 1895, 1896 and 1898 confirmed the range of products even adding that 'spun glass was made, in the bulk, by Hawkes and Co.'

One engraver at the Hawkes factory can be identified as William Herbert who appears in the local directory in 1828. He was born about 1806 in the Stourbridge district and married a Dudley-born girl who bore them three daughters. Judging by the engraved decanter which he signed and dated 1833 (Plate 52), his skill was equal to engravers working in other parts of the country. The magnificent Regency style of cutting confirms Hawkes' reputation and complements the finer diamond cutting of the celery vase. In the same year of 1833 William Herbert signed a petition, with other glassmen and cutters, against an attack by Sir John Campbell on the acting magistrates. In 1842 his disappearance from the directories coincides with the closure of the Hawkes firm and tradition states that he removed to Bristol. The 1851 census return finds him working as a glass engraver and living in Bedminster, near Bristol. Other members of the Herbert family who are listed in the Dudley directories are Samuel who is first mentioned in 1820 and John who appears in 1839. John Herbert continued the family tradition in the area and was still working at Stourbridge in 1873, described as a tobacconist, British wine dealer, painter, glass engraver, gilder and signwriter.

Throughout most of its life the Hawkes factory was hampered by the Glass Excise. Prices were increased in 1825 as a result of the changes in the way the tax was charged and in 1835 the evidence that Hawkes gave to the Commission of Inquiry clearly outlined the effect of the tax:

> I was out of business for a short time, for three years; I gave it over to my brothers, and they were so disgusted with it that they retired. I renewed the business with the hope that some alteration would take place, and I carry it on for one of my younger sons, to whom I thought I was doing an act of justice.

Some time between 1827 and 1837 the firm became known as Hawkes and Greathead, the new partner being William Greathead who later helped to establish the firm of Davis, Greathead and Green. In 1837 Richard Green joined the firm at the age of fifteen and by 1840 was promoted to the position of traveller for the firm. He was the third partner of Davis, Greathead and Green, thus echoing the words that 'indeed anything advanced in the glass trade at this period emanated from the Hawkes works; and many manufacturers graduated at his Dudley works'.

At the height of its importance, the factory consisted of two glasshouses, a cone-shaped one described in 1801 as having eleven pots and a square house added in 1838. The firm also operated a seven-pot furnace in Liverpool in 1803, which was recorded as a six-pot furnace in 1805. A wage book from the last year of the factory gives six chairs each with the usual four men, with names which tally with the parish registers of Dudley and Sedgley. A typical example of wages was:

	per week	moves over	two moves over
Jh. Webb	30s.	2s.6d.	£1.15s.0d.
Josh. Hand	20s.	2s.	£1. 6s.0d.
E. Parsons	6s.	6d.	7s.
Thos. Rushton	4s.	4d.	4s.8d.

In 1843 the Midland Mining Commission reported 'the great distress amongst the glassworkers results from the termination of Mr. Hawkes' works, some of the largest in the Kingdom for flint glass'. Most of the equipment was transferred to the Richardson glassworks at Wordsley, evidence of the close links between the three Richardson brothers and the Hawkes factory. Thomas Hawkes died in 1858 and was buried at Himley Church on the outskirts of Dudley. His glasshouse stood empty and was allowed 'to fall into disrepair, and for nearly 50 years it was an eye-sore to the inhabitants of Dudley and a source of wonder to observant strangers'. In 1874 the press reported the dangerous state of the building; two years later the idea was put forward that the old building should be demolished and the site used for the building of a public baths. However, nothing was achieved until 1884 when the issue was raised again after the building was offered for sale to the Town Council who voted, by twenty-two votes to nine, to buy it. Until then the works had been used as a hide and skin market but on the night of 14 December 1885 the dome fell in. On 23 June 1886 work began on removing it altogether although the arguments about the use of the site were still filling the pages of the local press in 1888. Today the cobbled site is still open space and serves as a car park for the centre of the town.

THE DIXONS GREEN GLASSWORKS

Francis Buckley, whose *Glasshouses of Dudley and Worcester* provides much of the early history of Dudley's glass industry, was the first to publish the earliest reference to glassmaking in the town when he quoted the 1713 *London Gazette's* listing of Hugh Dixon as a bankrupt glassmaker. In 1729 an Edward Dixon, glassmaker of Worcester, was jailed at the Fleet Prison, London, as an insolvent debtor. It is generally thought that this Dixon family gave their name to the area of Dixons Green and the glassworks just to the south of Dudley. For the last fifty years of the eighteenth century the works were operated by members of the Green family including Jonathan, John and Joseph, although the relationships are not clear. In 1803 Joseph Green had a ten-pot furnace and the map of 1808 shows one cone but with a notable lack of outbuildings.

From 1804 the works changed ownership at regular intervals with Edward Davies and William Hodgetts working it for the longest time from about 1820 until 1833 when they seemed to have closed it down. Shortly after that the cone collapsed due to mining subsidence. Hodgetts and Davies decided to cut their costs and removed to the Red House Glass Works at Wordsley. In 1868 the site was levelled and sold as prime building land.

THE PHOENIX GLASSWORKS

The earliest mention of this glasshouse, situated in Hall Street near the centre of the town, appeared in 1772 when 'James Horton (glass cutter) hired servant to Philip Penn absconded his master's service on the 25th May. At the same time went away Daniel Newton (apprentice)'. Philip Penn was succeeded about 1780 by William Penn who appears again in 1807 when he was given access to deposits of glasshouse pot clay at Lower Gornal. In 1818 John Roughton took the works, having left the Holly Hall factory some time after 1813.

In 1820 the works were bought by the brothers Isaac and Thomas Badger who were already engaged in the local iron trade and soon became involved in the politics of the glass industry (Plate 50). Surviving documents reveal that they did not have the popularity enjoyed by Hawkes. As leaders of the Tory clique which dominated the town and its politics, the anti-Chartist brothers used their position as magistrates to reinforce their position. Isaac was described as 'audacious but unlettered' and Thomas was tried for assault upon William Davis, a whitesmith, in 1835. When Thomas gave evidence to the Commission of Employment of Children in 1846 he thought that '10 to 12 is the right age for children to begin work; 10 years is not too young if the boy be strong and healthy'. Faced with the comment in 1852 by William Lee, the Superintending Inspector of Health, that 'as far as the duration of life is concerned Dudley is the most unhealthy place in the country', Isaac Badger claimed that the high death rate was due to industrial

Plate 53. Designs for wineglasses from the archives of John Jones, London. The glass on the bottom right is from the Badger glasshouse. Prints and Drawings Department, Victoria and Albert Museum.

accidents, ignoring the fact that over two-thirds of all deaths in Dudley were of children less than five years old. Isaac Badger, the father, had laid the foundations of their fortunes as a builder at the end of the eighteenth century and this was taken up enthusiastically by the two brothers who became notorious slum owners. Their outlook on the rest of the town's problems was equally insensitive. When Thomas died in 1856 he left nominally £40,000-£50,000, a substantial sum for those days.

Little can be identified of the firm's products but two designs for simple cut tumblers were registered in 1849 and 1850. Bristol Art Gallery has a small group of glasses including a decanter and jug which are said to have been made at Badger's but cut by the firm of William and Thomas Powell of Temple Gate, Bristol, in about the late 1820s. If this uncorroborated statement is true perhaps the reason may be that the disputes leading to the lockouts in 1831, resulting from the employees casting their votes in the elections, prevented any cutting in

Dudley. The story also points to the accepted route for export of glass from the Black Country, i.e. by canal to Stourport, then on to the River Severn and direct to Bristol. One wineglass by Badger's appears in a collection of designs for glass, silver, brass and porcelain in the Prints and Drawings Department at the Victoria and Albert Museum (Plate 53). The sheets, dated between 1837 and 1864, belonged to John Jones, a designer at Copeland's and perhaps the same Jones who is mentioned as a glass dealer of Grosvenor Square in *Kelly's Directory* of 1842. The ruby glass with matching cut pattern may also have come from the Dudley factory.

The firm disappears about 1860, possibly due to the effect of having to close down the works for a time in 1859 when all the factories took this course of action in an effort to modify the rules of the Glassmakers' Union. The cone was still standing as late as 1903 when it was used as a furniture works and warehouse by Charles Hale and featured in an advertisement with an aerial view of the premises.

THE CASTLE FOOT GLASSWORKS

As the name suggests, the factory was placed at the foot of Dudley Castle hill opposite the end of the present Tower Street. A drawing and a watercolour of the late nineteenth century by Paul Braddon, in Dudley Art Gallery, reveal it was set within a pleasant wooded area. Dates of 1780 and 1789 are given for its foundation. By 1818 it was run by Benjamin Cooke, Joseph Price and James Wood, but the partnership was dissolved in 1820 leaving Wood the sole proprietor. Two years later he was joined by the Guest brothers, Joseph and Edward. The partnership flourished until 1842 when the owners became Charles Henry Homer and John Renaud. A plan of the works drawn in 1844, and still naming the firm of J. & E. Guest Glass Manufactory, gives a detailed description including one glasshouse with a mixing room, three metal rooms, two pot rooms, mould room, packing room, machine room and one room set aside specifically for the use of the Excise Officers. The total area covered 1,233 square yards (1,031 sq m) with an annual rateable value of £140.

Under the Guest-Wood partnership the firm is supposed to have invented hollow-stemmed glasses as well as producing very fine cut glass which 'equalled the cut glass of any works near to them, as to quality, design and finish'. Ideas may have been copied from Belgian glass for Edward Guest had visited the glassworks at Val St. Lambert where he noted that the men 'had their dinners and it was nothing else but cabbage cooked in various ways'. Some extent of the profits accumulated by the Dudley industrialists is revealed by the large sums which the Guests gave to various institutions. When Joseph Guest died in 1867 he left the Dudley Blue Coat School £2,000, Dudley Female School of Industry £2,000, the General Hospital and the Queens Hospital in Birmingham £2,000 and £1,000, Dudley Dispensary £1,500, Dudley Grammar School £2,000, and St Thomas' Church Restoration Fund £300. Glassmaking was a sideline for the Guests, their money being made as nail ironmongers. They kept a low profile politically and as Liberals were opposed to the likes of the Badgers and Hawkes.

The partnership between Homer and Renaud continued until 1856 when Homer gave up his interest, leaving John Renaud in sole charge. Like many of his fellow glass proprietors he aspired to public office, eventually becoming Mayor of Dudley in 1856. Nothing definite is known of their glass but they did have a London showroom suggesting a high quality product. A Dudley resident still possesses a decanter and wineglass cased in ruby and cut, and a small decanter, cased with blue, cut and engraved with swags of flowers, which are said to have been made at the works. At the opening ceremony of the Dudley Fountain in October 1876 the Countess of Dudley tasted the water 'from a light and exquisite goblet of chaste and classical design, ornamented with an engraving of the fountain (manufactured by Messrs. Homer and Renaud)'. In 1896 the range of goods was:

> of a very high class and indicates the labour of artistic workers with original ideas. There are some quite original designs in heavy cut glass — the originality pertaining alike to the shapes and the decorations. Heavier work seems to be their strong feature though they show some graceful shapes, prettily decorated in light wines etc. Messrs. Renaud appear to confine their attention to table glass, and the success they have attained seems amply to justify that limitation. In heavy cut deep dishes and bowls, and wine and spirit decanters, they are showing some elaborate productions, the cutting and engraving being essentially different in character from the ordinary styles of such work. There are some elaborate water sets and sets of jugs of novel and pleasing shape. We noticed some fruit dishes of novel shape and beautifully cut. Taken all round, the cutting, both as to design and execution, is of a very high order of artistic glass work.

However encouraging that report may have been the works were nearing the end of their life. The final blow came in 1899 when the Glassmakers' Union encouraged the men to apply for a rise in wages which could not be met by E.J. Renaud as the firm had been running at a loss for a number of years. Consequently the men were given their notices, the furnace was put out and the works sold in 1900. Two years after the closure the main glasshouse was demolished. In August 1919 Edward John Renaud died and was buried next to his father, who had died in 1893, in the family vault at Oldswinford.

THE HOLLY HALL GLASSWORKS

The factory was situated at the Holly Hall crossroads, on the site now occupied by the Holly Hall Clinic building and its grounds on Stourbridge Road. It appears to have been the smallest of the town's factories and changed hands more often than any of its neighbours. First mention of it appears in a lease of 1783 following the death of the proprietor, John Keelinge. An earlier reference of 1754 to a runaway apprentice from Thomas Griffin of Holly Hall has given rise to the speculation that this may have been the Holly Hall works. George Ensell reputedly took over the works after Keelinge's death and a page from Joseph Richardson's furnace notebook, at Stuart Crystal, states that Richardson, a furnace builder, put in a nine-pot furnace for George Hinsole (*sic*) at Dudley in 1782. Following Ensell's bankruptcy in 1786 Zachariah Parkes took the works until 1800. He was joined by James Grainger and John Roughton but the latter retired and the firm became Parkes, Grainger and Green by 1817. A further change of partnership left the firm as Major Parkes and Co. until 1821 when Parkes relinquished it to Edward Page. By 1828 Joseph Stevens was in possession but no mention of the firm exists after 1854 although the buildings stood until the 1870s.

If the history of the owners is a jumble of names and dates at least one of the surviving reports, from the *Birmingham Gazette* of 1784, provides more useful information in the form of an extensive list of glass from the works. The sale notice describes the stock as:

> consisting of above 140 doz. decanters, barrel and Prussian shaped, cut and plain; 80 doz. goblets, sorted sizes, square and round feet, cut and plain; 800 doz. wines, cut and plain; 1100 doz. pint, half-pint, and quarter-pint Weight and Tale tumblers; 640 doz. punch glasses and tumblers; 40 doz. cut and plain ale glasses; 41 doz. rummers, cyders and carofts; 116 doz. castors and cruets, cut and plain; 262 doz. salts and salt linings, cut and plain; 154 doz. sorted smelling bottles; 206 gross white and green phials, sorted sizes; 43 gross Lavender's, Daffy's, Turlington's and Smith's Bottles; 216 doz. bird fountains and boxes; 52 street lamps. Together with a large quantity of salvers, butter-boats, trifle dishes, scollop-shells, mustards, patty pans, candlesticks, compleat apparatus, blue basons, cream jugs and many other articles.

THE EVE HILL GLASSWORKS

In 1865 Thomas Lane and his son Josiah founded a glassworks in Birmingham which by 1869 was well established at Hampton Street. By about 1888 Josiah Lane decided to set up another works in Dudley, possibly due to the fact that the Birmingham works were in a dilapidated condition. Perhaps a more important reason for the new venture was the cheapness of coal in Dudley. It would appear that the glassworks was already in existence when Lane settled in Dudley but nothing is known of its history until that date. It was situated in Parkway Road, close to the roundabout at St James's Church at Eve Hill.

Plain glass was made with some of the decoration carried out at the Birmingham works which were kept on. The main production concentrated on lamp glasses with speciality lines of plain and fancy gas globes, paraffin gas globes, chimneys, fancy shades for electric light fittings as well as confectionery glass and stationers' equipment (Plate 54). The firm patented three designs in 1883, 1886 and 1894 including a 'Patent Beehive Comet', a globe which had a corrugated top. Other items ranged from cut glass tableware to friggers including ruby pipes and apparently a range of paperweights, although none has been identified. An advertisement of 1912 shows a wide range of colour and decoration on lampshades including satin finish, opalescent patterns and cutting. Business seems to have been good as the firm employed about sixty-five hands in 1905.

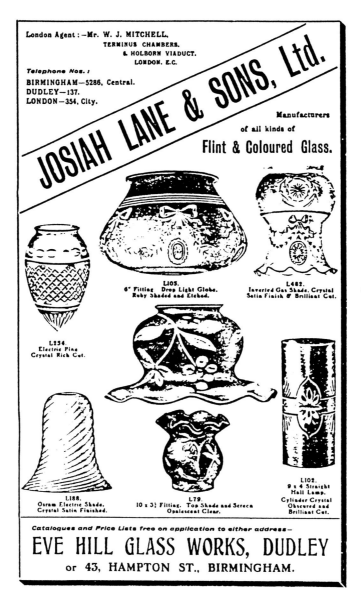

Plate 54. Advertisement of Josiah Lane, 1912, from the Dudley Chamber of Commerce Handbook.

By the 1920s the story had changed drastically. Josiah Lane, then a councillor for Dudley, told his work-force that the audited accounts for 1922 and 1923 showed an average loss of £25 per week. Although he anticipated closure fairly quickly the firm was able to continue until 1932. It was the last of the Dudley glassworks ending a two hundred year old tradition.

CUTTING SHOPS

In Dudley the decorating out-shops were already in existence at the beginning of the nineteenth century and increased in number as the glassmaking factories also extended their production. Glass cutters were the most common but engravers also set up small businesses. J. Lee is described as glass engraver and liquor merchant in 1809; others included John Bourne as well as the Herbert family associated with Hawkes' factory. Of the cutters the local directories mention John

Benson, Daniel Silvers, Thomas Silver, Joseph Parkes, Cornelius Pitt, Joseph Whitehouse, Skidmore and Careless, and Joseph Wright. Much of the work ended up in Sheffield where it was given plated mounts. In his book *A History of Old Sheffield Plate,* Frederick Bradbury gives a list of glass cutters and manufacturers from Birmingham and Dudley who supplied just one company, that of M. Fenton & Co., later known as Watson and Bradbury. John Benson from Dudley, who is credited with the introduction of steam power to glass cutting, was by far the largest supplier:

1803-4	£128. 0s. 1d.
1804	£219. 7s. 6d.
1804-5	£275. 0s. 4d.
1805	£217.11s.11d.
1805-6	£158.18s. 7d.
1806	£323.19s. 4d.
1807	£432. 1s. 6d.
1808	£455.19s. 2d.
1809	£687. 0s. 0d.
1810	£684.18s. 3d.
1811	£745. 9s. 3d.
1812	£581.12s. 7d.

The high level of payments to Benson suggests a well-established and extremely successful practice. Other Dudley suppliers were:

Lee & Large	
1804-5	£ 57. 2s. 4d.
1805	£ 34. 2s. 0d.
Wm. Large	
1805-6	£ 55. 0s.11d.
Large and Hodgetts	
1806	£ 60.18s. 7d.
1807	£ 31. 4s. 4d.
1808	£ 5. 5s. 0d.

One of the most important cutting shops was run by Richard Wilkes at the Campbell Street Glass Works during the last thirty years of the century. His stand at the Worcestershire Exhibition of 1882 brought forth the following comment by a contemporary reporter. 'Mr. Wilkes seems to have brought the art of glass-cutting and engraving to the scene of perfection. The richly cut toilet sets, salad and punch bowls (both gilt and silver mounted), biscuit boxes, scent bottles, here displayed, show the wonderful progress of this particular art and industry'. Wilkes cut a great deal of glass for the firm of Stevens and Williams, as did William Woodcock who by 1905 was 'almost the only glass cutter in Dudley'. His designs in the Stevens and Williams pattern books, at numbers

Plate 55. Tankard engraved with Dudley Castle and a crest, a monogram of JS, and 'Dudley Union Ppesant God Save the King'. Dudley, c.1830-37. Height 6⅛ in. (15.5cm).

19159-19170 dated 22 July 1893, show the typical hobnail cutting of this date suggesting that the independent cutting shops were used for the ordinary ranges of cut glass while the factory's own cutters carried out the more elaborate patterns.

IDENTIFICATION OF DUDLEY GLASS

Even though large amounts of cut glass still appear in antique shops and salerooms it is almost impossible to attribute any piece to a Dudley factory. Engraved glasses give slightly more scope for identification but only rarely is there strong evidence that they came from the town's workshops. A jug at Cannon Hall Museum near Barnsley is wheel engraved with a waggon and horses passing a signpost with two arms pointing to London and Dudley, giving a fifty/fifty chance that it was made at a Dudley glassworks (Plate 115). A tankard with a view of Dudley Castle and the strange inscription 'Dudley Union Ppesant — God Save The King' must date from before 1837 when Queen Victoria came to the throne but the exact meaning of the inscription has not been discovered (Plate 55). An 1888 engraved jug celebrates the coming of age of the Earl of Dudley. With the celery vase and the stagecoach decanter, the tankard and the coming of age jug are the only known pieces to have strong Dudley connections.

Reasons why the industry sprang up in Dudley must include the availability of raw materials and fuel, an experienced work-force and access to ever growing markets. Vast coal deposits, controlled mainly by the Earls of Dudley, would have provided an easily accessible and endless supply of fuel. The prospects of large profits must have been a keen inducement for Dudley was expanding in the second half of the eighteenth century with an increasing work-force. Three of the glasshouses were associated with areas of new building. The new breed of industrialists would see glassmaking as another venture to increase their existing profits from nail and chain making.

By the middle of the century a number of factors contributed to the gradual demise of the industry in the town. Growing competition from the Wordsley factories would have reduced profits in an industry that is notorious for large turnover with relatively small return. The likes of Thomas Hawkes and the Badger brothers were, after all, only financiers and not glassmakers of the standing of the Richardson brothers or Thomas Webb, whose strong personalities linked to a vital knowledge of glass enabled them to modify their designs to the changes of fashion and competition from abroad. How much the Glass Excise helped to put some of the Dudley works out of business is extremely difficult to assess. It may be that the abolition of the tax did more harm for the date of 1845 seems to coincide with the decline of the Dudley factories and the almost meteoric rise of firms in Wordsley and Brierley Hill. The evidence, in the shape of the glass itself, suggests greater experimentation with colours and techniques on the part of the Wordsley factories. The lack of a recognisable, surviving, comparable body of glass from the Dudley factories must lead to the conclusion that most of their products were of a mundane, everyday nature which could never hope to surpass the achievements of their Stourbridge competitors and as a result have fallen into obscurity.

Although so little is known about the Dudley factories and their products, a study of their development provides a fascinating microcosm of the industry and reveals a hard and realistic fact of life, still apparent in the industry today, that a glassworks needs to produce a vast bulk of useful wares in order to survive and even then cannot be certain of success. The history of the glass trade is as much about the skills of these 'jobbing' glassmakers as about the more appealing art glass products.

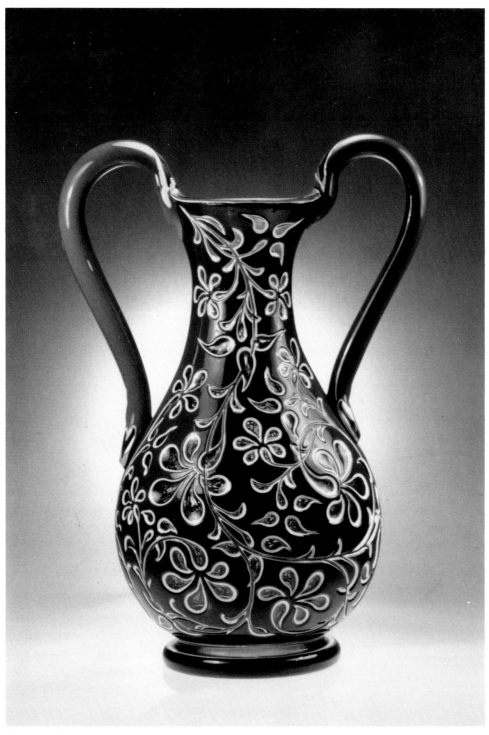

Plate 56. Vase, cut through four layers of ruby, clear, white and blue glass. Probably Saint Louis, France, c.1848. Height to top of handles 12 ¾ in. (32.3cm). The Jones Museum of Ceramics and Glass, Maine, U.S.A.

————— CHAPTER FOUR —————

The Bohemian Connection

In the early years of the nineteenth century the glassmaking centres in Bohemia developed the idea of casing or overlaying a layer of clear glass with a coloured glass which was cut through to reveal the clear layer underneath. Although it is difficult to give a precise date for the introduction of cased glass, a date as early as 1804 has been given by Leonard and Juliette Rakow in an unpublished article 'Bohemian Cased Engraved Glass, English Cased Cameo Glass and Related Paper-Weights'. By the 1820s and 1830s the industrial exhibitions held in Prague had led to the discovery of new colours and by 1836 clear glass was being cased with two or more colours. Cased glass was itself a reaction to the popularity of English cut glass but in its own turn the Bohemian glass was quickly imitated by other European glass centres and some American factories.

The French factory of Choisy-Le-Roi, under the direction of George Bontemps who later assisted Chance Brothers in the production of window glass for the Crystal Palace, is credited with making cased glass from 1825 and with the discovery of filigree glass in 1837. From 1836 the Society for the Encouragement of National Industry was motivating the French glass industry to experiment with new colours with the result that Baccarat and Saint Louis had introduced coloured glass by 1837. Two, three and four overlay pieces, marbled glasses, and copies of lava and malachite glasses were shown by the Saint Louis factory at the Exhibition of the Products of French Industry in 1844. Superb examples of three and four layer cased pieces from 1848 are illustrated by Gerard Ingold in his book on the history of Saint Louis. The quality of the large double-handled vase in the Jones Museum Collection would suggest the same pedigree (Plate 56).

In the 1840s large imports of Bohemian glass were reaching America where the cased technique was also known as plating. A notice in the *Boston Daily Journal* of 15 July 1848 informed the public of 'BOHEMIAN GLASS, The subscribers have just received a very large supply and assortment of this fancy Glass Ware, and offer for sale some of the richest and rarest patterns ever imported — pure crystal, ruby, blue, turquoise, and other tints, cut, engraved and enamel'd.'

In England the picture was much the same. Apsley Pellatt offered a large assortment of foreign glass for sale in 1847 at his Falcon Glass Works and at his branch in Baker Street. English literature on glass during the 1840s reveals an obsessive fascination with Bohemian glass. An article in the *Art Union* of 1848 entitled 'The Glass of Bohemia' describes in idyllic terms the factories, workshops, cottages and churches which the author, one C.E., visited some time before 8 November 1847. The glass factories

are all small, in fact only one large apartment, in the centre of which is a furnace,

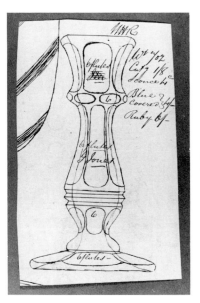

Plate 57. Design by William Haden Richardson, with his initials, for a cased blue or ruby candlestick, c.1844. Height of design 5in. (12.7cm).

a circular structure divided into eight compartments containing the melted metal for as many colours; one man and one boy are stationed at the door of each compartment, the former to extract the fluid with his pipe, the latter to hold the wooden mould (of beech) in which the article is blown and shaped. The number of hands employed in an ordinary fabrique, are: Eight men who work with metal, take it from the fire, and blow it in the moulds, etc.; four to stir the metal, etc.; two breakers; four day labourers.

After descriptions of the gilding and enamelling processes and a visit to the studio of an engraver, Charles Antoin Gunther, the author completed the tour with an account of the export of the products.

There are two classes of person engaged, on a large scale, in the exportation of Bohemian glass — the Fabricant and the Collector; generally speaking, however the latter is the direct exporter, and he also superintends the cutting, painting and packing. The Fabricant is more frequently engaged in furnishing the Collector, and to a great extent, with the glass in its original and more simple forms as it comes from the furnace, and it is then cut and painted by the cottagers who surround the dwelling of the Collector; so that many of these villages are entirely formed by the Collector and his people. Others however employed in the same way, cluster round the Fabrique; but even their productions for the most part go to the Collectors, who have their correspondents in Spain, Turkey, Greece, America, England, etc.

Reacting quickly to the foreign competition, English firms had successfully produced high quality cased and engraved glass by the 1840s. In London the cased glass made by Apsley Pellatt relied heavily on classical shapes decorated with the popular anthemion motif. In the Midlands the factories of Bacchus, Rice Harris and Richardson were generally acknowledged to be the foremost exponents.

In April 1846, the *Art-Union* magazine wrote:

We have intimated that Messrs. Richardson are directing considerable attention to the improvement of coloured glass; in this art we yet lag behind our neighbours; chemistry has at present done little for it in this country; these gentlemen have, however, already made great advance in rivaling [*sic*] the productions of Bohemia; and we have little doubt that, a few years hence, we shall see at least equal the best of the imported articles; their specimens of opal glass are remarkably successful; and of cutting, engraving, and polishing, they supply examples second to none that have ever been produced in this country.

The earliest English designs for cased glass appear in the Richardson pattern books about 1844 (Plate 57). Fortunately some of the glasses matching those designs were kept by the family and presented to Broadfield House Glass Museum (Plate 58). At the Manchester Exhibition of 1845-6 Richardson's displayed blue, green and red cased glass described as 'laudable attempts to rival the produce of Bohemia' (Plate 59).

These surviving Richardson glasses play a vital role in expanding our appreciation and knowledge of English cased glass in an area where the attribution to Bohemia, England or France can be extremely arbitrary to say the

Plate 58. Group of blue cased glass by Richardson's, c.1844. The candlestick matches exactly the design in Plate 57. Height of scent bottle 11 ¼ in. (28.5cm).

least, as demonstrated in the group in Colour Plate 5. The triple cased blue, white and clear vase on the left may be a Saint Louis example together with the carafe, tumble-up and stand, in white on clear glass, the latter with the slightly larger and broader cuts which were favoured by the Saint Louis factory. To confuse the issue, both have provenances from the Richardson family collection, although French pieces including Clichy scent bottles are in the same collection. The goblet on the right received a 'St. Louis' attribution in a saleroom catalogue though an attribution to the Bacchus factory is more likely with the thicker glass and colour

Plate 59. Blue cased and cut scent bottle shown by Richardson's at the Manchester Exhibition of 1845-6. Illustration from the Art-Union, January *1846.*

twist stem which does not have the mechanical precision seen on French examples. Single features such as the trefoil lip on the cased white jug provide the collector with another guideline to identify English examples. The remaining decanter, vase and candlestick in this group have strong English claims based on the Richardson identified pieces. The lack of gilding or enamelling, so apparent in this group, cannot in itself be taken as an absolute guide to the identification of English examples especially when one examines the Midland made glasses shown at the Great Exhibition. Heavy mitre cutting was practised on cased glass with the most stunning examples surviving from the Bacchus factory (Colour Plate 6). The decanter of ruby glass cased with white, a combination used elsewhere by Bacchus, was made about 1850 and the design of hobnail cuts suggests a Bacchus attribution for the jug and two goblets. The matching saucer for the jug and the red and white opaque twist stems of the goblets complete one of the most exquisite sets of cased and cut glass to have been made in England in the middle of the century.

A cheaper and quicker alternative to cased glass was the use of an overall surface stain fashionable during the Biedermeier period in Austria and made by the Bohemian factories. The best known stained glasses are the large goblets or vases engraved with stags and deer in woodland settings (Colour Plates 7 and 8). The vases were blown in clear glass which, after annealing, were cut with broad facets on the stem and foot. Following the cutting the exterior surface was painted with a ruby, amber or blue stain, fired into the glass to make it permanent. The glass was then passed to the copper wheel engraver who revealed the clear glass beneath as he engraved his standard woodland scenes. Staining can be distinguished from casing by the very sharp delineation between the stain and the engraved image due to the thinness of the stained layer. Cased glass, as on the Muckley goblet (Colour Plate 7), is much thicker in comparison and produces a more shaded effect, especially where the engraving is very shallow. The shape of the glass can also be a clue in determining between stained and cased. The heavily cut and stained stem and feet of the deer vases could never have been achieved with cased glass. Even a very thick layer of ruby glass on that part of the vase would have resulted in the clear glass showing through on the angular knop and the heavily scalloped foot after it came through the cutting process. Stained glass can often be recognised by the painterly, flowing effect of the stain as it has been applied by the brush. The stain was applied occasionally to imitate cased examples, as on two decanters said to be engraved by Thomas Wood of Stourbridge and shown at the Great Exhibition (Colour Plate 7). The Musician decanter shows an imitation of broad facet cuts on the lower and upper parts which is more often the hallmark of cased and cut examples.

One vase which has recently come to light suggests that English imitations of Bohemian glass may have been made earlier than is normally accepted (Plate 60). The urn-shaped vase, stained with amber and engraved with a bold band of fruiting vines, is accompanied by a hand-written note which reads:

Plate 60. Vase and cover, cut and stained amber. Probably made at Thomas Webb's and possibly engraved by John Herbert, c.1837. Height 10½in. (26.5cm). Private Collection.

Made at Dennis glass works for Herbert a painter of Collis Street for Queen Victoria Coronation. Their was a pr but the other one was no good & this one is shaded green on it so it was spoiled. Mr. Moody of Collis Street bought this one.

If the note is accurate it confirms the speed with which English factories reacted to foreign developments. The painter mentioned in the note is almost certainly John Herbert, a relation of William Herbert, the engraver at the Hawkes factory in Dudley. First recorded in 1839, he appears in Littlebury's *Worcestershire Directory* of 1873 as 'glass engraver and ornamental painter Collis St. Dennis Park'. One reading of the note suggests that the vase was made as well as decorated at Webb's but another interpretation of the phrase 'made for Herbert' can be taken as meaning that the blank, possibly stained, was made for Herbert who engraved the fruiting vine motif. Coincidentally the vase now belongs to a private collector who also lives in Collis Street, Amblecote, one of the boundaries of the Dennis glassworks of Thomas Webb.

Colour Plate 5. Cased and cut glass from the 1840s. Left to right. Vase, clear glass cased with white and blue, English or French, late 1840s, height 4¾in. (12cm). Candlestick, pink glass cased with white, English, probably Midlands, early 1840s, height 9in. (23cm). Decanter, clear glass cased with red, English, probably Midlands, c.1845, height 12¼in. (31cm). Vase, white glass cased with blue, English, probably Midlands, c.1845, height 12⅜in. (31.5cm). Carafe, tumbler and plate, clear glass cased with white, probably French, c.1845, height complete 9⅝in. (24.5cm). Jug, clear glass cased with white, probably Richardson of Wordsley, c.1845-50, height 7⅞in. (20cm). Goblet, the bowl and foot of clear glass cased with white, with a red, white and blue opaque twist stem, probably Bacchus of Birmingham, late 1840s, height 7in. (18cm). Candlestick, Hickman Collection, goblet Michael Parkington Collection.

Another exciting, Bohemian inspired glass to survive is a stained goblet engraved with a fruiting vine motif (Colour Plate 7). After the goblet was made and engraved the design was recorded in the Richardson pattern books. Some of these pages were cut up into smaller illustrations, but one loose page has survived showing the goblet (Plate 61). The inscription alongside the drawing reads 'Ruby covered goblet, hollow stem and foot with 6 flutes, 6 broad points and 7 fine Vandyke points between, weight 14oz. cutting 2/-, engraving 5/-, sells 13/-.' This page is dated December 1844 and the engraver is given as Philip Pargeter.

Colour Plate 6. Cased and cut glass by George Bacchus and Sons, Birmingham, c.1850. Heights: decanter 12in. (30.5cm), jug 12¼in. (31cm), goblets 8½in. (21.5cm); plate 6½in. (16.7cm) diameter. Michael Parkington Collection.

Pargeter was to achieve greater fame in the 1870s as the owner of the Red House Glass Works where, under his direction, the cameo blanks were made for John Northwood's copy of the Portland vase.

On some of their broad fluted decanters Richardson's used a stain which was painted on alternate panels and engraved through with sprays of flowers (Plate 62). Stained and cased pieces from the company appear in the catalogue to the Bingley Hall Exhibition held to celebrate the visit to Birmingham by the British Association in 1849 (Appendix 3, Nos. 41 to 47). The list mentions other

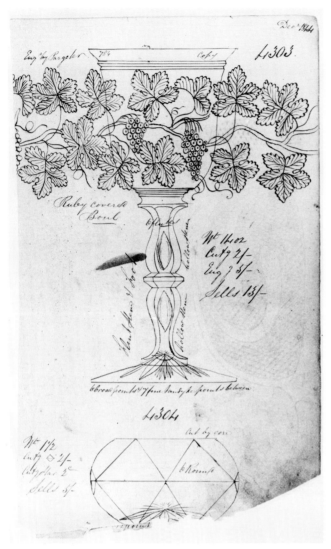

Plate 61. Design from the Richardson pattern books of the Pargeter engraved goblet, dated December 1844. Pattern no. 4304 below is for a salt cellar that sold for 5s.

Plate 62. Decanter cut with broad flutes, alternate ones stained ruby and engraved with roses, thistles and shamrocks, c.1840s. Probably by Richardson's. Height, including stopper, 13 ¾ in. (35cm). Michael Parkington Collection.

Bohemian influenced glass which can be matched with varying degrees of accuracy to pieces in the Benjamin Richardson III Collection at Broadfield House Glass Museum, including 'No. 99 Blue Vase, fluted all down and gilt' and even more fascinating 'No. 126 Mahogany colour, glass Salt, cut flat diamonds' (Colour Plate 10). The salt matches the pattern which appears under the Pargeter goblet drawing (Plate 61). A white, opaline gilded bowl, cover and stand (Plate 75) is very similar to a mid-nineteenth century bowl from Bohemia illustrated on page 235 by Pazaurek in *Gläser der Empire und Biedermeierzeit*. The German roemer shape was given a fresh interpretation in the late 1840s with the additional benefit of gilding (Colour Plate 10).

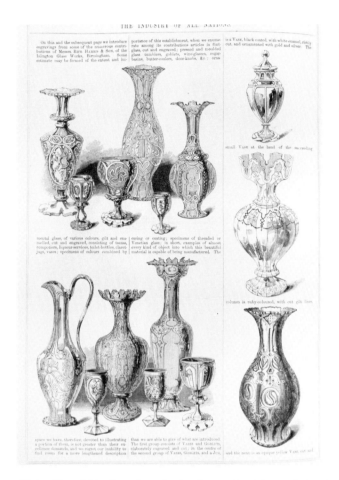

Plates 63 and 64. Pages from the Art Journal *catalogue of glass by Rice Harris of Birmingham shown at the Great Exhibition.*

The full impact of the Bohemian influence became apparent in the glass displays at the Crystal Palace Exhibition. From the evidence of the illustrations in the contemporary catalogues the Birmingham firm Rice Harris was the most fervent producer of Bohemian imitations with Bacchus and Sons following close on its heels (Plates 63, 64 and 65). The text for the Rice Harris pieces helps to identify the techniques:

> The first group [Plate 63] consists of Vases and Goblets elaborately engraved and cut; in the centre of the second group of Vases, Goblets and a Jug, is a Vase, black coated, with white enamel, richly cut, and ornamented with gold and silver. The small vase at the head of the succeeding column is ruby-coloured with cut gilt lines, and the next is an opaque yellow Vase, cut and scalloped with chased gilt flowers; the Vase that follows is deeply cut in a novel style of ornament. In the upper group on this page [Plate 64], to the left is a Vase of ruby glass, with cut plates, and gilt

Colour Plate 7. The technique of firing a coloured stain on to clear, cut glass to give the impression of cased glass was developed by Bohemian glassmakers on pieces like the tall vase engraved with stags and deer, made in the second quarter of the century. Amongst English versions of the process, dating to the 1840s, is the pair of decanter bottles, which, according to family tradition, are said to have been engraved by Thomas Wood and shown by him at the Great Exhibition. The catalogue entry for his display lists nine items: Blue cased dish; champagne bottle; stained ruby bottle; flint decanter; tumbler; ruby hock glass; stained claret; flint claret; flint wine.

His presence at the Great Exhibition as an independent engraver, the existence of the porcelain commemorative mug and the appearance of his name in the Webb pattern books from the 1840s to the 1860s, suggests that Thomas Wood was one of the most important free-lance engravers of the period. The dark ruby stained goblet, engraved with vine leaves, is by Phillip Pargeter and is recorded in an 1844 pattern, illustrated in Plate 61. The goblet on the right of the group shows the difference between cased and stained glass. The bowl, cased with ruby glass, was engraved by W.J. Muckley at the Richardson factory in about 1850. Heights, left to right: 4in. (10cm), 11¾in. (30cm), 12in. (30.5cm), 11¾in. (30cm), 8in. (20.5cm), 7¾in. (19.5cm). Pair of decanter bottles Private Collection.

chased ornaments; and by its side a large Goblet and Cover, of ground crystal, covered with ruby and white, richly cut in three shields; on one are the Royal arms of England, and on the other two the monograms of the Queen and Prince Albert respectively. In the centre of the lower group is a large alabaster Vase, nearly five feet high, elegantly and tastefully ornamented with gilt scrolls; on either side stands a Jug and Goblet, of opaque white, enamelled, heightened with gold in the ornament and handle, and in the left of the group is a Vase of dark, opaque blue, cut and scalloped, and ornamented in oak-leaves and acorns in silver. The whole of these works are executed in the highest degree of finish.

Colour Plate 8. Five vases showing the problems of attribution to Bohemian, French or English factories. The three vases on the left are Bohemian, dating in style from about 1840 to the early 1860s. The white and ruby cased and gilt vase may be French, or English, or Bohemian. At least stylistically it can be dated to the 1840s. The vase on the right, dating from the middle of the century, in clear glass cased with layers of white and blue is most likely to be Bohemian, although in the past it has been attributed to the Richardson factory as it was in the collection of Benjamin Richardson III. Heights, left to right: 24 ¾ in. (63cm), 18 ½ in. (47cm), 14 ¾ in. (37.5cm), 17in. (43cm), 16in. (40.5cm). Second and fourth vases from the left Hickman Collection.

The text for the Bacchus illustrations only mentions

> the large vase in the first group [Plate 65], where, if we imagine the lozenge-shaped ornaments of a deep ruby colour, cased with white enamel, and the wreaths of green ivy, we may form some idea of the rich effect produced.

The collector's problem of identifying the precise technique from the black and white drawings was commented on in the *Art Journal* catalogue when it stated that 'several of these objects lose no little portion of their rich appearance in the

The extensive GLASS works of Messrs. BACCHUS
and SONS, of Birmingham, furnish some beautiful
examples of their manufacture, of which we
engrave two groups, remarkable both for their
novelty of form and of ornamentation. Several
of these objects, it will be readily supposed, lose
no little portion of their rich appearance in the
engravings, where black only is made to take the

Plate 65. Page from the
Art Journal *catalogue
showing glass by Messrs
Bacchus and Sons shown
at the Great Exhibition.*

place of the most brilliant colours; this is especially to be observed in the large vase in the first
group, where, if we imagine the lozenge-shaped
ornaments of a deep ruby colour, cased with white
enamel, and the wreaths of green ivy, we may
form some idea of the rich effect produced. There
are few objects of British manufacture which have,
of late years, been marked by more decided im-

provement than is to be found in our "glasshouses;" and Birmingham is now a formidable
rival to London in this branch of industrial art;
moreover, it is rapidly, and rightly, advancing.

engravings, where black only is made to take the place of the most brilliant colours'. Unfortunately this scheme of using black to denote bright colours was not always adhered to, which makes the engravings difficult to de-code accurately. The use of the word 'enamel' in the texts would appear to mean a layer of glass rather than painted enamel.

None of the Rice Harris or Bacchus glasses has yet been found and identified. The close similarity of these and other English pieces to their Bohemian counterparts makes it extremely difficult on occasion to give precise attributions when trying to decide on a country of origin. A group of five vases (Colour Plate 8) covers the main types which appear on the market. The amber stained and engraved vase and cover on the extreme left is a type that is easily recognised as Bohemian and should give no problem to the collector. The white vase, enamelled with kittens, illustrates the often repeated theory that Bohemian glass was blown in a mould with an overblow being left on the vase which was later ground down. The flat rim would invariably be gilded. In England the glass would be transferred on to a pontil rod and the rim finished off by shearing, which results in a rounded rim. The centre vase of the group shows the other characteristic of Bohemian glass — the oval enamelled portrait painted to very high, almost photographic, standards. The style was still in production by 1862 when it was seen at the International London Exhibition of that year. The ruby vase, cased with white and gilded, is more difficult to attribute, with France, England and Bohemia being equal candidates. Equally difficult is the clear vase, cased with blue and white, and enamelled and gilt. One hesitates to say that this level of ornate decoration was exclusively a Bohemian characteristic until more English pieces are identified.

Bohemian glass was a non-lead glass and therefore the weight and ring of the glass, or rather the lack of it in the foreign examples, often helps to differentiate between the products of the two countries. Under short-wave ultra-violet light the two types of glass should fluoresce quite differently, with lead showing a blue/purple colour, but this can be misleading or difficult to assess, especially where the glass may be covered with enamelling or gilding, or if the coloured casings react in different ways. Bohemian pieces are sometimes painted on the base with a Continental-looking number which known English pieces do not have. Seen in combination these various clues can help towards an initial attribution. As certain characteristics, such as the style of painting, become recognised and one develops an eye for them the expertise in identification will increase.

The obsession for Bohemian-inspired cased and decorated glass reached its zenith at the Great Exhibition and disappeared very quickly after that date. Other Bohemian influences continued throughout the nineteenth century and were to be responsible for some of the magnificent engraved and rock crystal glassware made during the 1870s and 1880s.

Plate 66. Benjamin Richardson I, 1802-1887.

Plate 67. William Haden Richardson, 1785-1876. Artist unknown. Oil on board, 14½ in. x 11½ in. (37cm x 29cm).

CHAPTER FIVE

The Richardson Dynasty

Of all the nineteenth century glass firms the one deserving greatest recognition as a pioneer and innovator of styles and techniques is the Richardson works of Wordsley. During the first twenty-five years of its one hundred year history, the firm of W.H., B., & J. Richardson created consistently high quality utilitarian and decorative glassware which resulted in the award of a Prize Medal at the Crystal Palace Exhibition. The Richardson award confirmed the Midlands in general as the most important centre of English glassmaking, a situation which lasted for the rest of the century. The main reason for the success of the three Richardson brothers was their finely attuned sensitivity to the mainstreams of fashionable taste, current artistic styles and events both at home and abroad. Their pattern books of the 1830s and 1840s reveal every fashionable style including the Gothic revival, chinoiserie, the rococo revival and neo-classicism. The brothers were also excellent judges of glassmakers for they employed some of the future innovators at their glassworks. Philip Pargeter, John Northwood, W.J. Muckley and Thomas Bott all began their careers at Richardson's.

Although the firm's name includes the initials of all three brothers it is always Benjamin who is credited as the guiding force of the factory. He is often referred to as the 'Father of the Stourbridge Glass Trade' and there can be no doubt about his importance as a major force in glassmaking (Plate 66). But it is strange that the other brothers have been ignored completely as having any possible influence at the factory. Unpublished evidence in the form of letters between William Haden and his brothers would seem to call for a reassessment of the pre-1851 situation. The oldest brother, William Haden was a knowledgeable glassmaker with firsthand experience in various works in the Midlands (Plate 67). A notebook of his, dated 1819, in the Stuart Crystal archives states that he entered the trade in 1802 in Bilston and worked for Hawkes of Dudley from 1810 to July 1828. Every aspect of glassmaking is covered in the notebook including purchase of raw materials, recipes, rates of pay, prices and countrywide journeys to retailers.

On Christmas Day 1829 he achieved his ambition to become a glasshouse owner when he took over the Wordsley Flint Glassworks in partnership with his brother Benjamin and Thomas Webb. According to the agreement which still survives in the Staffordshire Record Office, Webb contributed £3,000 while the brothers each found £1,200. After seven years, when the partnership was renewable, Thomas Webb left the company and was paid £7,000. Although Webb was the main financier of the scheme it is difficult to assess his influence in the running of the works or on the design of their products. The third brother, Jonathan, was certainly at the factory by 1842 but he may already have joined

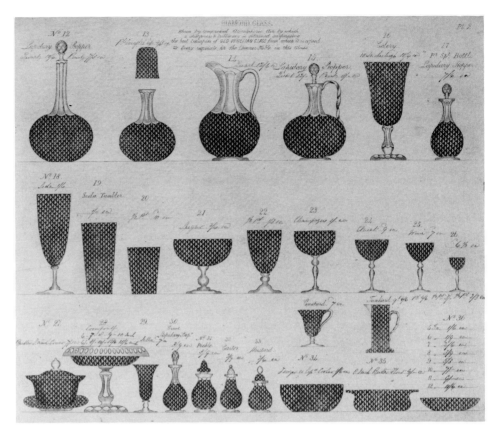

Plate 68. Page from printed Richardson catalogue of diamond glass blown by compressed air, c.1851.

the partnership by 1836. The obituary of his son, John T.H. Richardson, written in 1914, states that 'Mr. Jonathan Richardson joined his brothers as a partner in 1836, when the late Mr. Thos. Webb seceded from the firm of Webb and Richardson'. In 1838 when Jonathan and Sarah Richardson baptised their daughter Martha Jemima, his occupation was given as 'Glass Master formerly Clark and Book-keeper'. It may be that Jonathan, like his brothers, had worked at the Hawkes factory. When they set up on their own account it would be natural for the oldest brother to be in control. William H. was seventeen years older than Benjamin who was born in 1802. Jonathan was four years younger still. Using modern day comparisons one could perhaps see William Haden in the role of 'Managing Director' while Benjamin could be seen as 'Works Director'. Too little is known, as yet, of Jonathan's role to place him accurately in this line-up. This situation continued until 1852; from 1853 Benjamin took over the leadership although William continued to act in an advisory capacity.

William's surviving letters reveal a personality who was hard-working, indefatigable, acutely aware of his competitors, inventive and fascinated by technology. On 2 April 1842 he even recorded his visit to the Tipton Lead Ovens complete with drawings of the ovens and a description of the process. Another letter showed a drawing for pressure moulding equipment which has precedents in equipment designed by Ismael Robinet, a glassblower at Baccarat, during the 1820s and copied by George Bontemps in 1833. William's idea was obviously carried out as proved by the Diamond Glass service containing twenty-seven separate items 'blown by compressed Atmospheric air, by which a sharpness and brilliancy is obtained surpassing the best examples of OLD VENETIAN GLASS from which it is copied' (Plate 68). Apsley Pellatt in his *Curiosities of Glass Making* described the manufacture of his 'Venetian Diamond Moulded', a technique which must have been very close to the one used by Richardson. 'Equally good effects are produced by modern glass makers in a more direct manner by making brass open and shut, or dip moulds, so as to give at one operation the entire diamond impression, thus saving the tedium of forming each diamond separately with the pucellas'. The extra pressure of compressed air allowed much crisper modelling of the glass inside the mould while saving the lungs of the glassblower. Richardson's had introduced press-moulding into their works in the 1840s and the potential allowed by modern equipment must have appealed greatly to them. The French processes which were copied by Richardson's and other English firms are discussed by Miriam Mucha in an article entitled 'Mechanization, French Style, Cristaux, Moule's en Plein' in the September 1979 *Bulletin* of the National Early American Glass Club.

At the age of sixty-five William Haden was still visiting clients in London, where he spent much of his time, sending back his ideas for new moulds and machinery and exhorting his brothers to greater efforts. Over half of the 108 dealers supplied between 1837 and 1851 were in London, including the firms of Damell, Mortlock, Hancock and Co. and Thomas Goode. The major overseas customer was George Ellis of Montreal and Boston. A listing of some of the glasses sent to Ellis includes green hocks, finger cups, sugars and covers, butters, ice plates, jellies, custards, salts, violet matchboxes, blue tapers, blue eye glasses, smelling bottles, inks and graduated measures, diamond moulded decanters and whisky bottles.

One letter of September 1850, which mentions the diamond moulded pattern, is typical of the vital role William Haden played in filling the company's order books:

Dear Brothers,

Since I wrote to you ¼ to six this Evg. I have been to Mrs. Conne and seen the Decanters and Carofts [Carafes], wine Coolers and have prevailed on her to Keep the Decanters — she wishes the Diamond Moulded Crofts remade — Thos. Webb at Platts has the mould. Yours is no ways like this. However one of each is coming down for you to see and compare.

Do see if you cannot get into casting Diamd. Moulds and dont be discouraged at one or two failures and then if you succeed you may get up moulds as none else can until they find your way out. If you cannot succeed and will not try I will get a core carved out here and get it tried myself. It should be heated to redness (or nearly so) quietly and as soon as ready cast on — not suffered to cool — I can procure you blocks of C and send you down or you can try the Composition Varied sent to Johns until you succeed.

This day I have thought of a plan to make drams all of one size or nearly so — and over is the idea which can be tried at a very small cost say 5/-. If we could succeed in this then we could sell setts of Drams. I lose no time in communicating it to you I leave you to try to carry it out.

I have seen J.G. Green this Evg. and told him Cause why we did not attend to

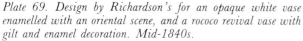

Plate 69. Design by Richardson's for an opaque white vase enamelled with an oriental scene, and a rococo revival vase with gilt and enamel decoration. Mid-1840s.

Plate 70. Design by Richardson's for an opaque white vase enamelled with an oriental scene.

his orders that it was entirely owing to the long Credit and that we are not able to give this Credit and were compelled to work for those who paid us quick — I am to draw a bill upon him tomorrow @ 8 months for £150 to fall due in May — said there is only one bill of the long standing bills now out and would be met in December look over these bills and see if correct and if so get his things made as soon as you can and sent off this is what I have agreed with him...I have been very unwell this day am better now so very much bother will cut me short — do stir of the stock — I have agreed to give young Phillips 2½p on any safe paid shipping orders he can get for us say if you approve of this and be ever after sending off the orders and I will try what can be done.

W.H.R.

The Mrs. Conne mentioned in the letter was probably Emily Conne, recorded as an engraver in 1860 and the wife of Nicholas Conne, also an engraver, who worked from 1823/4 until 1854. An Augustin Conne showed engraved glass at the 1851 Great Exhibition. The only known signed goblet by A. Conne shows a glassblowing scene with the motto 'United to Believe/Not Combined to Injure/Industry And Benevolence Unite Us In Friendship'. Its present whereabouts are unknown but it is illustrated in Plate 165 in *English and Irish Antique Glass* by Derek Davis. In the same 1851 Exhibition the glass displayed by J.G. Green, especially the trefoil lipped decanters, was almost certainly supplied

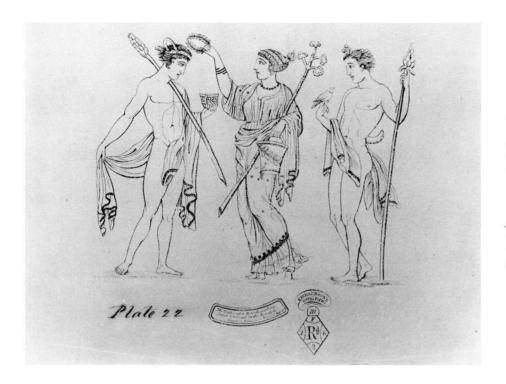

Plate 71. Transfer print
used on Richardson vases
showing the Richardson
mark and the Diamond
Registration for 6 July
1847. This was probably
used as a reference or
record by the Richardson
factory as it is printed on
to a sheet of paper to show
the figures in the same
positions as they appear on
the finished vase.

by Richardson's, perhaps as blanks and engraved by J.G. Green's own workers
(Plate 102).

During the 1840s Richardson designs were at their most brilliant and
inventive, often showing an awareness of foreign events on a broad scale. Two
designs from the Richardson pattern books for enamelled vases show quaint,
picturesque Chinese scenes reflecting the enthusiasm for the chinoiserie mania
sweeping Europe at the time (Plates 69 and 70).

In 1839 the seizure of opium stocks in British warehouses in China gave
Palmerston the opportunity to send out sixteen men-of-war and twenty-seven
troop carriers to Canton. The result was the first of the Opium Wars. Following
the treaty of Nanking in 1842 the island of Hong Kong was ceded to the British,
four ports were opened and access was suddenly available to China. The
botanical collector Robert Fortune visited the country and recounted his vivid
descriptions in four books in the 1840s and 1850s. The Richardson designs may
have been based on Fortune's accounts. In the sale of the contents of Richardson
Hall in 1953 the catalogue listed 'China Illustrated (4 Vols)'.

The Richardson brothers capitalised on another national event when the
Portland vase was smashed in the famous incident at the British Museum in 1845.
Transfer printed vases with the Portland design were soon on the market.
Although the designs in the pattern books show only baluster vases, small white
opaline versions of the Portland vase shape have appeared occasionally bearing
the Richardson mark (Colour Plate 9).

Before 1851 the firm used two marks, one with the words 'Richardson
Stourbridge' in a circle, surrounding the letter P and a number, although very
occasionally the 'Richardson Stourbridge' words are missing. The other, more
common mark said 'Richardson Vitrified', often with the extra words 'Enamel
Colors' (the latter word usually spelled without the 'u'). Transfer printing was

Plate 72. Vase transfer printed with the design in Plate 71 with a blue enamelled background, 1847. Height 12in. (30.6cm).

used extensively until 1851 and a number of transfer prints still exist in the Richardson archive complete with the title of the scene and the factory mark to be fired on the foot (Plate 71). The transfers were either printed straight on to the smooth opaline surface or set against a roughened matt surface with the figures in terracotta red, or with the addition of background colour after the print was fired on to the glass (Plate 72).

The appearance of rococo revival designs in the Richardson pattern books, intermingled among the chinoiserie and neo-classical patterns, confirms the ability of the factory to cater for every taste (Plates 73 and 74). The rococo revival was ignored by influential critics of the time but, nevertheless, from the 1820s until about 1870 it became the most popular commercial style, finding its way into most homes on everything from furniture to ceramics. The Richardson glasses, with their acanthus ornament, urns and cornucopiae, and assymetric, C- and S- scrolls framing bouquets of flowers, are typical of the bolder and more robust Victorian version of its eighteenth century predecessor. To enhance the mass appeal of their rococo designs, many of the Richardson items were given a coloured background.

Colour Plate 9. Page from a Richardson design book showing classical themes including the subject matter found on the Portland vase, c.1845-50. The designs were transfer printed on to the glass. Page size 17in. x 10⅝in. (43cm x 27cm).

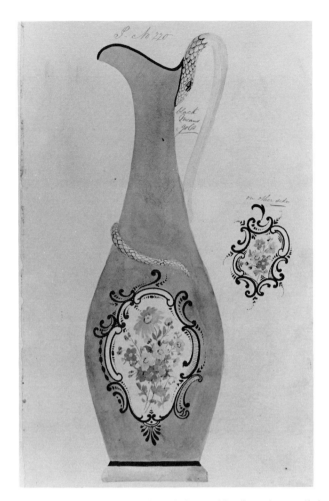

Plates 73 and 74. Richardson designs with gilt and enamelled rococo revival scrolls and flowers.

In 1847 the Richardson family received the first of many official awards. The Society of Arts awarded them their Gold Medal 'which was handed to Mr. Benjamin Richardson by H.R.H. Prince Albert for their specimens of Enamelled Colours on glass.' The following year the Society awarded them their Silver Medal 'handed to them by the Marquis of Northampton (the Prince being prevented from attending) for the Beauty and Purity of their glass and for the merit of their works in Engraved Glass'. A year later they received the Society's Silver Medal 'handed to them by H.R.H. Prince Albert for their Combination of Cut Glass with Venetian ornament'. Justifiably proud of their achievements they described themselves in an advertisement of 1849 as

Manufacturers of Every Description of Engraved, Cut, Frosted, Enamelled and Stained Glass comprising every variety of the Newest and Most Approved Style of English and French patterns. Also Manufacturers and Patentees of a new Vitreous-Stained Figured Glass of the most Beautiful and Transparent Colour, with Richly Executed Designs of Fruits, Flowers, Figures, etc. in shades of the greatest delicacy, and admirably adapted for Churches, Chapels, Halls etc. Also of the Registered New Pattern Waterlily Lamp Shade And a Variety of other Beautiful Cut Glass Shades. Druggists Glass of Every Description.

Plate 75. Left to right. Bowl, cover and stand, opal white with gilding, c.1850. Height 4in. (10cm). Leaf dish, opal white and painted, marked 'Richardson's Vitrified Enamel Colors', c.1847-50. Length 9in. (23cm).

Plate 76. Three Richardson wineglasses of the 1840s. The 'Tendril' wineglass (left) was made for Felix Summerly's Art Manufactures. The glass with the red, white and blue twist stem is found in the Richardson design books. The broad flat cutting on the wineglass was still in fashion at the time of the Great Exhibition. Heights (from left to right) 5¼in. (13.3cm), 7in. (17.7cm), 5in. (12.5cm).

In light of the Richardsons' speed to compete with their overseas rivals it is interesting to note the reference to French patterns in the 1849 advertisement. The Richardson leaf dish (Plate 75) is an identical copy of a French bowl shown by Yolande Amic on plate 21 of *L'Opaline Française au XIX*ᵉ *Siècle*. Examples of early nineteenth century Clichy latticinio glass were in the collections of the Richardson family and may have been brought to the factory in the 1840s to be used as models. The factory was certainly capable of producing coloured canes, judging by the stem of one engraved wineglass which is recorded in the Richardson archive (Plate 76). There is a strong likelihood that Richardson's

Colour Plate 10. Richardson glassware from the 1840s, showing painted, gilded and transfer-printed decoration. The salt cellar matches the design illustrated in Plate 61 while the pressed glass dolphin of the tazza is reminiscent of the dolphin candlesticks seen on New England glass of the same period. On the English version the tail is not connected to the fin on the underside of the body of the dolphin. Heights, left to right: 7⅞ in. (20cm), two decanters both 12½ in. (32cm), 2⅛ in. (5.4cm), 9in. (22.7cm), 5⅛ in. (13cm), 5in. (12.5cm).

used the Venetian technique of heating a row of canes, picking them up on the blowing iron and forming them into vessels (Colour Plate 23).

As one of the leading glass companies of the period it was inevitable that Richardson's should become involved with Felix Summerly's Art Manufactures. Henry Cole established the firm, under the alias of Felix Summerly, in 1847. To many glass enthusiasts it answered a plea expressed by artists and critics for a return to the glassiness of the material. One of Cole's most talented designers, a close friend and an established artist in his own right was Richard Redgrave who strongly advocated the influence of plant forms as decorative elements. Echoing Redgrave's belief, a contemporary writer declared that 'with respect to glass how often it is covered with a ground surface or cased with opal, forgetting that its beauty and its utility also consist in showing the crystal clearness of the water or the ruby brightness of the wine that mantles in it.' Richardson's made three designs for Cole which were the epitome of these ideals. The 'Tendril' glass,

Colour Plate 11. Richardson cut glass from 1851 and 1878. The cutting on the decanter on the extreme left matches the design on the service of Richardson glass illustrated in a catalogue of the Crystal Palace exhibition (see Plate 80). The other two decanters are of the same period and may have been shown at the Great Exhibition. The finely cut jug, carafe, wineglass, tumbler and salt cellar were part of a larger service shown by the firm at the Paris International Exhibition of 1878 and recorded in a photograph album. Heights: decanters, left to right, 13 ¾ in. (35cm), 14 ½ in. (37cm), 13 ¾ in. (35cm); jug 8 ¾ in. (22cm), carafe 6 ¼ in. (15.8cm), tumbler 3 ⅞ in. (9.8cm), wineglass 5in. (12.5cm), salt cellar 1 ¾ in. (4.5cm). 1878 glasses, Hickman Collection.

designed by Redgrave, consisted of a thin gilt thread of glass (the tendril) growing up the stem of the clear glass and spreading its leaves and tendrils on to the base (Plate 76). 'Bubbles Bursting' consisted of a design of cherubs cavorting in fountains of water by H.J. Townsend and was engraved on a champagne glass and soda water glass. The third design was for a set of decanters including a port and sherry which had applied green glass bands on the necks to bear the name of the contents (Plate 77).

RICHARDSON GLASS AT THE GREAT EXHIBITION

Contacts between Cole and the Richardsons were renewed at the Crystal Palace Exhibition when Cole wrote to the brothers, on behalf of Queen Victoria, with an order for a glass 'with a Venetian foot' (Plate 78). Coming after the award of a Prize Medal, the royal order set the final seal of approval on the great

Plate 77. Pair of decanters made by Richardson's for Felix Summerly's Art Manufactures, c.1847-8. Height 13 ¼ in. (33.5cm). Hulbert of Dudley Collection.

achievement of the Richardson brothers after only twenty-one years' existence as glass manufacturers. Such was their pride that they enquired of the exhibition officials if it was possible to strike two extra copies of the Prize Medal in order that each brother could own one. Two pages of the *Art Journal* catalogue to the exhibition illustrated some of the Richardson pieces (Plates 79 and 80). Lampshades made by the company were illustrated in the page of light fittings exhibited by Blews and Son of Birmingham. One of the many catalogues to the exhibition summarised their display:

Cut crystal glass; consisting of centre-dish and stand, complete; with the following articles to correspond; 10 and 8 inch oval dishes, 9 inch plate, sugar basin, quart decanter, and goblet.

Jugs, decanters, butter stands and covers, sugar-basins, oval dishes, celery glasses, goblet, and claret bottle etc.

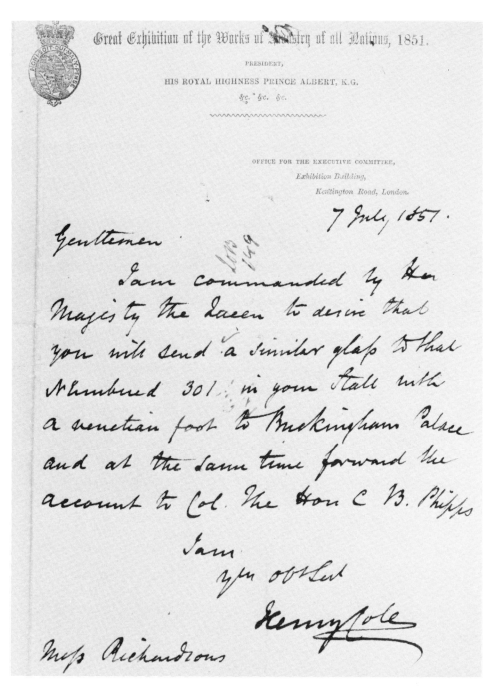

Plate 78. Letter dated 7 July 1851 from Henry Cole to Richardson's ordering a glass with a Venetian foot for Queen Victoria.

A great variety of cut and engraved glass applied to useful and ornamental purposes.

A variety of articles in coloured, frosted, and painted glass. Opal vases, painted with enamel colours; subjects — Ulysses weeping at the song of Demodocus — Judgement of Paris — Diomed casting his spear at Mars — Dream of Penelope — Loch Oich — and from Aesop's Fables, the latter gilt; and various others.

Flower vases of gilt; ruby, black, and flint-glass, cut and gilt; opal glass, painted — Pet Fawn — in enamel colours; opal glass, ornamented with enamel colours — Grecian figures.

Colour Plate 12. Richardson glass from the late 19th and early 20th century. Left to right. Two 'Ceonix' vases, c.1904-5, heights 4⅞ in. and 5⅛ in. (12.5cm and 13cm), Hulbert of Dudley Collection. Vase of green glass with pink trailing, possibly the 'Iris Threaded Glass' introduced in 1891, height 8⅜ in. (21.2cm). Bowl from the 'Firestone' range illustrated in the Pottery Gazette *in 1905, height 6½ in. (16.7cm), Hickman Collection. Vase with a filigree effect, c.1890s, height 11¼ in. (28.8cm), Hulbert of Dudley Collection.*

A large collection of vases, jugs, cups, dishes, decanters, and glasses, exhibiting various modes of ornamentation, modern and Venetian.

Match pots with cover for taper, opal glass, ornamented with enamel colours and crystal glass as specimens.

Using the two pages of illustrations of Richardson glass from the *Art Journal* catalogue, plus the rather vague listing of their display, it is possible to find and identify some of those glasses or ones which at least come very close to the published drawings. Two very exciting and important glasses have survived from the exhibition and are treasured as Richardson family heirlooms (Plates 81 and 82). Both glasses are illustrated in the catalogue (Plate 79) and provide firsthand evidence of the quality of the Richardson exhibits and show why they were awarded a Prize Medal. Apart from proving the accuracy of the line illustrations

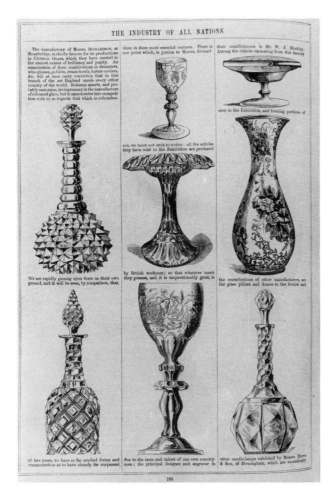

Plates 79 and 80. Pages from the Art Journal *catalogue of Richardson glass on display at the Great Exhibition.*

in the catalogues, the vase and the goblet illustrate another phase of the naturalistic theories of design which went hand in hand with a growing interest in gardening. On the opaline vase the scrollwork, a major feature of the rococo revival, becomes a minor element in the overall design which is dominated by the cascading bunches of accurately depicted flowers and fruit. The three-dimensional flowers carved deeply into the bowl of the goblet could be found in equal profusion on carpets and furnishings and in the Staffordshire earthenware dishes, inspired by Bernard Palissy, with every manner of flora and fauna depicted in vivid and lifelike detail. This over-blown portrayal of nature was anathema to Henry Cole, Richard Redgrave and their disciples who aired their views in the pages of the *Journal of Design,* edited by Redgrave himself. One can appreciate something of that concern when one compares a Richardson vase, enamelled with an abundance of English flowers, to the 'Water Lily' goblet, designed by Redgrave, with its self-effacing allegiance to natural forms (Colour Plate 41). Books of designs, including A.W. Pugin's *Floriated Ornament* of 1849, Owen Jones' *Grammar of Ornament* and his later *Chinese Ornament,* and the writings of Christopher Dresser, tried to establish sets of theories for the transformation

Plates 81 and 82. Vase and goblet which match the illustrations in the Art Journal *catalogue. The engraved work on the goblet is by W.J. Muckley. Heights: vase 20¼in. (51.5cm), goblet 14¼in. (36.2cm). Private Collection.*

of nature into ornament. However, the manufacturers of decorative arts were not about to miss the chance of profits from the popular appeal of floral decoration regardless of the moralising tracts written by the arbiters of taste. A later development of the enthusiasm for plants was the ubiquitous fern decoration seen on engraved glass.

The engraved glass on the Richardson stand, including the surviving goblet, was primarily the work of William Jabez Muckley who was described as the firm's 'principal designer and engraver'. The floral goblet illustrated in the catalogue is unusual in that it comes apart, the bowl and cut knop fitting by a peg into the stem where it curves over in the cut petal formation. Another goblet said to have been part of the exhibition is engraved with the same deep roses but through a layer of ruby glass (Colour Plate 7). The only signed example by W.J. Muckley is a magnificent goblet engraved with a splendid royal coat of arms

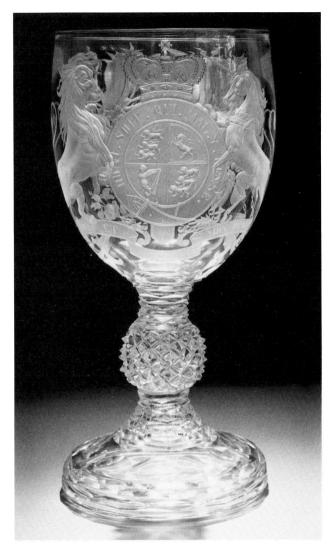

Plate 83. Goblet engraved with the royal coat of arms and bunches of roses. Signed W.J. Muckley; c.1850. Height 13in. (33cm).

Plate 83A. Reverse of the goblet in Plate 83.

with roses on the reverse (Plates 83 and 83A). The prickly cutting on the stem is similar to the body of the decanter illustrated in the exhibition catalogue (Plate 79) and to a salt cellar from the Richardson collection (Colour Plate 45).

Some confusion has arisen in the past over Muckley's identity and his date of birth. In his second edition of *Nineteenth Century British Glass* Hugh Wakefield suggested that the engraver and the W.J. Muckley who was an accomplished painter and became Art Master at the Manchester School of Art were two separate characters. In his earlier book Wakefield also gave the date of birth for the engraver as possibly 1837 which would mean that a fourteen year old was responsible for the quality of glass seen in 1851. The Wordsley parish registers record the baptism date of William Jabez (or Javus) Muckley as 5 July 1829. It is much more acceptable to imagine him at the age of twenty-one, rather than fourteen, as one of the most accomplished English engravers of his day. Muckley does not appear after the 1851 Exhibition and it may be that he did leave the Richardson works to settle in Manchester. The coincidence of the identical names seems too great otherwise.

One recent discovery of a white opaline vase enamelled in sepia and bearing the traces of a Richardson mark matches the description from the official catalogue of an 'Opal Vase painted with enamel colours: subject — Ulysses weeping at the song of Demodocus' (Plate 84). Apart from its importance as a highly probable 1851 Exhibition piece the vase also opens up the possibility of an attribution to the decorator Thomas Bott. There is much speculation about the work of Bott for Richardson's. Many of the enamelled vases with floral decoration are often attributed to Bott but with no basis in any existing evidence. When he worked at the Worcester Porcelain Factory one of his preferences was for monochrome enamelling and it may be that he established this technique during his time at the glassworks. A further tantalising connection with Bott and the Ulysses vase came in the shape of a pattern book belonging to Thomas Bott which appeared in a Christie's sale. One page showed a vase in the same shape as the Ulysses piece but with geometric decoration. The tentative connection between Bott and sepia enamelling raises the possible authorship of the rest of the sepia pieces by the Richardson factory (Colour Plates 10 and 41).

Cut glass from the 1851 Richardson exhibit was made to exacting standards judging by the illustrations in the catalogue. The cut pillars on the illustrated dessert set and the claret jug (Plate 80) precede the rock crystal style by some thirty years. A set of three decanters cut in a matching pattern to the claret jug must be contemporary pieces (Colour Plate 11). The profile of the decanters and the stoppers matches one of the catalogue illustrations, especially in the way the shape spreads out at the base.

THE NEXT FIFTY YEARS

Royal patronage and an international reputation would normally guarantee continued success but in this case it was not to be. The Richardsons' greatest achievement was marred by financial difficulties which had appeared as early as 1848 when Benjamin mortgaged his interest in the trade as security for liabilities of £4,450. The cost of their stand at the Crystal Palace Exhibition must have added an extra burden. By February 1852 the firm was bankrupt. William Haden's own comments reveal his sense of injury: 'In Feb. 1852 I was made unjustly bankrupt thro' a Vilanous old Banker and Faculty Lawyer who swindled me out of Thousands. Notwithstanding this every creditor was paid in full. It cost me 84/- for every 20/- owed'. The slight matter of bankruptcy could not dampen the Richardson determination to succeed. Benjamin and Jonathan had buried and concealed tools and moulds from the glasshouse which were used to re-establish the works. Within a year they displayed glass at the Dublin Exhibition of 1853. A new chapter of achievements began which placed them once again among the top innovators during the late nineteenth century.

Following the bankruptcy and the re-establishment of the firm it was known

Plate 84. White opaline vase, sepia enamelled with a scene of Ulysses weeping at the song of Demodocus, after an engraving by Flaxman; c.1851. Height 18½ in. (47.2cm).

Plate 85. Jug with vermicular pattern registered by Richardson's on 24 August 1854. Height 9¾ in. (25cm). Hulbert of Dudley Collection.

as 'B. Richardson' although it appears that William Haden was kept informed about developments. Little is known about the products during the 1850s and 1860s but the glass that survives from that period suggests it was a time of experimentation and preparation for the future. Acid etching was developed in the 1850s, as witnessed by the blue cased wineglass signed 'B. Richardson 1859' (Plate 155). The vermicular, or vermicelli pattern as it is sometimes called, was registered on 24 August 1854, number 96703, on a trefoil lip jug (Plate 85). The double twist loop handle on this jug was another Richardson innovation. On 27 July 1857 Benjamin Richardson had patented the idea for air trap decoration, that is of enclosing air bubbles inside a glass body by dipping the original gather into a dip mould which had diamond shapes or other protrusions inside it. These would press into the molten glass causing indentations which, when cased over with clear glass, would create the regular pattern of air bubbles. The summary of the patent stated:

Ornamenting; moulding; blowing. — Glass ornaments are formed by blowing glass

Plate 86. Photograph of the Richardson glass shown at the 1878 Paris Exhibition.

into a mould constructed to produce a design on the exterior of the glass; the design may consist of air bubbles formed in the glass. The moulded article is coated by dipping it in the glass of the same or different colour, or by enclosing it in a cup of glass blown to receive it, the blowing being continued until the article is shaped as desired.

In September 1863 Benjamin wrote to William Haden to report on signing the deed for the new partnership of the company which was fully operational in 1864 under the name Hodgetts, Richardson and Pargeter. During this partnership the firm produced a wide range of cut, engraved and acid etched glassware but without introducing any new ideas. Philip Pargeter left in 1870 to take over the running of the Red House Glass Works and the firm then became Hodgetts, Richardson and Son. Under the new partnership the firm began to contribute new techniques and designs such as the threading machine, patented by W.J. Hodgetts on 6 May 1876, which revolutionised that type of decoration. In addition, the company, under Henry Gething Richardson's name, registered new designs for glass each year from 1872 until 1876 and again in 1879, 1881 and 1882.

Following the successful reproduction in cameo of the Portland vase by John Northwood in 1876 (see the chapter on Cameo Glass) Richardson's appointed Joseph Locke and invited Alphonse Lechevrel from France to enable them to compete for the new cameo market. The hard-won results of their efforts were displayed at the Paris Exhibition of 1878 when the firm ended a self-imposed ban

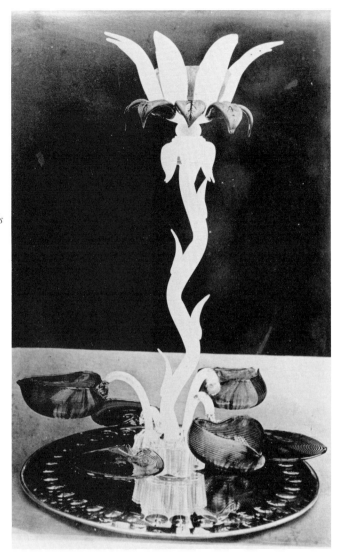

Plate 87. Photograph of a centrepiece from the 1878 Paris Exhibition album. The lower trailed holders were in green, the stems clear frosted, the top flower petals in green and the bowl inside in orange mottled glass. The price was 54s. (code ah/-).

on taking part in international exhibitions. The display was stunning and re-established, yet again, the Richardson company as one of the major English glass producers. Before the glass went off to Paris it was photographed at the factory (Plate 86), probably in the room marked 'Photo Room' on the plan of the site (Plate 4), and the photographs placed in albums. One of the albums has survived with a total of seventy-two photographs, making it a unique record of contemporary styles and fashions (Plates 87 to 93).

The album is the largest collection of photographs of glass exhibited by a company at one particular exhibition. It forms a time capsule of shapes and techniques in 1878 which veer from the lavish to the tortuous. The group photograph shows the cameo vases by Lechevrel and Locke, including the Portland vase, surrounded by cut lustres, engraved jugs, trailed centrepieces, heavy cut glass services, fantastic flower stands and a birdcage (Plate 86). Individual photographs were taken of each piece or set of glasses and often tinted to show the colours of the objects. Sixteen flower stands, in varying degrees of

Plate 88. Tiered centrepiece threaded with amber glass shown at the 1878 Paris Exhibition. The price was 189s. (code Rso/-).

complexity, formed a large part of the stand (Plates 87 and 88). Threaded decoration was a prominent feature, not unexpectedly, to show off the benefits of the newly patented threading machine by Hodgetts. Another dominant pattern was the rope twist or incised twist technique used for handles, feet and stems (Plates 89 to 91). Acid etching was used either to create floral and figurative scenes on clear glass, or to etch two layers of coloured glass (Plates 91 and 92). Two pages show brown and green glasses which may have been a version of Webb's bronze glass. A dispute between Webb and the Richardson factory, who were said to have infringed Webb's patent for bronze glass, ended with a letter from Richardson's to Webb's claiming that they had stopped experiments with iridescent glass at the time of the 1878 Paris Exhibition. Four cut glass services varied from bold hobnail patterns to the intricate diamonds cut over the entire surface (Colour Plate 11). The cameo vases by Locke and Lechevrel formed the centre of attraction with the Frenchman's 'Raising an Altar to Bacchus' as the high point, although for some unknown reason it does not appear in the group

Plate 89. Three glasses from the 1878 Paris Exhibition. The right-hand tazza was made in pale green glass. Prices were (from left to right) 7s.6d. (d/r), 10s. (Rn/-), 15s. (Ra/-).

Plate 90. Part of a service shown in Paris in 1878. The threading was in turquoise blue, a characteristic colour at Richardson's. Prices were (from left to right) 45s., 40s., 87s., 40s. and 35s.

Plate 91. Acid etched decanter and jugs from the 1878 Paris Exhibition. Prices were 18s., 15s. and 16s. respectively.

Plate 92. Liqueur pot, clear glass cased with blue and acid etched, with matching cups and saucers on a gilt plateau. The complete set sold for 166s. (code Rrr/-). From the 1878 Paris Exhibition album.

photograph. A typed slip of paper next to the photograph of the Bacchus vase in the album describes the cameo:

> The subject here represented is a Term, which a Satyr and two Bacchantes are uplifting on a pedestal. The scene is ingenious; the brow-horned Satyr bears on his robust shoulders the god's statue ending in a Sheath; whilst the young Bacchantes, scantily clothed, and with dishevelled hair, give help for the installation of the rural deity. A third personage in the back-ground holds the portable altar upon which sacrifices will be offered.

In the whole album the two pieces that do not have price codes are Locke's Portland vase and Lechevrel's 'Raising an Altar to Bacchus'.

When the photographs were stuck into the album, each item was marked with the price using a code known only to the Richardson family. The code was an ingenious idea thought of at the very start of the business and used throughout its existence. The firm's own name was the code with the letters numbered from 1 to 9 and finishing with 0:

R i c h a r d s o n
1 2 3 4 5 6 7 8 9 0

The two letter r's were differentiated by upper and lower case so that Rr/- stood for 16s. The use of codes seemed to be widespread amongst the Stourbridge firms and prevented the work-force knowing too much about charges and profits. At Webb's the code was the word PROVIDENCE with the last E changed to an H to avoid duplication.

The history of the firm after the success of the Paris Exhibition and the award of a Silver Medal was a repeat of the events following the Crystal Palace Exhibition. Although the firm continued to make a wide variety of decorative and utilitarian glassware there were no great innovations as witnessed at the two main rival factories of Webb's, and Stevens and Williams. It was as if every scrap of energy was channelled into the success of an international exhibition leaving the company exhausted for years after until it revived to become a fresh force. By 1882 Henry Gething Richardson (1832-1916) was running the company under his own name following the retirement of W.J. Hodgetts in 1881 due to ill-health.

An impression of the firm's products from the last twenty years of the century is gleaned from the pages of the *Pottery Gazette*. In March 1884 a 'new fancy glass' appeared 'in cream and new magenta colours, with a very graceful floral treatment'. Little can be made of that reference in isolation but the appearance of the extraordinary 'Convolvulus Vase' in 1885 (Colour Plate 33) suggests that furnace applied decoration may have become a speciality. In 1891 the novelties for the coming season included the 'Convolvulus Glass' and the 'Iris Threaded Glass', made in different styles and colours suitable for floral decoration. A vase in green glass with pink threads, said to be from the Richardson factory, may be an example of the 'Iris Threaded Glass' (Colour Plate 12). Latticinio or filigree glass was also made in the 1890s (Colour Plate 12).

By 1897 the newly organised London showroom in Holborn Circus

Plate 93. Trailed decanters, carafe, vase and jug, tinted brown on the photograph perhaps to suggest bronze glass. Other versions were available in emerald green and pale green. Prices were: top row 10s.6d. and 9s.; bottom row 3s.6d., 8s. and 6s. From the 1878 Paris Exhibition album.

concentrated on lighting fixtures. Globes, moons and shades for gas, oil and electricity were decorated by etching, enamelling and tinting, cutting and engraving. Services of etched, engraved and cut glass remained an important money earner in the middle price range while richly cut glass and 'Old English Cut Glass' catered for a more expensive market. Flower stands, centrepieces and posy holders formed a large part of Richardson's output at the end of the century. The mixture of flower vases and stands, lighting fixtures, and cut, engraved and etched services was similar to the combination of goods which Smart Brothers advertised in their printed catalogue (Colour Plates 36 and 37). The Richardson flower holders seemed more imaginative than Smart's and often combined separate vases on brass supports. An established favourite in 1897 was the 'Fir Cone' range in which small posy vases shaped as opalescent fir cones were grouped along glass or metal branches. In 1898 the 'Campanula' range was added to the 'Fir Cone'. Opalescent blue bell-flowers were arranged either singly or in groups of up to a dozen, on straw colour or light amber rustic feet. Yellow and flint opalescent flowers were available later. An 'Amberina' glass was used for flower holders of all kinds including a hyacinth glass with an indentation in the side to take a stick to support the flower.

In May 1899 the *Pottery Gazette* reported the large number of cut goods available in the London showroom but focused on the new 'Bamboo' ware for flower holders. This design was similar to the Stevens and Williams 'Bamboo' ware and consisted of two or more bamboo tubes supported and connected by horizontal

H. G. RICHARDSON & SONS.

Plate 94. Photograph from the Pottery Gazette *of August 1906 showing Richardson's 'Sunflower' range of flower holders.*

glass bars. The following year an 'Acorn' range was brought in and in 1906 the 'Sunflower' range kept pace with the constant demand for flower holders (Plate 94). Two designs published in the *Pottery Gazette* in 1905 showed that the factory still had the potential to invent 'interesting novelties in art glass' (Plate 95). 'Ceonix' was the name given to a series of vases where the effect was achieved simply by the marbled colours in the body of the glass. The second design was for vases and bowls with festoons of 'Firestone' placed against a satin finished ground (Colour Plate 12). Identical festoon decoration was used by other firms but not as far as is known in the 'Firestone' opalescent effect.

Light fittings continued to be a prominent feature of the company's products in the early twentieth century. A light green colour, called 'Fumée Verre', was used for a silky effect on light shades. In the late 1920s the firm reverted to cameo production with the 'Cameo-Fleur' design, wrongly called 'Pseudo-Cameo', of etched blue, green, amber or amethyst flowers against a clear stipple etched or cut background. Thomas Webb's continued production of the design when they

HENRY G. RICHARDSON & SONS, STOURBRIDGE.

Plate 95. Photograph from the Pottery Gazette *of July 1905 showing the 'Ceonix' range of marbled glass flanked by two 'Firestone' vases with festoon decoration.*

took over the Richardson company in 1930. After a glorious hundred year history it was ironic that they should be taken over by the company whose founder had provided more than half the capital for the original partnership in 1829.

OTHER MEMBERS OF THE RICHARDSON DYNASTY

There is no doubt that the Richardson family influenced the course of glassmaking in the nineteenth century. The unpublished letters from the family archives reveal the hitherto undocumented role played by William Haden Richardson but a great deal of information still needs to be collected to form an accurate picture of other members of the family. Benjamin Richardson II was involved in the glassworks, yet nothing is known of his contribution. When the *Pottery Gazette* reported on a visit to the London showroom in 1897 Benjamin Richardson acted as the guide. Whether this was Benjamin II or Benjamin III is not certain. The third Benjamin was born in 1864 and became the last of the family to be involved in the glassworks. His donation of the Richardson Collection of Glass to Stourbridge, now incorporated in the Dudley Metropolitan Borough Collections at Broadfield House Glass Museum, provides a major source of information on the company's products. At his death in 1952 many important records and documents were removed from Richardson Hall and burnt. Fortunately some were rescued by Herbert Woodward, the Keeper of Glass at the then Brierley Hill Glass Museum.

From the large Richardson family two sons were involved in glassmaking operations away from the Stourbridge area. John T.H. Richardson (1835-1913), the son of Jonathan and Sarah, joined the Tutbury Glass Company in 1863 as a managing partner. By 1871 he had established the works in Tutbury, Staffordshire, known as the Royal Castle Flint Glass Works which ran until 1899 when it was taken over by Corbett and Company. Advertisements of 1879 and 1881 in the *Pottery Gazette* show two glasshouse chimneys surrounded by extensive outbuildings. The products were described as 'flint, emerald, and ruby glass, cut and engraved for home and export trade.' In August 1899 the factory was honoured with a royal visit from the Duchess of York who was staying at Tutbury Castle. According to the *Pottery Gazette* of 1 September 1899, the Duchess expressed 'surprise at the expeditious and workmanlike manner in which the molten glass was manipulated, particularly ornaments such as swans, Jacob's ladders, and miniature Wellington boots. One of the men made with lightning rapidity a small model of a pig, whereupon her Royal Highness humorously remarked that that was not the kind of animal described in the song, "When the pigs begin to fly". "Oh! your Royal Highness," said the man, "we can soon get over that difficulty," and at once the pig was adorned with a pair of wings. The incident provoking much laughter, in which the Duchess heartily joined, and requested that it should be despatched with other articles to York House'.

In his obituary notice in February 1914, J.T.H. Richardson was credited with introducing 'many improvements in the manufacture of glass and travelled largely in connection with its development.' In 1870 he produced a shearing machine which would have displaced highly paid workmen, but the Glass-makers' Union would not allow it to be used in England, although it was adopted in other countries. In 1873 he patented a rubbing machine for blowing tumblers (Plate 273), and at about the same time a footboard which turned out cast feet equal to blown ones (Plate 15). He also originated several other appliances which are still in use. The Tutbury works was still in operation in the early 1980s under different management, although by that time it was reduced to badging milk bottles and stamping out bulkhead light fittings.

Of the same generation as J.T.H. and Henry Gething, William Haden Richardson II (1825-1913) began his career in the metal industry. He operated a business manufacturing gas tubes and fittings but his interest in glass led to an offer from James Couper and Sons to join them at the City Glass Works in Glasgow. In 1853, at the age of twenty-eight, he accepted the invitation to take over the management of the works of which he became the sole proprietor in 1900. Under his direction, the company employed Christopher Dresser to design the 'Clutha' range based on Roman and other ancient glass. W.H. Richardson II maintained an active interest in events in Wordsley where he supported a number of causes. He contributed to the founding of the Wordsley School of Art and established a 'W.H. Richardson Scholarship', funded by the income from the Drill Hall which he had purchased and presented to the village. Today it still operates as a community centre for the area. In accordance with his wishes he was buried in the Richardson family vault at Holy Trinity Church, Wordsley, the resting place of many other great glassmakers.

Plate 96. Pane of transfer printed glass entitled 'Taking The Duty Off Glass' with a scene of a monkey wearing a bonnet, smashing windows, mirrors and decanters, c.1845, 6½in. x 6¼in. (16.5 x 16cm).

——————— Chapter Six ———————

The Glass Excise

The introduction of the Glass Excise in 1745 imposed a financial burden and a set of administrative restrictions which severely hampered the operations and the growth of the glass industry. 'It is a matter of astonishment how Flint Glass works existed at all under such a concentration of commercial and manufacturing hinderances as were imposed by the Excise regulations' mused Apsley Pellatt retrospectively in 1849. Eventually, a Commission of Inquiry was set up to enquire into the management and collection of the excise, and its report, published in 1835, recommended the abolition of the tax. Another ten years elapsed before the tax was lifted. Its abolition was greeted with at least one satirical cartoon (Plate 96). The feelings of the glass trade were summed up in a note on the Remission of Glass Duties printed in the *Art Union* of March 1845:

> All lovers of Ornamental Art, and of its combination with the Useful Arts, must have been highly gratified by the total abolition of the excise on glass, announced by the Premier as part of his financial arrangements for the present year. In the whole range of fiscal duties, it would be scarcely possible to discover an impost every way so objectionable as that which is now about to be abolished... The materials of which glass is composed are, for the most part, worthless for any other purpose; the value added to them by the skill, the labour, and the ingenuity of manufacturers may consequently be regarded as the creation of so much new capital to be added to the stock of national wealth. Hitherto our manufacturers have been actually prohibited from making any improvements in their products, not only because their experiments were rendered costly by being subjected to taxation, but also because their processes were stringently regulated by the Board of Excise,...
> It was obviously impossible that any manufacture should flourish when persons utterly ignorant of the business had the power of prescribing the routine that was to be observed in every part and process of the fabrication. So far are the English glassmakers from deserving blame because they have in some branches of the art allowed foreigners to outstrip them, that it is highly creditable to their ingenuity and ability that they have been able to maintain the struggle at all.

When the tax was introduced the duty was on materials. Flint and white glass, and crown and plate were charged at 9s.4d. per cwt (50.8kg); bottles and green glass at 2s.4d. A further duty was levied on imports of crown, plate, flint, bottles and flasks, and green glass. A repayment of the full duty, known as the drawback, was allowed on exported glass. In 1777 the former duties were repealed and replaced with a new duty, still on raw materials, for plate, flint, enamel, stained or paste glass and phials. The charge was doubled to 18s.8d. per cwt. By 1794 the duty on materials for the category including flint glass was raised by 10s.8¾d. In the following year new rules were prescribed regarding the process of manufacture with fines of £20 rising to £500. The Act also gave the excise officers the power to interfere with the manufacture 'for the purpose of examining the state of the materials to be charged with the duty.'

In 1807 extra regulations tightened the method of taking the gauge of the materials in the pots, and in 1809 duties on broad glass and crown glass were raised.

In 1811 an important change was made to the method of calculating the duty, following a campaign by the glass manufacturers. The duty was no longer calculated on the weight of raw materials but on the weight of the finished goods. The new duty, fixed at 2s.9d. per cwt on flint and phials, was to last until 1825. Under the new system articles could be made as thinly or as thickly as was required, thereby disproving the often quoted argument that all glass made during the Excise period was by definition light and thin. Evidence from the glass manufacturers proves that there was more profit on heavy, cut glass than on the plainer range of goods. Joseph Price of the Durham Glassworks, Gateshead, stated that 'The disadvantages we labor [sic] under press far more heavily on the plainer articles...than on a richer cut article which sells for a higher amount.' In addition the 1811 Act required every lehr and annealing arch to have its own licence as well as a licence for the glasshouse in general.

A fresh spate of regulations was passed between 1814 and 1819. They dealt with the definition of 'persons who shall be deemed makers of glass', set a new duty of 8s.2d. per cwt on imported bottles, then repealed the same levy, exempted the makers of certain small glass wares or ornaments from taking out a licence as glass manufacturers, altered the laws concerning the quantity of goods made from certain quantities of materials and made changes in the drawback. The 1819 Act made special reference to the difficulties experienced in the preparation of quality optical glass and allowed at least three Treasury Commissioners to alter the regulations if they felt it necessary to ensure the availability of better glass for optical instruments.

The next Act of Parliament, in 1825, ordered that 'every glassmaker, for each and every glasshouse, is required to take out an annual licence amounting to £20'. An invoice of July 1838 sent to the Richardson factory shows the licence fee and a glass duty of £218.6s.8d (Plate 97). The same year saw the duties replaced with a rate of £12.10s. on every 1,000lb. (453.6kg) of material for flint and phial glass. The drawback was set at £29.3s.4d. on each 1,000lb. exported. Any glass left in the pot by Saturday evening was ladled out (a process known as draghading in the nineteenth century), measured and an allowance given on the tax payable.

A second 1825 Act introduced two ideas which brought further condemnation from the glassmakers. The Act re-introduced the charge on raw materials in the pot but retained the clause which required the articles to be weighed after they were made. A duty was charged on the difference in weight between the raw materials and the finished article. If the weight of finished articles from a pot was less than 50% of the weight of fluxed materials gauged to be in the pot, an extra duty was charged on the difference at the rate of 6d. per lb. (.45kg). Further

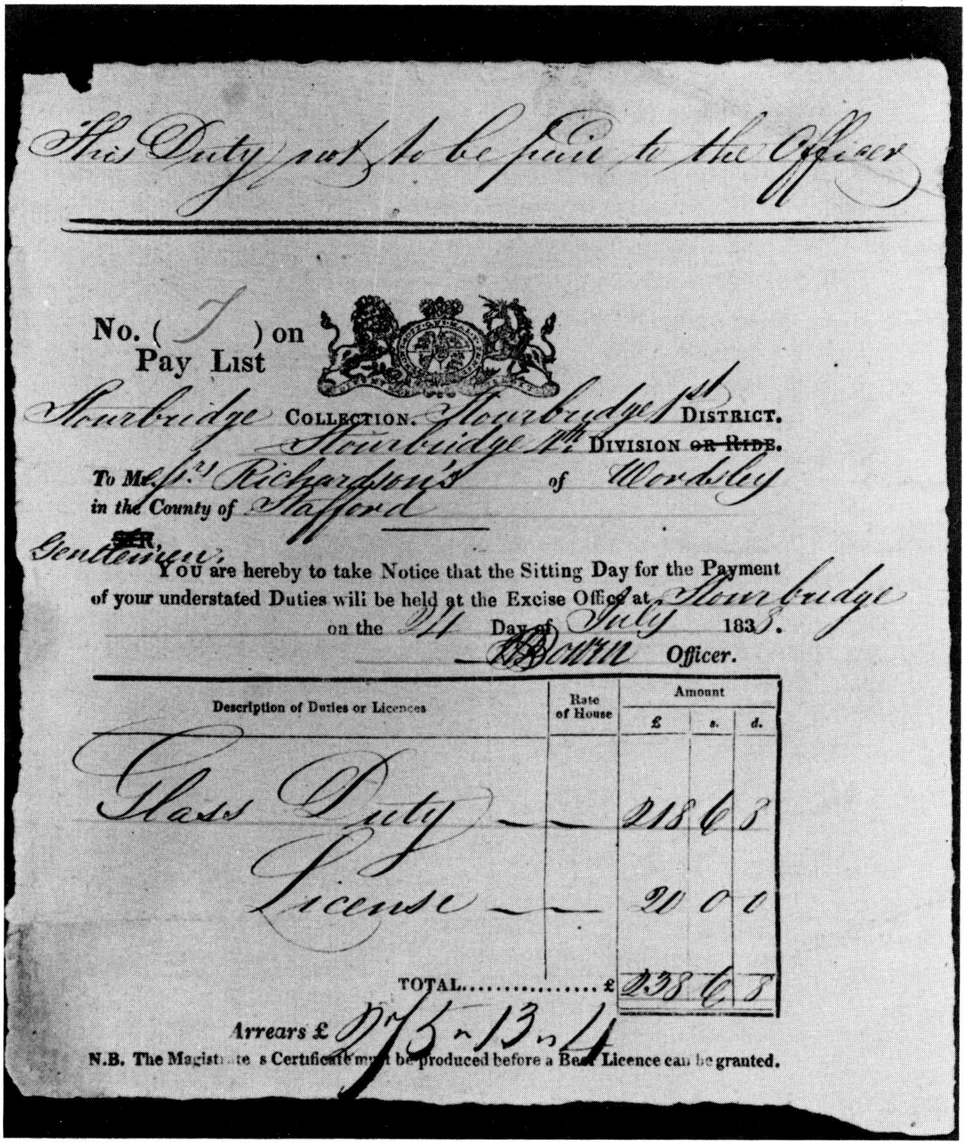

This Duty not to be paid to the Officer

No. (7) on
Pay List

Stourbridge COLLECTION. Stourbridge 1st DISTRICT.
Stourbridge 1st DIVISION ~~OR RIDE~~.
To Mess.rs Richardson's of Wordsley
in the County of Stafford

Gentlemen,
You are hereby to take Notice that the Sitting Day for the Payment of your understated Duties will be held at the Excise Office at Stourbridge on the 24 Day of July 1838.

B Bourn Officer.

Description of Duties or Licences	Rate of House	£	s.	d.
Glass Duty		218	6	8
License		20	0	0
TOTAL		238	6	8

Arrears £ 975-13-4

N.B. The Magistrate's Certificate must be produced before a Beer Licence can be granted.

Plate 97. Bill for payment of glass duty of £218.6s.8d., and the glasshouse licence of £20 issued to Messrs Richardson on 24 July 1838.

inconvenience was caused by the time-scale set for the weighing procedure which was fixed at six week intervals, during which time no glass could be processed. The other feature of the Act was the inclusion of Ireland which until then had enjoyed a total exemption. The immediate effect was to reduce the number of factories in Dublin from four in 1825 to one in 1833. The ten factories in Ireland in 1833 paid a total of £22,399 in duty compared with £45,491 in Scotland and £680,084 in England. The figures confirm that the dominance of the Irish factories in the cut glass market has been greatly overestimated.

In 1832 the duty was altered again to a rate of 20s. on every 100lb. (45.36kg) weight of fluxed materials inside the pot. The 50% figure for charging on the differences in weight was reduced to 40%. The glass manufacturer was now able to declare goods to be imperfect and withdraw them from the charge but a new regulation forced him to pass every type of flint glass through the annealing arch, regardless of expense and inconvenience.

The constant alterations to the laws attempted to close any loopholes in preceding Acts until they created a complex administrative set-up which was the bane of the glassmakers. Furnaces and pots, lehrs, pot rooms, working areas and any rooms used for preparing or keeping glass had to be numbered, measured and recorded in the survey-book, which was the master record of duties paid, and notices served for the various operations. Annealing ovens had to be rectangular with only one entrance covered by an iron grating with proper locks and fastenings, supplied at the expense of the glasshouse owner. The industry was divided into five distinct categories which were restricted to their own speciality. If a factory made anything other than its specified range the rate of duty was set so high as to deter any future production.

Notices in writing had to be given by the glassmakers to the excise officers for every operation, including charging the pots (twelve hours), unstopping the pots prior to glassmaking, heating annealing arches and ovens to take finished articles (six hours), opening the weighing room door for weighing and fixing the duty (six hours) and setting the pots in the furnace (six hours). One glassmaker, giving evidence to the Commissioners, estimated that sixty or seventy notices had to be issued each week. When the finished glass was set into the annealing ovens the amounts were notified and the iron grates were locked and sealed by the officers. Notices requiring the glass to be weighed were compared closely to the first declaration to prevent any illegal removal of glass from the lehr and thus evasion of a charge. In weighing the glass the turn of the scale was given in favour of the excise who allowed one pound weight (.45kg) on each hundredweight (50.8kg) back to the maker.

Three excise officers covered each glasshouse, working a rota of eight hour shifts. The officer in attendance, or stand officer, tried to ensure that every article was entered into the annealing lehr or taken to the room for unannealed glass and none was withdrawn prior to weighing. The regulations took into account possible frauds by the excise officers themselves. At the changeover period between shifts the two officers surveyed or patrolled the glasshouse together. One of the officers not working on the stand was known as the coursing officer. His responsibility was to attend the execution of all the notices in the glasshouse, to record the condition of pot arches, lehrs and weighing rooms and to have responsibility for holding the keys to the weighing room door. The coursing officer and the stand officer organised the weighing of the glass, signed the account book with a record of the gross weight and initialled each lehr pan with chalk as it was removed from the annealing arch.

In 1834 the gross receipts from this complex and unwieldy system came to £916,822. After allowances were re-paid to the factories, and the costs of collecting and supervising the duty were deducted, the Commissioners estimated that no more than two thirds of the gross would benefit the exchequer. It is little wonder that the three Commissioners of the Inquiry, led by Sir Henry Parnell MP, urged 'the expediency of that repeal at the earliest possible period, and by expressing our conviction that no tax can combine more objections, or be more at variance with all sound principles of taxation, than this duty on glass'.

The effect of the duty on the progress of English glassmaking is difficult to judge accurately. The evidence provided to the Inquiry by the glassmakers and the surveying officers is sometimes contradictory, difficult to understand and no doubt biased. In the mass of evidence two points of general concern continued to be raised. A major worry was the problem of fraudulent glasshouses and 'little-goes' or cribs, which could undercut and steal trade from factories which paid the full duty. The fraud included claiming the drawback on exports of glass on which no duty had been paid. Between 1832 and 1834 159 prosecutions were recorded in England, Scotland and Ireland. The most common charges were 'Making glass illegally', 'Removing glass illegally', 'Concealing glass to evade the duty', 'Receiving glass with fraudulent intent', and 'Being found in an unentered Glass Manufactory'. Penalties ranged from 'Goods condemned' to imprisonment. The highest fine was of £2,000 in 1832 for the 'Opening by art and contrivance four Annealing Arches, after having been locked by the Officers.'

The other, much greater, problem, which affected the long term prospects of the trade, was the restriction on experiments. Apsley Pellatt explained the situation in the course of his evidence given on 2 April 1835:

> Are you checked in making experiments in colours by the Excise regulations? — Yes, materially so; particularly in the most difficult colours, red and amber, in which we are inferior to the foreign. For instance, the copper red is a very delicate colour, and requires the pot to be open or shut at the command of the manufacturer whenever he requires it; complying with the usual regulations of the Excise would prevent any chance of success.

The duty charged on the difference between the weight of glass in the pot and the finished articles forced the glassmakers to get as many articles as possible out of a pot or risk paying large sums of excess duty. This was no inducement for taking risks. When asked whether the duties interfered with invention, Richard Shortridge of Newcastle replied: 'Yes: we are compelled to produce forty per cent. of manufactured goods out of a pot charged with the metal, and if we do not, we pay the duty for the deficiency. Suppose a man chose to try experiments, by making one article or another, he could not produce his forty per cent.'

New techniques upset the rigid operation of the excise. A request by the Richardson brothers, to reheat pieces and apply extra glass, was referred to the Excise Office in London for clarification. After a delay of three months, they replied on 2 September 1842:

> Sir,
>
> The Commissioners having considered your application dated the 11th June last requesting permission to attach fresh legs or pillars to certain 'Flower Glasses' of an extraordinary length by heating them and sticking fresh metal thereto and depositing the same in the Lears to be again annealed.

I am commanded to acquaint you that your request is granted upon condition that those parts of the Flower Glasses remaining perfect when taken from the Lears be weighed and charged with Duty as well in the first instance as when subsequently drawn from the Lears.

Hampered at every turn and faced with potential heavy costs on experimental pieces, the glassmakers stayed with tried and tested products of which cut glass was the most profitable. Thomas Badger of Dudley reported that 'Since the year 1826, upon the cut glass, we have made a handsome profit, and this has been swallowed by the loss upon the plain; I venture to say we have not made 2 per cent upon our own capital'.

In recommending the abolition of the tax, the Commissioners of the Inquiry showed an interest in the possible effects and future development of the industry. Apsley Pellatt anticipated 'an enormous increase in all the pressed or moulded glasses imitating cutting, it is generally of great weight — also on massive cut goods which incur great waste'. The author of the 1845 *Art Union* article had expressed the hope that the 'liberated powers will give to this manufacture a variety, an extension, and an excellence such as it has not attained in any other country'. Little could the writer have imagined how well that wish would be fulfilled in the next sixty years.

—————— CHAPTER SEVEN——————

International Exhibitions

The aims of the international exhibitions of the nineteenth century were as varied and complex as the objects on display. Organised by committees of established figures and royalty, the exhibitions were an attempt to impose the moral, religious and educational beliefs of the day on manufacturer and customer alike. The Great Exhibition of 1851 was the first of the international ventures. It was supposed to raise the artistic level of British manufacture and, on a more ambitious level, to promote world peace. Other exhibitions were organised as a matter of one-up-manship between monarchs and emperors, as was the case with the Paris Exhibition of 1855, while others were intended to revive the flagging fortunes of a country. The Paris Exhibition of 1878 was a good example of the efforts to inspire a country after a period of war, an idea which was echoed in the twentieth century with the 1951 Festival of Great Britain Exhibition.

If the aims of the exhibitions were somewhat fallacious and patronising, of more interest now are the objects which were displayed at those events. Glasses from the exhibitions periodically appear on the market but their importance and provenance often go unrecognised. In the last few years the Richardson vase with the scene of Ulysses weeping at the song of Demodocus (Plate 84), the Last Supper goblet (Plate 109) and the fragment of the Morrison tazza (Plate 110) have been identified from illustrations or entries in the catalogues. Sometimes they have been discovered through sheer coincidence and in some instances only identified after the purchase was made. Even with the wealth of illustrations in the exhibition catalogues available to assist with identification, the majority of the glasses that were displayed remain lost or unidentified. For the collector who is prepared to expend a little effort and do some homework on remembering shapes and designs from the exhibition catalogues, the reward can be the discovery of glasses which have a fascinating association with an international movement.

THE PRECURSORS

National exhibitions of objects and the processes leading to their manufacture had been held by England, France and Bohemia in the eighteenth and early nineteenth centuries. In 1761 the first ever industrial exhibition was held under the auspices of the Royal Society of Arts whose mandate was to encourage 'the arts, manufactures and commerce'. In the nineteenth century small exhibitions and displays were held in the provinces while in London, in 1845, a successful 'Exhibition of Manufactures' was held at Covent Garden. Similar efforts were held in France from 1797 and then at irregular intervals until the 1840s. In Bohemia the early nineteenth century exhibitions fulfilled the aims of the organisers and resulted in the development of new colour technology for glassware to compete against English cut glass.

The credit for the first purpose-built exhibition hall went to Birmingham. When the annual meeting of the British Association for the Advancement of Science was to be held in Birmingham in 1849, a temporary building was erected for the occasion. The event almost became the first international exhibition but support from foreign exhibitors failed to materialise. Midlands glass factories made full use of the opportunity to exhibit a wide selection of wares. The catalogue for the exhibition, held at Birmingham Central Library, lists every glass shown by Bacchus and Co., F. and C. Osler, Rice Harris, Lloyd and Summerfield, and W.H., B., & J. Richardson. The brief descriptions make it difficult to identify any of the Birmingham glass today. Fortunately the Richardson family preserved examples for their private collection from the displays which match the catalogue entries (Appendix 3). Two other companies were listed which have since been forgotten. James Jackson exhibited ceramics made by John Rose of Coalport and glass from the Cut Glass Co., Charles Street, Birmingham. Thomas Lane exhibited 'Patent Enamelled Pearl Glass' consisting of panels for use in doors and windows or as pictures. Subjects included views of famous London buildings, country houses and Continental landscapes. In 1849 a short note in the *Art-Union* magazine referred to Lane's 'Japanned Glass' which was much admired by Queen Victoria and Prince Albert. Thomas Lane may have been the same person who established the Eve Hill Glass Works in Dudley.

The temporary structure for the 1849 meeting was replaced in 1850 with the neo-classical Bingley Hall. The building served as an exhibition venue until the 1980s when it was gutted by fire and not rebuilt. The site now forms part of the new International Convention Centre which, together with the National Exhibition Centre outside the city, has restored Birmingham's premier role as an exhibition venue.

THE GREAT EXHIBITION OF THE WORKS OF INDUSTRY OF ALL NATIONS, 1851

From its initial design by Joseph Paxton on a scrap of blotting paper at a railway meeting in Derby, the Crystal Palace, as it was nicknamed by *Punch* magazine, was surrounded by extraordinary facts and figures. The building of the Palace in Hyde Park was a triumph for Midland engineering. The iron girders were supplied by Fox and Henderson while the job of glazing was given to Chance Brothers. The statistics of glazing the Crystal Palace are evidence of the enormity of the task faced by the Birmingham firm to provide the glass panes. In one week eighty men installed 18,392 panes of glass. A single worker could put in 108 panes in a single day. In total Chance's made 956,194ft.11in. (291,448m) of glass in sheets measuring 49in. x 30in. (124.5cm x 76.2cm) which were cut into three panes of 49in. x 10in. (124.5cm x 25.5cm) wide. In January 1851 63,000 panes of glass were made in a fortnight and between August 1850 and February 1851 300,000 panes weighing 400 tons (406.5 tonnes) were fixed in position using a glazing platform designed specially for the task which ran along the gutters cut

Plate 98. Group of glasses shown by W. Naylor at the Crystal Palace. From the Art Journal *catalogue.*

into the iron bars. The building was completed in seventeen weeks. A specially designed transept enclosed a row of elm trees which the pressure of public opinion had managed to save. The problem of birds flying through the building was solved by the Duke of Wellington's idea to use sparrow-hawks to remove the offending creatures.

When the building was opened by Queen Victoria on 1 May 1851, it contained 26 acres (10.5 hectares) of displays and over 100,000 separate exhibits of manufactured goods and natural history. None of the riots and insurrections which had been feared as a result of crowds pouring into the capital ever happened and the exhibition proved to be an outstanding success. By the time it closed on 11 October 1851, 6,039,195 visitors had passed through the doors at a daily rate of nearly 43,000. The success of the venture was a personal triumph for Prince Albert who became a favourite of the British people. The net profit of £186,437 was used to buy the area in South Kensington that now contains the Victoria and Albert Museum, the Science and Natural History Museums, the Royal Albert Hall and the Royal Colleges of Art and Music. Once the exhibition finished the Crystal Palace, originally intended to be a temporary structure, was dismantled and re-erected at Sydenham on the outskirts of London. It was destroyed by a spectacular fire in 1936.

The glass exhibitors numbered 157 and were housed in the Central North Gallery with chandeliers suspended above the displays. The Crystal Fountain made by F. and C. Osler and standing some 27ft. (8m) high formed the centrepiece of the entire exhibition. Two American firms exhibited and there were representatives from France, Germany, Italy, Austria and Bohemia. English tableware firms included Molineaux, Webb & Co.; W.H., B. & J. Richardson; Davis, Greathead and Green; Thomas Webb; Lloyd and

Plate 99. Page showing glasses by Lloyd and Summerfield of Birmingham with ornate applied handles and Venetian style opaque twist stems. From the Art Journal *catalogue.*

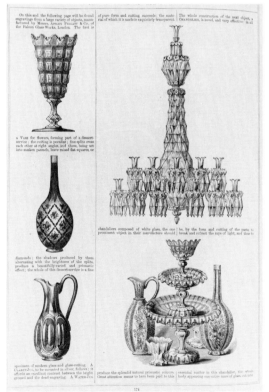

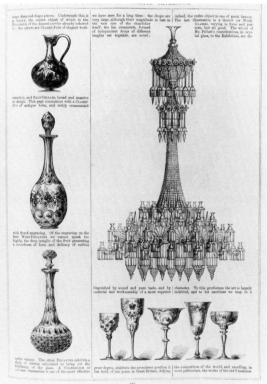

Plates 100 and 101. Pages from the Art Journal *catalogue of the Great Exhibition showing a selection of glass and two chandeliers by the Falcon Glass Works of Messrs Apsley Pellatt.*

Summerfield; George Bacchus and Sons; F. and C. Osler; Rice Harris and Son; E. Varnish and Co; William Naylor; J. Powell and Sons; J.G. Green; and Apsley Pellatt and Co. Irish glass was represented by examples of Waterford cut glass shown by George Gatchell. Every type of glass could be found from flat glass to bottles and tableware.

Some glasses were no doubt part of a commercial range while others were made expressly to capture the attention of the public. The display by W. Naylor typified the love of decoration that was a predominant feature of the exhibition (Plate 98). The Venetian influence appeared on the convoluted stems of glasses by Bacchus, and Lloyd and Summerfield (Plate 99). Apsley Pellatt exhibited 'a great variety of articles, in cut, engraved and frosted glass, and curious imitations of Venetian frosted and gilt glass. The frosted glass, though it may be a revival of an old taste, is now not only a novelty, but has a unique and beautiful effect'. The Pellatt stand also contained models of diamonds including the famous Koh-i-noor. Their chandeliers were commended for looking like 'one entire mass of glass cut into diamond-shape pieces' (Plates 100 and 101).

The critics were divided in their comments about the English glass on display. The cut glass exhibits were described by Somers Clarke as 'mere lumps, cut and tormented into a thousand surfaces, suggesting that the work was made from the solid'. He saw mid-nineteenth century cut decanters as 'a massive lump of mis-shapen material better suited to the purpose of braining a burglar than decorating a table'. Describing the enamelled glass by Richardson's, Ralph Wornum thought it appeared 'to be an attempt at combining two antagonistic elements, the opaque and the transparent; the best of colours, not viewed as transparencies, must appear dull, and even dirty, when compared with the brilliant refractions

Plate 102. Group of engraved glasses shown by J.G. Green at the Great Exhibition. From the Art Journal *catalogue. In September 1850 William Haden Richardson called on J.G. Green 'and told him Cause why we did not attend to his orders that it was entirely owing to the long Credit.' The shape of the jugs in this group suggests they are from the Richardson factory. The 'Neptune' jug, on the left, is in the Victoria and Albert Museum.*

Colour Plate 13. Five vases in the Etruscan style, fashionable from 1847 to 1851. Of the five, only two are definitely known to be English; the one on the extreme left is by Richardson and the one in the centre is by Bacchus. Both have transfer-printed marks. The others can be described as of uncertain origin. Heights, left to right: 12in. (30.5cm), 13¾in. (35cm), 16in. (40.5cm), 14in. (35.5cm), 12in. (30.5cm).

which constitute the chief charms of glass...except upon opal or opaque glass'. The stand of J.G. Green was commended for its 'most delicate engraving...upon some of the most exquisite shapes, constituting another illustration of the accomplished finish of Greek forms'. The clear, engraved glass shown by J.G. Green foreshadowed the preference for engraving later in the century (Plate 102).

Alongside the cased, coloured and engraved glass was the important style known as Etruscan, which reached its peak in 1851. In June 1847 the *Art Union* magazine promoted the new style which it praised for its vitality and novelty while retaining the spirit of the originals. The article was illustrated with vases, jugs, goblets and bowls decorated at the works of a Mr Giller, on blanks made by the Thomas Webb factory (Plate 103). At the Great Exhibition the Etruscan style of decoration appeared on many of the glass stands. One page of the

Colour Plate 13A. Newly discovered glasses from the Great Exhibition period with three souvenirs of the Crystal Palace. Pair of vases in the Etruscan style by Davis, Greathead and Green of Amblecote, height 18 ¼ in. (46.25cm). The vase on the right of the pair matches the design in Plate 106. Cut glass goblet by Richardson matching the design illustrated in Plate 80, height 9 ½ in. (24cm). Jug with blue ribs and engraved panels of flowers, Richardson c.1845-6. According to family tradition it is said to have been displayed at the Great Exhibition. The jug, with a matching goblet, was illustrated in the Art-Union *magazine, April 1846, in an article entitled 'Tour in the Manufacturing Districts, Stourbridge. The Manufacture of Glass'. The blue glass in the pillar-moulded ribs was picked up, on to the clear glass, in the form of blue glass rods arranged round the interior of a dip mould. Height 13in. (33cm). Private Collection. Three souvenirs of Paxton's Crystal Palace. Ruby stained goblet with an engraved view, probably Bohemian, height 6 ⅛ in. (15.5cm). Sulphide paperweight, probably by Apsley Pellatt and Co., diameter 2in. (5.1cm). Hulbert of Dudley Collection. Ceramic pot lid inscribed THE GRAND INTERNATIONAL BUILDING OF 1851/For the Exhibition of Art and Industry of all Nations', diameter 5 ¼ in. (13.3cm). Donald M. Smith Collection.*

catalogue was devoted to the glass of Molineaux, Webb and Co. in Manchester and featured at the bottom right a vase described as 'opalescent...engraved after Flaxman's design of Diomed casting his spear at Mars' (Plate 104). The format of the catalogue illustration is very similar to that used for other opaque white glass with enamelled decoration and the Molineaux, Webb vase was almost certainly in that technique. Only one Etruscan vase is known which may be from

Plate 103. Pages from the Art-Union *magazine, June 1847, showing Etruscan glasses decorated by Mr Giller using Webb blanks.*

the Manchester company (Plate 105). In the past the vase has been incorrectly attributed to the Stourbridge firm of Mills and Walker because of a faint painted mark of 'M,W & Co' on the base. The Stourbridge company operated much later in the nineteenth century by which date this style had disappeared, and therefore the Manchester attribution to Molineaux, Webb and Co. is more creditable.

Of the large numbers of Etruscan style glasses which are known, only those from the Bacchus and Richardson factories are marked with any regularity (Colour Plate 13). The remainder, apart from the solitary Molineaux Webb piece, require other detective methods to provide possible clues to origin. A large group of vases feature a distinctive orange-red colour which may be the characteristic of one particular factory, as yet unidentified. The vase with ochre and black enamelled decoration surrounding the figure riding the griffin is one of a type also not yet identified although it raises some tantalising possibilities for attributions (Colour Plate 13, second right). Known vases of this type are invariably of thick and heavy glass suggesting a British origin. Some of the decorative borders bear a slight resemblance to the Giller/Webb pieces but connections can also be made to Richardson designs, especially the vertical pattern of scroll-work seen on the extreme left of the page of Portland vase designs (Colour Plate 9).

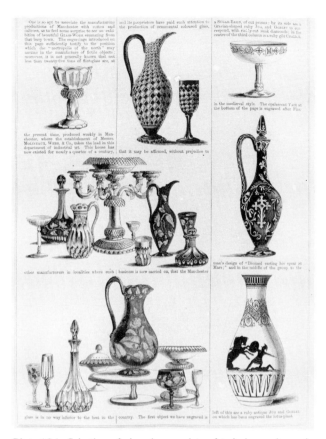

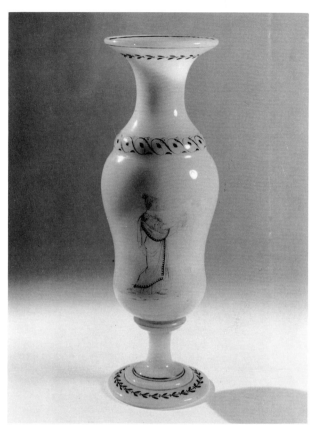

Plate 104. Selection of glass in a variety of techniques shown by Molineaux, Webb & Co. of Manchester at the Great Exhibition. From the Art Journal *catalogue.*

Plate 105. Vase in white glass transfer printed and enamelled with a classical figure. Marked 'M, W & Co', probably for Molineaux, Webb & Co., mid-19th century. Height 11 ¼ in. (28.5cm). Hulbert of Dudley Collection.

The stand of the firm of Davis, Greathead and Green, who operated the Dial Glasshouse in Amblecote (Plate 3), included Etruscan style vases which were displayed on polished black glass slabs. The list of the glass on display mentioned:

> A great variety of vases, jars, and scent-jars, and scent-jars for holding flowers, &c., in the Egyptian, Etruscan and Grecian styles; many of them cut, coated, gilt, painted in enamel colours, after the antique, with figures, ornaments, flowers, landscapes, and marine views, of the following colours, viz., ruby, oriental blue, chrysoprase, turquoise, black, rose colour, opal-coated blue, cornelian, opal frosted, pearl opal, mazareen blue, &c., Topaz, flints, &c.

Three vases from the display were illustrated in the official catalogue and provide the only clue for the identification of the firm's Etruscan vases (Plate 106). In February 1991 a pair of vases were discovered at a Midlands antique fair which match the shape and decoration of the tall central vase in the illustration (Colour Plate 13A). The figures and the geometric decoration are hand-painted and not transfer-printed as was assumed from the style of the illustration. The regular nature of the anthemion scroll-work on the reverse of both vases suggests that it was painted through a stencil. Both vases show a large amount of wear in the enamelled areas, which may explain the lack of facial details on the figures.

Colour Plate 14. Page from J.B. Waring's Masterpieces of Industrial Art and Sculpture at the International Exhibition, London 1862 *showing glass from the stand of Dobson and Pearce, including the Morrison tazza, the most expensive piece of contemporary glass at that date.*

Plate 106. Illustration from the 1851 Exhibition catalogue showing three vases by Davis, Greathead and Green in Etruscan style.

With the discovery of the two vases, the collector now has a benchmark to assist with the identification of the other pieces shown at the Great Exhibition by Davis, Greathead and Green and which have still not been located.

The Great Exhibition was used by artists and manufacturers of fine and decorative art objects as an international arena to exhibit styles and techniques which had developed in the 1840s and earlier. After 1851 many of those styles either waned in popularity or disappeared completely. For all its grand intentions the Exhibition had not encouraged any innovative work. The progress made in colour technology in the 1840s, for example, had to wait until the 1870s for a revival. Of greatest benefit to the English glass companies was the ability for the first time to compare their products side by side with Continental examples.

During the rest of the decade two other exhibitions were held in Europe, in Dublin in 1853 and in Paris in 1855. One result of the Dublin exhibition was the formation of the Irish National Gallery. The Richardson family sent a similar selection to Dublin to the one it had displayed at the Crystal Palace. Apart from

Plate 107. Stereoscopic photograph of engraved Venetian pattern glass by Naylor & Co. at the 1862 London International Exhibition.

Plate 108. Jug engraved with heraldic crest, swags and scrollwork. Shown on the stand of Naylor & Co. at the 1862 London Exhibition. Height 13¼in. (33.8cm).

a large candelabrum by F. and C. Osler, there was little British glass in the French exhibition. French firms accounted for half of the 140 glass exhibits. The most highly praised exhibits were those of Clichy, Saint Louis and Baccarat. The Baccarat display is recorded in a list preserved by the company and included several paperweights.

INTERNATIONAL EXHIBITIONS IN THE 1860s

The 1862 London International Exhibition was larger and perhaps more impressive than its predecessor of 1851. It attracted an even greater audience, calculated at 6,200,000. The building, however, situated on the present site of the Natural History Museum, lacked the popular appeal of the Crystal Palace and was universally condemned. One magazine called it 'a wretched shed'.

Clear glass with engraved decoration formed the highlight of the glass section, at least on the English stands. The Bohemian influence had disappeared to make way for thinly blown Venetian-style glassware with applied decoration of prunts and rope-twist handles and stems. A stereoscopic photograph shows a selection of glass from the display by Naylor & Co. described as 'Venetian pattern' (Plate 107). Of superb quality were a jug and a goblet which have been identified from the colour illustrated guide to the exhibition entitled *Masterpieces of Industrial Art and Sculpture at the International Exhibition, 1862.* The jug is finely engraved with lion

Plate 109. Goblet engraved with a scene of the Last Supper. Shown on the stand of Naylor & Co. at the 1862 London Exhibition. Height 10½in. (26.5cm).

Plate 109A. Detail of goblet in Plate 109.

crests amidst scrollwork and swags of flowers and leaves (Plate 108). The goblet is engraved with a scene of the Last Supper, a theme which was popular among Bohemian engravers in the first half of the nineteenth century (Plate 109).

The finest example of engraved glass at the exhibition was to be found on the stand of Dobson and Pearce. The Morrison tazza consisted of an engraved bowl set with turquoise and gold, placed on an engraved stem and foot with gold mounts. A colour plate in the *Masterpieces of Industrial Art and Sculpture* guide shows two views of it, one in profile and another with a view of the elaborate engraving of the bowl (Colour Plate 14). Described by *The Times* as 'the most extraordinary specimen of art manufacture of its kind in the whole exhibition', the tazza was purchased for 250 guineas, a record sum for a contemporary piece of glass. After its purchase the tazza disappeared and was not found until 1986, when a fragment of the bowl was discovered in a private collection in Quarry Bank in the West

Plate 110. Fragment of the Morrison tazza shown by Dobson and Pearce at the 1862 London Exhibition. The tazza had been lost since the exhibition until this fragment was discovered in 1986. Diameter 8in. (20.6cm). Private Collection.

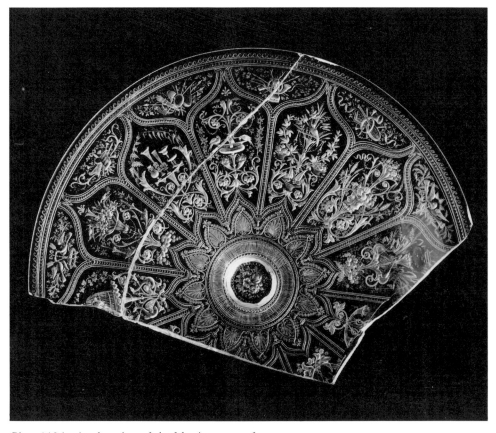

Plate 110A. Another view of the Morrison tazza fragment.

Plate 110B. Detail of the Morrison tazza.

Midlands (Plate 110). The history of the bowl in the intervening years is unknown. It was presented to the present owner by an elderly lady who felt it was of some merit but did not know its history. The diameter of the bowl, in its complete state, would be 8¼ in. (21cm), yet the detail of the engraving is finer and more intricate than pieces twice or three times as large. The goldfish bowl in one of the panels is no bigger than ⅜ in. (1cm), yet contains six well-defined fish (Plate 110B, top right).

One innovation at the 1862 Exhibition was the flower stand or centrepiece. Dobson and Pearce had registered the first design for a flower stand in June 1861 and continued to lead the way with new designs from 1862 onwards. When Pearce went to work for Thomas Webb's in Stourbridge the speciality lines of centrepieces as well as flower stands were probably to Pearce's designs. The 1862 Exhibition also saw the first of the many engraved fern patterns on glass which persisted into the 1870s and 1880s.

The Bohemian glass displays were little different from the 1851 Exhibition in London, although the 1862 Exhibition marked the international début of the Viennese firm of J. & L. Lobmeyr. A fascinating glass from the English engravers' point of view must have been the cased goblet showing Cupid amongst scrollwork engraved by F. Zach. Zach remains a mysterious figure but the quality of his work is evident from known signed pieces (Plate 111).

Plate 111. Large goblet cased blue over clear and engraved by the Bohemian engraver F. Zach, c.1860. Similar scenes entitled 'The Kiss of the Waves' appear on German enamelled porcelain plaques later in the century. Height 12 ¾ in. (32.5cm).

At the Paris Exhibition of 1867 Prize Medals went to the French factories with Baccarat receiving the Grand Prix. The firm showed a magnificent punch bowl and cover with matching tray and glasses, in blue cased glass with fine acid etching. The set is now in the collections at the Corning Museum of Glass. Italian firms exhibited revivals of fifteenth and sixteenth century glasses with attention focused on the displays of Antonio Salviati whose glass was featured in the earlier 1862 Exhibition in London. The British contingent was small, represented mainly by Powell and Sons and J. Defries who showed some ornate chandeliers.

INTERNATIONAL EXHIBITIONS IN THE 1870s

The three major exhibitions of the 1870s were held in Vienna in 1873, in Philadelphia in 1876 and in Paris in 1878. At the Vienna Exhibition Bohemian factories dominated the displays with coloured, cut, gilded and enamelled glass. J. and L. Lobmeyr were the established leaders in engraved glass but also showed a variety of rock crystal glass, enamelled glass copies of seventeenth and eighteenth century German glass and imitations of Near Eastern glass. The French enamelled glass of P.J. Brocard mixed Persian and oriental designs in rich, thickly applied colours. W.T. Copeland of London exhibited a stunning claret jug, now in the Victoria and Albert Museum, engraved with Renaissance motifs by the Bohemian Paul Oppitz who was working in England. Cut and engraved glass continued to be promoted by English exhibitors at the Philadelphia Exhibition. J.G. Green of London had exhibited at Vienna and simply moved the entire stand to America. Green was joined by J. Millar from Edinburgh. Contemporary writers singled out the glass of Lobmeyr and Green for special comment.

Like the earlier Paris Exhibitions of 1855 and 1867, the 1878 Exhibition was an attempt to keep up with other exhibitions despite heavy costs and political upheavals following France's defeat in the Franco-Prussian war. Ironically the aim of the exhibition yet again was world peace. It came at just the right time to show the innovations of the early and mid-1870s from Europe and England. In this sense the 1878 Exhibition, like all its predecessors, merely showed the status quo at the time.

The impressive Richardson display discussed in an earlier chapter epitomised the wealth of techniques which surpassed the European exhibits. The displays of Thomas Webb were filled with new techniques such as bronze glass and styles which covered every period of history, many of them copied directly from Owen Jones' *Grammar of Ornament* and similar 'crib' books. The only technique missing from the English displays was rock crystal. Two claret decanters with Celtic motifs, designed by Webb's chief designer James O'Fallon, may have been in rock crystal but they only survive through drawings which do not give details of technique. The decanters received special comment and helped Webb's to win the Grand Prix. John Northwood's cameo vases were displayed but some of the potential impact was lost as they were shown on separate stands. The Portland vase was shown on the stand of R.P. Daniell, a London dealer; the Milton vase was shown on the stand of J. Green; and the Pegasus vase was shown in an unfinished state on the Webb stand. The English cameo glass would have been seen by Emile Gallé who showed enamelled and engraved glass in oriental patterns. Only one French critic prophesied the great future ahead of Gallé. In comparison with his work the displays of Baccarat and other French firms, although grandiose in size and concept, were criticised by some as old-fashioned. The centrepiece of the Baccarat display was a Temple of Mercury, made entirely of glass pieces which highlighted the silver figure of the god. The Temple has survived and stands in the middle of a lake at an estate in Barcelona. The accusation of 'old-fashioned' may have been better levelled at the firm of Salviati who showed sixteenth and seventeenth century replicas and copies of Roman glass.

At the end of the decade the first international exhibition was staged in Australia. The 1879 Sydney International Exhibition was attended by Thomas Webb's who won a Gold Medal for their stand, described in the pages of the *Pottery Gazette* on January 1880:

This firm make a magnificent display of glass and china, and, owing to the splendid position allotted to them, and the elegant manner in which their exhibits are arranged, their stand is one of the most imposing in the whole building. Occupying a space of 1,200 square feet [111.5sq m], directly in front of the principal entrance to the building, Messrs. Webb's stand is generally the first to attract the attention of the visitor. From an arch over the centre of the stand is suspended a magnificent chandelier for thirty-six lights; it is of the air-twist design, with snake drops. The price of this magnificent piece of workmanship is 400 guineas. Candelabra and candlesticks are shown in great variety, also wall mirrors. The toilet services shown are remarkable for tasteful design and substantial, but not heavy, appearance; they are jewelled ruby and diamond. The cut glass services shown are chiefly designed by Mr. Charles Webb (the head of the firm); they are much admired for their elegant and yet massive appearance. A large display of fancy glass, from the designs of Mr. Wilkes Webb, was much admired by Lord Loftus. Some of the jardinières exhibited are decorated in a high style of art; some are mounted on glass pillars, having a very pleasing effect. The engraved glass services shown are of elegant design, and the workmanship is admirable. Specimens are shown in Byzantine, Greek, Persian, Indian, and Gothic styles. Mr. B.B. Gribbon, manager of Messrs. Webb & Sons' house here, superintended the erection and arrangement of the stand which, by the way, is the one the firm had in the Paris Exhibition last year.

INTERNATIONAL EXHIBITIONS 1880 TO 1900

The buildings erected for the Melbourne Exhibition in 1880 continue to provide the city with an exhibition and conference site. Thomas Webb's won another Gold Medal for engraved glass, some of which was engraved by two employees sent from England. The engravers decided to stay in Australia and established their own workshops. Another exhibition was held in Melbourne in 1888.

In England the International Health Exhibition of 1884 was an unlikely venue for cameo and rock crystal glass. Examples of both techniques were bought by the Victoria and Albert Museum. Webb's won yet another Gold Medal, and collected more gold awards at the International Inventions Exhibition in 1885 and the International Exhibition of Science and Art in 1886.

The next Paris Exhibition came in 1889 and witnessed the aesthetic and technological developments made by Emile Gallé since the 1878 Exhibition. The other legacy of the Fair was the Eiffel Tower. Gallé followed up his success with another dazzling display at the 1900 Paris Exhibition, centred on a reconstruction of a glass furnace. He was joined by Louis C. Tiffany who, like Gallé before him, was made a Chevalier of the Legion of Honour. The only English glassmaker to be honoured in this way was Thomas Wilkes Webb at the 1878 Exhibition.

The nineteenth century saw forty separate international exhibitions take place in settings as varied as Antwerp and Calcutta. Since 1900 an equal number of World Fairs and Expos have continued the attempts by countries to promote and increase world trade. However, few of them have captured the imagination of the public as much as the very first international venture, the Great Exhibition of 1851, described by William Makepeace Thackeray as 'the grandest and most cheerful, the brightest and most splendid show that eyes had ever looked on since the creation of the world'.

CHAPTER EIGHT

The Fine Art of Copper Wheel Engraving

A separate apartment is devoted to the operations of the glass engraver, who is seated at a bench before a small lathe; and to this lathe he attaches one of a series of little metallic disks or wheels, generally made of copper, and varying from an eighth of an inch to two inches [.32cm to 5cm] in diameter. The edge of the rotating disk he touches with a little emery moistened in oil, and then holds the glass vessel against the edge of the disk, by which very minute scratches or indentations are produced. By dexterous changes in the position of the glass, and in the form and size of the disks employed, he combines these indentations so as to produce beautiful intaglios or sunken pictures.

This is strictly a branch of the Fine Arts and as such places the engraver on a different level from the other workmen.

George Dodds' description of a glass engraver, in his *Days in the Factories* of 1843, is little different from the arrangement used by present day engravers (Plate 112). Some of the lathes still in use have been passed down from the engravers who brought them from their native Bohemia when they moved to

Plate 112. Cyril Kimberley engraving a rock crystal glass goblet, commissioned by Broadfield House Glass Museum, at Thomas Webb and Sons, Amblecote, 1979.

Plate 113. 19th century engraving lathe with a selection of copper wheels. The sloping stool allowed the engraver some leverage and support while operating the treadle.

England. Quite often the brass lathes will have the name and date of the maker engraved on the foot. Two lathes which formerly belonged to Joseph Keller are marked 'Made by Franz Anton Flegel, Meistersdorf, Bohemia, 1866'. The main differences between nineteenth and twentieth century equipment are the means of driving the lathe and the number of different grades of emery powder. Throughout the nineteenth century the lathes were powered by the engraver using a foot-operated treadle under the table. This would turn the flywheel connected to the pulleys driving the spindle carrying the copper wheel (Plate 113).

The marvellous skills of the Victorian engravers are all the more astonishing when one realises that they not only had to hold quite heavy items and manipulate them under the wheel but had to control the treadle at the same time. Heavy pieces would be suspended from slings to allow the engraver an occasional break from supporting the weight of the glass on his arms. Modern engravers invariably use a motor to drive the lathe but at the expense of the fine control of the speed available by treadling. This reduction of control, combined with fewer grades of

Plate 114. Rummer engraved with two scenes of a boxing match, c.1820. Height 7¼in. (18.5cm). Cannon Hall Museum, Barnsley.

Plate 115. Jug engraved with a waggon and horses and a signpost marked London/Dudley, possibly Dudley c.1800. Height 6½in. (16.5cm). Cannon Hall Museum, Barnsley.

abrasive emery powder dabbed on to the wheel in an oil mixture, has resulted in the range of shadings and nuances on modern engraving being less diverse than they were a century ago.

EARLY NINETEENTH CENTURY ENGRAVING

The engraved glass from the first forty years of the century provides a charming document of English social history whether it be sporting life, architecture or industrial scenes. The engravers were totally at home with their subject matter and there is no sign of the foreign influences which played such an important role from the 1840s onwards. The naïve and refreshingly innocent view of ordinary daily events more than makes up for any lack of finish. Like Thomas Hardy's novels, the engraved glasses are evocative reminders of a way of life long since vanished. A boxing match is brought to life through the clever juxtaposition of two separate pieces of action (Plate 114). As the eye moves between the two one gets the same result as a children's flip book where the sequence of still images moves as the pages are flicked through at speed. A similar effect is achieved on the scene of the waggon and horses approaching a gate while on the opposite side of the glass a signpost points the waggon master on the route between London and Dudley (Plate 115). The appeal of the glasses is enhanced by the great

Plate 116. Rummer with hollow knop stem enclosing a coin. Engraved with a horse and jockey and the initials GW. Inscribed in diamond point on the underside of the foot 'T. Hudson Engr. Newcastle No. 5 1843'. Height 7¾ in. (19.7cm).

Plate 117. Rummer with lemon squeezer foot engraved with a named view of the Bell Rock Lighthouse. Possibly North-East, c.1811. Height 9½ in. (24cm). Cannon Hall Museum, Barnsley.

probability that they were part of the events they depict, the jug perhaps used by the waggon master at home or in his local hostelry, or the boxing match rummer presented to the winner of the contest.

One of the strongest wheel engraving traditions was established in Newcastle and Sunderland by the middle of the eighteenth century and was responsible for a number of important glasses in the first half of the nineteenth century. Some of the well-known Sunderland Bridge rummers and other commemorative glasses may have been the work of Robert Haddock, recorded in Sunderland directories from 1854 to 1869, and Robert Pyle who appears from 1827 to 1853. In Newcastle, the Hudson family were involved with glassmaking and engraving in the 1780s when Robert Hudson was recorded as a 'glass cutter and engraver'. His son, Thomas Hudson, continued the engraving tradition although he was recorded as an 'Innkeeper' at the Black Bull Inn next to his father's glass and china shop at High Bridge in 1827. One of Thomas Hudson's specialities was the portrayal of racehorses, no doubt from the Newcastle race meetings held on the Town Moor. One goblet engraved with a horse and jockey scene bears the initials GW within a panel and is signed on the base 'T. Hudson

Plate 118. Rummer engraved with a view inside a forge, probably Midlands, c.1810-20. Height 4⅞ in. (12.4cm).

Plate 119. Halfpenny token issued by John Wilkinson, Iron Master, in 1787. Diameter 1⅛ in. (2.9cm). Peter Glews Collection.

Engr. Newcastle No. 5 1843' (Plate 116). The motif of the basket, on the reverse, above the panel with the initials, is found on other rummers with North-East connections and may be a hallmark of North-East engravers. The motif appears on a magnificent rummer engraved with a named panel of the Bell Rock Lighthouse (Plate 117). The Bell Rock or Inchcape Rock Lighthouse was constructed between 1807 and 1811 on a notorious sunken ledge in the fairway to the Firth of Tay due east of Dundee. Two other rummers showing the Bell Rock Lighthouse were sold at Sotheby's in 1970 and 1972, one of them also decorated with the Nelson Monument in Edinburgh, constructed between 1805 and 1816. The scrolling leaf pattern and the thistle and rose decoration around the rim of the present example are identical to recorded glasses with Boston associations. One rummer is engraved with the Boston Stump and dated 1815. The other rummer is engraved with Boston Bridge and Church and is dated shortly after 1807 when the Boston Bridge was constructed by Thomas Telford. The most likely origin for a group of glasses that encompass both Scotland and Lincolnshire would be North-East England.

Apart from Thomas Hudson, only two other Tyneside engravers are known from signed glasses. John Watson signed four examples between 1823 and 1834 and John Williams' signature is found on two. Many other engravers have been identified from trade directories and church records. They constituted a thriving business of engraved glass which was to re-emerge at the end of the century in the form of the disaster glasses.

Less common glasses depict industrial scenes copied from trade tokens of the period. One rummer features an interior scene of the tilt hammer in an ironworks belonging to John Wilkinson which is copied directly from a halfpenny token, first issued by Wilkinson in 1787 (Plates 118 and 119). Another goblet from the

Plate 120. Rummer engraved with a blast furnace, probably Stourbridge, c.1820-40. Height 8¾in. (22cm).

Plate 120A. Detail of the engraving on Plate 120.

period between 1820 and 1840 provides one of the most accurate records of a four furnace blast plant (Plates 120 and 120A). A possible source for the picture may have been a token issued by the Priestfield Furnaces at Bilston in 1811 (Plate 121) but the engraving on the glass is so accurate that the engraver may have worked from a contemporary drawing or even sketched the factory himself if the glass was a special commission by the owner. The two pairs of furnaces are exactly as one would expect of the period with the charging incline complete with waggon, blast regulator, haystack boilers and tunnel heads. The slag heap on the right even shows the cakes of slag.

Plate 121. Trade token of Priestfield Furnaces, Bilston 1811.
Dudley Museum and Art Gallery.

Plate 122. Decanter, diamond point decoration of rows of flowers
and the inscription

WATER
Mary Fillingham
Leadenham
Nov 15
1829

On the reverse the inscription reads:
Let mirth abound, let social cheer
Invest us all assembled here;
Let blithesome innocence appear
To crown our joy;
Nor envy, with sarcastic sneer,
Our bliss destroy.

There is a diamond point drawing of a head in profile on the pontil mark, also the initials 'BH' and
the signature 'T. Stubley Engraver'. Height without stopper 12½ in. (32cm), with stopper 14¼ in.
(36cm). Michael Parkington Collection.

Although wheel engraving was the normal type of decoration, other engraved
techniques were used in the first half of the nineteenth century. Rare examples
occur with diamond point engraving (Plate 122). One group of rummers and
tumblers carry naïve diamond point decoration of hunting and shooting scenes,
railway engines and coats of arms intermixed with doggerel verse. Many are
signed 'Sutherland, London' and have the common characteristic of the royal
coat of arms. They range in date from 1847 to 1863. At Yarmouth William
Absolon decorated coloured rummers and tumblers with crudely engraved

Plate 123. Green rummer, engraved with horse and trap and the motto 'A TRIFLE FROM YARMOUTH', with on the reverse 'PLENTY TO A GENEROUS MIND'. Early 19th century. Height 4⅞ in. (12.4cm). Michael Parkington Collection.

Plate 124. Dark green bottle, coarse stippled decoration of wheat sheaves and mason's tools with the name and date William Kemp 1838. Probably made in Alloa, Scotland. Height 9½ in. (24cm).

coaching and farming scenes, intended for a souvenir market (Plate 123). In Scotland, the bottles made by the Alloa glassworks were decorated with names, dates and simple designs of tools and wheat sheaves, possibly with Masonic connections, using a coarse type of stippled decoration (Plate 124).

THE BOHEMIAN ENGRAVERS

By the late 1840s the influx of examples of Bohemian engraved glass swept away the English tradition. In 1849 probably the finest example of Bohemian engraved glass was in England in the possession of Apsley Pellatt who described it in his *Curiosities of Glassmaking:*

> A most beautifully engraved vase by a Bohemian artist, is in the possession of the author; the workmanship is even more elaborate than that of the Portland Vase; the subject is from Le Brun's painting of the conquest and final overthrow of the Persians at the battle of Arbela, by Alexander the Great. For depth of workmanship and artistic execution, as a modern intaglio engraving, this vase is unrivalled.

Pellatt thought so highly of the vase that he included it, next to the Portland vase, the Naples vase and the Auldjo jug, in the illustration in the frontispiece of his

Plate 125. Vase and cover, signed and dated August Bohm 1840. The vase, engraved with a scene based on the Lebrun painting in the Louvre of Alexander defeating the Persians, is Bohm's masterpiece. Plaster casts of the panel were treasured in Bohemia. Height 23in. (58.4cm). Private Collection, on loan to Broadfield House Glass Museum.

Plate 125A. Detail of Bohm vase.

book. The engraved panel on the vase was the work of August Bohm and must rank as his masterpiece (Plate 125). On the reverse is an engraved inscription in French which, translated, reads:

> Valour overcomes every obstacle. Alexander crosses the Granicus, attacks the Persians whose forces far outnumber his and puts their vast hordes to flight.

Signed and dated 'Gravirt v. Aug. Bohm aus Meistersdorf in Bohmen 1840', the vase was considered so highly that plaster casts were taken and kept in Bohemia to encourage other engravers. The impact it had on English engravers is readily visible in the deeper engraved work of W.J. Muckley shown at the Great Exhibition (Plates 82 and 83). The Bohm vase was itself on display at the Great

Plate 126. Claret jug with rope twist handle. The engraved female classical figure is signed J.B. Millar; Scottish, c.1870. Height 11½ in. (29cm). Private Collection.

Plate 127. Jug engraved with a scene of Edinburgh Castle, Scottish, late 1860s. Height 12½ in. (32cm). Jack and Penny Pacifico Collection.

Exhibition. Modern day engravers, like their nineteenth century predecessors, express amazement at the quality of the carving with its depth and wealth of minute detail.

During the 1850s many Bohemian engravers made their way to England to

Plate 128. Jug engraved with a classical figure on a stylised boat. The Holyrood glassworks of John Ford, c.1868-70. Height 8⅛ in. (20.7cm).

Plate 129. Jug engraved with fox and duck by Schiller at Stevens and Williams in 1873. Height 9½ in. (24cm). Private Collection, on loan to Broadfield House Glass Museum.

capitalise on the increasing prosperity of the country. One accepted route for the immigrant engravers was through the Edinburgh workshop of J.H.B. Millar, himself a Bohemian and a skilled engraver judging by a signed example of his work (Plate 126). By 1869 the workshop employed forty men and boys who executed every type of engraved decoration. Other Bohemian engravers, including Emanuel Lerche and F.J. Marschner, settled in Edinburgh. In Glasgow four Bohemian engravers have been traced, including Vincent Keller who was employed at the James Couper factory but may have engraved glass for the firm of James Baird in the 1870s and 1880s. One of those decorators may have been responsible for the jug engraved with a scene of Edinburgh Castle and a train emerging from the tunnel beneath it, with typical Bohemian flourishes on the rim and foot (Plate 127). Engraved glass of a high standard came from the Holyrood Flint Glass Works, run by John Ford (Plate 128). Without the benefit of the Millar signature or the identification of the Ford jug in the pattern books held by Huntly House Museum in Edinburgh, the engraving on both jugs and features such as the rope twist and shell handles would normally be attributed to Stourbridge.

Some of the most talented of the Bohemian engravers settled in the Stourbridge area, adjacent to the factories of Webb, and Stevens and Williams. An engraver

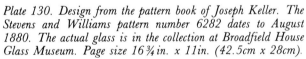

Plate 130. Design from the pattern book of Joseph Keller. The Stevens and Williams pattern number 6282 dates to August 1880. The actual glass is in the collection at Broadfield House Glass Museum. Page size 16¾in. x 11in. (42.5cm x 28cm).

Plate 131. Design by Joseph Keller, c.1880. Decanters with this type of rim were called cup mouth decanters. Page size as Plate 130.

named Schiller appears regularly in the Stevens and Williams pattern books, certainly from 1860 until about 1876 when an engraver called Baasler seems to have taken over. The bulk of Schiller's work consisted of scrolls, borders, medallions, hanging festoons, ferns, and anthemion motifs, but a number of figurative subjects are recorded. In 1871 some of his subjects included 'Tam O'Shanter', 'Willie brewed a peck o'malt' and 'The Jolly Beggars'. One jug has been identified from a series which Schiller carried out in 1873 on the subjects of 'Fox and escaped duck' (Plate 129), 'Fox and hawk with bird' and 'Mock bird and butterfly'. On 4 November 1875 a tankard 'very richly engraved The Four Seasons' was recorded by Schiller who was paid 90s. and the piece sold for £7.

From the mid-1870s a great deal of the engraved work at Stevens and Williams was masterminded by Joseph Keller. A volume entitled *A Collection of Patterns for the Use of Glass Decorators, Designed by Joseph Keller* includes designs for rock crystal glass and polished bright engraving, which were executed either by Keller or other engravers working for Stevens and Williams as well as other factories (Plates 130 to 132). Keller's name appears occasionally in the Webb design books.

At Thomas Webb's the records from 1840 until the end of the century list over

Plate 132. Design by Joseph Keller showing the faint moulded ribbed effect known as optic, with shallow rock crystal or polished bright engraving. Page size as Plate 130

twenty names of engravers giving some impression of the amount of engraved glass produced by one factory (see Appendix 7). Amongst the names are Frederick Engelbert Kny and William Fritsche.

Frederick Engelbert Kny came to the Dennis glassworks in about 1860 and his name appears for the first time in the Webb books in 1865. According to Geoffrey Beard, he had worked for a short time at James Powell & Sons before joining Webb's. His last mention in the records was in 1896. The directories record him as a glass engraver at Platts glassworks from 1889 to 1892, then as Kny Brothers from 1893 to 1910. He died in 1906. There are few signed glasses by Kny and therefore his reputation is not as great as that of Fritsche. The Elgin vase (Plate 227) and his work on rock crystal glass, including the earliest rock crystal designs (Plates 229 and 230), are some of the finest examples of engraved work in the nineteenth century. His versatile talent earned him the position in charge of the engraving shop at Webb's, where he was to be joined by Fritsche in 1868.

Plate 133. William Fritsche, from a group photograph probably taken at Webb's. Exact date not known.

Plate 134. Claret jug engraved by William Fritsche, late 19th century. Height 13⅛ in. (33.3cm). The Jones Museum of Ceramics and Glass, Maine, U.S.A.

WILLIAM FRITSCHE

William Fritsche was the greatest of the Bohemian engravers working in England or America in the late nineteenth and early twentieth century (Plate 133). Only the great August Bohm could challenge him in his native Bohemia. The late Cyril Kimberley, who worked at Webb's and was no mean engraver in his own right, regarded Fritsche as a legend, a view echoed by every engraver and collector who knows his work.

Fritsche was born in Meistersdorf in 1853 into a family of glass engravers. About 1868 he came to Stourbridge where he spent his entire working life at Thomas Webb's. His name appears in the Webb pattern books in 1871 and by the 1880s features regularly in the pages. His mastery of the copper wheel took engraving beyond the limits of glass decoration and into the realms of fine art. His genius could transform the characteristic Bohemian woodland scene of stags and deer into a nightmare hunting scene, worthy of paintings by Landseer, in which even the trees conspire to trap the stag (Plate 134). Like George Woodall with cameo glass, William Fritsche never compromised the quality of his work and maintained the highest levels of achievement until his death (Plate 135). Whether he was engraving clear, cased or coloured glass, or working in collaboration with another studio on enamelled ware, Fritsche treated every piece with equal skill (Colour Plate 15). The two-handled bowl with engraved and enamelled overlapping panels in Japanese style is of special interest due to its similarity to signed Gallé pieces of the same shape. One bowl was sold at Christie's a few years ago while another Gallé signed example is in the collections of the Milan Historical Society in Milan, Ohio. In the Webb pattern books there are notes by some of the designs which prove that the factory was obtaining blanks from Baccarat in France. For example, an engraved floral design, no. 14737 by Kny, is inscribed 'Baccarat make all but Claret, Port and Sherry'. The coincidence of the identical shapes may be explained simply by the fact that the companies used a common source to obtain their blanks which they then decorated in their own individual manner. The practice continues today with some English decorating shops buying blanks from foreign suppliers.

For someone with such great talent little is known about Fritsche's everyday life. From the trade directories we have the intriguing detail that he was the proprietor of the Red Lion pub on Brettell Lane in Amblecote from 1886 until 1892 when he moved to Collis Street. It was to the Red Lion address that William Waldron, a Brierley Hill solicitor, wrote to Fritsche on 11 November 1890 about a patent infringement:

> Sir,
>
> I have been consulted by Mr. Jabez Facer, of Collis St., Dennis Park, Glass Etcher & Designer, in reference to your having infringed his Patent No. 11994 of 1889 for 'Improvements in polishing cut and engraved flint and coloured glass or plate or sheet glass'.
>
> My instructions are to apply to you for fair and reasonable compensation for such infringement, and to require you to abstain from any such infringement in the future.
>
> Unless, therefore, you see me on or before Saturday next and make some arrangement as to the matter, legal proceedings will be forthwith commenced against you by my client to enforce his legal rights.
>
> Yours obediently
> William Waldron

Facer was employed by Webb's, possibly on a free-lance basis, and his name appears frequently in the design books. His patent was for polishing glass using a mixture of equal parts of hydrofluoric and sulphuric acid, diluted with water. Considering that experiments with this formula were under way by other

Colour Plate 15. Engraved glass by William Fritsche. Left to right. Decanter and stopper, cut and engraved 'rock crystal' with the 'Indian cone' and a chipped background to the floral decoration, recorded as pattern no. 22252 on 16 February 1897; pencilled in the price book against this design 'W.F. January 1897'; height 9⅞ in. (25cm). Hock glass, the bowl cased in purple and engraved with deer and stags, signed W. Fritsche, late 19th century, height 7in. (17.6cm). Amber vase engraved with a portrait of Edward VII; Fritsche signed the vase in reverse on the ribbon beneath the portrait which is supposed to be viewed through the clear glass oval on the reverse of the vase; early 20th century, height 7⅞ in. (20cm). Two-handled bowl engraved by Fritsche and enamelled in an oriental style by Jules Barbe, signed W Fritsche in the corner of one of the panels and marked WEBB underneath one of the handles; c.1880s, height 4¼ in. (10.6cm). (Two similar bowls have been recorded with signatures by Emile Gallé.) Plate of clear glass cased with ruby and engraved with a band of Chinese lions amongst foliage, signed W. Fritsche, late 19th century, diameter 9in. (23cm). Decanter and stopper engraved with a warrior throwing a spear from a chariot, and the monogram AH on the reverse, signed W. Fritsche, 1870s, height 12½ in. (32cm).

glassmakers, Facer's efforts to restrict its use seem rather futile. If the dispute hints at the rivalry and competitiveness between decorators at the same factory one wonders what skulduggery took place between rival firms. Although the outcome of this personal dispute is not known, the use of the new recipe for acid

Plate 135. Vase engraved with a peacock and ducks by William Fritsche, c.1920. Height 15 ¼ in. (38.5cm). Hulbert of Dudley Collection.

polishing of glass soon became widespread.

William Fritsche died on 24 March 1924. He was buried in Amblecote Parish Church, next to his wife who had predeceased him by seven years. The marble cross inscribed with their names still stands as a place of pilgrimage for his admirers and as a memorial to one of the greatest engravers who ever lived.

TWO REDISCOVERED BOHEMIAN ENGRAVERS

The work of the great Bohemian engravers in Britain is fairly well documented and recorded. It is the work of their lesser-known countrymen which is more difficult to find and to assess. Fortunately it has been possible to identify two of these engravers through family documents which have been preserved by their descendants. Glasses which have survived with the documents serve to emphasise

Plate 137. Pages from the Pohl family Bible. Photograph courtesy P. & P. Chapman.

Plate 136. Portrait of Wilhelm Florian Pohl. Photograph courtesy Mrs. F. West.

Plate 138. Rummer engraved by Pohl with view of St Mary's Church, Sankey, and Woolf's House, c.1871-74. Height 6⅜ in. (16.25cm). Private Collection.

Plate 139. The Manchester Town Hall goblet engraved by Pohl, 1877. Height 15½ in. (39.4cm). City of Manchester Art Galleries.

Plate 140. Jug engraved by Pohl with The Devil's Glen, Co. Wicklow, 1870s. Height 8¾ in. (22.2cm). P. & P. Chapman Collection.

Plate 140A. Print of The Devil's Glen, Co. Wicklow, used by Pohl as source material for his engraving. Published by Newman & Co., Watling Street, London. No date is given.

the level of quality work produced by the more obscure engravers and underline the influences they exerted on English engraving. Wilhelm Pohl and Valentin Weinich were contemporaries who moved to Great Britain within four years of each other and whose careers followed almost identical patterns.

Wilhelm Florian Pohl was born on 31 May 1839 in Parchen near Steinschonau, Bohemia (Plate 136). His family Bible records that he was resident in Edinburgh by 1858, had moved to Warrington in 1863 and was in Manchester by 1875 (Plate 137). The facing page lists, on the lower half, the names and birthdays of his five children and reveals the tragic time in 1870 when the youngest daughter Christina died at the age of nine months in May followed in December by his first wife Christina Blyth Pohl. On 21 August 1871 Pohl married Sarah (surname unknown) at Saint Mary's Church, Great Sankey and set up home in 'Woolf's House' where their first daughter, Eleanor Ada, was born. Pohl featured these two important buildings in his life on a rummer that must date between 1871 and 1874 when the family lived in Bank Quay, Warrington (Plate 138). Of all seven glasses known by Pohl this one evokes the greatest emotions when seen against the entries in the family Bible.

In 1877 he engraved the impressive new Manchester Town Hall on a large goblet which was presented to the Mayor at the opening ceremony by the workmen of the Prussia Street Flint Glass Works of Andrew Kerr (Plate 139). Some time after the opening ceremony the goblet vanished without trace. The

Plate 141. Valentin Weinich with his son Ferdinand. Private Collection.

mystery surrounding its disappearance became a regular feature of the local Manchester newspapers in the 1920s. Following its reappearance in a County Durham antiques shop in 1973 it was purchased by the Manchester City Art Gallery and at this stage was identified by Mrs Florence West as the work of her grandfather. From this chance discovery another branch of the family made available the family Bible and other glasses by Pohl including the Devil's Glen jug (Plate 140).

A similar situation arising from a chance meeting with a descendant of Valentin Weinich resulted in the discovery of a number of Weinich's original documents including a trade card, a 'Deportation or Repatriation of Aliens' form, a First World War identity book and his death certificate. With the information given in these papers it is possible to piece together a detailed history of Valentin Weinich's life, even to his height of 5ft.4¾in. (1.64m) (Plate 141). He was born on 12 December 1844 in Blottendorf, Bohemia, and trained as a glass engraver. He moved to England at the age of eighteen but his steps are unknown until 1873 by which time he was living and working in Manchester at 111 City Road, Hulme. He had married an English girl, Janet Fields, and on 29 October 1873 their daughter Franziska was born. On 21 March 1878 Amelia was born; the third child Ferdinand was born on 11 May 1884.

Plate 142. Pair of ruby stained vases and covers engraved with horses and riders by Valentin Weinich. Height 15½in. (39.4cm). Private Collection.

In an exhibition of glass in January and February 1876, organised by the Glass Sellers Company and held at Alexandra Palace, Valentin Weinich, together with an F. Weinich of whom nothing is known at present, was awarded a Bronze Medal. Other Bohemians who won Medals were Paul Oppitz (Gold and Silver), F.E. Kny, W. Fritsche, J. Blumtritt, F. Kirchoff and A. Proft. Weinich's trade card proudly mentions his Bronze Medal award and describes him as a 'Practical Glass Engraver, Wholesale Cut & Engraved Glass Manufacturer, 111 City Road, Hulme, Manchester. Flower Stands, Water Sets, Water Bottles and Tops, Decanters, Wines, Tumblers, Sugars and Creams, Celeries etc. in Great Variety, Coat-of-Arms, Monograms etc. Engraved in First Style of Art'. According to family tradition Weinich had a shop in Blackpool to sell his glass, a close parallel with Pohl who is said to have worked on the sea front for two seasons engraving glasses with names and mottoes.

By 1910 Weinich had moved, as a widower, from Manchester to Stourbridge. In 1914 his address was 13 High Street, Amblecote, only a few minutes' walk from Fritsche's house. In Amblecote he worked at the glasshouse of Webb and Corbett where William Kny was a partner. Together with Herbert Webb of the same factory, Kny was a signatory to vouch for Weinich's good behaviour on the application form for exemption from Deportation or Repatriation of Aliens in

Plate 143. Goblet engraved with three roundels, two with birds and leaves and one with cornucopia and fruit, by V. Weinich. Late 19th or early 20th century. Height 9¼ in. (23.5cm). Private Collection.

Plate 144. Jug engraved with a panel of 'Satan Smitten by Michael', by V. Weinich. This subject matter does not appear to be recorded elsewhere on glass. Late 19th or early 20th century. Height 7½ in. (19cm). Private Collection.

1914. As an alien his identity card was stamped with regulations such as the War Office 'approval for munition work if otherwise eligible' and 'Valid Only For Work With T. Webb and Corbett'. His five changes of address in Stourbridge between 1918 and 1921 are also recorded. Valentin Weinich died on 6 April 1927 aged eighty-two years.

Of the four glasses in the family collection two vases with covers may have been brought from Bohemia (Plate 142). A goblet is engraved with three roundels, two with birds amongst leaves and fruit and one with cornucopia and fruit (Plate 143). A jug is engraved with a named panel of 'Satan Smitten by Michael' surrounded by scrolling foliage (Plate 144). Family tradition is certain that all four are the work of Weinich.

THE CRITIC'S VIEW

In the same way that Ruskin attacked cut glass, Christopher Dresser maligned the work of the engraver. His comment was written in number 25 of a series of

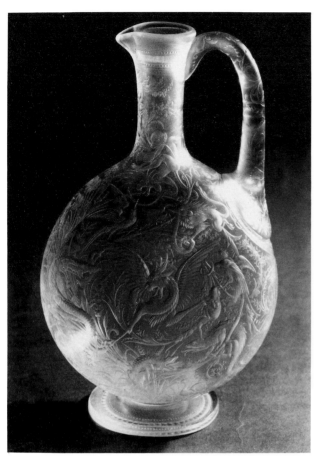

Plate 145. Claret jug similar to the one shown by Dobson and Pearce at the 1862 London Exhibition. Possibly the work of F.E. Kny at Thomas Webb and Sons. Height 11in. (28cm). Private Collection.

Plate 147. Claret jug engraved at the Hodgetts, Richardson works, c.1873-74. It appears in the pattern books of Hodgetts, Richardson and Son at pattern no. '5218 Richly Engd hn/- [40s.] Plain o/- [9s.].' Height 8¾ in. (22cm). Michael Parkington Collection.

articles on 'Principles of Design' in the *Technical Educator* between 1870 and 1873 and published in book form as *The Principles of Decorative Design* in 1873:

> Somewhat elaborate effects can be rendered in glass by very laborious engraving, whereby different depths of cutting are attained, but such work is the result of great labour, and rarely produces an effect proportionate to the toil expended upon it; and if a bottle so engraved is filled with a coloured wine, the entire beauty of its engraving is destroyed. Fig. 115 is a drawing of a most elaborately engraved bottle which was shown in the Exhibition of 1862. It represents, to a great extent, wasted labour.

The jug was included in the colour plate of the 1862 catalogue showing the work of Dobson and Pearce (Colour Plate 14) and a very similar piece has survived in a private collection (Plate 145). In the same way that Ruskin's comment on cut glass was ignored, Dresser's opinion also received little support and fine quality engraving continued to the end of the century and after.

A huge variety of subjects can be found on engraved glass of the late nineteenth century (Plates 146-151). For example, medieval knights fighting on a pilgrim jug

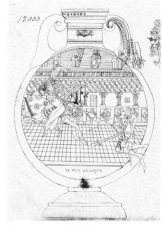

Plate 146. 'Ye-Men-at-Arms', design for a pilgrim bottle in the Webb pattern books c.1879-80. The actual glass is in the collections at Broadfield House Glass Museum.

171

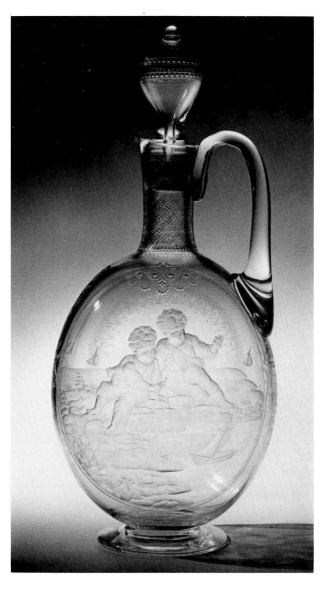

Plate 148. Jug with applied lion masks on the feet. Probably designed by James O'Fallon at Thomas Webb and Sons, 1870s. Height 5 ¾ in. (14.5cm). Michael Parkington Collection.

Plate 149. Claret jug engraved with a scene of two boys sailing toy boats. Stourbridge, 1870s. Height, including stopper, 14 ¼ in. Jack and Penny Pacifico Collection.

from the Webb factory have counterparts in ceramic versions of medieval scenes from Minton's (Plate 146). A claret jug engraved with an oriental scene of a mandarin walking amongst pagodas is a surprise from the Richardson factory, not noted for their engraving at this date (Plate 147). The bizarre personality of James O'Fallon, the Art Director at Thomas Webb's, created strange compositions often of insects depicted as humans or, as in one instance, classically draped females cavorting with insects and one riding a grasshopper (Plate 148). A scene on a decanter showing two boys sailing toy boats with the real ships in the background is reminiscent of the mawkish sentimentality of John Everett Millais' *Boyhood of Raleigh* (Plate 149). Geometric patterns were popular on the sets of a water jug and two goblets placed between every two guests at the dinner table (Plate 150). The jug and goblets are not, as has been suggested, a marriage set for the bride and groom. When William F. Cody visited Amblecote with his travelling rodeo show in 1903 one engraver was quick to capture his likeness for a high class souvenir tumbler (Plate 151).

Plate 150. Water goblet with twisted stem and geometric engraved bowl. Stourbridge, possibly Boulton and Mills, 1870s. Height 7½ in. (19.3cm). Author's Collection.

Plate 151. Tumbler engraved with a portrait of Buffalo Bill, c.1903. The engraving is attributed to W.O. Bowen who worked at J. & J. Northwood's decorating shop in Wordsley and later became its manager. Height 5¼ in. (13.6cm). Hulbert of Dudley Collection.

DISASTER GLASSES

The last forty years of the century witnessed a strange and macabre phenomenon in engraved glass which echoed the purely English nature of engraved glass at the beginning of the century. Peculiar to the North-East, these glasses commemorate various disasters such as hangings, drownings, colliery accidents, outbreaks of war and shipwrecks (Plate 152). The rummers, jugs and miniature tankards are inevitably of poor quality with simple engraving and the occasional flourish of leaves or ferns. It is the very combination of poor quality glass engraved with the history of the events which gives the glasses their nostalgic and poignant appeal. Similarities in the layout and style of the lettering suggest that they were the products of a small group of engravers based around Newcastle and Sunderland.

The purpose of the glasses seems to have been to raise money for the disaster funds set up to help the bereaved families. The majority record pit accidents such as the Hetton Colliery explosion of 20 December 1860 when twenty-two lives

Plate 152. Two disaster glasses. The taller glass is engraved 'The S.S. Regiau Wrecked Upon The Bondicarr Rock Between Broomhill and Amble 1884'. The smaller glass is engraved 'William Jobling Gibbetted at Jarrow Slake August 3rd 1832'. Both glasses date from the early 1880s. Heights 5 ¾ in. (14.5cm) and 3 ¾ in. (9.5cm). Author's Collection.

were lost and the Seaham Colliery explosion on 8 September 1880 when 164 pitmen died. One of the worst disasters was the Victoria Hall tragedy in Sunderland on 16 June 1883 when 191 children, rushing downstairs to receive prizes, died after they were trapped against a locked door in the hall. Some small handled mugs commemorate a fatal pony trap accident to Lady Grey near Alnwick in Northumberland in 1908. Other glasses reflect the political turmoil of the day. A rummer inscribed 'William Jobling Gibbetted at Jarrow Slake August 3rd 1832' refers to the wrongful arrest and hanging of Jobling for the murder of a magistrate during the upheavals surrounding the Reform Act (Plate 152). The Jobling glasses are later commemoratives as no other disaster glasses are known from this early date and the style of manufacture and engraving suggest that they were made in the second half of the nineteenth century.

CHAPTER NINE

Acid Etching

The full potential of acid etching on glass as a commercial proposition was developed in the Stourbridge area during the 1850s and it quickly became one of the most popular means of decoration. In the first half of the century, however, the history of etching is shrouded in mystery and very few English etched glasses are known to have existed before 1850. The use of hydrofluoric acid for glass etching is usually accepted to have been discovered by Carl Wilhelm Scheele in Sweden in 1771. Even though a great deal of written information appeared on the subject after that date the technique seemed to be considered more of a curiosity, dabbled in by enthusiastic amateurs. One of the early nineteenth century references appears in Rees' *Manufacturing Industry* where he mentions hydrofluoric acid for etching and engraving on glass vessels by fuming. In 1849 Apsley Pellatt in his *Curiosities of Glassmaking* doubted the usefulness of the medium when he wrote 'etching by fluoric acid has been introduced, but its bite is not sufficiently rough, and is not found effective for general purposes'.

The basic process consisted of coating the glass with an acid resist, scratching the design through the resist to expose the glass and dipping it into hydrofluoric acid to give a line decoration. Because it was used in many instances to decorate cheap, mass-produced glass, the whole technique has often suffered quite wrongly from a total condemnation. It was regarded by some nineteenth century contemporaries as a quick and cheap alternative to wheel engraving, but some of the effects required many hours of laborious effort in the decorating shops where the wax resist was applied and the decoration scratched through by an army of women, and in the acid shops where the dipping took place (Plates 153 and 154). Not least of these tasks was the application of the wax coating. In his book about his father, John Northwood II described this first stage in acid etching:

> The layout comprises firstly a heating chamber — this is often an iron-sheeted cupboard heated by steam or gas and containing shelves to hold a quantity of articles. This heated chamber is of a temperature somewhat near the melting point of the wax. The cold articles are placed in this chamber before they are ready for their wax coating. The wax composition is usually a beeswax and rosin mixture and is melted in a heated sheet-tin bath which has a perforated shelf on one side, just above the surface of the wax. The operator takes out the heated article and immerses it in the hot wax and brings it out and stands it on the perforated shelf to drain. The hot wax runs off and down into the bath again, leaving a thin coating of wax on the surface of the article. This is then taken out and left to harden ready for the process of decorating it.

Plate 153. The Stuart etching shop in 1902; applying the resist. Photograph courtesy Stuart Crystal.

Plate 154. The Stuart etching shop in 1902 showing the upright etching machines. Photograph courtesy Stuart Crystal.

The decoration itself was applied either by free-hand drawing using sharp metal or wooden points, sometimes known as stilettos, or by tracing the design on to the glass via a variety of etching machines. Machine work could always be enhanced by adding extra details in free-hand which the machines could not be programmed to achieve. Dipping the glass into the acid vat was the most obnoxious stage from the worker's point of view. John Northwood II described it in vivid detail in his reminiscences, published in the Spring 1954 issue of the Stevens and Williams works magazine *Crystal:*

> The worst was the aciding. In those days there were no fume extractors or ventilating fans and one had to have his acid vat out in the open air, in bad weather under an open shed, no heating whatever the cold. We used to work in our overcoats and mufflers in the winter. The article could not be left in the bath of acid which was very strong, but had to be continually kept on the move by hand. Our faces and hands used to suffer from the strong fumes.
>
> To hold the article we shaped a wood stick to fit the mouth or neck of the vase or bottle and dipping the end of it in melted pitch, plunged it into the neck of the glass which then formed a handle to hold it and at the same time prevented the acid from entering the article.
>
> For bowls, plates, dishes and other articles, we made a stubby shaped handle out of wood and pitched it to the bottom of the article. We had to keep removing the scum formed on the glass where acid was acting to prevent it eating down in an uneven way. To do this we had sticks of wood with a pad of cotton-wool tied on the end which we called a 'mop'. The operation was to stand over the vat and whilst moving the article in the acid with the one hand, we rubbed the mop over the surface of the glass with the other. So you see we could not get very far away from the fumes. It was always an unpleasant job and no one wanted it. If possible some used to pay others to do this part for them.

The Northwood etching shop was the first and the most important of the Stourbridge decorating workshops. One can trace back a line of descent for etching from John Northwood through the Richardson family to Thomas Hawkes' Dudley works where the first commercial application of acid etching is said to have occurred.

During the 1850s Benjamin Richardson developed the full potential of acid etching and laid the foundations for future expansion. In her book *Victorian Glass,* Ruth Webb Lee states that 'the first English [etching] machine was made in 1855 in a very primitive way by one James Smith, an engineer in the employ of W.H. Richardson of Wordsley, being constructed out of an old lathe which had been used for turning gun butts'. Whatever the accuracy of this unverified statement it is clear that Richardson had made significant discoveries in the use of different acids and their applications. On 20 June 1857 Benjamin Richardson patented his process for etching through cased coloured glass. It was very similar to an 1853 patent in which cut-out stencils were used to paint the resist design on to the glass. The corrosive action of the acid removed the exposed parts leaving a relief coloured design. The method is recorded in the shape of a blue cased wineglass which is etched on the base of the foot 'Mr. B. Richardson, Wordsley, 1857' (Plate 155).

Plate 155. Wineglass, cased blue over clear, acid etched. Signed on foot 'Mr. B. Richardson, Wordsley 1857'. Height 5½in. (14cm).

Richardson's 1857 patent also included his discovery of the addition of sulphuric acid to hydrofluoric to produce a bright polish rather than a matt finish. This combination formed the basis for acid polishing of glass at the end of the century. Richardson's patent and the existence of his signed 1857 glass provide an important landmark in the commercialisation of etching in Stourbridge. It suggests that until that date only a matt effect was obtainable. The large degree of experimentation required to get to this stage meant that the technique was regarded as a major addition to the decorator's repertoire. Richardson's may have been the only glassworks at this date with a separate acid shop. The site of that shop is clearly marked in the plan of the works (Plate 4).

The potential of operating a successful free-lance decorating workshop was quickly seized upon by John Northwood who had served his apprenticeship at the Richardson works. By 1859 he had established the workshop in partnership with his brother Joseph, Tom Guest and Henry Gething Richardson. Guest and Richardson had left the partnership by 1861 and the company operated as J. and J. Northwood. It was to become the largest producer of etched glass in Stourbridge during the nineteenth century. At the height of its success it

Plate 156. Interior of the J. & J. Northwood etching shop about 1885. The workshop was situated at the corner of Barnett Street and Barnett Lane in Wordsley.

employed between fifty and sixty staff, mainly women, and closed only in 1926 when the staff were moved to Stevens and Williams. A photograph of the interior shows the women standing by their geometric machines (Plate 156). In the early 1880s the workshop was the main cameo decorating centre for Stevens and Williams.

The success of the Northwood venture depended on the inventive ability of John Northwood to create machines which speeded up the tracing of the patterns through the acid resist. By 1861 the first of these machines, for template etching, was in use. Only one example of this machine remains in existence, originating at Stevens and Williams who presented it to the Science Museum (Plate 157). This small machine, measuring 16in. high by 12in. deep (40.5 x 30.5cm) was intended to stand on a workbench. The large central wooden drum was covered with a thin sheet of brass which held rows of brass pins spaced at different intervals. It was connected by a drive shaft to the turntable which carried the glass. The spring pawl which can be seen on the left of the upright T-bar could be adjusted vertically on to any of the rows of pins and gave the number of repeats for any pattern on to the glass depending on the size and shape of the pattern. Each time the drum was turned and the pawl clicked over a pin the operator would trace the pattern through the templates which were clamped into the horizontal bar above the drum. The template bar could be moved backwards and forwards to take account of different sized glasses while the height of the glass could be adjusted by a small hand-wheel, just visible in the photograph, that was fitted with a screw spindle underneath the central drum. The mechanics of the template machine were similar to the marking-up machines used to draw the guidelines on the glass for the cutters.

Plate 157. Template etching machine invented by John Northwood about 1860-61. Science Museum.

Templates were made from tinfoil unless they were to be in constant use in which case thin brass or copper sheet was employed. Separate templates had to be cut for the different sized glasses in a suite of glass which was to be etched with a template design. On one service which was etched by Northwood for Thomas Webb and shown at the Paris Exhibition of 1878 the modifications to the template designs can be seen on the decanter (Plate 158) and the shorter and smaller handled flask (Plate 159, right). This particular design appears in the Webb pattern book under number 12147 and included a carafe and tumbler (known as a tumble-up) and at least five wineglasses. Two templates illustrated by John Northwood II (Plate 160) can be matched to a frieze of horsemen on a jug which was a Richardson blank (Plate 161). With a complex pattern such as this the

Plate 158. Carafe etched by Northwood and shown at the Paris Exhibition of 1878. Height 8½in. (21.5cm).

Plate 159. Wineglass and miniature jug etched by Northwood about 1878. Heights: wineglass 4½in. (11.5cm), jug 5¼in. (13.5cm).

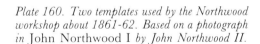

Plate 160. Two templates used by the Northwood workshop about 1861-62. Based on a photograph in John Northwood I by John Northwood II.

machine operator needed to exercise some skill where the different horses and riders overlapped each other. For example, the small gap which was created between the outlines of the legs, where one line would be etched inside the gap against the body of the horse and the other scratched around the outside of the part below the belly of the horse, would be connected when the jug came off the machine. Other details to be added free-hand at this stage were the fine points such as features of the heads of riders and horses, modelling of the cloaks and extra details in the horses' manes and tails. Templates were strung together and hung from nails in the timbers of the ceiling of the workshop for easy storage and access. Like many pieces of equipment in the glass trade, few have survived to

Plate 161. Richardson jug etched by Northwood with a frieze based on the Elgin marbles, about 1862. Height 9in. (23cm).

the present day, having been discarded by glass companies as so much unwanted junk.

By 1865 a new etching machine, once again the brainchild of John Northwood, was in operation in the Barnett Lane workshop in Wordsley. The geometric etching machine looked even more like an instrument of torture than its predecessor (Plate 162). The machines can be clearly identified in use, set with their flat ends against the wall, in the interior photograph of the workshop (Plate 156). The glass to be etched, already covered with its layer of acid resist, was placed horizontally in the machine, its top resting against the wooden chuck and its base clamped in position by the small hand wheel seen at the top right of the machine. A circular tin disc on the end of the poppet holding the glass in position allowed it to rotate freely when the machine was put into action. The design was scratched by a needle or needles held in a special holder that was spring loaded to allow a degree of movement as the glass rotated underneath the needle. The needle holder, set on the end of a complicated piece of gearing, could be moved to the necessary position by the hand-wheel seen on the bottom right. The long cone arrangement of toothed wheels, on the left of the machine, led to the drive mechanism which rotated the glass held in the chuck. A small cog-wheel engaged the cones and took the drive from there to the headstock and the needle. By turning the large hand-wheel, at the front left, both operations acted simultaneously, the one revolving the glass while the needle in the headstock, set off centre, revolved and scratched the wax away from the glass. Different

Plate 162. *Geometric etching machine invented by John Northwood in the early 1860s. Length of baseplate 45¼ in. (115cm). Science Museum.*

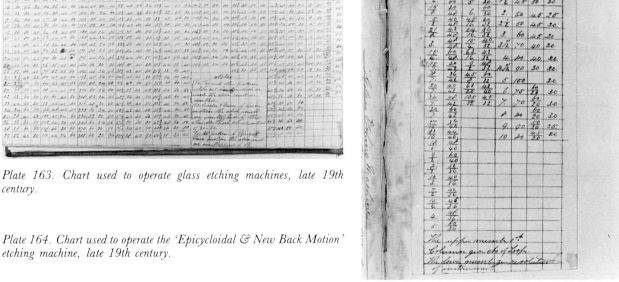

Plate 163. *Chart used to operate glass etching machines, late 19th century.*

Plate 164. *Chart used to operate the 'Epicycloidal & New Back Motion' etching machine, late 19th century.*

combinations of needles gave a wide variety of patterns. Extra needle holders could be slotted into the V-shaped grooves cut into the baseplate.

The complexity of these machines is evident from the two tables of numbers and operating instructions, found in the back of a Richardson pattern book,

Plate 165. Jug and custard cup by the Northwood workshop, showing variations of geometric etching, late 1860s. Heights: jug 5½in. (14cm), cup 3¼in. (8.5cm).

which give the gear combinations to obtain different patterns (Plates 163 and 164). Six surviving letters dating between 1902 and 1905 from George Plant and Son, Makers of Amateur's Lathes and Appliances, Glass Etching Machines etc., of King's Heath, Birmingham, provide answers to queries from H.G. Richardson about the addition of cams or the position of the 'jigger' arm to alter certain patterns.

The first patterns to come off the geometric etching machine were the favourite Greek key motif and the 'Circle' design which was a band of overlapping circles. Once the decorators became adept at operating the machines patterns became more complex (Plate 165).

The effects produced by Northwood's machines consisted only of outlines. If the areas inside the figures were to be shaded the glass was passed to the engraving shop. Broad copper wheels were used to matt the surface but this was a time-consuming process and Northwood eventually came up with an acid, known as 'white acid', which performed the task in a fraction of the time. An early jug from the Northwood workshop, signed and dated JN 1862, shows the engraved shaded parts inside the regular acid outline, where the wheel has left a slightly irregular surface (Plate 166). In contrast, acid shading can be easily distinguished by its very fine, uniform, flat texture. Northwood may have seen shaded foreign glasses and used them as his starting point to develop white acid, a process which was known on the Continent well before the 1867 date of Northwood's use. The process seems to have been discovered in the early part of the nineteenth century by the Swede, J.J. Berzelius, one of the nineteenth century's greatest chemists. From 1808 onwards he laid the foundations of quantitative chemical analysis which made an immediate impact on glass

Plate 166. Jug with acid etched outlines and engraved shading. Signed and dated JN 1862. Height 12½ in. (32cm).

Plate 167. Goblet etched by the Northwood workshop about 1869. Height 7in. (18cm).

technology. The rational analysis of chemicals and their effects ended the great confusion in terminology of earlier glass recipes. It was from such investigations into the properties of glass that Berzelius suggested the use of ammonium fluoride as an etching medium capable of giving a soft texture. Northwood's own experiments resulted in the use of alkali salts such as potassium carbonate or sodium carbonate to neutralize the effect of hydrofluoric acid. The white acid attacked the surface of the glass rather than eating into it.

Shading with acid lengthened the time the glass spent in the decorating room. After the glass was etched to create an outline, the resist and acid were washed off and the glass brought back to the decorating room where a new layer of resist had to be painted by hand up to the edges of the outlines, leaving the interiors clear to take the white acid. On complicated patterns, like the Egyptian motif (Plate 167), this was a time-consuming task. Some of the early Northwood pieces

Plate 168. Goblet etched by the Northwood workshop after a design by Flaxman. In the Stevens and Williams pattern book this shape is referred to as a 'French Ale' (pattern no. 2567 20/10/1869). Height 7½ in. (19cm).

Plate 169. Reproduction of the Portland vase in clear glass with etched decoration by Northwood. Height 9¾ in. (24.5cm).

were worked further by the engraver who polished small sections of the matt acid surface very slightly to give variety and life to an otherwise flat scene. The effect can be clearly noticed on a goblet from the 1870s showing the Flaxman inspired scene of 'Hector and Ajax separated by the heralds' (Plate 168). The polishing appears on parts of the cloaks of the heralds and on the shields of the two warriors.

Throughout the rest of the century the Northwood workshop continued to send out high quality etched glass and the use of acid was developed in a number of unusual applications. Apart from using acid to remove the unwanted white layer of cameo glass, Northwood made a Portland vase in clear glass, etched in outline and shaded, with the full Portland scene (Plate 169). The vase may have been a precursor of his cameo reproduction and perhaps was used almost as a sketchbook while he worked on the cameo version. Following the success of his Portland vase copy Northwood was commissioned by Wedgwood to cut and polish special examples of their Jasperware reproductions. A letter of 5 May 1877 quoted the prices for the work:

Plate 170. Wedgwood Rockingham ware etched and engraved by the Northwood workshop, 1880s. Photograph courtesy Richard Dennis.

Plate 171. Rockingham ware teapot and stand etched and engraved by the Northwood workshop, 1880s. Height of teapot 7in. (17.8cm).

Smoothing ground and figures but figures not cut . . . .£ 2. 0. 0d.
Smoothing ground and figures cut up for painting . . . .£10.10. 0d.
Polishing ground and handles and inside lip of vase all bright
as original, with figures cut up to show ground through as
well as possible . . . .£26. 5. 0d.

The special editions with Northwood's work bear his initials on the base. The Wedgwood contract led to extra work, this time on their Rockingham ware. Hydrofluoric acid was used to etch through the top glaze of brown, blue or green to the cream ceramic body underneath. Some items were engraved rather than etched (Plate 170). Where an object consisted of two or more parts, such as the

187

Plate 172. The Pilgrimage to Canterbury *by Thomas Stothard, 1806-7. Oil on board, 12½ in. x 37½ in. (32cm x 95cm). Tate Gallery.*

Plate 173. Vase etched with a frieze of the Canterbury Pilgrims after Stothard. Signed and dated W. Northwood 1883. Height 12¾ in. (32.5cm).

188

Plate 174. Une Bonne Histoire, *a print published by Goupil & Co. 1 April 1877 after a painting by Leo Herrmann of 1876. 10½in. x 14in. (26.5cm x 36cm).*

teapot and stand in Plate 171, the one part (the stand) was acid etched and the other wheel engraved.

Contemporary prints and paintings were used as popular sources of subject matter at the Northwood workshop. The subtle effects of light and shade required to reproduce the painted or printed image in acid meant that the piece had to be dipped a number of times. Items in the foreground would be shaded more strongly while the background features might only need one dip in acid. One of the most popular images was the Canterbury Pilgrims, based on the original painting *The Pilgrimage to Canterbury* of 1806-7 by Thomas Stothard and now in the Tate Gallery (Plate 172). In October 1817 the painting was published as an engraving by James Heath, entitled *The Pilgrimage*. Subsequent publications made the scene widely known and copied. In 1851 an adaptation of Stothard's picture was used on a large sideboard that was exhibited at the Great Exhibition. Stothard's first biographer, Mrs Bray, says of the engraving that 'few houses, where the master has a library, or has any pretensions to a love or knowledge of the fine arts, are without the print, framed and hung in a conspicuous place. Thousands have seen it, both abroad and at home, and everywhere is it equally admired and praised.' One of the prints still hangs in Sir Walter Scott's study at Abbotsford. The same print was the source for William Northwood's etched glass version which he signed and dated 1883 (Plate 173). The name of T. Stothard has also been added as acknowledgement of the source.

Equally popular were the satirical scenes of monks and clerics enjoying themselves (Plate 174). One print was the source for an etched jug signed with

Plate 175. Jug etched with an accurate copy of Une Bonne Histoire *after Herrmann, 1877-80. Signed in monogram, possibly J.L. Height 8½ in. (21.5cm).*

a monogram that can be read as JL (Plate 175). Figurative etched work of this quality is rare and must have necessitated a working drawing, taken in every detail from the original print, and transferred to the resist on the glass. The intricate and involved work of scratching the design through the wax, followed by a number of separate etchings, suggests that the jug and the Canterbury Pilgrims vase were one-off items and regarded as works of art in their own right. The glass artists were awarded the rare honour of signing their work.

Notable talents at the Northwood workshop included George and Tom Woodall, William Northwood and John Northwood II, Albert Gyngell who later became a landscape artist at Worcester, Benjamin Fenn, Joshua Hodgetts and James Hill. Hill can be seen on the left of the photograph of the workshop interior (Plate 156). A number of original drawings still exist by Hill (Plate 176) and are proof of the wide range of influences the artists were exposed to when they attended the Stourbridge School of Art. John Northwood II remembered that 'no expense was spared to equip a good library of Art books and portfolios and Art periodicals of the day. A large bookcase was filled with these and looking through some of them in later years one could not but remark what a large amount of use

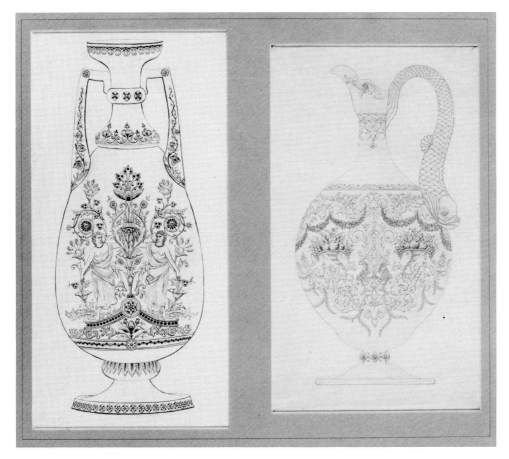

Plate 176. Two pencil designs by James Hill, 1878-80. Heights: vase 12 ¼ in. (31cm), jug 10 ½ in. (26.5cm).

they had. It was really a school which seemed to turn out skilled craftsmen like machines — nothing was too intricate or too difficult in decoration for them to transfer to glass'.

Two primary sources, the *Grammar of Ornament* by Owen Jones and the designs of John Flaxman, were used extensively on etched glass. The influence of Jones' *Grammar* is clearly seen on the Egyptian goblet (Plate 167) and the Renaissance arabesques and strapwork on the decanter, wineglass and jug (Plates 158 and 159). John Flaxman's illustrations to the *Iliad* and the *Odyssey* had been strong favourites with designers ever since they were first published in 1793 and a new edition of the illustrations in 1870 may have revived interest in the neo-classical style. The cool and precise qualities of Flaxman's designs transferred perfectly into the medium of acid etching (Plates 168 and 183). Another edition of Flaxman's *Classical Outlines* was published in 1879 with a foreword by John Sparkes, the headmaster of the National Art Training School at South Kensington, who urged that:

> The student may see great form, dignity and beauty in attitude; exquisite skill in so arranging a drapery that it may aid the lines of the composition; and not hide the construction of the figure beneath, expressed in the fewest lines and the most simple arrangement. Another rare quality is the sweet and purely innocent beauty of form and attitude in his female figures. No artist has ever before or since his time treated this most difficult section of all so perfectly. This is perhaps most evident

Plate 177. *Jug etched by Guest Brothers, 1871. Height 10½in. (26.5cm).*

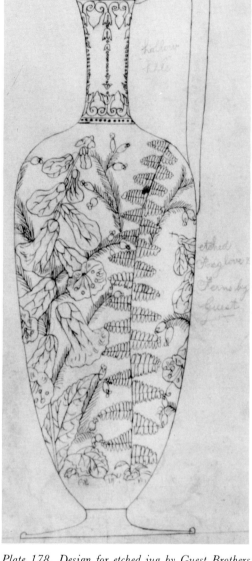

Plate 178. *Design for etched jug by Guest Brothers in the Thomas Webb pattern books, early 1870s.*

in the undraped forms, which embody an expression of childish unconsciousness and give the impression of purity and simplicity met with to the same extent in no other artist.

In her excellent article on Flaxman's influence on glass decoration, in the May 1987 issue of the *Burlington Magazine*, Barbara Morris suggests that it was 'this innocent appeal and the almost sexless quality of the nude figures that made the compositions an ideal source for the late Victorian designer'.

The other great firm of glass etchers in Stourbridge was Guest Brothers, one of whom, Tom Guest, had been a partner with Northwood in 1859. By 1864 or 1865 the name 'Guest and Brothers' appears in the pattern books at Thomas

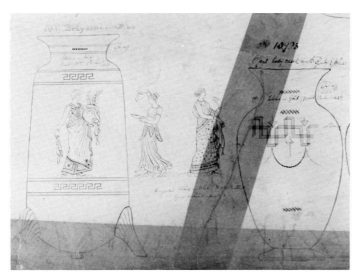

Plate 179. Design for etched and infilled decoration by Guest Brothers
in the Thomas Webb pattern books, 1878.

Plate 180. Goblet with white threads worked on pull-up machine, etched
with flowers and leaves infilled with gilding. Designed by John
Northwood at Stevens and Williams about 1885. Height 5in. (13cm).

Webb beside patterns described as etched. Situated a mile or two from
Northwood's workshop, the firm continued until 1918 and seems to have
employed up to thirty staff. Little else is known about the factory or its products.
One surviving decanter jug bears the inscription 'Presented by Guest Brothers
to Serg$^{t.}$ Westwood, XV Staffordshire Rifle Volunteers, 1871' (Plate 177). The
reason for the presentation remains a mystery but the quality of the etching
confirms local tradition that Guest's produced some of the finest etching in the
district.

For other examples of etching by Guest's one must go to the pattern books of
Thomas Webb. The first Guest patterns appear at number 6962, dated about
1865, and continue until 1896 with pattern number 22622 (Plate 178). A series
of designs dated to July 1878, about pattern number 10982, show vases of cased
glass with one or two colours, laid over opal (Plate 179). The text reads 'Etched
with gold, Guest Patent' and 'Figures etched in white'. No specimens have yet
been identified with these patterns but a bronze glass vase with etched outlines
bearing traces of infill is almost certainly a Webb/Guest product (Colour Plate
40). Similar work was produced by Northwood in the 1880s, often on latticinio
glass (Plate 180). Guest's also employed the infilled etched technique on pottery
vases. Some of the commemoratives made by Richardson's for Queen Victoria's
Diamond Jubilee also featured coloured infill decoration.

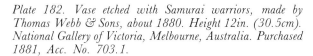
Plate 181. Pilgrim bottle flask, cased with blue over white and etched with a classical head. By Northwood for Thomas Webb, late 1860s. Height 10¼ in. (26cm).

Plate 182. Vase etched with Samurai warriors, made by Thomas Webb & Sons, about 1880. Height 12in. (30.5cm). National Gallery of Victoria, Melbourne, Australia. Purchased 1881, Acc. No. 703.1.

Other workshops which carried out work for Webb included Northwood, a decorator named Sutton, and a company referred to as H.W. & W. in the pattern books, probably Hingley, Weaver and Whitworth of the Wordsley Glassworks, Stourbridge. A pilgrim flask, cased with blue on white and etched with a classical head surrounded by laurel leaves, was decorated for Webb by Northwood (Plate 181) and identified from the Webb pattern books. Not all of the Webb's examples can be attributed to these firms but what is certain is the high standard required by the company. A superb vase, showing Samurai warriors, was acquired by the National Gallery of Victoria in Melbourne in 1881 direct from the Webb stand at the Melbourne Exhibition where they were awarded Gold Medals in three classes (Plate 182).

Two other firms whose work was of a consistently high nature deserving greater recognition were the Philip Pargeter works at the Red House Cone and Grice Brothers. The Pargeter design books show a wide range of etched patterns including a number of subjects which can be identified from Flaxman's

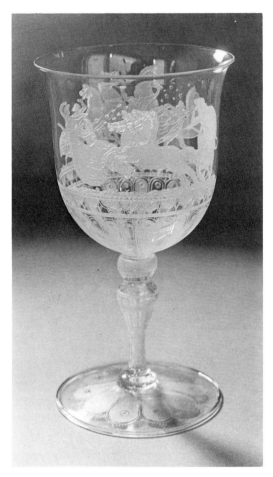

Plate 183. Goblet etched with a scene of 'Juno and Minerva Going To Assist The Greeks' after Flaxman. Made at the Pargeter works, early 1870s. Height 6½in. (16.5cm).

Plate 184. Photograph of John Northwood I with Edwin Grice (right), probably taken about 1880.

engravings. One goblet which matches the designs has been blown almost paper thin with a hollow stem and a fragile foot with a very thin folded rim (Plate 183).

Even less is known about the firm of Grice Brothers. According to Sam Thompson, who was in charge of the acid workshop at Stevens and Williams for many years, Grice Brothers' important contribution was the development of vertical etching machines. One of the brothers, Edwin (Plate 184), had worked alongside John Northwood during the latter's cameo period and assisted with carving the applied heads on the Pegasus vase, now in the Smithsonian Institution. The Grice workshop was eventually bought out by Stevens and Williams. Two existing pieces, a decanter and a plate, which both came from the Grice family, show strong oriental influences (Plates 185 and 186). The etched panels on the decanter alternate with spiral bands of fine cutting. The etching on the plate is through a thick layer of blue glass, a use of the technique which is seen on a French jug and goblets where the red glass has been left in high relief (Plate 187).

Plate 185. Decanter and stopper etched by Grice Brothers, 1880s. Height 12½ in. (31.5cm).

Plate 186. Plate cased with blue on clear and etched with a Japanese influenced design. By Grice Brothers, 1880s. Diameter 9½ in. (24cm).

Although the decorating shops continued to supply the firms with etched work the larger companies could afford to establish their own acid facilities. The invaluable photographs taken in 1902 at the Stuart factory recorded the layout of their acid decorating room (Plates 153 and 154); the bare fabric of the building is still in existence and the photographs have been used to reconstruct the setting as part of the Red House Cone Museum. The photographs are the only record of the vertical etching machines (Plate 154).

As acid etching quickly spread through every glassmaking centre, cheaper variations on the technique were developed to satisfy a demand for bulk orders from hotels, railways and shipping lines and for all types of souvenirs. The idea of using transfer prints to apply the resist bypassed the labour intensive methods developed by Northwood, although these did continue right through the century in parallel with the new methods. In 1853 a Charles Breese of London patented

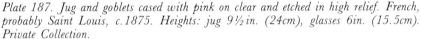

Plate 187. Jug and goblets cased with pink on clear and etched in high relief. French, probably Saint Louis, c.1875. Heights: jug 9½in. (24cm), glasses 6in. (15.5cm). Private Collection.

Plate 188. Tumbler etched using transfer print resist method. Possibly by the Northwood workshop, late 19th century. Height 4in. (10.5cm).

a process of printing a negative on paper with printing ink and transferring this to glass to be etched. Examples were shown at the Paris Exhibition of 1855 while in England the Patent Etching and Ornamenting Glass Company at the Globe works in Sheffield is known to have used a similar process. The Stourbridge companies were also quick to capitalise on the idea (Plate 188).

The stages of the process began with the required design cut into the copper plate without being reversed as the image would print the right way round on the glass. The plate was then covered with the resist which was forced into the design and the excess removed so that it filled only the intaglio design. The plate was passed through a press and the resist picked up on to fine paper. The design was transferred to the glass and the paper removed. At this stage the remainder of the glass which was not to be etched was blocked out with the same resist. Finally the glass was dipped into the acid bath. The length of time the glass remained in the acid composition depended on the depth of the etch required as well as the strength of the acid.

Transfer printed etching became widely used for commemoratives and souvenirs in the last forty years of the century and some extremely fine work was achieved using lithographic stones which were themselves etched with acid. Glass etchers apparently also experimented with glass and zinc plates.

From the idea of applying the resist by transfer printing, it was a short step to dispensing with the resist and transfer printing the design directly on to the glass.

Plate 189. Posy vase in opalescent yellow glass etched with the Royal Mail Steam Packet Company emblem. Stourbridge, late 19th century. Height 2 ¼ in. (6cm).

Most of the badged glassware for shipping lines and hotels was decorated in this way (Plate 189).

The process involved the use of an engraved copper plate, and an acid paste, containing starch and gum tragacanth, plus a fluoride liquid which attacked the glass. The engraved lines of the plate were filled with the paste by using a palette knife and the design was transferred with tissue paper to the glass. The fluoride etching paste ate into the glass and after about two minutes the transfer was removed and the remnants of the paste washed away to reveal the permanent mark on the glass. Items which have been badged with fluoride paste can normally be distinguished by the much fainter impression of the image when compared with the transfer printed resist versions which were still dipped in acid.

Badged glass, like the Steam Packet posy bowl which at first glance seems of little consequence, can provide a fascinating link with the social and economic life of the Victorian period. The British and North American Royal Mail Steam Packet Company, to give its full name, was formed by Samuel Cunard and began operating in 1840. Born in Halifax, Nova Scotia, Cunard secured a seven year contract from the Admiralty who wished to speed communications between Great Britain and the colonies. The service startled the North American colonies when the inaugural crossing, with Cunard on board, took only twelve days and ten hours to reach Halifax from Liverpool. Boston was quickly added to the link providing fast transatlantic communication.

One of the first glassworks to use etching in Manchester was the well-known firm of Molineaux Webb. The manager of the acid shop was James Fone, seen in a family photograph with his wife on the left, and his brother and his wife on the right (Plate 190). A notebook of his, in the family's possession, records various acid recipes including a hot and cold process for printing resist, a mixture for dull etching, bright acid for lampshades and a mixture for bright polishing which consisted of 'Equal parts Hydrofluoric acid and Cold Water let Stand until

Plate 190. Photograph of James Fone (left) and his wife, brother and sister-in-law, early 20th century. Private Collection.

Plate 191. Wineglass etched by James Fone, 1867. Height 7in. (17.5cm). Private Collection.

Cold then add equal parts of Sulphuric Acid Mixing by degrees. *Very Good'*.

Some of the dangers of the early experiments are recounted in a family anecdote about James Fone's experimental mix of acid for etching and polishing. An appointment between Mr Fone and Mr Webb was arranged for early one morning, when the new mix was to be tried. However Mr Webb proceeded to blend the ingredients before Mr Fone arrived, but only succeeded in producing an explosion which damaged the etching shop and part of the cutting shop. Two dated glasses in the family collection were decorated by James Fone. The first is dated 1867 and has the initials MF for his wife Martha, who would have been nineteen years of age at that date (Plate 191). Fone may have worked at Stourbridge prior to his time in Manchester and this glass may possibly be a Midlands product. The other glass, a definite Manchester example and dated 1871, bears the initials JF for their first daughter Jane, born in Manchester on 1 December, eleven months after James and Martha were married in Congleton on 2 January 1867 (Plate 192). Both glasses show free-hand work and geometric machine patterns.

In Scotland the works of John Baird of Glasgow specialised in glass for advertising and produced badged souvenirs for the Scottish National Exhibition

Plate 192. Wineglass etched by James Fone in 1871 at Molineaux, Webb & Co., Manchester. Height approximately 7in. (18cm). Private Collection.

in Edinburgh in 1908 and perhaps for later exhibitions in Glasgow (Plate 193). French and Belgian factories exported vast quantities of etched glass into England which were sometimes advertised in the pages of the *Pottery Gazette*. The factories of Saint Louis and Baccarat used the technique as early as the 1860s. A tumbler etched through a thin amber layer (Plate 194) is similar in technique to an 1866 tumbler in the Saint Louis collections with a blue layer on a frosted background, etched with a scene of stags in a woodland setting. Many etched souvenirs of English events are of European make.

Figurative and geometric etched glass was made in large numbers by the Danish factories of Kastrup and Holmegaard. Little attention has been paid to this source of etched glass which can be identified from existing catalogues. At Holmegaard bright needle etching appears in a catalogue of 1900. The glasses were decorated on the only automatic guilloche or pantograph machine to be used in Denmark. Bought from a German company in the Rhineland, it remained in use until 1910. At the Copenhagen works of Kastrup the etched subjects included

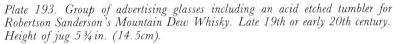

Plate 193. *Group of advertising glasses including an acid etched tumbler for Robertson Sanderson's Mountain Dew Whisky. Late 19th or early 20th century. Height of jug 5¾in. (14.5cm).*

Plate 194. *Tumbler etched through amber stain, Saint Louis, France, about 1866. Height 5½in. (14cm).*

stags, birds and inscriptions placed on carafes and decanters, goblets and mugs, recorded in a catalogue of 1910. An invaluable book, illustrating these etched pieces as well as other blown and moulded items which could be mistaken as English, is the *Danish Glass* catalogue which was produced by the Victoria and Albert Museum in 1974 for the touring exhibition of the Peter F. Heering Collection of drinking glasses, decanters and pocket flasks from 1814 to 1914. It is essential reading for all collectors of English nineteenth and early twentieth century glass.

Acid etched glass, with its fascinating variety of effects, can sustain the interest of the most demanding collector. In the words of one nineteenth century writer, 'etching should rank with engraving, and it is an absurd prejudice which displaces it'. If the Victorian decorative arts are sometimes accused of being too brash, loud and extravagant then acid etching provides the other extreme of delicate and sensitive decoration combined with a high degree of technical sophistication.

Plate 195. Photograph of John Northwood I taken by George Woodall. Printed from Woodall's original glass plate negative.

CHAPTER TEN

Cameo Glass

When John Northwood I (Plate 195) finished his copy of the Portland vase in 1876 he laid the foundations for one of the greatest contributions Stourbridge was to make to the history of glass. Of all the English glassmaking districts Stourbridge was the only one with the wealth of talent necessary to produce cameo decoration and it enjoyed an absolute monopoly. The exquisite cameo glasses from Webb's, Richardson's, and Stevens and Williams ranked in excellence with that other great period of cameo production, the first century A.D. in the Roman Empire. From the outset Roman cameo glass was used as the model for the revival in Stourbridge. The presence of the finest example of cameo glass from the ancient world in the British Museum inevitably played a crucial part in the story.

Since it was discovered in Rome in the sixteenth century the Portland vase had been the centre of intrigue and legend. In 1783 it was acquired by Sir William Hamilton who sold it to the Duchess of Portland. Two years later it was acquired by the third Duke of Portland who lent it to Josiah Wedgwood. In 1810 it was put on display at the British Museum. Eight years later two Birmingham men failed in their attempt to reproduce it. Interest was revived on a national scale following an incident in the Museum in 1845 when the vase was smashed, while on display, into 189 pieces. In the publicity surrounding the event, Benjamin Richardson is said to have offered a £1,000 prize for the first accurate Portland reproduction. The restored vase continued its stay at the British Museum due to the generosity of successive Dukes of Portland until it was bought for the nation in 1945.

With the eclecticism of nineteenth century design and the fashion for revivals of historic styles it was inevitable that cameo glass should receive a great deal of attention. The technical know-how amassed by generations of glassmakers in Stourbridge made the reproduction a possibility. All that was needed for success was a total belief in the idea. In 1873 Philip Pargeter, the owner of the Red House Glass Works (Plate 2), felt his glassmakers had the skill to make the blank. He put forward the notion to John Northwood I and asked him if he could carry out the carving. Three years later the fruit of their vision stunned the glassmaking world (Colour Plate 16).

Faced with the total absence of any Roman evidence to help explain the cameo process, Pargeter and Northwood relied on techniques which had developed simultaneously in Stourbridge since the 1840s. Northwood's own training and experience had brought expertise in acid etching and in relief carving, which he perfected on the Elgin vase now in the Birmingham Art Gallery. The benefit of the etching process in cameo glass was the speedy removal of the unwanted parts

Plate 196. Cup casing at the Webb Corbett glassworks, Amblecote, 1979. A bubble of clear glass is being inserted into a red glass cup which is resting on a dip mould.

from the top layer of glass. The method of blowing cameo blanks, itself an extension of the cased technique introduced in the 1840s, became known as the cup casing method. It provided the certainty of a uniformly thick, top layer to allow for the high relief carving. Before the glass was blown, it was essential that both colours were physically compatible with virtually identical coefficents of expansion and contraction. For the Portland vase shape the cup was made in white glass and would form the outside layer of the vase. By the early 1880s the Roman influence of the blue and white combination gave way to other colours although white remained the favourite colour for the outside casing. At the Webb Corbett factory in the 1970s their cameo pieces featured coloured glass decoration on a clear glass body. The following description of the cup casing method is based on the process used by the team headed by Malcolm Andrews, at Webb Corbett's (Plate 196).

The blowing process for cup casing begins with the making of the cup by the servitor of the team. Once the cup has been completed it is broken off the blowing-iron and placed on a small dip mould to await the inside layer of glass. It is important to pre-heat the mould to minimise the difference in temperature which could result in the cup cracking. While the cup is in the process of being

Colour Plate 16. The Portland vase, the Milton vase and the Shakespeare portrait tazza by John Northwood I. Completed in 1876, the Portland vase established the cameo tradition in Stourbridge. Northwood went on to carve the Milton vase, completed in 1878, and the Shakespeare tazza, about 1880, with two other portrait tazzas of Newton and Flaxman. A second Shakespeare tazza was discovered in the late 1970s. Heights 9⅞in. and 13in. (25cm and 33cm), and diameter 9¼in. (23.5cm). Portland vase and Shakespeare tazza Dr and Mrs Leonard Rakow Collection; Milton vase Mr and Mrs Billy Hitt Collection. Photograph courtesy of The Corning Museum of Glass.

formed another member of the team makes two gathers of glass on another blowpipe which is passed to the head of the chair, the gaffer, for final blowing and shaping prior to placing it in the cup. The time between the cracking-off of the cup and the insertion of the bubble is only a matter of seconds. Any delay would result in a fall in temperature which would give a poor and uncertain join between the two. The bubble is placed in the bottom of the cup and pressed down to ensure good adhesion and to prevent any air bubbles which would make the final blank useless. The size of the bubble is only slightly smaller than the cup shape so as it is pressed into the cup the glass is forced upwards making contact all the way with the cup. The gaffer does not inflate the bubble but relies on the pressure of the glass being pushed into the cup to make the necessary join. The bubble is taken to the glory-hole to be re-heated to ensure the two layers have fused.

From this point the complete bubble is worked to give it the final shape and proportions. Once it has been re-heated it is rolled on the marver to give a smooth, uniform surface. This constant reworking of the glass means that a thicker layer of the outside casing has formed at the base of the bubble and has to be removed in order to give a uniform thickness of glass in the final blank. The gaffer will use the pucellas or jacks to draw off the unwanted surplus at the base and snip it off with the shears. During the shaping process each member of the team will take it in turns to re-heat the blank in front of the glory-hole, allowing their team-mates a deserved respite from the heat. The next dangerous stage is to transfer the shape on to the pontil rod to allow the final shaping of the neck and rim and the addition of handles. The glass on the pontil rod needs to be of the correct temperature to fuse to the base of the vase. If it is too hot the vase will drag on the pontil and fall off. If it is too cold the join will not be adequate to take the weight of the vase and it will also drop off the pontil rod. After the transfer to the pontil rod, further re-heating will allow the gaffer to shear off the unwanted glass on the rim and to make the final shape. When the gaffer is satisfied with the final look of the blank it is knocked off the pontil rod and taken to the annealing lehr where it is cooled overnight to remove stresses and strains.

Although the glassmaking team now breathe a sigh of relief at the successful completion of their task, the cameo will always retain an element of suspense. Even after proper annealing, cameo glass retains some stress between the layers which can cause fracture or splitting years after completion. Where a fracture did occur or if a section of the top layer had flaked off the body, the glass would be saved in the damaged state rather than have hours of work thrown away (Plate 197). The time between start and finish depends on the size and shape of the glass and whether it has more than one casing. At the Webb Corbett factory large chalices and bowls could take up to thirty minutes to complete.

The same method of cup casing was used on cameos with three or more layers. Each subsequent layer increased the risks of air traps and incompatibility. On some nineteenth century pieces the inner and outer coloured layers are separated by a clear glass. Other multi-layered glasses may have two layers of the same colour separated by other colours.

Variations of the cup-casing method were used for many other types of Victorian glassware apart from cameo. Quicker versions of the method were required for small or cheap items or when a large run of items needed to be made. In one process, described in a 'Tour in the Manufacturing Districts', published

Plate 197. Unfinished and broken cameo vase, possibly from John Northwood's workshop, mid- to late 1870s. Height 13½ in. (34.3cm).

in the *Art Union* magazine in April 1846, the cup remained on the blowing-iron:

The glass-worker dips the end of his rod into the melted glass, which forms the foundation of the article he is about to make, and after collecting a sufficient quantity, his assistant having gathered a portion of coloured glass of the kind required for the outer coating, and formed this into a cup at the end of the rod, is ready, on the former's having made the requisite preparations, to insert the cup of coloured material on the top of the glass already mentioned, as being attached to the master's rod; the coloured glass is disconnected from the rod by means of a smart tap, and the cup covers and remains firmly attached to the internal substance. It is introduced to the heating furnace, after which, in the language of

Colour Plate 17. Stourbridge cameo glass from the 1880s. Left to right. Citron and white cameo vase, carved by Joshua Hodgetts at Stevens and Williams, height 12in. (30.5cm). Blue and white cameo vase, probably engraved by Benjamin Hollis at Thomas Webb's (see Plate 220), c.1884, height 5½in. (14cm). Red and white cameo vase, Stevens and Williams, recorded in their pattern books, no. 12548, about March 1887, and priced at £4.10s.; height 14¼in. (36cm). Red and white cameo vase carved at the Richardson glassworks, early 1880s, height 6⅞in. (17.5cm). Yellow, red and white cameo vase, probably Thomas Webb's, height 8¾in. (22.2cm), Mr and Mrs Evans Collection. Red and white cameo vase carved with damsons, Richardson's, early 1880s, height 6½in. (16.5cm); the vase is recorded in a series of photographs from the factory, pattern no. '9706 Damson sh/- [84s.]' (see Plate 204). Cinnamon and white cameo vase, recorded at Stevens and Williams at pattern no. 11409 'Cinnamon Cameo £9 Nor. 16 guineas 5/5/86', signed W. Northwood, height 9½in. (24cm).

the trade, it is 'marved', or rolled on the cast metal slab, in use by all glass-blowers, the effect of which is to place in complete contact or adhesion the two different colours.

Some colours were too strident if used on their own, but by casing them on to clear glass a finer, diluted shade was obtained. The expensive coloured glass batch could also be made to go further by casing it on to a base of clear glass. For items such as wineglasses with coloured bowls, an even faster method of casing was developed using a long tube of coloured glass about 2in. (5cm) in diameter. The end of the hot coloured tube was first pinched to form an egg-cup

Colour Plate 18. Stourbridge cameo glass showing variations on the basic technique. Left to right. Vase cased with ruby over citron, carved to reveal white flowers trapped in the citron layer, marked Thomas Webb and Sons Gem Cameo, late 19th century, height 5½ in. (13.8cm). White vase cased with a rainbow striped layer and etched with leaves, marked Stevens and Williams Stourbridge Art Glass; possibly the 'new rainbow colour' introduced at the factory in 1894 although the ground rim and the insipid shade of the white body gives sufficient reason to question the English attribution; height 6⅛ in. (15.5cm). Amber and citron cameo vase with the chipped background introduced at Stevens and Williams in 1887, height 7½ in. (19cm). Red, blue and white cameo vase carved with a bird behind irises, the background acid etched, marked as the left-hand vase; the entire pontil area including the mark has been badly etched, an effect not often seen on pieces which carry a definitive factory-originated mark; recorded in the Woodall price book as 'F118 GW £3-15s-0d (Sale price) £10-10s-0d' and noted by the side of the sketch 'Woodall's estimate ec/- [79s.]'; height 9⅞ in. (25cm). Decanter and stopper, cut and engraved rock crystal glass with a cameo band of pink and white, Thomas Webb's, height 11⅝ in. (29.5cm). Michael Parkington Collection with the exception of the Stevens and Williams chipped background vase.

shape. A gather of glass was made on a blowing-iron, formed into a small bubble and pushed into the coloured shape to create the cased effect. The fused shape was cracked off the end of the tube and the wineglass could be finished in the normal way. The end of the tube was formed into another egg-cup shape and the whole process was repeated.

The alternative to cup-casing was to dip a formed shape of one colour into a pot of another colour. The process may possibly have been used to form the

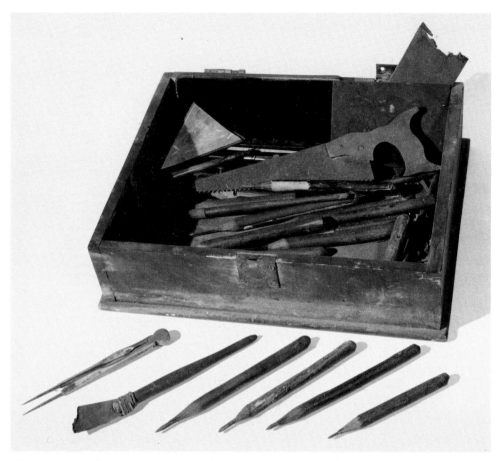

Plate 198. Box of carving tools used by George Woodall. Private Collection.

Portland vase if the cup-casing method was unknown to Roman glassmakers. Another variant was to gather the different colours directly on to the blowing-iron. A very thin layer of coloured glass, sometimes referred to as flashing, could be obtained by this method.

The carving and modelling of the cameo blank requires two distinct operations. Before the glass is painted with an acid resist in the required design, the glossy surface of the white glass is deadened in acid to give a key for the drawn design. Once the resist has set the vase is dipped into hydrofluoric acid which gradually removes the unwanted white glass. This process needs to be repeated a number of times depending on the thickness of the white glass as the build-up of deposits during the etching retards its own action. The remaining white silhouette is modelled using small steel points set into wooden holders to scrape and carve the glass. The rough and ready nature of the modelling tools which still survive is hard to equate with the subtle and evocative effects of modelling which they created (Plate 198).

Credit for blowing the cameo blanks for Northwood's Portland vase went to the chair headed by Daniel Hancox, assisted by Joseph Worrall (servitor), Charles Hancox (footmaker and son of Daniel), and Benjamin Downing

Plate 199. The base of Northwood's Portland vase. The signature and date can be seen above the foot rim. Photograph courtesy Sotheby's.

(footmaker). As is normal in a glasshouse with a special commission, a number of blanks would be made in order to give the decorator the choice of the best one and to have a replacement in the event of an accident to the first. Unfortunately, like the original Roman vase, Northwood's version was also to suffer damage when it cracked due to the stresses within the glass. The crack affected the body of the vase and did not damage the carving on the base (Plate 199). John Northwood II believed that 'the carving had made the opal coating very irregular in its thickness, and this rendered the vase more sensitive to any change in temperature'. A firsthand account of the damage was given by Edwin Grice in an interview in 1913:

> We had got the vase into a very forward condition, having worked upon it for two years, and we contemplated another journey to compare it with the original. Before we started early for London we had a terrible mishap. The night had been very frosty, and when the vase was being lifted carefully into the box something went crack. We afterwards found that the holding of the vase in warm hands had caused uneven expansion, producing a fracture. It put a damper on our spirits, as you may guess. It had cracked right up the body and across one part of it.

On completion in 1876 the vase was widely publicised and exhibited. It was displayed at the Red House works for two weeks and then taken to Pargeter's London showrooms. In January 1877 it was exhibited in Stoke-on-Trent. With

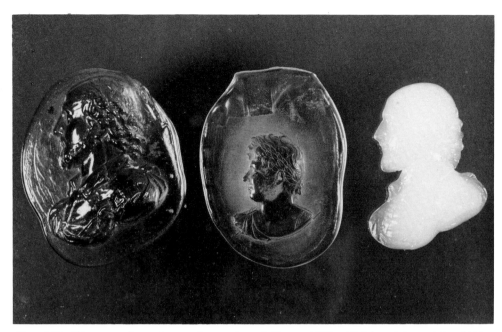

Plate 200. Three experimental pressed portrait medallions, 1870s. Heights, left to right, 3½in. (8.9cm), 3½in. (8.9cm), 3in. (7.4cm).

Plate 201. Cameo vases by Alphonse Lechevrel 1877-78. From left to right: Raising an Altar to Bacchus; Venus arising from the Waves; Hercules restoring Alcestis to her husband Admetus. Heights, left to right, 15½in. (39.5cm), 11¼in. (28.3cm), 14in. (35.4cm). When George Woodall was asked to remove the handles from the Venus vase and its pair he removed Lechevrel's signature and added his own but a monogram AL, in diamond point, can still be seen on the vase.

the Milton vase it formed the centre of attraction on Thomas Webb's stand at the Paris Exhibition in 1878. In 1905 it was back on display in Stourbridge. The vase remained the property of Philip Pargeter who estimated that it had cost him over £500. When it came up for sale at Sotheby's Belgravia in 1975 it fetched the then record price for a piece of glass of £30,000.

In the next five years Northwood created another five cameo pieces which confirmed his outstanding skills. The Milton vase and the three portrait tazzas of Newton representing science, Shakespeare representing literature and Flaxman representing art were produced in collaboration with Philip Pargeter (Colour Plate 16). The Pegasus vase was the last of the series made to a commission from Thomas Wilkes Webb and is now in the collections at the Smithsonian Institution in Washington. In the late 1970s another, hitherto unrecorded, tazza of Shakespeare appeared on the market. As a result of this impressive body of work, Northwood became an internationally acclaimed celebrity and was enticed to take the prestige job of Artistic Director at Stevens and Williams in 1881. In that role, he established the company as one of the three great Stourbridge glasshouses of the nineteenth century.

Written accounts of the cameo revival accept without question that all of Northwood's cameos were made by the cup casing method. However, the thickness of the cameo heads on the tazzas suggests that an alternative method may have been employed. Glassmakers are not prone to waste unnecessary effort when speedier and equally effective alternatives are available. A vast amount of thick, white glass would have to be etched away in order to leave a small amount for the portrait heads. Several glasses suggest the alternative method which may have been used. The most important glass from this group is a jug, decorated in relief with a white cameo bust of a Roman emperor, which, perhaps not coincidentally, was in the collection of John Northwood II (Colour Plate 22). It is obvious from a close examination of this jug that no other white glass could have been applied to the jug; therefore the medallion had to be applied as a separate piece. Three portrait medallions may have been trials in which the glass was pressed into a mould, then carved in a cold state to sharpen the details (Plate 200). On completion the medallion would be set in a metal mould with its flat back facing into the open mould. By blowing a bubble of glass into the hot mould it was possible to pick up the pre-carved, glass medallion which became a unified part of the object. The same technique was used by Apsley Pellatt for his Crystallo Engraving (Plate 248). In his specification the ceramic insert was removed after it had impressed the design into the glass, but Pellatt realised the other possibility and would use it on his Crystallo-Ceramie pieces, where the sulphide was left on the surface rather than enclosed within the glass. Precedents for the technique had appeared in Bohemia in the nineteenth century. A lithyalin beaker with a white relief portrait bust of Schiller on the surface of the glass is illustrated in *Porträtgläser* by S. Baumgärtner.

Within a year of Northwood completing his Portland vase the major Stourbridge factories had set up their own workshops to capitalise on the demand

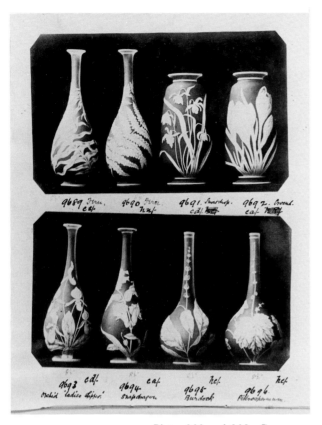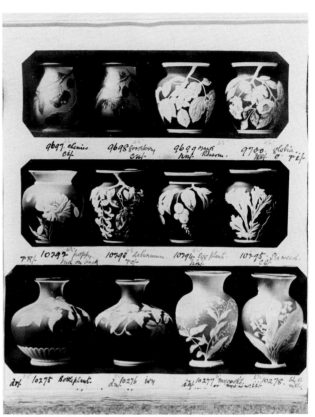

Plates 202 and 203. Cameo vases illustrated in a Richardson pattern book, early 1880s.

for cameo. Thomas Webb's employed George and Tom Woodall who had trained with John Northwood. The Woodalls were to lead a team of cameo decorators who created the most consistently high quality work in the 1880s and 1890s. Stevens and Williams eventually subcontracted the Northwood workshop to supply their company with cameo.

At the Richardson's works Joseph Locke quickly produced a second Portland vase copy while in 1877 Benjamin Richardson took the unique step of inviting the Frenchman Alphonse Lechevrel to work specifically on the new technique. Born in Paris in 1850, Lechevrel trained as a gem engraver and medallist with Henri François whose own work deeply influenced him. François' work in onyx included classical subjects such as Venus disarming Cupid, Venus playing with Cupid and Venus emerging from the Waves. Two of Lechevrel's vases for Richardson featured Venus arising from the Waves and the Birth of Venus (Plate 201). Before arriving in England, Lechevrel carved several gems and semi-precious stones with subjects of Minerva, Medusa, Perseus, Bacchus and Cupid, making him an ideal choice to work on Stourbridge cameo which relied heavily on classical mythology, at least in its early years. His experience with hard materials stood him in good stead with the equally intractable glass. Lechevrel stayed at Wordsley for two years and his production seems to have been limited to a dozen pieces including 'Raising an Altar to Bacchus', probably his

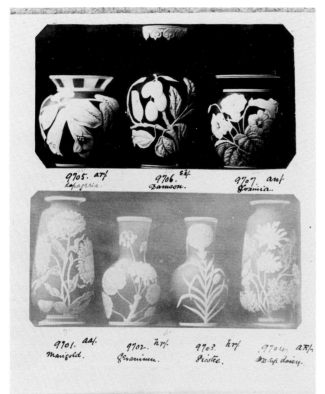

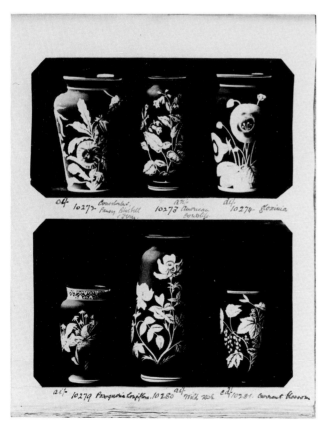

Plate 204.

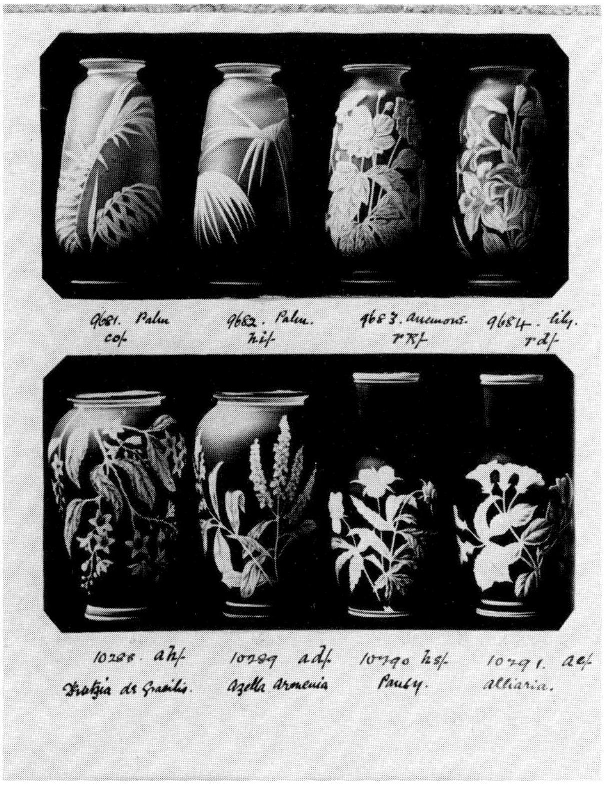

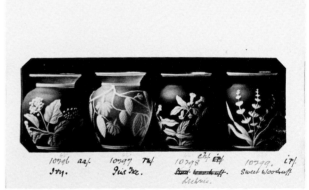

Plate 205.

Plate 207.

Cameo vases illustrated in a Richardson pattern book, early 1880s.

Plate 206.

215

masterpiece and one of the finest restrained expositions of the technique.

At the 1878 Paris Exhibition the price of Lechevrel's vases started from £150 for 'Venus arising from the Waves' to £250 for 'Hercules restoring Alcestes to her husband Admetus'. At the other end of the market, Richardson's, in line with the other firms, produced large numbers of floral vases, often termed 'commercial cameo' (Plates 202 to 207 and Colour Plate 17). During the early to mid-1880s, prices for these small vases, between 4½in. and 8in. (11.5cm and 20.25cm) high, were from 22s. (£1.10) to 88s. (£4.40). The word 'commercial' should in no sense be seen as a derogatory term, for the quality of modelling is exceptionally high with crisply serrated leaves and rounded flowers that almost cascade from the surface. Usually attributed to Webb or Stevens and Williams, Richardson commercial cameo vases do not carry a Richardson mark of any type but may occasionally have a diamond point inscription on the base with the name of the flower and, very rarely, with the price code.

At the Brierley Hill works of Stevens and Williams cut, engraved and coloured glass predominated and no cameo work seems to have been undertaken during the late 1870s. By the early 1880s the pattern books are crammed with cameo designs, coinciding with the appointment of John Northwood I as Artistic Director. The range of objects consisted of vases, claret jugs and clareteens, scent and smelling bottles, decanters, watch bottles (i.e. shaped as watches), lamps, salts and inkpots, menu balls and even parasol handles. The number of colours was no less varied and included claret, orange, nut brown, cinnamon, gorse yellow, poppy red, plum, rose, pale blue, rose du barry, turquoise, amber, emerald, peacock blue and topaz. Cameo glass followed the same stylistic influences from Islam and the Orient which were so marked in the firm's rock crystal glass. The double gourd shape was extremely popular, as was the elegant, tall, thin-necked vase based on Persian forms. Over all these grew a profusion of blossoms. Chrysanthemums, peonies, sunflowers, poppies, azaleas and passion flowers intermingled with convolvulus, snowdrops, primroses, daisies, tiger lilies, clematis and maidenhair ferns (Colour Plate 17).

As the public demand for cameo glass increased so the Stourbridge firms were equal to the challenge, each developing its own characteristic and recognisable styles. A number of variations were introduced by Northwood during the mid-1880s, including the occasional use of cameo on his latticinio glass. 'Dolce Relievo' appeared in 1884. It consisted of a cream ground with a purple top layer etched with acid. The shapes echoed the Middle Eastern favourites with subject matter predominantly of figurative decoration based on classical themes (Plate 208).

Another variation involved the addition of silver deposit decoration to the finished cameo. The best designs on cameo were open trellis patterns entwined with prunus blossoms or chrysanthemums, evocative of Japanese gardens (Plate 209).

Engraving skills developed on rock crystal glass were often transferred to cameo decoration. One specific technique was the chipped, hammered or

Plate 208. Cameo vase in 'Dolce Relievo' from Stevens and Williams, c.1884. Height 10¾ in. (27.3cm). Photograph courtesy Sotheby's.

Plate 209. Cameo vase with white flowers on a red background with silver deposit decoration, c.1890. Height 4½ in. (11.5cm).

'pecked' background which appears as a frosted or cracked surface. Production was low because it involved chipping the glass against a rotating S-shaped metal tool, fixed on the end of a spindle and set in an engraving lathe. In the Stevens and Williams books this decoration, patented as a 'chiselled' ground, first appears as pattern 12981 on 24 September 1887 (Colour Plate 18).

All the payments for cameo glass at Stevens and Williams were made to Northwood. The actual carving and modelling took place at his decorating workshop in Wordsley where his nephew, William Northwood, and Joshua Hodgetts were the top artists. William worked in a variety of styles, from classical themes of Venus and Cupid to complicated oriental patterns (Colour Plate 17). Joshua's favourite motifs were flowers and birds executed in a strong oriental manner (Colour Plate 17). According to family tradition (see Appendix 9), Hodgetts had access to an important local collection of oriental art and in some of his vases he would carve the entire vase on the wheel, in Chinese fashion,

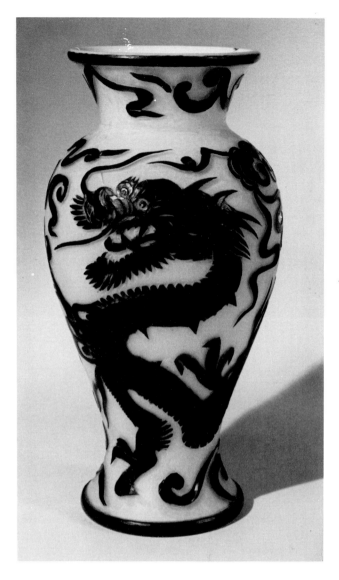

Plate 210. Black and white cameo vase carved on the engraving wheel. Signed by Joshua Hodgetts, late 19th century. Height 8¼ in. (21cm).

rather than employing acid to speed the operation (Plate 210). Hodgetts later moved to Stevens and Williams where he became the leading intaglio engraver when that technique was introduced in 1891. Intaglio quickly became the predominant style but cameo variations continued to appear. As late as 1897, when intaglio designs filled the pattern books, 'Transparent Cameo' was introduced at pattern numbers 24242-24244, dated roughly to October of that year. The pieces were carved by none other than Joshua Hodgetts, the intaglio specialist (Colour Plate 19). Transparent cameo was probably made in other colours but only emerald green and amethyst have been found. The reduction in cameo production at Stevens and Williams in the 1890s, due mainly to high costs, left the market open to the brilliant achievements at Thomas Webb & Sons.

The director of the firm in the 1870s was Thomas Wilkes Webb, one of three sons of the original founder. In 1880 he commissioned John Northwood to produce the Pegasus vase as his final piece of cameo work. By that time Webb

Plate 211. Photograph of George Woodall. From a glass plate negative on loan to Broadfield House Glass Museum.

Plate 212. Photograph of the Woodall cameo team. Back row: Tom Farmer, Harry Davies, Tom Woodall. Front row: William Hill, J. T. Fereday and George Woodall.

employed the brothers George and Tom Woodall who had trained with Northwood. In his diary, Tom Woodall remembered his own part in the Portland vase saga:

> Whilst I was with Messrs. Northwood Mr. Philip Pargeter, then of the Red House Glass Works, commissioned Messrs. Northwood to execute a copy of the Portland Vase. He made several trials and succeeded in getting a good copy as to shape etc. from one of Wedgwoods excellent copies in Jasperware. I made the first drawings and painted resist for aciding this out which was a fairly long job as it was fairly thick an outer casing to get the necessary relief. Mr. Northwood then took it in hand.

With such a sound background George and Tom had taken over the running of the cameo department in 1874 (Plates 211 and 212). Due to the greater number of pieces of cameo signed by George Woodall it is always assumed that he was the more talented of the two brothers. The pieces that are signed by Tom reveal an equal talent. However, Tom was more interested in music and he was more self-effacing than his brother who enjoyed and played up to the reputation of an international celebrity. For ten years, between 1889 and 1899, the brothers' joint signature of 'T & G Woodall' appeared on a range of vases and plaques. There is a well-known local Stourbridge anecdote about how George removed Tom's signature from their joint efforts and there may be a grain of truth in this story. When George carried out some repairs on two Lechevrel vases in about 1920 he seems to have deliberately removed Lechevrel's signature and replaced it with his own (Plate 201). However, the quality of George Woodall's cameos is evidence enough of his supreme talent as the greatest cameo carver of the time.

Plate 213. 'The Moorish Bathers' by George Woodall. Dr and Mrs Leonard S. Rakow Collection, on loan to the Corning Museum of Glass.

Plate 214. Photograph by George Woodall of an early design for 'The Moorish Bathers', printed from his glass plate negative.

Colour Plate 19. 'Transparent Cameo' decanter and stopper (left) and an intaglio cut decanter and stopper, both in amethyst over clear and both cut by Joshua Hodgetts at Stevens and Williams c.1897 Heights 11in. (28cm) and 12 ⅜in. (31.5cm). Michael Parkington Collection.

Looking through photographs of his work it becomes clear that George Woodall chose his subject matter not simply for its fashionable taste but because it was the most difficult scene to transpose into layers of cameo glass. The more difficult the subject, the more easily did Woodall conquer the problem. George Woodall's masterpiece, acknowledged as such by himself, is 'The Moorish Bathers' (Plate 213). It is a plaque of the standard 18in. (45.75cm) diameter cased with white over a raisin coloured body and carved with a scene of six women swimming and lounging on the sides of a pool, surrounded by exotic architecture and foliage. Motifs like the row of columns which ends in a hardly visible doorway revealing a shaft of light, the Persian carpet with a feather fan and a

Plate 215. Cleopatra plaque by George Woodall, from one of his glass plate negatives.

Plate 216. 'The Pearl Necklace' by George Woodall, c.1910. Height 6¼ in. (15.9cm).

smoking incense jar, or the illusion of clear water lapping the steps of the pool, where no clear glass layer exists, have been deliberately chosen by Woodall to test and show off his extraordinary powers. In 1898 the *Pottery Gazette* featured the Bathers plaque and after many superlatives it concluded:

> we have remarked upon the fact that this beautiful piece of cameo carving has taken some years in executing. If we asked Mr. Woodall himself how long it took him to produce 'The Moorish Bathers' he would probably say — all his lifetime. Messrs. Thomas Webb and Sons and firms like theirs are entitled to great credit for fostering and encouraging talent such as is possessed by Mr. Woodall and other artists. But the nominally high cost of works of art does not detract from the satisfaction of the artist who can say of his work with pride 'I have done it as well as it can be done' or of his principals, who are conscious that they have produced a specimen of glass sculpturing that has never been surpassed.

Woodall's other, little known, talent was his work as a professional photographer. Not only did he record each finished piece but he also photographed the important cameos at every stage from the first drawing on the blank through each major alteration to the composition (Plates 214 and 215). One of the first sketches for 'The Moorish Bathers' shows how the design underwent drastic alterations before it was finished (Plate 214). Another negative shows the fountain and the table at the front gradually assuming less importance until, in the finished version, only an edge of the fountain was retained while the table disappeared completely. A series of photographs of one of his Cleopatra plaques illustrates his preference for altering the design as he worked directly on the piece.

Plate 217. Photograph of cameo vases by George Woodall printed from his own glass plate negative, each vase with Woodall's number as recorded in the Webb/Woodall price book. All the vases are in white glass on a brown background. The dates of the W numbered Vases are in the very late 1880s and early 1890s; the GW series began in late 1899, dating GW21 to early 1900.
Top centre; W2510 vase 8½in. (21.5cm) 'Ceres Receiving from Bacchus a Restorative Cup', marked 'Thomas Webb and Sons Gem Cameo'; the retail price of the vase was £35, reduced to £27.10s.0d. when it was sold on 11 November 1902. Left to right; W2403 two-handled vase 15½in. (39.4cm), 'The Fruit Seller', signed G. Woodall 1889 and marked 'Thomas Webb and Sons Gem Cameo'. Woodall was paid £28 for the carving, the retail price was £60. W2872 vase 9½in. (24.1cm), 'Hebe', the number may be an error as no.2827 in the Woodall price book shows this exact design. Woodall was paid £10.10s.0d. for the work and the retail price was fixed at £27 and reduced to £22.10s.0d. when it was sold to a person named Finigan on 15 November 1915. GW 21 vase 6in. (15.2cm), 'Ceramia', Cost £8 Sold £18.' W2609 two-handled vase 15½in. (39.4cm); no title given in the price book but known as Cupid and Psyche; signed G. Woodall and marked 'Tiffany & Co, Paris Exhibition 1889, Thomas Webb and Sons Gem Cameo'. Woodall was paid £25 for the vase which was priced at £65, later reduced to £55.

This rash, dare-devil approach required supreme confidence and planning for once a section of white glass was removed it could not be replaced. The photographic images he took of the female beauties of Kingswinford may have provided the source material for the plaque entitled 'The Pearl Necklace', a rare treatment of a contemporary subject (Plate 216). Many of Woodall's glass plate negatives still exist in private or museum collections, but tragically some were lost during the last war when the shortage of window glass resulted in the emulsion being cleaned from the plates which were then used for glazing.

Woodall's subject matter was not restricted to the classical although it did form a substantial part of his *oeuvre* (Plate 217). He collected source material of

223

Plate 218. Clear glass plaque engraved with St. John the Baptist by George Woodall. Height 5in (12.7cm)

Plate 219. George Woodall outside his studio in Kingswinford. The building still stands on Stream Road, Kingswinford, and is now occupied by a branch of the Trustees Savings Bank

Colour Plate 20. Cameo vase with applied pads of coloured glass carved with two canoeists shooting the rapids, Thomas Webb and Sons, late 1880s, marked in semi-circle 'Thomas Webb & Sons', height 8½in. (21.7cm), Michael Parkington Collection. Although this type of carving is often attributed to Daniel and Lionel Pearce, at least one design for similar work in the Webb pattern books gives the initial F for the engraver who was probably Jacob Facer. The unfinished smaller vase shows the pads of red, white and blue glass before they were modelled; Thomas Webb's, height 6⅞in (17.5cm)

everything from magazine cuttings of Egyptian scenes to engravings of Venus and Cupid. He was equally at home with standard floral cameo work (Colour Plate 18) or using the copper wheel to engrave a religious subject (Plate 218). In 1911 Woodall retired from Webb's but continued to model his glass visions of classical beauty at his home in Kingswinford which is still recognisable today (Plate 219). The Woodall pattern and price books from the Webb archive stand as a constant reminder and a fitting tribute to the exquisite artistry of the greatest cameo carver. When George Woodall died in 1925 he had preserved for fifty years the great tradition established by Northwood.

Plate 220. Bronze Medal and exhibitor's pass presented to Benjamin Hollis of the Thomas Webb glassworks, International Health Exhibition, 1884.

The Woodall brothers recruited four other skilled engravers, William Hill, Tom Farmer, Harry Davies and J.T. Fereday, to form the 'Woodall team' responsible for all unique cameos made by Webb's. In the late 1890s the team posed for a group photograph (Plate 212) on the occasion of the completion of two masterpieces, 'The Great Tazza' and the matching 18in. (45.75cm) plaque. Made up of no less than five separate layers of dark green, pink, white and two layers of light green, the design was taken from an illustration in Owen Jones' *Examples of Chinese Ornament* published in 1867. Jones' earlier *Grammar of Ornament* was already the established 'bible' of Stourbridge etchers and engravers. Other reference books used by the Woodall team contained engravings of works by Flaxman, Canova, Guido Reni and Boucher. Such was the dedication by Thomas Wilkes Webb to cameo production that at one stage the firm employed seventy decorators working on floral vases under the direction of the Woodall team. The back-up work-force retains the anonymity imposed by the factory system, which only allowed the likes of Woodall and Fritsche to sign their work. The discovery of a Bronze Medal and an exhibitor's pass to the International Health Exhibition in London in 1884 has identified at least one of these forgotten artists (Plate 220).

The oriental inspiration led Webb's and the cameo team to introduce technical innovations not seen before on Stourbridge cameo. Single blobs of colour were applied on to the glass which removed the need to case the entire piece with each separate colour. The technique, known as padding, was taken up and extended by Emile Gallé with his *marquetrie sur verre*. The majority of padded vases bear a

Plate 221. Photograph of Daniel Pearce by George Woodall.

strong oriental influence in which the separate pads of colour are used cleverly to accentuate the design (Colour Plate 20). Although these pieces do not bear an artist's signature, apart from the Webb mark, they are generally accepted to be the work of Daniel and Lionel Pearce who joined the Webb firm in 1884 (Plate 221). The father and son team deserves greater recognition than has been credited to it, especially as their designs were the few Stourbridge cameos to come anywhere near the free flowing art nouveau style of Gallé and his European contemporaries.

Born in 1817, Daniel trained as a designer at the Somerset House science and art classes and was awarded a medal for proficiency. About 1845 he entered into partnership with Mr Dobson and the two set up a glass trade business in St James's Street in London. According to Pearce's obituary in the *Pottery Gazette* in March 1907, the firm:

> cultivated a high class trade and their shop was a favourite resort of the nobility (who were the wealthy in those days). He had opportunities of submitting to his customers some of the finest productions in glass, and there is no doubt he did much to encourage the taste for engraved glass. This taste developed greatly as the great exhibition of 1862 approached. A small tazza, executed from a design by Mr. Pearce, was priced at £25 — a very high price at that date.

Colour Plate 21. Daniel Pearce and his son Lionel played a dominant role at Thomas Webb's in the late 19th and early 20th century. In the family group photograph set into the lid of the velvet covered casket, Daniel Pearce is seated on the right, next to his wife, with their daughter, now Sister Magdalene, standing beside Lionel. The pair of blue cased and acid-etched vases were until recently kept in the family, are said to be the work of Daniel Pearce, and date to the late 1880s. Lionel Pearce was the designer of the 'Sylvandale' vase produced about 1900-04. Heights: pair of vases 12 ¼ in. (31cm). box closed 4 ¾ in. (12cm), vase 8in. (20.5cm). Pair of vases Hulbert of Dudley Collection.

This tantalising reference is the only mention of a glass designed by Pearce in the whole obituary. The famous Morrison tazza, displayed by Dobson and Pearce at the exhibition, was the most expensive piece of contemporary glass made up to that date (Plate 110). Although the price of the tazza was £250 and not £25 as stated in the obituary, the slip is reasonable after a gap of forty-five years. Pearce's continued presence and high class work in the glass trade as opposed to Dobson's anonymity seems to confirm that Daniel acted as the glass expert for the partnership. On the strength of that evidence, Daniel Pearce has a strong claim as the designer, even if not the engraver, of the Morrison tazza.

Shortly after the 1862 Exhibition finished, Pearce left the Dobson partnership and became part of Phillips and Pearce in Bond Street. His designs included complete table decorations, glass chandeliers, novelties such as glass birdcages, and Wedgwood centrepieces incorporating Flaxman figures. After the partnership with Phillips was dissolved, he operated under his own name at North End, Hammersmith, where his basic stock in trade consisted of table decorations, flower holders, and fountains and jardinières. Pearce's reputation as a top designer is made evident by the commission from Webb's for him to design several pieces for the Paris Exhibition of 1878. 'In addition to many beautiful magnum jugs, special vases, elaborately engraved, and many fine chandeliers, Mr. Pearce designed the show table and stand for the firm's exhibit, so that to him belongs some of the credit for the Grand Prix which was awarded the firm'. The *Pottery Gazette* continued with the statement that:

> In 1884 Mr. Pearce gave up his Hammersmith business, and joined Messrs. Webb & Sons at the Dennis Works, Stourbridge, a firm of whom he had always spoken of as making the finest glass in the world. Cameo glass cutting was then in vogue at Dennis. This was artistic work after his own heart, and he used his best exertions in conjunction with those of Messrs. Charles, Wilkes and Walter Webb, to encourage its development. Mr. Pearce continued his connection with the Dennis Works until he retired, five years ago at the venerable age of 85. Since then he has lived in retirement until he passed peacefully away on the 7th of last month.

The full extent of Daniel's contribution to Webb designs needs further examination through the pattern books.

Lionel Pearce was to become designer in chief at Webb's, possibly on the retirement of his father. Little is known about his career and there seems to be confusion over his date of birth. Geoffrey Beard gives his dates as 1852 to 1926 but from fragments of information in Pearce's marriage certificate and an undated obituary a date of 1854 for his birth may be more accurate. Due to the generosity and helpfulness of descendants of Daniel and Lionel Pearce, it is possible to publish this information for the first time and to bring together important family treasures including a velvet covered box with a family photograph and a pair of blue cameo vases by Daniel Pearce (Colour Plate 21). The photograph set into the lid of the casket shows Daniel on the right, while Lionel is in front of an easel, working on a female portrait in Japanese style. The green and blue landscape vase signed by Lionel Pearce could be mistaken for a French early twentieth century example. It is dated about 1900 from the particular etched Webb mark on this piece which was used from 1889 until about 1905. Two similar vases from the same series, referred to as 'Sylvandale', were acquired (one by gift of Thomas Webb's) by the Art Gallery of South Australia in 1904.

Thomas Webb's cameo glass displayed the widest range of subjects from portraits of statesmen, politicians and monarchy to horse races and scenes of the Antarctic. New shapes were developed regularly while the colour combinations, including three and four layers, were both rich and subtle. Combinations of different techniques opened up new avenues not explored by the other cameo producers. Deep, rock crystal pillars excelled as a contrast to simple bands of two colour cameo, applied in a variation of the padded technique (Colour Plate 18). Another combination was to trap white enamel floral designs within the coloured

Plate 222. Group of ivory vases and bowls, the photograph made from a George Woodall glass plate negative.
Top shelf, left to right:
Vase, pattern no. I 677, by Jacob Facer, carved with fish in a pinwheel design, two fish eating smaller fish, height 5½in. (14cm), 'Sale price £5 5s. 0d.'; bowl, pattern no. I 632, by George Woodall, carved with animals among arabesque foliage, diameter 6½in. (16.5cm), 'Sale price £10 15s' reduced later to £7.
Middle shelf, left to right:
Vase, no. I 615, by Kretschmann, carved with a seated oriental sage, dimpled sides carved with landscapes, height 8in. (20.5cm), 'Sale price £8 8s.'; vase, with carved and gilded fish — an identical example is illustrated in English Cameo Glass (Pl.C.362), height 11¼in. (28.7cm); vase, no. I 613, by Kretschmann, carved with an oriental figure resting on a bamboo stick, height 9in. (22.9cm), 'Sale price £9 17s.6d.'.
Bottom shelf, left to right:
Vase, no. I 80, height 5in. (12.8cm), 'Sale price 65s.'; vase with snake handles — this shape exists in pattern books with different engraved subjects; bowl, carved with ducks on water; vase, possibly no. I 689½, by Kretschmann, 'Sale as 689 but with different design inside panels' — carved with a seated figure, the birds carved from applied jewels of coloured glass, height 9in. (23cm), 'Sale price £25'; vase, carved with meandering floral pattern — three similar shaped vases in the designs are all by Woodall.

body. The top layer was carved to reveal the trapped white pattern (Colour Plate 18).

Ivory glass was not strictly a cameo process in the sense that there was only one layer of glass, but many of the pieces were etched and carved to give the impression of cameo and are normally included in that category (Plate 222). In the Webb archives a section devoted to ivory glass has survived and is reproduced in *English Cameo Glass* by R. and L. Grover. It records 735 individual patterns

Plate 223. Medallion cameo scent bottle with a pink and white cameo panel carved with flowers, a bird's nest with eggs and the characteristic trompe-l'oeil *effect of one corner peeling away. Stuart and Sons, c.1887. Height 6¼ in. (16cm). Private Collection.*

with detailed illustrations and information about the carvers, the production costs and selling prices. Ten examples of ivory glass were photographed by George Woodall who was responsible for many of the 735 designs (Plate 222). His photograph shows the dominance of the oriental influence on the ivory range and hints at some of the wonderful combinations of different techniques which went into creating this extraordinary body of work. Apart from the etching, staining, enamelling, gilding and casing which can be found on ivory glass some of the most beautiful effects were achieved with the padded cameo technique. Tiny beads of colour, transformed by the engravers into birds, spiders, flies, jewels and flowers, juggling balls and a mirror, gave a vitality and three-dimensional quality to the landscapes and scenes of oriental sages which they decorated. Although the ivory glasses were sometimes referred to as 'Curio' in the pattern books, they are some of the most technically accomplished and aesthetically pleasing masterpieces of Stourbridge cameo glass.

Two other firms which made interesting contributions to cameo were Stuart and Sons, and Boulton and Mills. In 1881 Frederick Stuart purchased the Red House works from Philip Pargeter and began a glassmaking tradition which continues as a family concern to the present day. In 1887 the firm patented the idea of 'Medallion Cameo', described in the *Pottery Gazette* as the 'latest Art Production for this season, a most delicate and entirely novel effect in Vases,

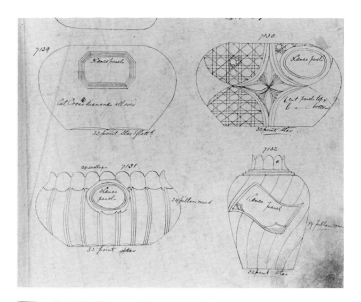

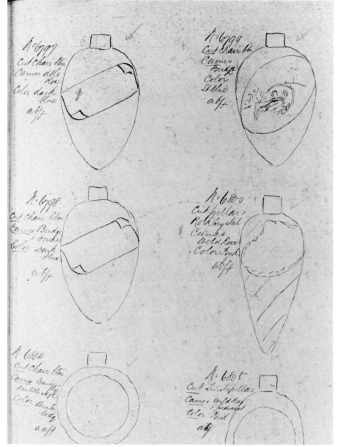

Plates 224 and 225. Designs from the Stuart pattern books for medallion cameo vases and scent bottles, c.1887. Photograph courtesy Stuart Crystal.

Bowls, Scent Bottles etc., etc.' The novel effect consisted of a small pad of cameo applied to a clear glass body (Plate 223). The cameo panels are often set at an angle while on some of the jugs they are placed assymetrically around the base of the handle. The Stuart pattern books record a number of different shapes with the emphasis on scent bottles (Plates 224 and 225). Subject matter was restricted

Plate 226. Blue glass plaque with applied layer of candle wax carved in imitation of white cameo glass. Paper labels state 'Northwood' and 'National Bronze Medal'. Dated 1889. Diameter 21 ⅛ in. (53.7cm). The age of the student is given as thirty-one on one of the labels identifying him as William Northwood 1858-1937.

mainly to flowers and leaves, sometimes with a bird's nest and eggs. One of the scent bottle designs mentions a rare landscape scene of a 'cameo bridge'.

The cameo products of Boulton and Mills have not been identified but the firm advertised an 'Autumnal Tinted Cameo' in the pages of the *Pottery Gazette* in the 1880s. It may have been clear glass overlaid with white, acid etched and enamelled with apples or other fruits (Colour Plate 41). Many firms began to use enamel on mass-produced glass in an attempt to provide a cheaper alternative to cameo glass. The ubiquitous 'Mary Gregory' glass was just one of the many variations.

One question often asked by glass collectors is how the artists translated the design into the finished article. When faced with a large and complex design some of the cameo carvers would have a trial run before embarking on the main glass. The trial was carried out on a glass which was given a thick layer of candle wax and it was this material, approximating in colour to the white glass, that was modelled. The process formed part of the training of glass apprentices at the Wordsley and Stourbridge Schools of Art. Waxed examples sometimes have one or two labels from the Schools of Design or are accompanied by prizes in the form of books which were intended to encourage the student in his work (Plate 226).

CHAPTER ELEVEN

Rock Crystal Glass

Rock crystal glass, together with cameo, was the speciality of the Stourbridge factories. Its development follows almost the same pattern and time-scale as that of cameo which is perhaps not unexpected when both styles were made by the same companies. From 1878 until the turn of the century it formed the most significant form of copper wheel engraving.

The term itself can be confusing and sometimes leads to the assumption that the object is carved out of rock crystal quartz whereas all rock crystal glass is made from full lead glass. The rock crystal title refers simply to the influences which inspired it, namely the deeply sculptured ornate carvings in quartz from the Orient.

There is also some confusion about the definition of rock crystal glass. The general consensus of opinion agrees that there are three main characteristics: deep cutting, copper wheel engraving and final polishing. Firstly the glass has to be shaped by cutting, usually with pillars or roundels, from a thick blank to provide the basic shape. The pillared decoration by the glass cutter is extremely skilful, difficult and time-consuming as it is cut out of the solid with a mathematical precision that belies its hand operation. Because the cutting is later covered by engraving this essential part of the process is often greatly underrated. The glass is next passed to the copper wheel engraver who carves the finer details which complement the deeper cutting. For example the engraving may consist of leaves and flowers which grow out of the stems formed by the deep cutting. The third requisite is the polishing of the cutting and the engraving to restore the original polish to the glass.

As the style became more popular and demand outstripped supply, cheaper and quicker methods of production were brought in. Deep pillar cutting was imitated by blowing the glass into moulds and then putting simple cuts around those blown moulded pillars to give the impression of thicker glass. These glasses can be recognised by running one's finger around the inner surface which will have the ghost impression of the outer mould effect. The later glasses are much thinner and shallower in comparison with the earlier pieces and are referred to in the pattern books as 'bright polished' rather than rock crystal.

Large pieces of colourless rock crystal quartz had been carved into luxury vessels in Europe since the Middle Ages. The purity and brilliance of rock crystal and its scarcity led glassmakers to search for an alternative. The English answer was the discovery of lead glass whereas the Bohemians developed a potash-lime glass which was in use by 1690 and proved an excellent replacement for the hard stone. In Japan the pure, brilliant quartz held a deeper significance for its owners. An article on Japanese rock crystal in the *Illustrated Household Journal* of

Plate 227. The Elgin vase, clear glass carved in high relief with a frieze of horsemen after the Elgin marbles. Made at Thomas Webb and Sons, engraved by Frederick E. Kny c.1875. Height 7½ in. (19.3cm).

November 1880 describes the bronze 'Dai' or stand in the form of a dragon supporting in its claw a large globe of rock crystal with two smaller balls occasionally set near the head and tail of the dragon. 'Pure, flawless, transparent, a perfect sphere, it seems like a bubble of spring water hovering in the air...Pure quartz in its smaller forms, is the congealed breath of the white dragon. In its larger and ice pure forms, it is the solidified saliva of the violet dragon'.

The influence of oriental designs, which were to play a major role in the creation of the rock crystal style, was first seen at the Vienna International Exhibition of 1873 and highlighted in the report on the English glass exhibits produced for both Houses of Parliament. The section on the glass of Pellatt and Co. stresses:

> an infusion of Japanese art which is steadily moving into European designs was apparent in a very charming service with engraved panels in which were storks and vases with plants, and the conventional key bands and scrolls of Japan work...reminded the observer of some of the highest qualities of Chinese engraving on pure rock crystal...Another service in Japanese style...A third set, entirely different in design, which was rather more in Chinese than in Japanese

Plate 228. Vase carved in relief by Giuseppe de Giovanni with a scene of 'The Childhood of Bacchus', the young boy being initiated into the delights of wine by the kneeling Pan, watched by Mercury with his foster-father Silenus standing in the background accompanied by two nymphs. Signed and dated on the base 'G. de Giovanni 21st April 1870 London'. Place of manufacture unknown. Height 5½in. (14cm). Photograph courtesy Phillips.

style, consisted of decanters formed upon the model of jade or rock crystal vases.

The engraved glass at the Vienna Exhibition was almost certainly left matt but in the next five years polished engraving in imitation of rock crystal was introduced. At the Paris Exhibition of 1878 the *Art Journal* catalogue stated:

Another development is that of deep, bright cutting, sometimes in relief, like a cameo, sometimes sunk, as in intaglio; in either case thick glass is employed and the deepest portions are sunk to the depth of a quarter of an inch or more. This method has been adopted with great effect both by the French and English manufacturers and engravers. Our neighbours...have adopted some square and rhomboidal forms similar to those often employed by the Chinese and Japanese potters and have produced bold floral patterns with birds and other objects in this deep engraving, which is brilliantly polished. . . Our own countrymen have largely employed figure subjects, generally taking them from the antique. In Messrs. Webbs' collection is a portion of the frieze of the Parthenon executed in relief and polished, around the neck of the vase, producing an object of truly high Art.

That vase was almost certainly the Elgin vase, carved in high relief in about 1875 by Frederick Kny (Plate 227). Public and artistic interest in the Parthenon frieze was generated when Lord Elgin brought some of the marble sculptures to England in 1812. Plaster casts were made for him of the portions which remained in Greece. It is not known whether Kny and his fellow engravers used this collection as their inspiration, although it is doubtful. A more probable and easily available source for their iconography was the sets of miniature plaster casts, representing the Parthenon frieze, made between 1817 and 1821 by the Scottish sculptor John Henning (1771-1851). The popularity of the sets encouraged a pirated version which was issued in large numbers. The accuracy of Henning's casts varies enormously as he arbitrarily restored missing fragments and paid little attention to the correct juxtaposition of figures. One classical engraved vase in the Hulbert of Dudley collection bears some features which can only have derived from Henning's casts. Equally the frieze on the Kny Elgin vase is virtually identical in height to the Henning casts.

Kny's vase was preceded by John Northwood's Elgin vase which had been commissioned in 1864 by Benjamin Stone. Finished by 1873, the two-handled vase features a continuous band of the Parthenon horsemen in relief between anthemion and scrollwork borders. Another vase, carved in relief, is contemporary with these vases by Kny and Northwood. It was described in the *Art Journal* in 1875:

> A glass vase in size and shape about that of our ordinary pint measure, only without a handle, sculptured in bas relief, after the style of the Portland Vase in the British Museum, will, we are sure, create great interest in art circles. It is to be regretted that the young artist, Signor de Giovanni, did not come to this country earlier in the year so that his beautiful work might have been seen and admired by appreciative judges and connoisseurs. His production has occupied four years and its art merits are of the highest order. The central relief of the vase consists of six figures representing the education of Bacchus.

The vase continued to attract attention in the press in the nineteenth century. The *Daily Telegraph* gave a detailed account of it on 6 August 1878 and the *Art Journal* mentioned it again in 1885. After a long period of obscurity the vase re-emerged at a Phillips sale in London in 1988 (Plate 228). In 1945 the vase belonged to Mr Louis Deleuse whose will states that the late King of Italy offered £5,000 for it. Guiseppe de Giovanni was a Neapolitan engraver who was probably working in England in the 1860s and 1870s although no other examples of his work are known.

Although the three vases were difficult and laborious to produce and could

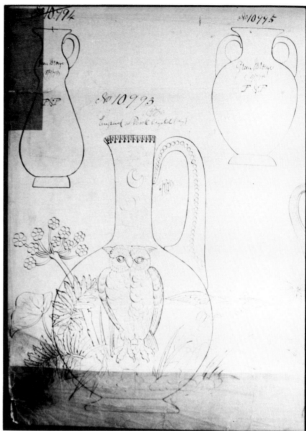

Plates 229 and 230. Two pages from the Thomas Webb pattern books showing two of the three earliest recorded patterns for rock crystal glass. Inscribed 'Engraved as Rock Crystal (Kny)' and dated 6 July 1878. The other shapes on the pages are for bronze glass. Thomas Webb and Sons.

never be made commercially, they showed the change in taste away from the shallow engraving practised between the 1850s and 1870s and proved that the skills were available to execute cameo and rock crystal work.

THE ROCK CRYSTAL GLASS OF THOMAS WEBB AND SONS

The earliest known record of the term 'rock crystal' appears in the Thomas Webb factory pattern books, next to pattern numbers 10991, 10992 and 10993, inscribed 'Engraved as Rock Crystal (Kny)' and dated 6 July 1878 (Plates 229 and 230). It is not known who introduced the style at Webb's although Fritsche is usually given the credit, but without documentary proof. Fritsche and Kny were responsible for the bulk of rock crystal from the factory and its introduction may have been a joint venture by the two great Bohemian engravers. No other English firm had introduced rock crystal at this time and Webb's maintained their lead throughout the next thirty years.

The Dennis Glass Works was responsible for the magnificent ewer carved by William Fritsche, which is the most spectacular example of rock crystal glass ever produced (Plate 231). A letter from A.S. Johnson, FRGS, reveals the awe with which the ewer was regarded at the time of its completion in 1886:

THEODORE B. STARR,
JEWELER,
206, FIFTH AVENUE,
MADISON SQUARE,
NEW YORK.

THE FRITSCHE EWER

It is often, in this somewhat carping nineteenth century of ours, laid to the charge of the workman today that he has lost the great love of his work which in the old days — days which some folk always consider so much better than our own — produced the noble work in wood and stone and metal which made the Dark Ages the Art Ages too. That this statement is not of universal application, the Fritsche Ewer, the subject of this note, will prove. This superb piece of glass the finest specimen of the so-called 'Rock Crystal work' that has ever been executed, was both designed and manufactured by one man. W. Fritsche the artist of the ewer, for he is as true an artist as ever breathed, was born in 1853, in Bohemia. In the very heart and home of glass making and engraving, in the village of Meistersdorf, — the village of Master, — a quiet little place which gained its name generations back from being the place where the best art-workers of that day lived. His father and forefathers for many generations had been glass-makers, working in their little upland farms all through the summer; thus gaining that love and knowledge of nature, with suggestions and transcripts of which they decorated the beautiful art-work which they produced in the villages during the long cold months of winter. This, too, was the young Fritsche's education. It is difficult to conceive any training more likely to make an artist of a sensitive and imaginative boy. In 1868 he came to England, and proceeded to Stourbridge, the great glass-making centre, where some short time afterwards he entered the glass-works of those consistent fosterers of art, Messrs. Thomas Webb & Sons. There he has been employed in art-work ever since. Twelve years ago he introduced the manufacture of Rock Crystal Glass at the Dennis Works with great success. It has since been copied extensively by other makers.

The manufacture of this glass is not of recent invention; it has been made in Bohemia for at least two hundred years, but the decoration of it has always consisted of deep cutting and engraving alone. Some fine specimens of this work are to be seen in the collection in the South Kensington Museum [Victoria and Albert Museum]. The decoration of the Fritsche Ewer is different. On this the design is in very high and bold relief.

Mr. Fritsche generally designs his own work. A sketch of the outline of the required article is given to the glass-blower, who makes the piece in clear flint glass of enormous thickness. This is then treated just as real rock crystal is; the design is carved straight out of the solid. The weight of this ewer, before it was decorated was just twice what it now is half of the material having been actually cut away in the carving of it. The difficulty of such a work is very great, and the patience required to undertake and carry out a piece of the size of this ewer, which measures sixteen inches in height, is only to be sustained by the artist's intense love of his work. Mr. Fritsche has been engaged upon this ewer for two years and a half. Of course this does not mean that he has devoted the whole of that time to it, for the strain of working with such delicacy of touch and carefulness of handling as this piece required is too great to be endured for a long time together.

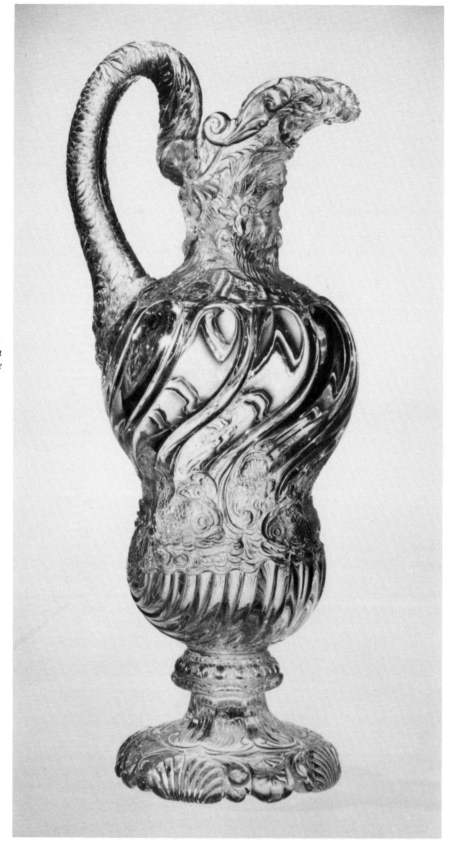

Plate 231. Ewer, cut and engraved rock crystal with marine scenes. The neck is decorated with a mask of a river god in high relief; the body is engraved with dolphins and the foot with shells. Thomas Webb and Sons, engraved and signed by William Fritsche, 1886. Height 15¼in. (38.7cm). The Corning Museum of Glass.

The conception of the scheme of decoration is very poetic. It is as beautiful in thought as in execution. The whole ewer may be said to represent the progress of a river from its birth in a rocky hill-side till it loses itself at last in the blue infinity of the sea. The neck of the ewer represents the mountain birth-place of the stream, where, amidst a tangle of loose leaves and wild brook foliage, the new born river gushes from the mother earth. This idea, so difficult of expression in this material, is treated with great poetry and skill. There is in the mystery of it a suggestion of the withdrawn remoteness of the little hill-side spring. The bold lip of the ewer is formed of broad leaves from which cool drops of water drip as dew in the early misty mornings before the sun dispels it. On the front of the neck is carved, in very bold relief, the beautiful head of the water god himself, garlanded with rushes and aquatic plants, and with his swirling beard flowing into the stream of clear water beneath. Around the base of the neck a graceful wreath of water-lilies lies, as it might on the surface of some sunny pool, a back-water of the stream. The rush and hurry of the rapid river are wonderfully expressed by the strong clear, curving volutes of the body of the ewer. The strength and simplicity of this portion of the design is in delightful relief to the richness and beauty of the decoration in other parts. As the river nears the sea the flow and swirl of it are just indicated by a little simple but exquisitely clever cutting at the base of the spirals.

The lowest part of the body of the ewer is formed of a great fluted shell, which is symbolic of the bottom of the sea. In this swim and sport a circle of vigorous dolphins, all moving with individuality and the greatest freedom. Each dolphin is different from the others: some are playing, some are rushing through the waves, and others are carved as though rising up to the surface to catch the stream of fresh water pouring on to them from the river above. The water of the sea is rough, and here and there splashes over the edge of the shell. The decoration of the foot is a bold treatment of shells and sea-weeds, from which rises a water-spout or sudden upheaval of the waters of the ocean, thus forming the pedestal, and consistently carrying out the artist's idea. A conveniently treated dolphin covered with scales and graceful submarine foliage, forms a very beautiful and natural handle.

It is pleasant to see that the Messrs Webb with that just appreciation of art which so distinguishes them, have insisted upon the artist signing this unique and magnificent piece of work with his own name instead of theirs, as is the usual unjust custom.

It is greatly to be regretted that this piece should have been allowed to leave England. It was purchased by an American firm and has, we believe, already left for the United States. Such a superb example of contemporary English art manufacture should have found a permanent resting-place in the South Kensington museum for certainly no such piece of carved glass has ever been produced before, either in England or abroad.

April 1886   Alfred S. Johnston, F.R.G.S.

On completion the ewer was shipped to the United States without having been displayed to English audiences. In 1976 the Corning Museum of Glass loaned the ewer for the first public display in England since its manufacture in Amblecote in 1886. The ewer formed the centrepiece of the first ever exhibition of English rock crystal glass held at Dudley Art Gallery in the West Midlands in August and September of 1976.

Plate 232. Vase, cut and engraved rock crystal with fish amid waves. Recorded in the Webb pattern books, no. 17415 'Flint vase engd. RC' and in the price book '25.3.89. 12" vase flint carved £34.00'. Thomas Webb and Sons, possibly engraved by George Woodall, 1889. Height 12in. (30.6cm).

Plate 233. Hock glass, clear glass with ruby casing on bowl and foot. Engraved rock crystal with stylised flowers set within ogival pillars. Webb pattern no. 17728 'Ruby bowl cut as 14660'. Thomas Webb and Sons, engraved by Frederick E. Kny, 1889. Height 5¾in. (14.7cm). Thomas Webb and Sons.

The visual resemblance of rock crystal glass to flowing water resulted in the regular appearance of marine subjects. The idea of rock crystal as an oriental symbol for ice or solidified water was translated into English terms on the magnificent Fish vase, one of the masterpieces of English rock crystal glass (Plate 232). The stylised natural motif forecasts the brilliant graphic designs in the glass of René Lalique some thirty years later.

Oriental influences dominated rock crystal production at Webb's in the 1880s with Chinese designs gaining in popularity as the decade wore on. Whereas the unique vases such as the Fritsche ewer included some figurative subject matter, stylised floral motifs based on Chinese models were more commercial on large table services. A hock glass of 1889, cased on the bowl with ruby glass, is engraved with scrolling leaves in exactly the same manner as Chinese jades (Plate

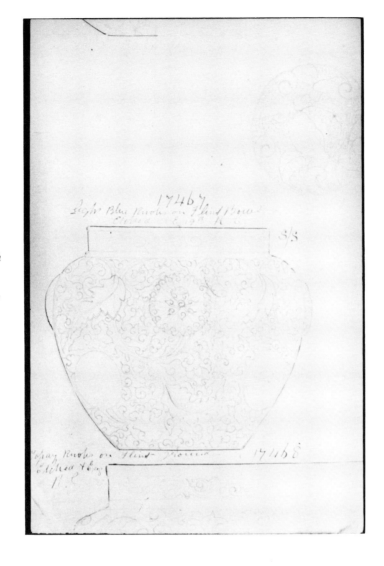

Plate 234. Pattern no. 17467 from Thomas Webb and Sons for a clear bowl applied with light blue knobs and 'Etched and Engraved R.C.', 1889. Thomas Webb and Sons.

233). The cameo variation of padding was used on rock crystal and is recorded on two bowls in the Webb books (Plate 234). The inscriptions at the side of the patterns which read 'Light blue (or Topaz) knobs on Flint glass etched and engraved as rock crystal' refer to the coloured flower heads engraved in the Chinese manner and set against the clear polished glass. The amount of etching is uncertain as no examples of these bowls have yet come to light.

Amongst the 'Persian', 'Japanese' and 'Indian' designs for rock crystal, the 'Indian cone' was a popular favourite with William Fritsche and appears on bowls, wineglasses and decanters (Colour Plate 15). Derived from Kashmir shawls, the cone represented a vase and a flower or a flower with roots. It was often used by Fritsche in combination with 'a new style of chipped work' which he introduced in May 1891, based on an idea developed by Stevens and Williams in 1887. On cameo work the effect is of a shattered surface (Colour Plate 18). On rock crystal glass, once the glass has been polished, the effect is of a sharply stippled background.

Less common but no less stunning in execution were the baroque-inspired rock

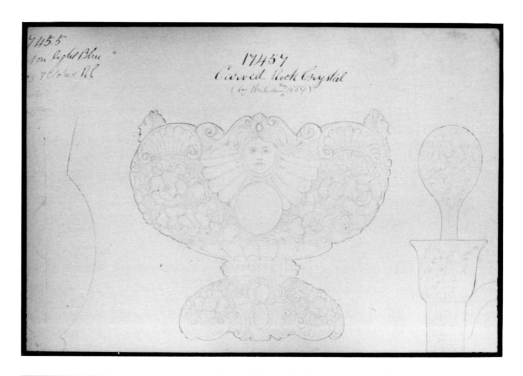

Plate 235. Pattern no. 17457 from Thomas Webb and Sons for a 'Carved Rock Crystal' bowl 'by Kretschmann, 1889'. Thomas Webb and Sons.

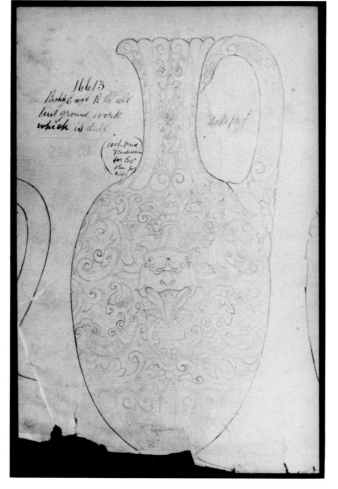

Plate 236. Pattern no. 16613 for an engraved rock crystal jug 'Richly Engd RC all but ground work which is dull'. A note mentions a payment of 100s. to the engraver in February 1890. Thomas Webb and Sons, engraved by F. Kretschmann, 1888-1890. Thomas Webb and Sons.

Plate 237. Jug with cut and engraved rock crystal decoration of fruit trailed across twisted pillars. Stevens and Williams pattern no. 8750 '23/1/84 Orchard'. Stevens and Williams, engraved by J. Orchard, 1884. Height 8in. (20.5cm). Royal Brierley Crystal.

crystal pieces by F. Kretschmann in the late 1880s with the variation on some of the pieces of 'ground work which is dull' (Plates 235 and 236).

STEVENS AND WILLIAMS

As the only serious rival to Thomas Webb in the production of rock crystal glass, Stevens and Williams created their own distinctive patterns within the overall framework of Persian and oriental influences. The company introduced the style a year later than their competitor with the first record of the term 'rock crystal' dated 1 December 1879. Two distinct periods of production can be identified at Stevens and Williams, the first ending about 1893 when the newly introduced intaglio technique was given priority, and then for about ten years after 1900 when some exceptionally fine work was produced in the art nouveau style.

A favourite motif, in the Japanese style, was the placing of polished engraving of fruits and prunus blossoms at right angles to the vertical or angled pillars (Plate 237). Squared-off handles and the use of thick collars are typical of the factory's

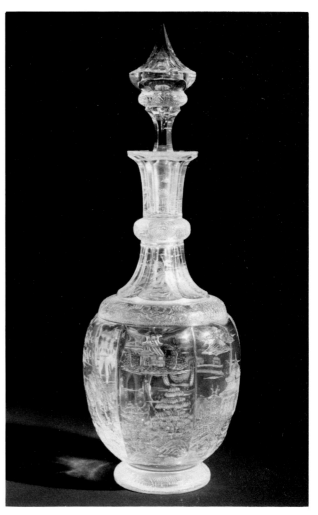

Plate 238. Page from the design book of Joseph Keller showing a willow pattern decanter in engraved rock crystal, c.1883-84.

Plate 239. Decanter, cut and engraved rock crystal with a willow pattern design from the Joseph Keller design book. Stevens and Williams, engraved by J. Orchard, February 1884. Height 12 ¾ in. (32.4cm).

work until the mid-1880s. By 1884 new designs showed a heavier emphasis with full pillars, usually rounded off at the top, forming the basis of many designs. One design features a rare appearance in glass of the willow pattern engraved across the broad pillars as well as extending on to the neck and pagoda stopper of a decanter (Plate 238). Although the pattern for the quart decanter appears in the design book of Joseph Keller, the engraver of the service was John Orchard (Plate 239). In February 1884 the cost of the decanter was '15/- shop, 4/- cutting, 65/- Orchard, 135/- each'. Orchard's name first appears in the design books on 30 October 1883 for a service with 'richly engraved Chinese ornament polished all over'. Shortly after that date he was to become chief engraver for the company. For the next twenty years his skills rivalled those of Fritsche and Kny. Typical of his artistic and technical finesse is a bowl from 1894, in the Stevens and Williams museum, with grotesque birds and floral sprays complemented by a pair

Plate 240. Bowl, the body with applied ring handles, and pillar cut and engraved rock crystal with grotesque birds and floral sprays, on a scalloped foot. Pattern no. 20398, '18s. cutting. 40s. Orchard, 120s each'. Stevens and Williams, engraved by J. Orchard, May 1894. Diameter 4¼ in. (10.6cm). Royal Brierley Crystal.

of Chinese ring handles in imitation of jade vessels (Plate 240). By 1900 when rock crystal glass at Stevens and Williams received a fresh impetus from the art nouveau style, all the glass was engraved either by, or under the direction of Orchard. His original designs, such as the decanter of 1903 (Plate 241), fully integrated the cut and engraved elements to create a glass which is as sculptural as the Fish vase from Webb's factory in 1889.

The art nouveau engraved glass from Stevens and Williams was the final swan-song of the rock crystal style which fell from favour by about 1906-07. From 1900 the firms of Webb Corbett and Stuart and Sons made their own versions of rock crystal with a mixture of art nouveau and neo-classicism under the direction of two of Frederick Kny's sons, William and Ludwig. After the First World War there was no place for the ornate rock crystal style which, in the new jazz age, represented a bygone era. Pieces were sometimes made to replace broken items

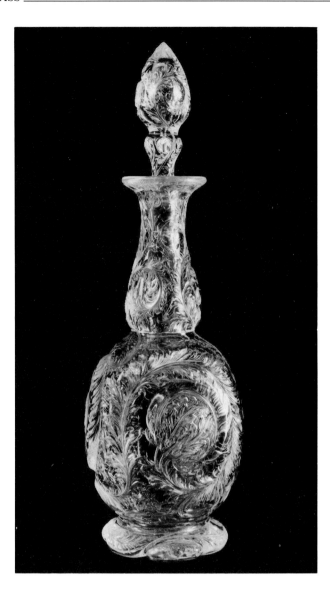

Plate 241. Quart decanter, cut and engraved rock crystal; the body decorated with spiral cuts, fringed with engraved floral work in art nouveau style. Pattern 31601 'Orchard 9/6/03'. Stevens and Williams, engraved by J. Orchard, 1903. Height 15½in. (39.5cm). Private Collection.

from large services and Webb Corbett retained one design in their catalogue into the 1970s. But, in the main, the style was forgotten by makers and collectors alike. In 1976 the exhibition at Dudley Art Gallery was instrumental in restoring the reputation of rock crystal glass. The publication of the exhibition catalogue made collectors and dealers aware of the quality of an area of Victorian glass which they had ignored for too long and prices rocketed accordingly. Now rock crystal glass is recognised once again as the finest cold-decorated work to come from the English factories in the late Victorian period.

─── CHAPTER TWELVE───

Patents and Techniques

TALE GLASS

In the Richardson pattern books one page has the fascinating heading of 'Tale Goods' above a selection of ale glasses, rummers and tumblers (Plate 242). Few references exist in the glass literature to this method of glassmaking although it was accepted practice in the early part of the nineteenth century. Even the writer of a short note in the *Pottery Gazette,* in January 1899, stated that 'glass makers themselves, we fear, do not know what is meant by tale glass'. The article went on to explain the term which was a 'method of quick manufacture, blown and opened by the tools without shearing. It was rough but useful and cheap, and it did use off the common oft-melted cullett, and it was known in the trade, sixty or seventy years ago, in such goods as tale goblets, ales, salts, wines, tots, etc.' The dates given by the magazine are confirmed by the 1840-42 catalogue of tablewares from Apsley Pellatt's Falcon Glass Works which lists among the cut glass lines:

4.	Cruets, castors, mustards, and soys, tale R.M. per doz.	7s.0d.
17.	Tale jellies, very slight, per doz.	4s. to 5s.0d.

The initials 'R.M.' in the description meant rough mouths, made without shearing the lip. Cruets described as 'stronger, cut all over, P.M.', meaning polished mouths, cost 16s. per dozen while 'very strong cruets' with 'cut panels and Polished Mouths' cost 24s. per dozen.

In the 'Nett Prices of Flint Glass of W.H., B., & J. Richardson, Wordsley, April 5 1839' the following glasses were listed as available in tale glass: 'basins for sugars; bell glasses; cans, lemonades; cruets and castors; custards, with or without handles; drams; egg cups; flutes; goblets; ice cups; inks; jellies; muffineers; mustards and tops; patty pans; salts; syllabubs; tumblers and wines.' The price list carried the proviso that 'Goods are to be charged by Weight, if they come to more by Weight than the Tale Price; and to be charged by Tale when that price exceeds the Weight Price'.

Another type of glass, or metal, which is mentioned in the price list and which is as little known as tale glass, is Kiln Metal. It was of a slightly better quality than the standard glass as it was charged at '1d. per lb. extra'. In August 1897 the *Pottery Gazette* described kiln metal as 'the lading [or draghading as the ladling process was also called] of the half-melted glass into water and refilling the pot with the same, with the addition of more batch'. The credit for the discovery of the process was given to Solomon Davis of Stourbridge, who was a manager at the glassworks of Wheeley and Davis in Brettell Lane. The availability of three grades of glass from one factory should make collectors aware of the problems of

Plate 242. Page from the Richardson pattern books showing part of the range of tale glass, c.1835-40. The shape of the two glasses on the bottom right of the page was known as a Princes Goblet.

attributing glass to provincial or London glasshouses simply by the quality of the metal itself or the method of manufacture.

JOHN DAVENPORT AND HIS NEW METHOD OF ORNAMENTING

In 1806 John Davenport (1765-1848) of Longport, Staffordshire, filed a specification for 'A new method of ornamenting of all kinds of glass in imitation of engraving or etching, by means of which borders, cyphers, coats-of-arms, drawings, and the most elaborate designs may be executed in a stile [sic] of elegance hitherto unknown, and which cannot possibly be equalled by the usual and customary mode of etching or engraving as hitherto practised' (Plate 243). The new method involved a finely ground, smooth glass frit, mixed with a paste of double refined loaf sugar and pure water, applied on to the surface of the glass by means of squirrel or camel hair brushes. At this stage the coating could be scratched and removed with a pointed instrument to give the effect of drawing on the glass. The glass was 'then exposed to a heat sufficient to produce a semi-vitrification of the coated surface, and to incorporate it sufficiently with the substance or body of glass so coated, but great care must be had not to extend the degree of heat further than is necessary for these purposes, because in that case a complete vitrification of the coating would ensue.' Davenport claimed that his invention would 'produce an effect similar but greatly superior to the effect heretofore produced by the usual method of grinding and polishing with wheels.' For the glass mixture he used three recipes, number 1 consisting of 160 parts cullet, 10 parts of pearl ashes, 40 parts red lead and 10 parts of arsenic. Mixture

Plate 243. Footed tumbler, decorated by John Davenport's patent process with a huntsman loading his rifle, with his dogs, in a wooded landscape, c.1806-10. Height 4½in. (11.4cm). The original use for this shape of glass is not clear. The shape is similar to the caddy bowls in the Richardson pattern book (Plate 38) but that use of this glass seems unlikely as the decoration would rarely be seen once the glass was placed into the tea caddy box. A more likely use would be to hold the spoons or glass sugar crushers used by the members of gentlemen's drinking clubs or political groups (Plate 50). The shape reappears in pressed glass, later in the century, for that purpose (Colour Plate 44).

number 2 used 120 parts of cullet, 160 parts of red lead, 60 parts of sand and 60 parts of borax. Mixture number 3 used 70 parts of red lead, 22½ parts of sand and 40 parts of calcined borax. The mixtures were fired in separate glasshouse pots to form a vitrified frit. By mixing equal parts of all three with the loaf sugar he obtained the 'most perfect and beautiful specimens'. Most of the examples of glass decorated in this way are usually marked with the word Patent on the base.

When John Davenport filed his patent on 1 August 1806 he had been involved in ceramic manufacture since 1794 and had expanded into glassmaking in 1801, using the services of an Edward Grafton from Brettell Lane in Brierley Hill. The company became well known for high class plain, cut and engraved tablewares. When the Prince of Wales visited the ceramic and glass factory in 1806 he was shown the new method of glass decoration and placed an order for 'a service of glass etched with Grecian border'. The invoice for the order describes the service of over 250 pieces as 'Etchd Feathers' and 'Etchd His Royal Highness Arms in full'. A further order from the Prince of Wales in 1808 consisted of panes and fan lights with 'etched figures from Flaxman'. The use of the word etched referred to the scratched designs through the applied fine paste of glass rather than the technique of acid etching. The firm continued to expand throughout the middle years of the century and traded throughout Europe and as far afield as South America. When John Davenport died in 1848 his younger son William carried on the business as William Davenport and Co. By the 1880s their fortunes

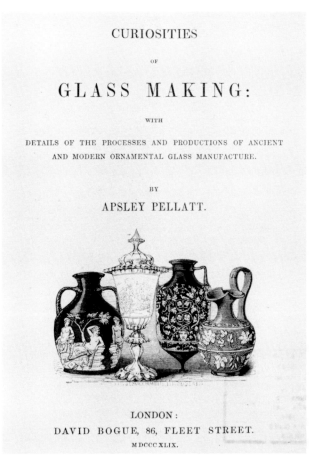

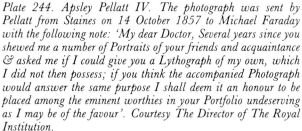

Plate 244. Apsley Pellatt IV. The photograph was sent by Pellatt from Staines on 14 October 1857 to Michael Faraday with the following note: 'My dear Doctor, Several years since you shewed me a number of Portraits of your friends and acquaintance & asked me if I could give you a Lythograph of my own, which I did not then possess; if you think the accompanied Photograph would answer the same purpose I shall deem it an honour to be placed among the eminent worthies in your Portfolio undeserving as I may be of the favour'. Courtesy The Director of The Royal Institution.

Plate 245. Frontispiece of Curiosities of Glass Making *published by Apsley Pellatt in 1849. The tall vase to the right of the Portland vase is almost certainly the Bohm vase, illustrated in Plate 125, which Pellatt mentions as being in his possession at that time.*

suffered a reverse and in 1887 the glass factory was closed and the glass moulds and glass cutters' machinery were offered for sale 'without reserve'.

APSLEY PELLATT IV (1791-1863)

Apsley Pellatt IV (Plate 244) played a major role in the transformation of the English glass industry which, by the middle of the century, could compete with and outclass many of the developments of its Continental rivals. His own experiments and achievements should rank with the successes of his contemporaries and his successors in the Stourbridge district.

In 1802-03 Apsley Pellatt III had taken over the Falcon Glass Works in Blackfriars in London and proceeded to experiment with various uses for glass as well as producing domestic glassware. About 1810-12 his son entered the business and by 1820 had patented his process known as 'Crystallo-Ceramie' or

Colour Plate 22. British and French sulphides. Left to right. Carafe with sulphide portrait of Gladstone, John Ford and Co., Edinburgh, c.1880, height 7½in. (19.3cm). Jug with rope twist handle and applied classical head in white glass, probably made at Philip Pargeter's Red House Glass Works possibly as a trial for portrait medallion cameos by John Northwood I, c.1875-1880, height 9in. (23cm). Two paperweights with sulphide portraits of the Comte de Chambord (left) and Prince Albert, Baccarat, mid-19th century, heights 3⅛in. (7.8cm) (left) and 3in. (7.5cm). Amber bottle with cutting around the sulphide of Queen Victoria, Stevens and Williams, 1887, height 4in. (10.3cm), Michael Parkington Collection. The pattern for this bottle is shown in Plate 267. Scent bottle and stopper by Apsley Pellatt, c.1820s, height 4¼in. (10.8cm).

'Cameo Incrustation'. In 1821 he published a *Memoir on the Origin, Progress, and Improvement of Glass Manufactures: including An Account of the Patent Crystallo Ceramie, or, Glass Incrustations*. Published more as a trade circular than as a serious or informative guide, it attempts to give a brief history of glassmaking throughout the world and ends with a description and a set of illustrations of glassware incorporating the glass incrustations or sulphides.

Much more useful and fascinating from a glassmaking point of view is Apsley Pellatt's 1849 publication *Curiosities of Glass Making* (Plate 245). The book was the

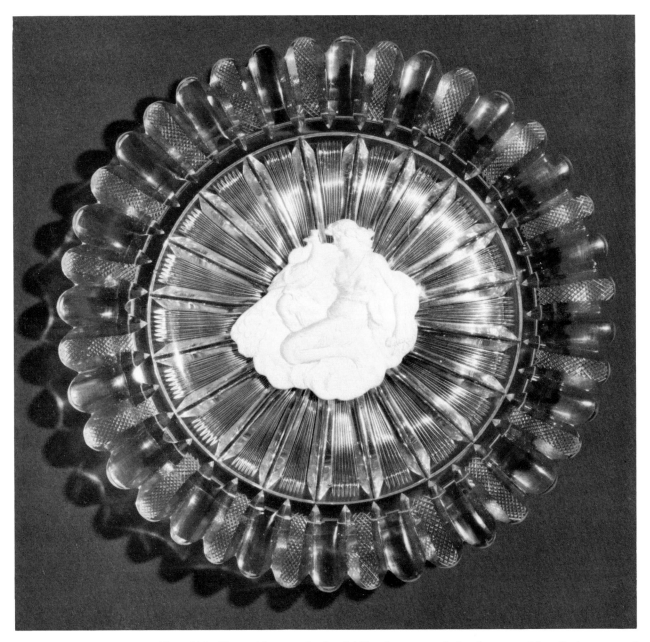

Plate 246. Plate with an enclosed sulphide, the reverse of the plate cut with radiating star and strawberry diamonds, probably by Apsley Pellatt, c.1820-25. Diameter 7in. (18cm). Photograph courtesy Christie's.

only publication throughout the century which provided detailed technical information about most aspects of glassmaking from the stages of manufacture to Venetian processes, including vitro di trino and frosted glass. With its thorough approach, *Curiosities of Glass Making* forms an invaluable record of the styles and techniques which preoccupied glassmakers in England in the first decade of Victoria's reign.

'Cameo Incrustations'

In glass collecting circles the name 'sulphide', as 'cameo incrustations' became known, is synonymous with Apsley Pellatt. However, sulphides were in production throughout the century in Europe and the United States (Colour Plate 22). The major French paperweight factories continue their production. On a smaller scale, in 1985 the visitor to Charles Gibson's studio in Milton, West Virginia could see paperweights made with sulphides of American trains.

Pellatt's formula for the sulphide consisted of white china clay and super-silicate of potash, described by him as 'sand exposed at a high temperature in a crucible, with a small portion of carbonate of potash, sufficient to fuse it partially, for grinding into an impalpable powder'. The mixed ingredients were moulded in plaster of Paris moulds to the required shapes and slightly baked. It was necessary to warm the sulphide before it was inserted into the glass. A glass bubble was blown, opened at one end to form a tube and the sulphide was inserted into the opening. The bubble was resealed by the glassmaker who sucked the air out and collapsed the glass over the sulphide. Another method, used for smaller and less important work, was to apply the sulphide directly on to the glass object and cover it with another gather of glass. The inherent problem in both methods was the danger of trapping small air bubbles around the sulphide which would glisten and shine and spoil the overall appearance. Also, if the compatibility between the glass and the sulphide was too great the piece would crack. Pellatt himself ends his description of the process in *Curiosities* with the obviously heartfelt remark that 'these incrustations require very careful annealing'.

After the glassmaking part of the process was finished the glass was elaborately cut. The process was used on seals, brooches and cloak pins, candlesticks and lustres, lamp fittings, jugs, plaques, door furniture, scent bottles and plates (Colour Plate 22, extreme right and Plate 246).

In the middle of the century French manufacturers, including Baccarat, used sulphides of famous people in the newly introduced paperweights (Colour Plate 22, centre). In Scotland the firm of John Ford and Co. made a huge range of sulphide decorated pieces including decanters, vases, paperweights and scent bottles. The subjects were of famous personalities and included Burns, Wellington, Gladstone, Byron and Sir Walter Scott and date from about 1880-81. Some of the sulphides are signed by Leonard Charles Wyon, an engraver at the Royal Mint (Colour Plate 22, extreme left). To celebrate Queen Victoria's Jubilee in 1887 Stevens and Williams created a small vase in amber glass with a sulphide portrait of the Queen (Colour Plate 22). The shape was recorded in the pattern books as no. 12237 (Plate 267). Thomas Webb and Sons made a range where the sulphide portrait of Victoria was applied on to the surface of bowls and vases and covered with a pad of hot glass.

'Crystallo Engraving'

In 1831, Pellatt took out a patent for a technique called 'Crystallo Engraving',

Colour Plate 23. Venetian-inspired techniques were copied by British glassmakers from the 1840s to the 1890s, following the publication of Apsley Pellatt's Curiosities of Glass Making *which gave precise instructions and methods of manufacture of many Venetian processes. Left to right. Jug made from pink and white opaque twist canes, probably Richardson's, c.1845, height 7¼in. (18.6cm). Stemmed bowl with white canes set in pink glass, Stevens and Williams, mid-1880s, height 8¼in. (21cm). Wineglass by James Powell and Sons, London, mid-1870s, height 5¾in. (14.8cm). Jug in dark green glass with applied trails and prunts, possibly from the Sowerby art glass range, c.1880, height 10in. (25.7cm). Jug with applied blue trails, Sowerby, c.1880, height 2¼in. (5.5cm), Michael Parkington Collection. Jug, crackle glass with a rope twist handle, English, late 19th century, height 8¼in. (20.8cm). Jug, blue glass with an applied white rim, possibly Sowerby, c.1880, height 6¾in. (17cm).*

which imitated copper wheel engraving by blowing the glass into a mould and forcing it against a plaster cake which left the intaglio impression on the glass (Plate 247). Pellatt described the process in his 1849 publication:

> In addition to Cameo Incrustation which was patented many years since, a subsequent patent was secured for taking fac-similes of casts or dies from intaglios, and impressing them upon hollow Glass vessels in intaglio. This plan of Glass

Colour Plate 24. With the revival of their glass industry from about 1835, Venetian glassmakers looked to their former glories for inspiration and models. Amongst the leading firms was the Venice and Murano Glass Company run by Antonio Salviati. In 1866, when the company opened a shop in Oxford Street, London, the Art Journal *described his glass as 'the most successful we have yet seen. . . all these pieces are so close an imitation that it behoves collectors of ancient glass to be on their guard for it is difficult for any but the most expert judges to discriminate between the old and the new'. The seven examples in this group serve to underline that comment.*
Left to right. Shallow dish in mosaic glass with applied rim, by the Venice and Murano Glass Co., c.1885; diameter 6½ in. (16.3cm). Vase with aventurine inclusions, and clear glass prunts and trails, late 19th century, probably Salviati, height 3½ in. (8.7cm). Two-handled vase with mottled surface decoration, probably Vetro Corinto by Francesco Ferro and Son, c.1880 (Rosa Barovier Mentasti illustrates similar pieces on page 217), height 10¼ in. (26cm). Beaker with the inscription 'Caro Bevi', late 19th century, height 3¼ in. (8.2cm). Goblet, the bowl decorated with fragments of turquoise glass, hollow lion mask stem, Salviati, 1870s, height 7in. (17.6cm). Wineglass with blue trails, late 19th century, height 4⅞ in. (12.4cm). Bowl enamelled with named portraits of Laurentius, Julius, Epolitus, Timoteus and Ciprianus, late 19th century, height 3½ in. (9cm).

engraving has been chiefly adopted where numerous copies of elaborate devices have been required; such as badges of regiments, or arms upon decanters and table Glass. The following is the mode of operating: dust Tripoli, very finely pulverized

Plate 247. Scent bottle with crystallo engraving of three Muses signed 'Pellatt & Co. Patentees', c.1830. Height 4 ¼ in. (10.7cm). Michael Parkington Collection.

upon the die or cast; then a larger coating of dry plaster of Paris and pulverized brick-dust, with another layer of coarser plaster of Paris and brick-dust; place the whole under a press, which when screwed to its utmost, allows water to saturate the pores of the impressed cake; and, when gradually dried, it will be fit for use. A brass mould, A [Plate 248], with a recess to receive the cake, and a hinged leverage to keep it in its position, B, is provided; so that the face of the cake, C, which is then embossed in relief, ranges with the circular form of the Glass vessel intended to be blown into it; and this, being heated to redness, is placed in the recess of the mould. In this state, the ball of hot Glass is introduced and expanded by the power of blowing, till it assumes the exact shape of the mould, and the cake adheres to the glass. The cake is then released by the lever, and the Glass reheated, with the cake adhering to it, as often as necessary to finish the article, (as usually practised by blowers in ordinary moulded Glass vessels); the cake and Glass vessel being annealed together, with its blow-over, which is afterwards finished by the Glass-cutter. When the Glass is cold, it is released from the cake by its absorption of cold water, and the intaglio impression upon the Glass will be found as sharp as the original die. A cake once used, seldom answers for a second impression.

The finished object was given the same fine cut decoration as the pieces which contained sulphides. The 'Crystallo Engraved' pieces usually carry the impressed name 'Pellatt & Co. Patentees' below the image. In September 1847 *Art Union* magazine illustrated one of the finest examples of the process, entitled the 'Queen's Plate' (Plate 249), and described it as 'a unique example of glass intaglio moulding. The head is, of course, a portrait of Her Majesty, and on the flange are groups of figures in procession, copied from Thorwaldsen's beautiful Procession of the Triumph of Constantine, executed in a masterly style on the under side of the plate.'

It is ironic that Pellatt should have developed an imitative process when later in the century his glassworks became renowned for traditional copper wheel engraving. Engraved decanters, wineglasses and vases formed the main display at the Great Exhibition while cut tableware and lighting fixtures were an equally important part of their production (Plates 100 and 101). A gift of over forty pieces of the company's engraved glass was presented by the firm to the Royal Scottish Museum in Edinburgh in 1864. Of equal quality are two engraved oil lamps which have the rare, if not unique, distinction of bearing the engraved signature 'PELLATT' below a crown (Plate 250 and Appendix 12, 21). At the 1862 London Exhibition engraved glass again featured prominently in the display by Messrs Pellatt, often in combination with applied jewels of coloured glass. Apsley Pellatt died the following year but the firm continued under various partnerships until 1890.

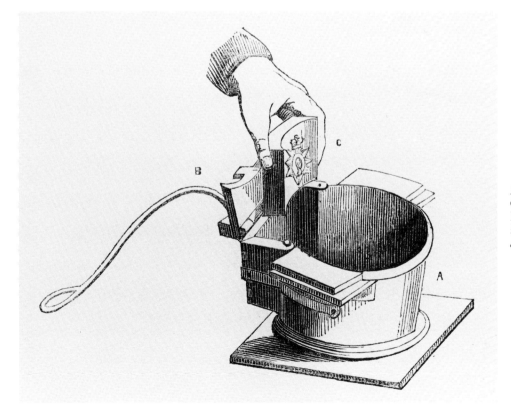

Plate 248. Drawing from Curiosities of Glass Making *showing the insertion of the cake for the crystallo engraving process.*

Colour Plate 25. Cased, cut and silvered glass by E. Varnish and Co., London. The goblet is engraved with the arms of the City of London above the motto, 'DOMINE DIRIGE NOS'. The coat of arms with the motto 'LEGES AC. JURA SERVARE' engraved on the reverse are those of Thomas Farncombe. As Lord Mayor of the City of London in 1849-50, he held a banquet for Prince Albert and Mayors from all the boroughs in the country to further the Great Exhibition of 1851. A goblet matching this one was on display in that exhibition. Heights: candlesticks 11 ½ in. (29cm), goblet 9in. (23cm). Michael Parkington Collection.

Plate 249. 'The Queen's Plate', crystallo engraving by Pellatt, illustrated in the Art Union *magazine, September 1847.*

Plate 250. Pair of oil lamps, engraved with swags of flowers, c.1860. Signed 'Pellatt' below a crown. Height 8in. (20.5cm). The description of the glasses as oil lamps is based on the wide, ground smooth rims, a feature not normally seen on vases. Michael Parkington Collection.

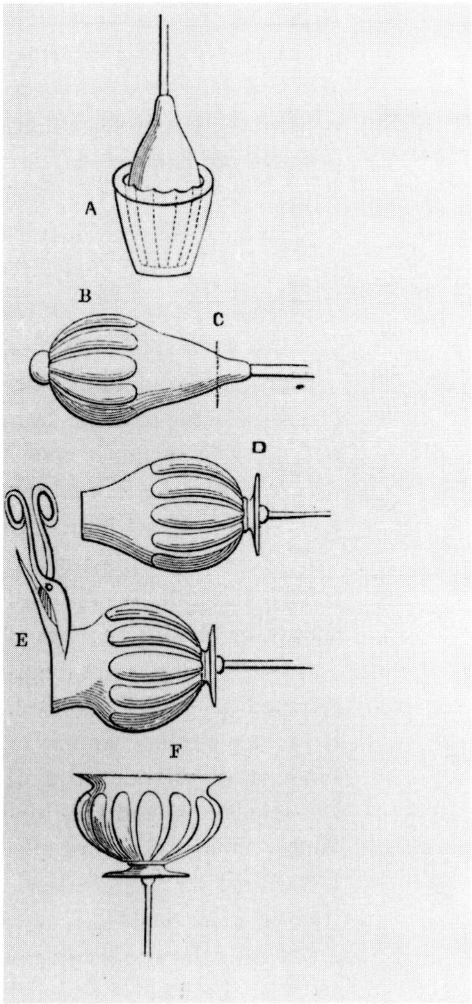

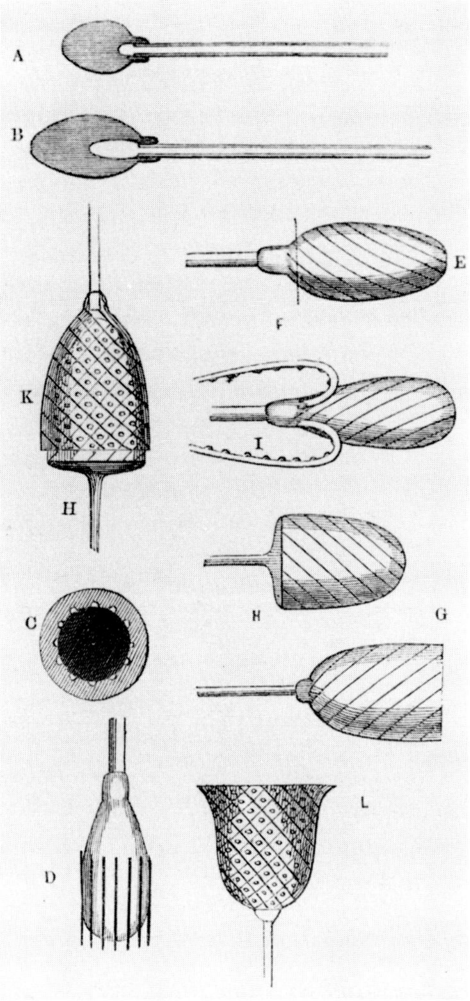

Plate 251. Stages in making a pillar moulded bowl, from Curiosities of Glass Making.

Plate 252. Stages in making 'Vitro di Trino' or vetro a retorti glass, from Curiosities of Glass Making.

'Moulded Roman Pillars'

In 1851 the Conservatoire National des Arts et Métiers in Paris acquired fifteen examples of glass from the Falcon Glass Works. Thirteen of those pieces survive including a pillar moulded bowl which is similar to a ruby bowl in the Michael Parkington Collection (Colour Plate 35). Except for the absence of a foot, this bowl matches the description for 'Moulded Roman Pillars' which Pellatt gives on page 104 of *Curiosities* (Plate 251).

Moulded Glass, as recently introduced by the English manufacturer, owes its refractive and cut-like effect to its inequalities of substance — the interior having no indentations to correspond with its exterior projections. It requires, in addition to the usual Glass-maker's tools, only a metal mould of about one-third the size of the object to be manufactured. The metal is first gathered upon a rod in the ordinary manner, except that the first gathering should be allowed to cool to a greater degree of hardness than usual; the second coating should be pressed into the mould, A, as hot as possible, that the exterior coating only shall be acted upon by the pressure of moulding, and that the interior shall preserve its smooth circular area. When about half formed, the projecting parts, B, have a centrifugal enlargement given to them by a sharp trundling of the iron at, or immediately after, the moment the workman is blowing; during the re-heating process, the piece is separated at C, has a foot welded to it, and is re-warmed, as D; sheared, as E; and when finished, by flashing, shaping, &c., as F, is called patent-pillar-moulding. The fire polish is given to it by frequently re-melting the surface of the Glass, after it leaves the mould. A little cutting or scolloping makes this refractive moulding still more ornamental, but, though it much resembles cutting, (as to its round pillars), it is inferior when sharp angles are required.

Ventian Glassmaking Techniques

At a time when Turner's views of Venice and the Grand Canal were exhibited in London, and John Ruskin had moved to the 'Jewel of the Adriatic' to write his *Stones of Venice,* it was inevitable that many of the processes described by Pellatt in *Curiosities of Glass Making* should be of Venetian origin. Of greatest help to fellow glassmakers must have been the explicit line drawings which showed every stage of each process.

In the following descriptions of the techniques Pellatt's original headings are used. The correct Venetian names for the techniques are explained in an effort to clear up some of the confusion created by the terms 'latticinio' and 'filigrano'. Both terms are generic names for glass decoration using white or coloured canes but the accepted practice now is to give each pattern a specific name.

'Venetian Filigree Glass'

Canes with intricate spiral patterns running through them, reminiscent of the opaque twist stems of eighteenth century wineglasses, were used to make 'filigree' glass, known as 'vetro a retorti'. The canes could be placed side by side and heated on a slab inside the furnace, at which point they would be picked up, by a blowing-iron, and formed into a cylinder. An alternative method was to line the canes inside a mould as in the 'vetro di trino' technique and pick them up on the iron (Plate 252D). From this point it was a question of skill on the part of the glassmaker to retain the symmetry of the canes to give a regular upright effect on the finished object (Colour Plate 23, extreme left). If plain, coloured canes were used for a simple, striped effect the technique was called 'vetro a fili'.

'Vitro di Trino'

As a term 'vitro di trino' or 'vetro de trina' is not regarded as accurate for this type of glass. Now known as 'vetro a reticello', the method took the vetro a fili or retorti techniques one step further by sticking together two bubbles of glass each decorated with canes of glass to form a network pattern (Plate 252). After the glass was gathered (A) and marvered (B), it was blown into a dip mould which was lined with upright canes of glass (C). The hot glass would pick up the canes which eventually would give part of the crisscross pattern (D). The canes are partially marvered into the surface and the bubble is twisted to give the spiral effect (E). It is now transferred on to the pontil rod, broken off the blowpipe (F) and opened out to form a cup shape (G). After it is opened out a glass disc or

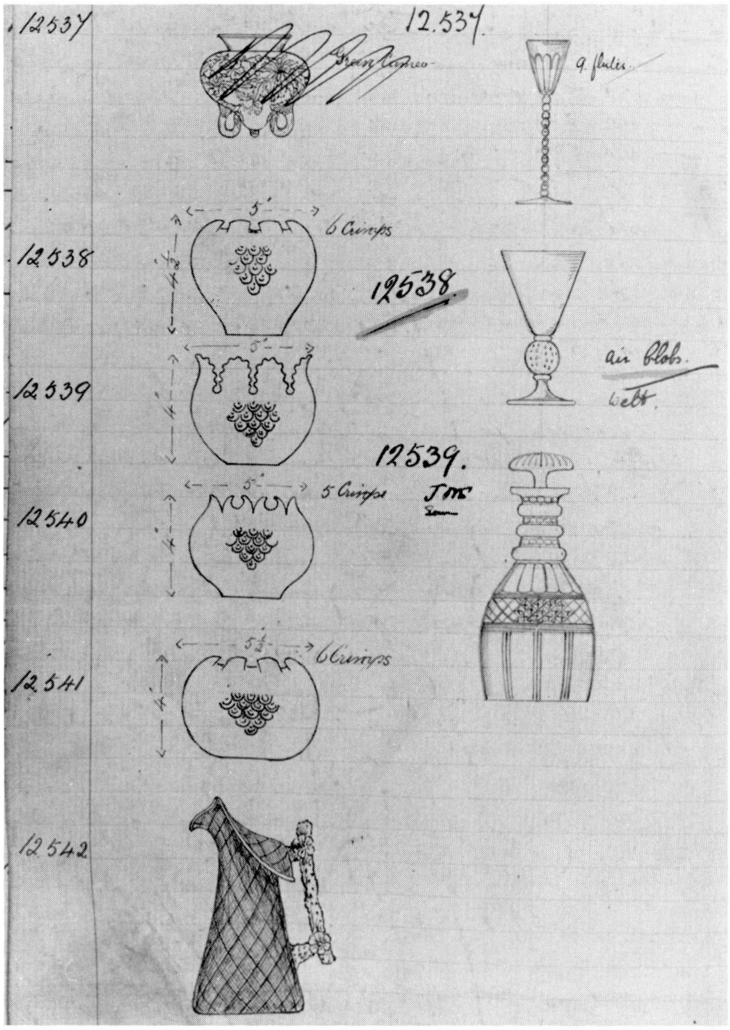

Plate 253. Page from a pattern book at Stevens and Williams showing design number 12542 for a latticinio jug with rusticated clear glass handle and applied glass flowers, March/April 1887. The four patterns from 12538-41 are for the firm's 'Tapestry' ware. In the early years of the 20th century some new designs were entered and given the pattern numbers of earlier pieces. Royal Brierley Crystal.

post, on another blowing-iron, is stuck on to the edge of the opened rim (H) and the previous pontil rod cracked off. With the canes on the outside surface, this shape will eventually form the inside of the finished piece. To make the outer layer another member of the glass making team repeats the process with another bubble up to stage (G). The second bubble is now turned over on itself to form a cup shape with the canes positioned on the inner surface (I). This shape is fixed to a pontil rod and the blowing-iron is cracked off from the inside. The outer cup (K) is placed over the inner shape (H) and fused together. The blowing-iron from the inner cup is cracked off and the two shapes are reheated and worked to give the final shape (L) which shows the criss-crossed canes. Because the canes are left slightly proud of the surface, they trap tiny air bubbles when the two surfaces are fused. In the 1880s the technique was used extensively at Stevens and Williams by John Northwood I on vases, jugs and bowls (Colour Plate 23 and Plate 253). The same effect can be achieved by cutting a bubble of glass, decorated with canes of coloured glass, while hot, into halves and fusing them together.

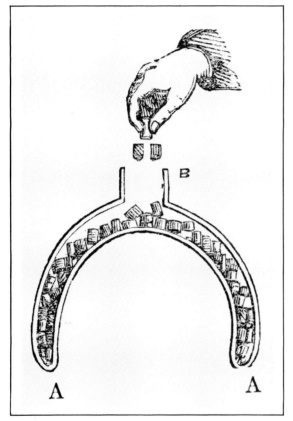

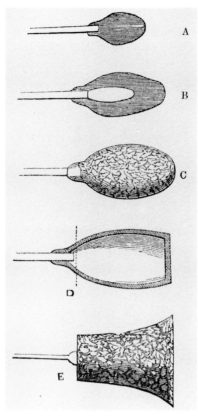

Plate 255. Stages in making 'Old Venetian Frosted Glass', from Curiosities of Glass Making.

Plate 254. Process of making millefiore decorated glass, from Curiosities of Glass Making.

'Mille-fiore'

The use of randomly spaced slices of millefiore canes is found on glass from the Roman Empire and the technique was revived by the Venetians at the beginning of the sixteenth century. Used by French glassworks in the first half of the nineteenth century, it was described and illustrated by Pellatt (Plate 254):

> It was formed by placing lozenges of glass, cut from the ends of coloured filigree canes, ranging them in regular or irregular devices, and encasing them in Flint transparent glass. The double transparent Glass cone A, receives the lozenges between the two surfaces. The whole is reheated; a hollow disk, communicating with the blowing-iron, adheres to the neck B, and the air is exhausted or sucked out of the double case. After being rewarmed, it becomes one homogeneous mass, and can be shaped into a tazza, paperweight, &c., at pleasure.

'Old Venetian Frosted Glass'

Developed initially by the Venetians, frosted, crackle or ice glass became a favourite mode of decoration of English and European glassmakers in the 19th century. Pellatt's concise description of the process (Plate 255) states:

> A, is the first gathering; B, the second, expanded by blowing; while at nearly a white heat, it is suddenly plunged into cold water; if immediately re-warmed and blown, the effect will be as C; flatten the bottom, and whet off at D; attach a ponty, as E, and finish the article as usual; but in the latter process, the less heat the better, or it will melt out the frosting.

Plate 256. Vase in pale lemon opalescent glass, with pinched waist. Marked 'Rd' in a circle, probably James Powell of Whitefriars, c.1880. Height 7¾ in. (19.5cm).

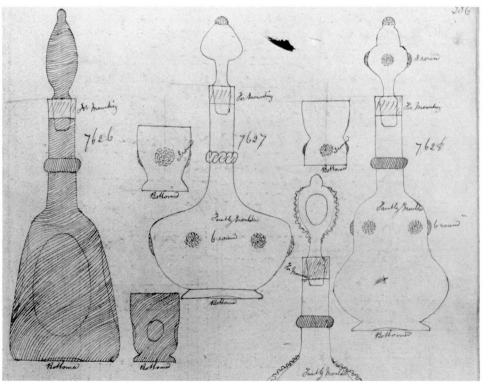

Plate 257. Page of designs for decanters with trails and prunts from Stuart and Sons, mid-1889. Stuart Crystal.

266

Although the appearance of crackle or ice glass suggests that the cracks and fissures run through the entire body, it is only the surface which contains the crackle effect. If the glass is blown out to any degree the openings become much more widely spaced. It was this process which was used by Stevens and Williams for their moss agate glass and by Webb's for their crackled bronze glass, but in many cases the clear iced glass was left plain (Colour Plate 23).

Other Anglo-Venetian Glass

The interest in Venetian glass which Pellatt helped to promote was taken up by various factories in England and Scotland. Some, such as Alexander Jenkinson's Norton Park Glass Works in Edinburgh, created exact Venetian copies in latticinio and applied floral work. Others used Venetian names to capitalise on the fashion but the products were far removed from the original inspiration. One unlikely producer of Venetian-style glass was the pressed glass company of J.G. Sowerby who introduced opalescent free blown glass about 1878 and marketed a 'Venetian' series in 1880 which consisted of plain shapes with a simple trailed rim, sometimes with extra threading (Colour Plate 23, extreme right). More fanciful ware was also made with a variety of decorative techniques which included applied prunts and trailed and pincered collars on to wrythen moulded shapes (Colour Plate 23, back centre). Sowerby's cream coloured glass was used on free blown pieces with blue trails (Colour Plate 23, centre).

The greatest commitment by a glassworks to the philosophy of critics such as William Morris, John Ruskin and Charles Locke Eastlake, who championed the cause of plain blown glass in the Venetian tradition, came from the Whitefriars factory of James Powell and Sons in London. One table service, consisting of simple shapes in green glass (Colour Plate 23, left centre), still exists at Wightwick Manor, the Arts and Crafts Movement period house near Wolverhampton. The Powell factory even introduced soda glass as a replacement for lead glass to ensure absolute truth to materials. Soda glass gave the ability to create paper thin vessels decorated with fragile applied threads of glass. A delicate opalescent effect was given to some wares in imitation of pieces which the Venetian firm of Antonio Salviati had first shown in London at the International Exhibition in 1862 (Plate 256). The elegant and delicate profiles of Powell glass in the 1870s, especially evident on some of their decanters which were simply decorated by moulding or trailing, were copied by Stuart and Sons in the 1880s (Plate 257). Until 1940 the Powell factory continued to produce designs based on historical examples which can be mistaken for late nineteenth century examples (Plate 258).

From the middle of the century glassmakers as well as collectors were able to enjoy antique Venetian glass at first hand. Much of it was made available by Felix Slade who had lent part of his collection to a Society of Arts exhibition in 1850. Other exhibitions followed in Manchester in 1857, in London in 1861 and 1862, and in Leeds in 1868. After Slade's death his collection was displayed in 1868 at the British Museum and published in 1871. Through his example museums began to collect old Venetian glass while magazine articles brought it to a wider

Plate 258. Wineglass from the tear series by Powell of Whitefriars. Designed in 1901 the pattern was based on a glass in an altarpiece by Hugo van der Goes in the Uffizi, Florence. Height 8in. (20.6cm). Vase with green applied peacock trails, Stuart and Sons, c.1900. Height 14½in. (37cm). Vase with moulded decoration, applied prunts and milled foot rim, by Powell's. Height 5⅞in. (14.9cm). Similar pieces were made by Powell's in 1906 and continued in production until 1932. Wineglass and vase, Michael Parkington Collection. Tall vase, Stuart Crystal.

Plate 259. Two 'Clutha' vases from the Couper Glass Works, Glasgow, late 19th century. Height left 8in. (20.2cm), right 7½in. (19cm). Vase on right Hickman Collection.

public. Contemporary glass from the revived industry in Venice, itself supported by English sources, was seen in museum collections and was available for purchase from shops in London. The legacy of this great enthusiasm for Venetian glass can still be found in antiques shops today, often unrecognised either as Venetian or as nineteenth century (Colour Plate 24).

In a similar vein of eclectic design Christopher Dresser relied on the decorative arts of cultures as varied as Roman, Persian and Middle Eastern, and Pre-Columbian for his 'Clutha' range of glassware. The designs appeared from about 1885 at the James Couper glassworks in Glasgow which were under the management of W.H. Richardson II. The most common colour was a bubbly green made in shapes which were inspired originally by Roman glasses but can rarely be matched to known Roman shapes. With the identification of more Clutha pieces, the range of colours and designs known to have been made by the factory to Dresser's designs included pink, white, green, red and blue glass

Plate 260. Wineglass cooler with honeycomb moulded decoration and silvered interior. Marked 'E. Varnish & Co London Patent', c.1849-50. Height 3¾in. (9.3cm). The body and the glass plug are marked in diamond point with the number 633a. Michael Parkington Collection.

applied in random swirling lines on assymetric shapes as well as more formal striped effects. The factory commissioned other designs from the Glasgow architect George Walton (1867-1933) who seems to have added patches of gold aventurine to designs which are similiar to Dresser's (Plate 259).

SILVERED GLASS

Double-walled silvered glass was patented by Edward Varnish and Frederick Hale Thomson on 19 August 1849. The process involved blowing the glass in such a way that it contained a cavity into which a silvering solution was poured (Colour Plate 25 and Plate 260). The technique seems to have been used for two or three years after the first patent. Often dismissed as a curious novelty it merits greater attention and admiration. In an effort to discover the techniques and inherent problems of blowing some of the more complex shapes, in January 1989 the International Glass Centre at Brierley Hill was approached for advice. From discussions with Chris Greenaway, the head of the college, John Davies, the glass cutting lecturer and Malcolm Andrews, the master glassblower, several possible methods were put forward but none seemed to be quite feasible. Following those discussions Malcolm Andrews decided to attempt to blow a goblet based on a Varnish glass in the collections at Broadfield House Glass Museum. His efforts, which proved totally successful, bridged a gap of 140 years. The stage of the process which the discussions had failed to discover was the moment when the glass is transferred from one blowing-iron to another. The trick of changing ends with the blowing-irons allows the shape of the bowl, foot and stem to be achieved and allows the top to be made, reheated and dropped in to form the double wall. The following description and the diagrams in Plate 261 are based on a video film of Malcolm Andrews, assisted by Pat Ricketts, recreating a piece of Varnish glass.

The making of the goblet took twenty minutes, during which period the glass

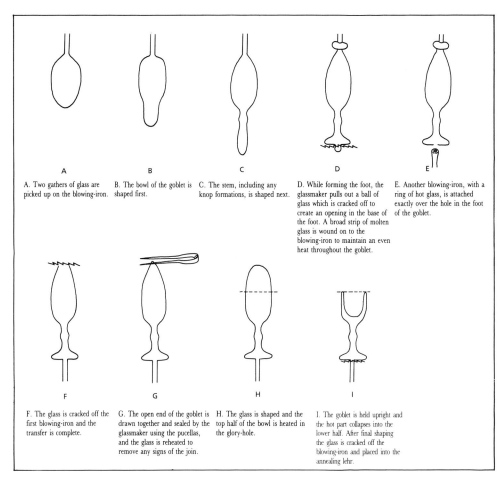

A. Two gathers of glass are picked up on the blowing-iron.

B. The bowl of the goblet is shaped first.

C. The stem, including any knop formations, is shaped next.

D. While forming the foot, the glassmaker pulls out a ball of glass which is cracked off to create an opening in the base of the foot. A broad strip of molten glass is wound on to the blowing-iron to maintain an even heat throughout the goblet.

E. Another blowing-iron, with a ring of hot glass, is attached exactly over the hole in the foot of the goblet.

F. The glass is cracked off the first blowing-iron and the transfer is complete.

G. The open end of the goblet is drawn together and sealed by the glassmaker using the pucellas, and the glass is reheated to remove any signs of the join.

H. The glass is shaped and the top half of the bowl is heated in the glory-hole.

I. The goblet is held upright and the hot part collapses into the lower half. After final shaping the glass is cracked off the blowing-iron and placed into the annealing lehr.

Plate 261. Stages in making a hollow walled goblet based on a Varnish blue cased silvered goblet in the Broadfield House Glass Museum.

had to be re-heated twenty times. After the first gather is made it is allowed to cool slightly to prevent the bubble from distorting when it comes to blowing it out. A second gather is taken to provide sufficient material for the shape of the glass (Plate 261A). It is blocked in wet paper (i.e. rolled on a wet, folded newspaper held in the palm of the right hand) to provide a smooth surface, the glass starts to be blown out and the bowl of the goblet begins to take shape (B). Once the bowl form is satisfactory, the most difficult part, the stem, is shaped (C). Any stem formations such as knops or balusters are extremely difficult to form as the glassmaker is trying to control the shape which is hot and hollow at the same time. It is occasionally blocked with wet paper to keep it straight. An assistant gives a little blow down the blowing-iron at this stage to expand the glass at the end of the bubble which will form the foot. The foot is now shaped with the pucellas and a further blow is given by the assistant which helps to form a small ball at the end where the pontil would normally be (D). The glassmaker cuts in the ball with the pucellas (i.e. narrows the join of the ball to the foot to assist with cracking off) and proceeds to crack it off the rest of the glass, thereby creating a small hole in the base. At this stage, while the glassmaker is working, the assistant wraps a gather of hot glass from the pot on to the end of the blowing-iron to maintain the heat at that end, otherwise the gradual cooling would make the glass crack and break off the iron.

The glass is passed to the assistant who keeps it warm while the glassblower takes another blowing-iron and forms a small ring of hot glass around the opening. The glassmaker and the assistant exchange their blowing-irons; the glassmaker puts a rubbing of French chalk around the hole in the foot, which will ease the cracking-off process, and the assistant sticks the second iron exactly over the aperture (E). The glass is broken off the first blowing-iron leaving a hole at the top of the goblet (F). The top of the glass is reheated and the opening sealed up (G). While the assistant blows into the iron to inflate the end part of the goblet, which will soon form the inner wall of the bowl, the glassmaker shapes the top of the bowl (H). The top half of the bowl is reheated in the glory-hole and once the right temperature is obtained the glass is held upright on the iron and the hot part of the bowl collapses into the lower half (I). Back on his chair, the glassmaker eases in the inner wall with wooden pucellas while the assistant helps by sucking gently at the other end of the iron. After a final reheat and a check to make sure that the shape is correct, the goblet is finished. It is cracked off the blowing-iron and placed into the annealing oven to cool overnight.

It is worth mentioning that the making of the modern goblet was in clear glass. Many of the nineteenth century pieces were cased in colours which would add to the difficulty and increase the making time.

In the nineteenth century the next stage was to silver the interior. A solution, consisting of silver nitrate and glucose, was poured into the cavity. When the excess was poured out a deposit of silver was left fixed to the inner layer of the glass. The silver was protected from tarnishing by 'a preservative coating of cement'. The hole in the base was first fitted with a metal disc which carried the name of the patentees and then with a circular, glass plug to provide the final airtight seal. The hole in the foot would have to be ground into a regular circle which would need to correspond in diameter to the metal disc and glass plug. The majority of silvered glasses by Varnish are scratched in diamond point with a number on the glass plug and on the foot of the vessel immediately adjacent to the plug. The exact relevance of the numbering, which does not always match on the plug and the body, is unclear, but it must have been used in some way to assist the worker to match the seal to the opening. The most commonly found mark on the seal reads 'E. VARNISH & CO. PATENT LONDON' (see Appendix 12, 20), but occasionally 'HALE THOMSON'S PATENT LONDON' or 'W. LUND PATENT LONDON' are seen. The silver mount of one scent bottle was inscribed Thomas Mellish, a partner with Hale Thomson when they took out another patent for silvered glass in 1850. These firms were retailers and dealers and the glass was made for them, presumably, at one of the London glassworks. Some authorities give James Powell and Sons as the probable makers but there is no conclusive proof.

The majority of English silvered glasses from the middle years of the century are cased and cut. Some smaller examples, including salt cellars, are stained yellow on the slumped part of the bowl. A hitherto unrecorded wineglass cooler was made in clear glass and decorated with honeycomb moulding (Plate 260). Rare examples with engraved decoration include a ruby cased Varnish goblet decorated with portrait heads of Queen Victoria and Prince Albert, in the collections at Osborne House. A green cased goblet is engraved with two sets of coats of arms (Colour Plate 25). The front is engraved with the arms of the City of London above the motto *DOMINE DIRIGE NOS.* The coat of arms on the reverse, above the motto *LEGES AC. JURA SERVARE,* are those of Farncombe of Kennington in Surrey. The owner was Thomas Farncombe (1779-1865) who was a wharfinger of considerable note on the Surrey side of the Thames, as well as a promoter, and for many years a director, of the London and Westminster Bank. In 1840 he became a sheriff of the City of London, from 1841-1849 he was elected an alderman and finally in 1849-1850 he became Lord Mayor. In his capacity as Lord Mayor he held a banquet in honour of Prince Albert and the Mayors of all the boroughs in the country to promote the Great Exhibition of 1851. A goblet matching the description of the one illustrated was on display at the Exhibition.

TRAILED AND THREADED GLASS

Trailing or threading is the oldest form of decoration known to glassmakers, dating back to 1500BC when it was the sole method of decoration on Egyptian sand-core vessels. Herring-bone patterns were produced even then by dragging a point through the horizontal threads, a technique taken up by nineteenth century glassmakers.

The terms trailing and threading can be confusing at first acquaintance. Some authorities have argued that they should be seen as two separate techniques: trailing as independent decoration on the surface and threading as part of the glass. In the glass world both terms are interchangeable, but if a definition is required perhaps it should rest on whether the decoration is applied free-hand (trailing) or with the use of a machine (threading). However, there will always be glasses which will be difficult to classify. Trailing by hand can give quite a precise spiral which could be hard to differentiate from machine threading, especially when the latter is blown out and the threads take on a handmade look as in the red, white and blue vase by Richardson (Colour Plate 27, second left).

Until 1876 all trailed decoration was applied by hand or by picking up canes from a dip mould (Colour Plate 26). Trailing by hand requires two glassmakers to work in close harmony. One glassmaker gathers a small amount of glass on the pontil rod, dabs it very slightly on to the main article and pulls out a thread. The other glassmaker rotates the blowing-iron and the thread continues to be pulled on to the glass. The method is seen to marvellous effect on the cider jug where the blue trail was started on the base and wound upwards to the neck. The so-called 'Nailsea' glasses, with looped decoration, were made by applying a spiral of coloured glass on to a gather of glass which had been blown out slightly. After the threads were dragged through with a point the glass was blown to full size and the loops enlarged accordingly. The technique, seen on the red looped

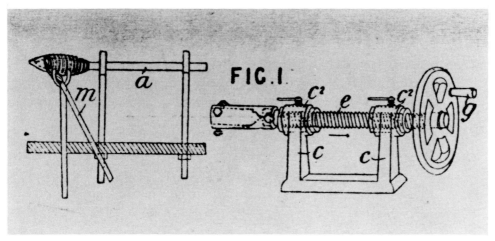

Plate 262. Design for a threading machine patent registered on 6 May 1876 by W.J. Hodgetts.

carafe, was used in most glassmaking areas and was certainly not peculiar to Nailsea or Bristol. Designed for a slightly more sophisticated buyer the decanter and stopper with white trails was made in exactly the same way. The addition of the three rings on the neck elevated the decanter to fashionable pretensions which belied its simple process. Similar in effect to the jug, decanter and carafe but made by a different method are the tobacco jar with red, white and blue stripes and the butter dish with its restrained lines. Although separated by some fifty years both were made by picking the canes up on a gather of glass from a dip mould. To ensure that the canes of the lid matched the body, the glassmaker would simply cut the hot glass into two pieces and finish one as the body, the other as the lid.

Machine Threaded Glass

From 1876 glassmakers had the option of applying trailed decoration by using a machine. In that year William J. Hodgetts, a partner in the firm of Hodgetts, Richardson and Son, patented his invention of a threading machine to speed up the hand process and ensure an absolutely regular spacing (Plate 262). The patent was registered on 6 May.

1914. Ornamenting. — Relates to means for ornamenting glass articles whereby an appearance similar to fine wicker or basket work is given to the surface. In forming the article, a bubble is blown in the ordinary way, and the 'iron' or pipe *a,* Fig. 1, is fixed in a horizontal position to the head of a screw *e* working through nuts *c²* in the framing *c* and rotated by a handwheel *g.* A fine thread of coloured or colourless glass is then coiled on the bulb from the end of the punty *m* by rotating the hand-wheel *g,* the coiling being preferably commenced at the end nearest the 'iron'. The bulb is then reheated and blown in ribbed moulds and afterwards shaped as a jug, vase, or other vessel or article in the ordinary way. In a modification by which threads crossing each other may be coiled on the bulb, the screw has a right-handed and a left-handed thread crossing each other, and is moved longitudinally by one or other of two half-nuts which can be turned down to engage the corresponding thread. Flat sheets of glass, obtained by blowing hollow cylinders which are then divided in a line parallel with the axis and flattened

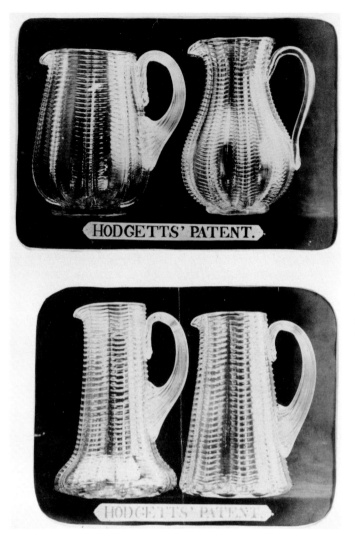

Plate 263. Page from the pattern books of Hodgetts, Richardson and Son showing jugs threaded on Hodgetts' machine. Three of the jugs show the new method of applying the handle, introduced about 1867. Known as a 'dab' handle, the lower part was stuck on to the jug first and finished at the top. The earlier 'pump' handle, on the top right jug, was applied at the top and pulled out and finished on the body of the jug. It was used throughout the 18th century and continued in use sporadically even after the introduction of the 'dab' handle. The three 'dab' handles are in the shell pattern which was patented by Thomas W. Webb in 1867.

out, may be ornamented in a similar manner, by first coiling the threads of coloured or colourless glass on the cylinder and then blowing in ribbed moulds.

The new machine was put into practice immediately and many Hodgetts' patent glasses were recorded in the company pattern books (Plate 263). Hodgetts' idea was quickly imitated and led to a flood of vases and bowls which relied for their effect on the new technique, often combined with crimping.

Another Wordsley man, William Henry Stevens, patented a version of Hodgetts' idea on 8 December 1878. The specification stated:

Upon a bed-plate is a headstock carrying the blowpipe socket, driven at any required speed by change-wheel gearing from a winch or handle. The same handle drives a leading screw, carrying a saddle holding the forks in which the puntey irons, generally two, are placed opposite each other. The height of the forks is adjustable to the size of bulb to be threaded. The pitch of the threading can be altered by varying the change-wheels, and the rotation of the socket may be reversed at will.

Plate 264. View inside the Red House Cone at Stuart and Sons in 1902 showing a threading machine in operation. The vessel is rotated in the blowing-iron clamped in the machine and the thread is pulled on to the vessel from the gather of glass on the end of the iron resting on the notched bar. Stuart Crystal.

In 1881 a patent by William H. Stuart referred to threading as part of the ornamentation of glass:

> Relates to flower vases, chandeliers, lamps, decanters, globes, &c Glass is blown into a bulb, which is rolled while plastic, on a surface sprinkled over with pulverized glass or enamel. A thread of glass is also spun or coiled spirally upon the bulb, which is then re-heated and shaped as required.

In 1902 a threading machine was recorded in use inside the Red House cone at the Stuart factory (Plate 264). It differs from Hodgetts' specification by having a separate fly-wheel and pulley to drive the threaded tube holding the blowing-iron. The metal rest for the pontil rod now has at least twelve notches providing the option to thread different parts of the same object without having to alter the position of the blowing-iron. This machine is still in existence at Stuart Crystal where it is occasionally put into operation.

In typical Victorian style the Stourbridge glassmakers took up the basic idea of threaded decoration, combined it with other techniques and produced a stunning array of objects (Colour Plate 27). The red, white and blue vase is close to Hodgetts' patent as it has been blown into a ribbed mould after threading. Dating from shortly after 1878, this vase is a splendid example of the glassmaker's art. The body, composed of alternate red and white stripes, must have been made by picking up those coloured rods with the blowing-iron from a dip mould. That shape was threaded and blown out slightly, especially on the lower half where the white thread has spread out and the gap between each line is wider. The foot was made separately, in white glass finely threaded with blue, and applied to the body. The finishing touches consisted of two collars, one in clear and the other in blue with snail-like horns. A more subtle approach was taken in the handled jug where the clear glass thread running over the entire jug is set off with great style by a single blue collar on the waisted neck. Clear threading on crystal was often known as 'silver threading' in the trade, because of the silvery look it created. It is seen mostly on 'match balls', the glass holders for matches, supplied to hotels and offices. The corrugated effect of the threading could be used as a striker.

The option to place a second thread over the first, as suggested by Hodgetts, was rarely taken up, but the red striped mug, from the Richardson factory, shows a variation on that idea. The mug has fascinated generations of glassblowers because of the sequence of transferring the glass from one pontil to another to allow for the two sets of threading as well as the additions of the foot and the handle.

Stevens and Williams created some delightful versions of threading which are peculiar to that company. A clever use of clear casing to trap air bubbles caught between the threads was patented on 6 September 1886 and known as 'jewelled' glass. A bubble of glass was threaded all over, blown into a clear glass cup to trap the air bubbles and then blown into a ribbed mould which squeezed the glass together to form solid stripes alternating with vertical rows of air bubbles. Made in clear and coloured glass, usually ruby, most jewelled pieces with vertical rows of air bubbles have the engraved registry number 'Rd. 55693'. At this date the glassblowers were in total control of the whole gamut of techniques and were constantly developing new combinations of ideas. The jewelled technique was given the full treatment in an awe-inspiring vase which combined four separate processes (Colour Plate 27, left). The first inspiration was to trail the clear glass bubble with green glass rather than clear. The trailed paraison was then cased with a heat-sensitive glass. Rather than using a ribbed mould the jewelled effect was obtained in a mould which gave a 'raindrop' effect. Once the vase was transferred on to the pontil rod, re-heating at the furnace mouth produced a warm red colouring which contrasted with the original green threads. To complete the *tour de force* the rim was given a very fancy double crimped rim. Pieces with the raindrop jewelled pattern often have the engraved registry number 'Rd. 81051'.

The Stevens and Williams pattern books, especially during 1889, show a

Colour Plate 26. Trailed decoration is often termed 'Nailsea' but was made by glasshouses in all parts of the country. Of this group the cider flagon probably has the best claim to a West country origin. The various levels of sophistication of the trailing reflect the markets that the products were made for. Left to right. Cider flagon, early 19th century, height 12in. (30.5cm). Tobacco jar, mid-19th century, possibly Stourbridge, height 6in. (15.2cm). Decanter and stopper, early 19th century, height 9¼ in. (23.5cm), Michael Parkington Collection. Butter dish and cover, c.1800, height 6in. (15.2cm). Carafe, early 19th century, height 8½ in. (21.5cm).

number of vases and bowls known as 'Moresque', in which the glass spiral was closely threaded on to shapes which had been blown into dip moulds carved on the inside with ogee shaped arches or other oriental and near Eastern patterns. Once the piece was blown out, the effect of the dip mould softened into a gentle optical effect and with the addition of a layer of close threading it gave the appearance of watered silk.

Very occasionally the collector will come across vases and bowls which have the appearance of jewelled glass but the bubbles have been dragged into a herring-bone pattern. After threading, these pieces were subjected to the pull-up machine to obtain the regular zig-zag pattern. Once the piece came out of the machine it

Plate 265. Vase with clear trails worked in a pull-up machine and cased with clear glass to give an air-trap, jewelled effect. Stevens and Williams, c.1887. Height 7in. (18cm). Hulbert of Dudley Collection.

Plate 265a. Clear glass bowl with rows of turquoise beads formed by the method outlined by H. Wilkinson in his patent specification of 1905. Stourbridge, early 20th century. Height 2¼in. (5.6cm), diameter 4¾in. (12cm).

was cased in clear glass and more often than not given a crimped rim (Plate 265).

Yet another variation of threading, this time in combination with enamelling, was pioneered by Stevens and Williams in 1887 (Colour Plate 41). The technique has been aptly called 'Tapestry' by collectors. The company's pattern books however show 'Tapestry' as being quite a different pattern, though the technique used to achieve the design has not been identified (Plate 253). After the bowl was threaded the enamelled flowers were painted on top to achieve the texture of woven tapestry. The painting required some skill if the colours were not to run along the channels between the threads. Enamel and gilded work at Stevens and Williams was the speciality of Oscar Pierre Erard.

Some Stevens and Williams threaded items were cut through with the intaglio wheel after the technique was introduced in 1891 by John Northwood. Other threaded vases were trailed with green glass in the same manner as Silveria or Fibrilose pieces (q.v.).

In 1905 H. Wilkinson of 10 Dennis Street, Amblecote, adjacent to the back entrance of the Thomas Webb glassworks, patented a technique using threaded glass which must have been known to nineteenth century glassmakers and which is sometimes used by studio glassmakers. A glass thread was wound on to a ribbed shape so that the threads only adhered to the tips of the ribs. By heating the glass and spinning it, the threads snapped and formed into rows of beads (Plate 265a). Wilkinson's specification states:

> My invention relates to a process by which the surface of the glass is ornamented with bead-like globules of glass. The usual method of ornamenting glass articles with beads is to put each one on separately. By my process the whole number are put on the glass at the same time. I first of all rib the glass, by the usual trade method of dipping it in a ribbed mould, 'or any mould having suitable projections', when a thread of glass, coloured or clear, is twisted round the body, or ribbed lump of glass before it is completely blown to its proper size; by the fact of the body being ribbed the thread only adheres to the rib or prominent part of the glass; I then hold the partly made article 'directly it is threaded', to melt, turning it all the time so that the thread between the parts adhering, is by centrifugal force kept away from the glass, 'or from sticking between the ribs'; I continue this heating for a short time, until the loops between the ribs melt, and separate exactly in the centre of the loop, at this period the section of the thread forming into a head will have two horn-like projections; continuing the heating and revolving the thread-like piece of the broken loop will melt back to where that section of the thread adhered to the rib, and form itself into a perfect bead by molecular attraction; this same process is going on all over the article, or wherever the glass was threaded; the article can be blown and shaped into any design after the process of forming the bead is finished. By using a hollow thread I obtain a hollow bead; in the same way a fancy thread makes a fancy bead; and the size of the bead depends on the size of the thread.

PULL-UP DECORATION
Technological innovation was the hallmark of the Stourbridge glassmakers in the

Colour Plate 27. Five examples of machine threaded decoration showing the inventiveness of the Victorian glassmaker. Left to right. Jewelled vase by Stevens and Williams, c.1886, height 5in. (12.5cm). Vase trailed with white over vertical bands of red and white, Hodgetts, Richardson and Son, c.1878, height 8¾in. (22.3cm). Bowl, late 19th century, height 2⅜in. (6cm). Jug threaded with clear glass and applied with a blue collar, Hodgetts, Richardson and Son, c.1880, height 9in. (23cm). Mug with double trail of red glass, Hodgetts, Richardson and Son, c.1880, height 4¾in. (12cm).

late 1870s and 1880s. Foremost among the pioneers of new techniques was John Northwood. After reviving the cameo glass tradition virtually singlehanded, and moving to Stevens and Williams as Artistic Director, Northwood delighted in inventing new machinery. His pull-up machine took the idea of threading one stage further by concentrating on the patterns into which the threads could be pulled. Unfortunately Northwood's machine, like so many others throughout the glass trade, has not survived, but his patent registration for it on 20 February 1885 contains a diagrammatic cross-section (Plate 266), and the following text:

Ornamenting glass articles in the process of manufacture, with threaded designs.
A cylinder A, divided into two parts and hinged in order to allow the insertion of

Colour Plate 28. 'Osiris' vases and bowls in Stevens and Williams pull-up technique patented by John Northwood I in 1885 and in full production in 1886-7. Heights, left to right: front row, 5⅛in. (13cm), 3½in. (8.7cm), 2⅜in. (6cm), 5½in. (14cm); back row, 10in. (25.5cm), 9¾in. (25cm), 6in. (15cm). Michael Parkington Collection.

the glass, is fixed over a hole in a bed of iron etc. I. In the interior of the cylinder are fixed a number of saw-toothed blades; between these are slots in which are inserted other similar blades H having longer teeth, and resting on the disc E attached to the screw D working through guides K on the cross-bar C and actuated by the hand-wheel F. The workman inserts the glass (previously threaded) on the blowpipe N, closes the cylinder by the handles M and catch L, and blows to expand the metal; the hand-wheel F is then turned rapidly, and the toothed blades rise and form a festoon design on the article.

In his book about his father John Northwood II expanded on the working of the machine:

John made a kind of circular mould composed of flat steel blades with their edges pointed to the centre, these thin blades having their edges made like a saw with sharp points. Every alternate blade was of a movable type, the other being fixed.

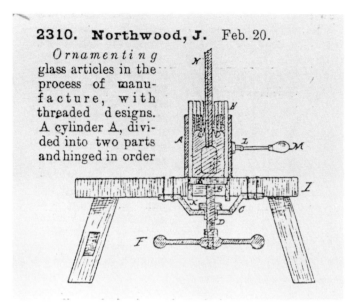

2310. **Northwood, J.** Feb. 20.

Ornamenting glass articles in the process of manufacture, with threaded designs. A cylinder A, divided into two parts and hinged in order

Plate 266. Design for the pull-up machine patented by John Northwood I in 1885.

The movable ones were connected at their base to a threaded iron upright spindle, which, by a hand wheel underneath, forced these blades upwards. The machine stood upon a low bench about 12 inches from the floor so that this hand wheel could be operated. To use it — first the workman got the body of the article he was making covered with the horizontal threads and then whilst hot and pliable he placed it in this mould and proceeded to blow it up larger until the surface with the threads on pressed up against the points of the saw edged blades, then the handwheel underneath was operated by a boy; the movable blades pulled up the part of the threads they were engaged with while the fixed blades kept the other of the threads in a stationary position. When the body of the article came out of the mould it had the threads in a 'V' shape from the top of the article to the bottom.

It is interesting to note in the original specification that it was the long-toothed blades which were responsible for pulling up the threads; the extra tooth length presumably guaranteed the threads would be pulled up the full length and maintain their definition. Once the cylindrical trailed gather had been processed it received the final blowing and shaping. The first recorded pull-up examples appear in the Stevens and Williams pattern books exactly a year after Northwood's patent was registered, suggesting a number of production problems. By February of 1887 dozens of pull-up shapes appear in the books. Inscribed next to the first of the 1887 designs, at pattern number 12238, was the chosen title for the range, Osiris (Plate 267).

The superb quality of Osiris pull-up can be seen in seven examples from the Michael Parkington collection (Colour Plate 28). Each piece has a contrasting interior colour on to which the second layer was cased and the threads wound on. The majority of pieces have a silky smooth finish obtained by acid. Rare examples were cased in clear glass, often trapping air bubbles where the saw points had dug in. Examples are almost always marked on the base with the word PATENT raised in the original glass surface which has been removed elsewhere by the satin acid finish. Many pieces also received crimped rims on machines invented by Northwood. One vase in the Michael Parkington collection was blown into a ribbed mould to produce a high relief, horizontal zig-zag effect.

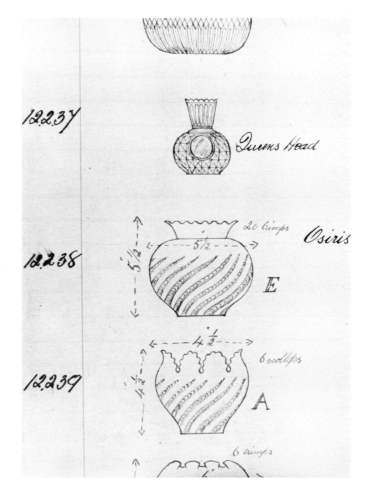

Plate 267. Page from the Stevens and Williams pattern books showing the first designs for pull-up decoration vases known as 'Osiris', dated 1887. Royal Brierley Crystal.

Before any piece of Osiris was started careful decisions had to be taken about the size of the cylinder to fit the pull-up machine, the positioning of the horizontal threads on that cylinder and the amount of pull-up to give those threads, all of which would affect the final appearance of the piece. For example, to achieve the long thin 'fingers' of coloured threads on some of the pieces, the horizontal threads would have been placed very low down on the master cylinder, the blades pulling them up almost the entire length of the cylinder. On other examples where the entire vase is covered the cylinder had to be threaded completely and the knife blades only given a fraction of a turn on the hand-wheel to result in a shallow 'V' formation.

A SELECTION OF TECHNIQUES FROM STEVENS AND WILLIAMS

Silveria

About 1900 Stevens and Williams developed a range of glassware which was given the name Silveria and involved trapping a layer of silver foil between two layers of clear glass (Colour Plate 29). In conversations with Albert C. Revi in 1956 John Northwood II, who masterminded the technique, remembered that his father had been present at the glasshouse when the trials were carried out,

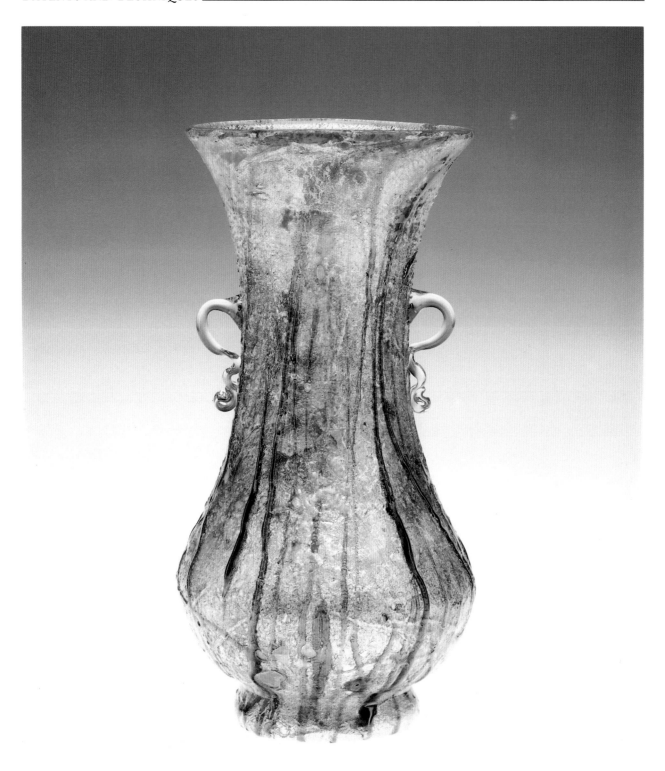

Colour Plate 29. 'Silveria' vase with green applied handles, Stevens and Williams, c.1900, height 14¼ in. (36cm). 'Silveria' is one of the most beautiful and sought after of all Stevens and Williams products; the size of this vase makes it especially rare. Michael Parkington Collection.

Colour Plate 30. Under the management of Joseph Silvers Williams and with the artistic directorship of John Northwood I, the firm of Stevens and Williams created some of the finest art glass of the late 19th century. Left to right. Bowl with open trellis work, pattern no. 7922 October/November 1882, height 2 ¾ in. (7cm). Bowl, cream coloured glass body applied with clear glass tubes, cased with a heat sensitive glass shading to red, and applied with 'Mat-Su-No-Ke' flowers and branches, and finally given a satin finish by acid, c.1885, height 5 ½ in. (14cm). Vase in moss agate, c.1888, height 5 ¼ in. (13.3cm). 'Fibrilose' vase, c.1900, height 12 ¼ in. (31cm), Private Collection. Flower vase with Rd. No. 55693, patented on 6 September 1886, for ornamentation using threading over dip moulding which was then cased with crystal, height 12in. (30.5cm), Michael Parkington Collection.

offering advice and encouragement. The idea of trapping gold or silver foil between two layers of glass is as old as glassblowing itself and is found on bowl fragments and portrait medallions of the second to fourth centuries A.D. in the Roman Empire. In the late nineteenth century a number of Stourbridge firms had produced their versions of the idea. Edward Webb at the White House Glass Works named his versions 'Argentine', 'Oroide' and 'Titania', while Joseph

Webb at the nearby Coalbourn Hill Glass Works developed a 'New Gold Glass' which was described in the *Pottery Gazette* in March 1883.

Silveria differed from its competitors in that the silver foil remained intact throughout the making rather than breaking up into fragments. The secret of the technique was to blow the first bubble of clear glass to the full size of the required object. The silver foil would be placed on the marver and picked up on to the hot glass. No further blowing took place in order to maintain the solid sheet of silver but the next problem was to case it in clear glass. It has been suggested that the bubble with its layer of silver was dipped into a pot of clear glass to make the covering. The problem with that process was the possibility of the silver being pulled off the original bubble. The solution was probably to blow a second bubble of clear glass, apply it to the base of the first bubble, crack it off and fold it over on to the silver, thereby giving a thin casing of clear which prevented any oxidation of the metal foil. At this stage of the process the glass would be rolled in ground glass colours to produce the subtle shades of blue, pink, yellow and green which create the characteristic shimmering effect of Silveria. The final steps were to shape the glass, apply the green glass fibrilose trails over the body and add any extras such as handles if it was felt necessary. One rare vase in the Broadfield House Glass Museum collections has been further decorated with applied flowers in clear, blue and red. Made for only a very short period, Silveria is one of the most beautiful and sought after of all Stevens and Williams products. Artistically it is reminiscent of the abstract effects achieved by Claude Monet in his later water-lily paintings.

Fibrilose

The green glass decoration which was one of a number of elements in Silveria glass was used as a separate technique on vases, bowls, jugs and decanters. The patent was registered as number 366502 on 20 November 1900 (Colour Plate 30).

Moss Agate

Another glass which utilised the idea of trapping different elements was 'Moss Agate', a deliberate and very successful attempt to imitate the actual mineral (Colour Plate 30). The effect of imitation stone in glass was achieved in the early 1880s by the French glassmakers Eugène Rousseau and Eugène Leveillé. At Stevens and Williams John Northwood I put his version into production about 1888 in shapes which are said to have been designed by Frederick Carder before his move to the United States. The exact method of manufacture has not been recorded and today there are two schools of thought regarding the process. In his book *Nineteenth Century Glass* Albert Revi suggests that a thin bubble of soda glass was blown and cased with a thick layer of lead glass. The bubble was then rolled on the marver to pick up the coloured glass which gave the striations. The colour was trapped by another layer of lead glass. When the glass was transferred on to the pontil rod cold water was poured into the bubble to give the crackled quality on the soda glass inner casing.

The other possible method was to blow a bubble of lead glass which was dipped very quickly, while still on the blowing-iron, into a bucket of cold water. With the crackled effect on the surface of the glass, the bubble would be warmed up again and then rolled on the marver to collect the coloured glass to give the streaky effect of moss agate. The crackle and the colour were trapped at this stage by the second coating of lead glass and the glass was finally shaped and formed to the desired pattern. An examination of a number of examples of Moss Agate does not provide conclusive proof about the sequence of crackling the glass or of the soda glass interior. Apart from reducing the amount of casing required, the second method would also remove the problem of compatibility between the soda and lead glass layers. After the health scare in the winter of 1990 when scientific experiments suggested that the lead content of lead glass could leach into the contents of decanters, at least one Stourbridge factory began to experiment with the idea of using a soda glass casing inside lead glass decanters. Their initial trials revealed the extremely fine tolerances necessary if the two types of glass were to be compatible.

Crackle or Ice Glass
In the Stevens and Williams pattern books the first use of crackle or ice glass, as a decorative technique in its own right, was recorded at pattern number 4784, annotated 'Iced by Water', for a stemmed and footed bowl, made in sizes ranging from 4in. to 8in. (10.2 to 20.3cm). The approximate date is February 1877.

Silver Deposit
The combination of glass with metal became a popular decorative technique in the latter part of the nineteenth century not only in England but in Europe and the United States. Some of the processes involved blowing hot glass into pre-formed metal shapes but others, such as the silver deposit patent from Stevens and Williams, involved a type of electro-plating (Plate 209). On 9 May 1889 Oscar Pierre Erard and Benjamin John Round patented their method of electro-deposition:

> 7761. Ornamenting glass and pottery surfaces. — A flux is formed consisting of 7 parts of calcined borax, 3 of sand, 4 of lead oxide, 1 of potassium nitrate, ½ of calcium phosphate, and 2 of white arsenic, the whole being melted, washed, and ground. The flux is mixed with silver in the proportion of 4½ to 10 parts, and the whole ground together and mixed with turpentine. The article of glass, porcelain, or the like to be ornamented has the design placed on in any known manner, and the work is then painted on those parts; or the flux may be dusted on separately, and the silver mixed with turpentine placed on afterwards. In any case the article is then burned in a kiln, and, after cleaning, any desired metal is placed thereon by electrodeposition.

The purpose of the flux was not only to provide a solid ground for the deposit but also to act as a good conductor of electricity. The next stage of the process was to attach a wire to the article and suspend it in a bath containing a silver

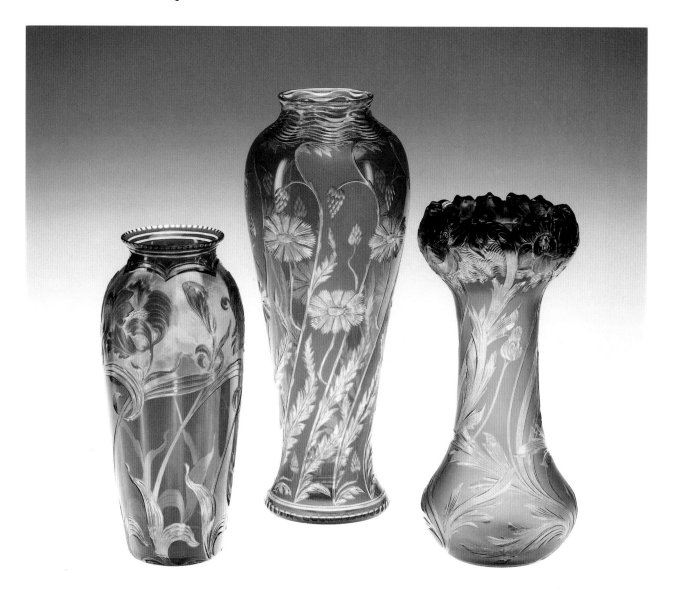

Colour Plate 31. Three masterpieces of intaglio cutting by Joshua Hodgetts at Stevens and Williams, early 20th century. The vase on the left is recorded in pattern book 34, no. 39960, 'Wallflower over citron Josh 25/- Sell 84/- 4/02/09'. In the photograph of Joshua Hodgetts (Plate 268), the vase which he is cutting is virtually identical to the green vase on the right. Another very similar vase is in the Jones Museum of Ceramics and Glass in Maine, U.S.A. Heights, left to right: 11 ½ in. (29.2cm), Hulbert of Dudley Collection; 15 ¾ in (39.8cm), Michael Parkington Collection; 12 ⅝ in. (32cm), Michael Parkington Collection.

solution. Anodes fixed inside the bath completed the circuit. A current of two volts was passed through the solution for a period of up to six hours to build up a suitable thickness of silver. On Stevens and Williams examples the silver was usually engraved with linear designs and buffed to a bright shine. Some silver deposit decoration was also carried out on ceramics at the glassworks. Two entries

Colour Plate 32. Plate, tazza and jugs with trapped enamel decoration by Richardson's of Wordsley, c.1879-80. Plate diameter 10in. (25.4cm), heights, left to right: 4¼in. (10.8cm), 9¾in. (25cm), 10in. (25.4cm).

in the pattern books, at numbers 24347 and 24348, read 'Coalport China silver deposit' and 'Rockingham Ware silver deposit' and date to the very end of 1897.

Intaglio

Intaglio is best described as a technique mid-way between copper wheel engraving and cutting. The small stone wheels on the intaglio lathe cannot reproduce the finesse and drawing-like quality of the copper wheel, yet intaglio has a greater flexibility than the geometric patterns of the traditional cutting wheel. A close examination of a standard intaglio cut will reveal a sharp edge on one side going into the surface of the glass at ninety degrees while the other edge slopes gradually upwards to the surface. Modern intaglio floral patterns will often have parts of the flower left in the original matt finish whereas nineteenth century intaglio was invariably polished. In the trade the process is referred to as 'tag'.

In the modern day glass factories in Stourbridge, the use of intaglio cutting has superseded copper wheel engraving and totally reversed the proportions which were the norm in 1890. At that date John Northwood I, in his position as Artistic Director, was still operating his etching and engraving works in Barnett Lane in Wordsley which had doubled as the cameo workshop for Stevens and Williams. The reduction in orders for cameo glass forced Northwood to look at alternative forms of decoration which would allow him to maintain his work-force in employment at both the workshop and the factory. Some form of cutting effect was considered which would complement the etched designs and led to the idea of using small stone cutting wheels which were fixed on to the copper wheel lathes. Although the machinery was not robust enough to take the heavier wheels the teething problems were overcome in the Barnett Lane workshop and the method was given the name 'stone-engraving'. However, the foot treadle operated lathes could not provide adequate speed and power for the deeper cuts and eventually sturdier equipment was developed which set the pattern for the standard intaglio lathe used today. A system of cone drives on the new lathes allowed the cutter to adjust the drive belt quickly and easily to give the desired speed to the wheel. Unlike the copper wheel lathe, in which the wheels are soldered to the spindle, the intaglio lathe had a fixed spindle and separate wheels with uniform threads.

From July 1892, when the combination of etching and intaglio first appears in the Stevens and Williams pattern books, intaglio decoration became as important to the company as cameo had been in the 1880s. Joshua Hodgetts, who had shown an aptitude for the new technique, became head of the intaglio department (Plate 268). Although Hodgetts had been a very capable cameo carver (Colour Plate 17, extreme left), his intaglio work on clear, and cased and coloured glasses resulted in some of the most elegant, stylish and sophisticated designs ever to come out of the Stourbridge district. During the mid- to late 1890s the exquisite nature of Stevens and Williams colours is recorded in the pattern books with entries such as 'new blue opalescent', 'new blue opaline', 'topaz cased', 'heliotrope cased', 'ruby cased', 'ruby over topaz' and 'amethyst over crystal'. It was on to these colours that Hodgetts and his team applied the classic intaglio decoration of swirling leaves and flowers (Colour Plate 19, right). About 1900, designs at the factory became heavily influenced by the art nouveau style. Rock crystal glass patterns were the first to alter but it was with the work of Hodgetts that the company outstripped its competitors. The sensitivity of the colour combinations and the virtuosity of the intaglio cutting found their perfect expression in the free-flowing art nouveau style (Colour Plate 31).

Trapped Enamel Decoration

In 1916 the Orrefors factory in Sweden developed the technique of Graal glass which involved reheating a carved cameo blank and trapping the cameo decoration under a layer of clear glass. Orrefors hailed the idea as revolutionary but Stourbridge had already patented the idea of reheating glass, at least for enamel glass, nearly forty years earlier. On 16 December 1879 Henry Gething Richardson filed a patent for trapping enamelled decoration between two layers

Plate 268. Joshua Hodgetts at work on the intaglio lathe carving a vase very similar to one in Colour Plate 31, early 20th century.

of glass:

> The design etc. is painted etc. in enamel colours etc. on the inside of a thin flint-glass vessel, which has a wide open mouth and is preferably of the same shape as the required vase etc. When the colours have set, the vessel is heated, and a hot opal etc. glass vessel, supported on a blowing iron, is introduced there, and — by blowing — is caused to expand, till the two vessels combine and enclose the design etc. and the produced vase etc. is then shaped by heating etc. and finished. Distortion in the design is prevented by making the expansible parts thereof proportionally less, and the contractible parts correspondingly larger. Or the design may be painted etc. on the outside of a glass vessel etc. which is heated and attached to a blowing-iron, and upon which heated flint etc. glass is gathered, so as to enclose the design; the vessel etc. is then shaped as required by blowing etc. The enamel colours etc. employed may be applied by a brush, by transfers, or by stencilling etc.

Four glasses in this technique have survived in the Richardson collection at Broadfield House Glass Museum. These may have been kept by the family since the time they were made (Colour Plate 32). The difficulties inherent in the various stages of this technique are enormous and would involve many experiments and trials, especially with the enamel colours which can alter hue or disappear totally when subjected to different temperatures. The wording of the patent quickly passes over the reheating of the glass vessel after it has been enamelled but this process is one of the most difficult to control.

Colour Plate 33. Left to right. The Convolvulus vase made by H. Sutton at H.G. Richardson and Sons, 1885, height 16⅛ in. (41cm). Vase with applied strawberries, probably made at Boulton and Mills, Audnam, c.1885, height 10⅝ in. (27cm).

When glass is first made it requires gradual cooling in an annealing tunnel or lehr to remove the stresses and strains within it. Reheating multiplies those stresses and the glass takes on the properties of a time bomb which can shatter at any stage during its re-working. The breakage rate is high, as was experienced by Orrefors in their production of Graal glass. The process of casing or trapping the decoration created its own problems depending on which of the two methods was used. The first method was to blow a bubble of clear glass which could be blown either inside or over the preformed shape. Casing from the inside was marginally easier although one had to ensure that no air bubbles were trapped between the two layers. Blowing the clear glass over a preformed shape involves sticking the bubble of clear glass to the base, cutting the clear bubble off the

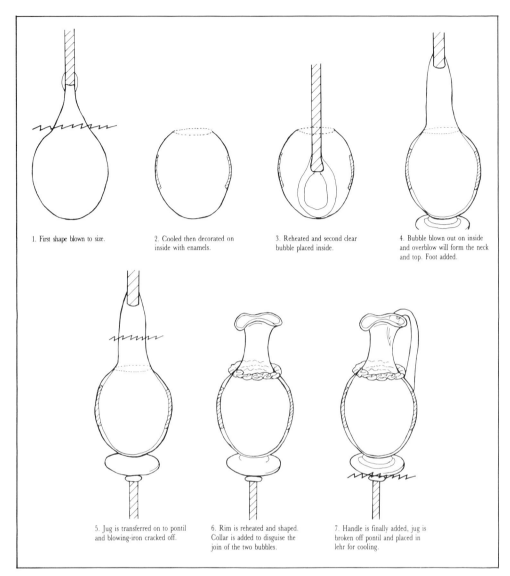

1. First shape blown to size.

2. Cooled then decorated on inside with enamels.

3. Reheated and second clear bubble placed inside.

4. Bubble blown out on inside and overblow will form the neck and top. Foot added.

5. Jug is transferred on to pontil and blowing-iron cracked off.

6. Rim is reheated and shaped. Collar is added to disguise the join of the two bubbles.

7. Handle is finally added, jug is broken off pontil and placed in lehr for cooling.

Plate 269. Stages in the manufacture of a jug with trapped enamel decoration.

blowing-iron, opening it out into a flat disc shape and gradually folding it back over on to the preformed shape. The second method, of dipping the already decorated shape into a pot of molten glass, could result in distortion of the enamel pattern while the thickness of the new layer was less controllable.

Having looked at the difficulties of the technique one can look at the jugs, for example, and see how they were constructed, stage by stage, and the reasons for the addition of the collar (Plate 269). Stage one was to shape the first clear bubble into an open-topped oval, the full size of the required final size, and allow it to cool. Once the glass was decorated on the inside, at stage 2, the oval shape would be gradually reheated. Another gather of glass, smaller than the existing oval shape, would be blown on a separate iron and pressed into the base (stage 3). The bubble would be quickly inflated and the overblow used to form the neck and lip (stage 4). The foot would be added at this point. The jug would be transferred on to the pontil rod and broken off the blowing-iron (stage 5). After reheating,

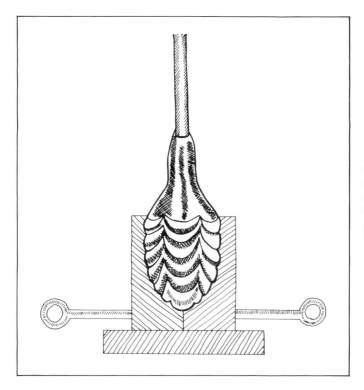

Plate 270. Using a dip mould to impart a pattern on to the molten glass, in this instance a draped effect. Based on an illustration in the Pottery Gazette *in June 1903.*

Plate 271. Group of four dip moulds, an open and shut crimping machine from Stevens and Williams, and canes used to create latticinio decoration. Photographed at the Glass Department of Stourbridge College of Art which was transferred to Wolverhampton Polytechnic in 1989.

the rim would be shaped and a collar of glass applied to disguise the ridged line of the top of the first shape (stage 6). The handle would then be applied and the jug cracked off the pontil and placed into an annealing tunnel or oven, to cool overnight. As the jug cooled in the lehr the glass was liable to crack due to the tension between the two layers.

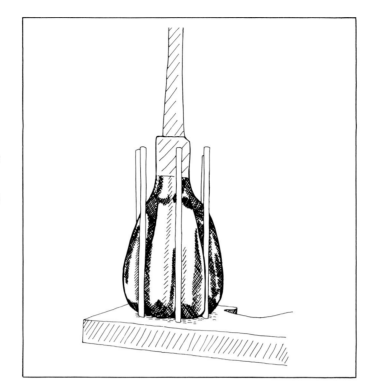

Plate 272. Blowing glass into a skeleton mould to achieve a lobed effect. Based on a photograph in 'Studio Glassmaking' by Ray Flavell and Claude Smale.

MOULDING

The invention of new moulds increased enormously from the 1870s as the glasshouse owners rivalled each other for new shapes to capture the public's imagination or to improve old processes. Most of the developments for press moulding came, as one might expect, from the North-East firms, but some interesting ideas came from the traditional hand-blown areas of the industry.

Small iron dip moulds were the simplest way of imparting a design or shape on to a hot bubble of glass (Plate 270). Four of these moulds can be seen in a photograph taken at the Stourbridge College of Art (Plate 271). The diamond or pineapple mould in the right foreground is in three, hinged parts, to allow the glass to be removed where the design is undercut. A bubble of glass blown into this mould and cased with another layer of clear glass would result in rows of trapped air bubbles. Rib moulds, used to impart a vertical rib pattern, were also used to make canes with opaque twist patterns. Thin, white or coloured canes were placed inside the vertical grooves of the rib mould. Hot glass on the end of the blowing-iron was pushed into the mould to pick up the canes on to the cylinder of hot glass. The canes were rolled and marvered into the surface and finally drawn out to give the characteristic spiral effect. These canes could then be chopped up and used to line the rib mould again to give numerous variations on opaque twist stems. Dip moulds were often the most readily available stand on which to hold or rest the cup during the process of cup casing for cameo glass (Plate 196). Many of the moulds depended on the ingenuity of the mould maker to create the necessary equipment welded together from any available scraps of metal. One of the simplest was the skeleton mould, formed of metal rods driven into a wooden or metal base (Plate 272). The lobed effect produced by this mould

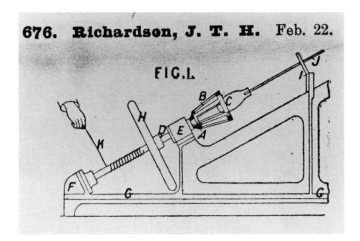

Plate 273. Design for the rubbing mould machine patented by J.T.H. Richardson in 1873.

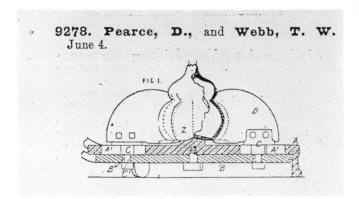

Plate 274. Design for a machine to give a double gourd shape to the glass, patented by Daniel Pearce and Thomas Wilkes Webb in June 1889.

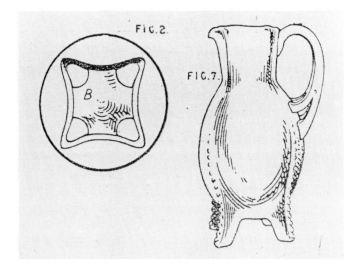

Plate 275. Designs from an 1894 patent specification by Lionel Pearce to produce feet and handles by the use of moulds.

was used for some rock crystal glass at the very end of the nineteenth century as it gave a ribbed or pillared effect similar to cut pillars but without incurring the time and costs of the cutting shop.

An unusual piece of equipment known as the revolving rubbing mould was patented by J.T.H. Richardson of the Tutbury Glassworks on 22 February 1873 (Plate 273). It related to:

> the manufacture of tumblers, goblets and other glass articles. The glass is blown on a tube J which is then placed on guides I on the frame G, and moved slowly downwards to bring the bubble into a 'rubber' formed with a base A fixed to a shaft D, and with fixed or movable bars B united by a rim C. The shaft D is then caused to rotate by sharply pulling a cord or strap K coiled upon it. A flywheel H mounted on the shaft serves, by its impetus to re-wind the cord K. The bars of the rubber are made of graphite, carbon, etc. and may be straight, spiral etc. in shape provided that in revolving they describe the contour of the vessel to be formed. The shaft may be horizontal or inclined and the apparatus is mounted on wheels to facilitate removal. Motion may be given to the rubber by any suitable means.

One example of this machine, missing its 'rubber' part, is in the collections at Broadfield House Glass Museum. Unfortunately there are no records of how successful it was in operation.

In June of 1889 Daniel Pearce and Thomas Wilkes Webb took out a patent for shaping double gourd vases which appear in cameo or ivory versions in the Webb's pattern books (Plate 274). The design stated that:

> Glass articles having a series of bulges are produced by shaping the roughly-formed article Z by means of thin templets [*sic*] D, provided with serrated wavy or other suitably-shaped edges. The templets are secured to slides C, which are caused to travel along radial slots A1 in a table A, by means of a rotating disc B, provided with slots B1 inclined to the slots A1, through which pass the pins C1 secured to the slides.

In 1894 Lionel Pearce invented a mould which allowed the feet of glasses to be made at the same time as the article was blown (Plate 275). On pieces made in this way, the solid feet merge into the body without any mould marks. The specification was for:

> Moulding jugs, decanters, glasses, wine glasses, vases etc. Consists in making the moulds B, Fig. 2, for blown glass-ware, with depressions in the bottom in order to form feet in one with the article produced. Handles as shown in Fig. 7 are formed with projections at one end by the use of moulds with corresponding depressions and are fixed on to the article in the usual way.

CRIMPED DECORATION

Crimping, or scalloping as it was sometimes known, became a popular way of treating the rims of every type of glassware from about 1874 onwards. A note by the side of designs for 'Bouquet holders, frilled feet' in the Stevens and Williams pattern books, dated 26/7/74, mentions 'machine frill' for the first time. Crimping machines speeded up the manual process and became incredibly varied to cater for every type of pattern. The crimping operation, which is the final stage in the making of a glass, may seem fairly simple but it requires a skilled workman to be able to crimp an article properly. The trick is to drop the article centrally on to the crimper, otherwise the crimped edge will be wider on one side than the

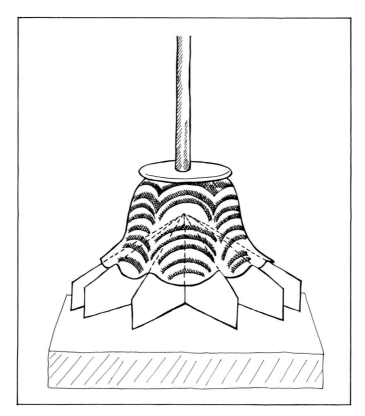

Plate 276. Using an arrangement of radiating metal plates to obtain a crimped effect on the rim of a bowl. Based on an illustration in the Pottery Gazette *in June 1903.*

other. In order to be able to gauge the centre of a crimp mould accurately the glassmaker would mark the centre of the mould with a piece of white glass or with a chalk mark. The white mark was easy to spot when the glassmaker had suddenly to turn away from the bright light of the glory-hole, where the piece was reheated, in order to drop the hot glass on the crimper. The simplest equipment consisted of a set of upright metal plates radiating from a central point upon which the rim of the glass would be pushed. If the glass was hot enough, it would sag by its own weight between the strips of metal, leaving the crimped points resting on the top edges of the metal plates (Plate 276).

One of the many variations and developments of the basic equipment was patented by John Northwood on 1 February 1884 (Plate 277):

> For crimping or scalloping articles, guide pieces A, A of wire etc. are fixed at an angle of about 60 degrees to a board or suitable base B in a circle. These are inclined alternately in opposite directions, so that when the glass vessel, having a plain top of suitable diameter, is heated and pressed on the crimper, the action of the pieces A produces the scalloped effect.

When a finer ruffled effect was required the crimper needed to be made of iron and able to open and shut (Plate 278). The teeth in the bottom part of the crimper corresponded to the grooves between the teeth in the two movable upper halves producing a fine crimped edge on the flattened rim of the glass. A crimping machine from the Stevens and Williams factory shows one of the many variations of an open and shut mould (Plate 271, left). The wavy rims made by these pieces

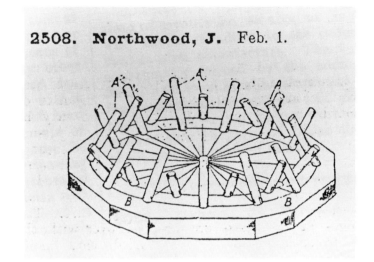

Plate 277. Design for a crimping mould patented by John Northwood I in February 1884.

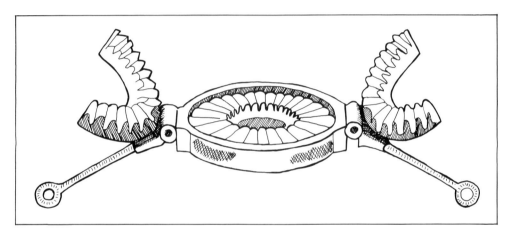

Plate 278. An open and shut crimping mould, based on an illustration in the Pottery Gazette in June 1903.

of equipment were termed single crimps. Double crimps were the more complicated profiles in which the glass was crimped first in one of the open and shut variety of crimp moulds, and then, while still soft, was dropped on to the basic pattern of plates or rods to give a broader, wavy effect. Both types of crimp moulds are still in constant use at the Fenton Glassworks in West Virginia for crimping the rims of their Silver Crest and other ranges (Plates 279 and 280).

The Fenton crimp moulds are placed on the floor of the glassworks next to the glassmaker's chair. The open and shut type of mould is operated by foot, the operation taking only two or three seconds to complete. A foot-operated example described as a 'New Glass Crimping Machine' in the *Pottery Gazette* in November 1886 was invented by William Leighton Jr. of Wheeling, West Virginia (Plate 281). The design of the inner former and the movable crimping 'fingers' allowed more of the glass vessel to be shaped at the same time as the crimp was applied.

Crimped tops could also be formed without the use of moulds if the glass was first blown into a vertical ribbed mould. From that process the ribs would have

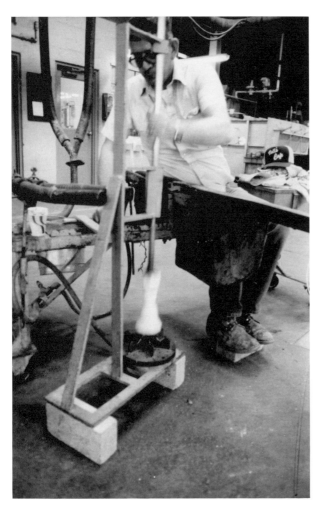

Plate 279. Crimping glass at the Fenton Glassworks in West Virginia, 1985.

Plate 280. Using a foot-operated open and shut crimping mould at the Fenton Glassworks in 1985.

a greater thickness of glass which would keep their shape longer. After reheating, the glass would be given a 'slight toss with the edge downwards'. The thin parts of the glass would fall inwards and form a very similar pattern to that produced on the single crimp mould.

CUTTING OFF MACHINES

Until the nineteenth century all rims of hand-blown glassware, such as wineglasses and tumblers, were sheared by hand, reheated and finished off to leave a nicely rounded rim. The modern process of cutting off dispenses with hand-shearing and relies on machines to cut off the overblow left after the bowl of the glass has been blown-moulded. The date of the introduction of the process is much earlier than is generally thought. The first patent was registered by Thomas George Webb, of the Molineaux Webb factory in Manchester, on 27 November 1868, and stated that 'the article is generally cut cold, and the

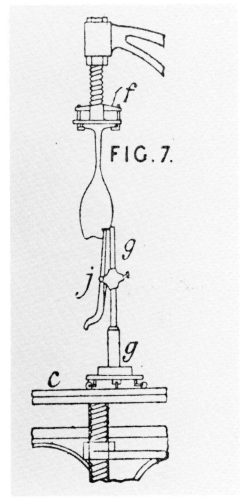

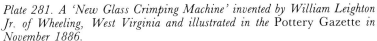

Plate 281. A 'New Glass Crimping Machine' invented by William Leighton Jr. of Wheeling, West Virginia and illustrated in the Pottery Gazette *in November 1886.*

Plate 282. Design for a cutting off machine patented by J.T.H. Richardson in February 1869.

operation may be performed after it has been separated from the blowing-iron. The cut edges are afterwards glazed by heat'.

In his patent of 26 February 1869, J.T.H. Richardson placed the glass upside down in the machine and foreshadowed the modern day practice which allows the cut-off waste to drop straight into a container and be removed for use as cullet (Plate 282). A diamond point cut the bowl of the wineglass on the inside while two small horizontal wheels revolved in the same position on the outside of the glass. According to a writer in the *Pottery Gazette* in 1884, Belgian factories used the process on cheap wineglasses which could be turned out much more quickly than if they were hand-sheared.

FURNACE APPLIED DECORATION

As the name suggests, this type of applied work was performed in front of the furnace while the glass was in a molten state. By the mid-1880s the skills were used, especially in Stourbridge, with total self-confidence, born of absolute control of the material.

The most staggering example of technical perfection, if not perhaps to modern aesthetic tastes, is the Convolvulus vase (Colour Plate 33). Two letters in the *Pottery Gazette* of 1897 have provided a date and maker for the vase. In June 1897 a writer with the *nom de plume* of Aurora sent the following letter, illustrated with a line drawing of the vase, to the Editor:

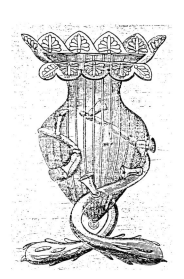

> Sirs, — Enclosed herewith I beg to hand you a rough sketch of a vase which is worthy of reproduction in your pages, and the original of which I feel sure should find a place in the Kensington Museum, or other places where 'Art' is recognised. Who has not heard of the famous 'Portland Vase' which has been exhibited far and wide? I feel sure that the artistic merit of the vase now illustrated would be as fully recognised and appreciated as the above, were its existence more fully known. I was in Stourbridge and called by chance upon the maker of this vase; we casually got into conversation and he showed it to me; I immediately felt that it was in its wrong place and decided to inform you of its existence. My sketch will not at all give you an adequate idea of the beauty of this specimen of 'Stourbridge art'; it is also unique, inasmuch as there is not another like it. As you will see, it is an egg-shaped body, round which three sprays are run, forming the tripod upon which the vase rests. Upon the sprays are stuck in a very natural manner convolvuli. Round the top two rows of leaves. It is a citron-coloured body, and the whole is oxided over giving it a pretty effect. It stands about 12 inches high and weighs about 11lbs. I called this vase the 'Convolvulus Vase', from the flowers by which it is decorated. We are taught to appreciate Venetian art glass, Bohemian ware, and other like things, whilst we do not fully recognise that 'Art' lies hidden in the most unlooked for places at home. I feel I cannot myself speak or describe to you the merits in this vase, but trust by bringing it to your notice you will be enabled to become acquainted with the same, when I am sure you will agree with me that really art of the highest merit still exists amongst the workers of the Stourbridge glass trade.
>
> Brierley Hill   Yours, &c.,
> May 11.   Aurora

Fortunately for glass history the hitherto mysterious glassmaker identified himself when he replied to Aurora's letter in the August issue of the same year:

> Sirs, — I thank you for the copy of the June issue of the Pottery Gazette which you kindly sent me containing a description and drawing of a vase in my possession. I beg to enclose you herewith a photo of same. The vase stands a little over sixteen inches high, and was made by me twelve years ago, at the works of Messrs. H.G. Richardson & Sons, at Wordsley. The feet and stems which support and encircle the base are crystal, the flowers (convolvulus) pink inside and opal outside and the body of the vase straw colour and opal inside with ribs from top to bottom; it is all in one piece, and has not been treated with acid or anything else in any way; it is entirely my own design and workmanship. The weight of the vase is 12 to 14lbs.
>
> Acorn Inn,   Yours, &c.
> Brettell Lane,   H. Sutton
> July 17.

Plate 283. Basket in cream glass cased over pink with applied amber coral-type handle and feet, possibly Boulton and Mills, Audnam, mid-1880s. Height 7in. (18cm). Hulbert of Dudley Collection.

Most factories in the Stourbridge district made their own versions of furnace applied decoration from the mid-1880s onwards. A ruby vase applied with lush strawberries (Colour Plate 33) bears a close similarity to a bowl still displayed in the Jaylynne cutting shop in Audnam run by the Hand family. Family tradition has it that the bowl was made at the Boulton and Mills factory by Mr Hand's grandfather and carried in a glass procession about 1890. Boulton and Mills were situated opposite the present site of the Jaylynne works. Although the Boulton and Mills factory was one of the more important glassworks in the area in the nineteenth century few records exist to allow exact identification of its products. A pattern book, illustrating engraved and etched jugs and goblets, flower stands and vases exists in the Broadfield House Glass Museum collections, but little is known of their coloured glass. The company's advertisements in the *Pottery Gazette* offer some tantalising names of as yet unidentified products. In 1886 they advertised themselves as the 'Original Makers of the Celebrated Old Gold and Crackled Primrose Glass'. Two years later they claimed to be 'Sole Makers of the new Patent "Nacre De Perle" Glass'. In February 1887 their specialities for the season were 'Autumnal Tinted Cameo', 'Algerine', 'Tunisian' and 'Verre D'Iris'. Local tradition maintains that the company specialised in opaque coloured, furnace applied decoration (Plate 283) and certainly the one or two

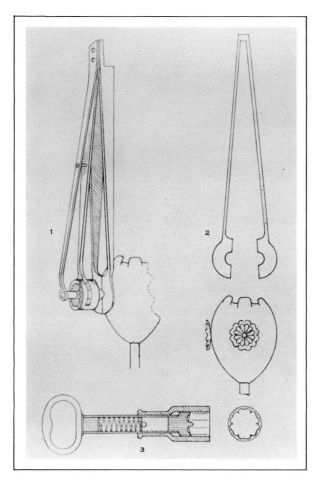

Plate 284. Spring pincers and a stamping device patented by John Northwood I in 1885.

Plate 285. 'Mat-Su-No-Ke' vase, shading from cream to brown, on a clear rusticated base, decorated with applied flowers using the spring pincers patented by Northwood, c.1885. Height 5in. (12.7cm).

items which have been traced in private collections in the area underline this theory.

In 1885, at Stevens and Williams, John Northwood I patented a set of spring pincers and a stamping device (Plate 284) which allowed for the quick application of flowers and rosettes, notably on the 'Mat-Su-No-Ke' vases and bowls. Influenced by Japanese decorative styles, the name translates as 'The Spirit of the Pine Tree' (Colour Plate 30, top left, and Plate 285). The pincers ensured that the applied flowers were held away from the surface of the glass giving a more natural and lifelike effect. John Northwood II described the technique as follows:

a boy brought a small quantity of hot glass to the maker who then stuck it on the branch of the spray where required, and then the boy, using the simple two-armed pincer [Plate 284, 2] pressed it together round the small lump, of hot glass and held it there whilst the workman, using the three-pronged pincers [Plate 284, 1], squeezed the two bottom prongs together round the small piece of hot glass and then pressed the third prong carrying the core, down into the die of the two, and so shaped the blossom. Several of these blossoms would be placed on one branch to

Plate 286. Vase in opaque white glass with a clear trailed, crimped rim, the body applied with leaves and flowers, the stems forming the feet, and with enamelled floral decoration. Engraved mark 'S & W' for Stevens and Williams, mid to late 1880s. Height approximately 12in. (30.5cm). Canadian Museum of Civilisation, Ottawa.

complete the design. The dies and core could be changed on the pincers to give various shaped flowers.

The stamping device (Plate 284, 3) was a mechanised version of the stamp or seal which was used to apply raspberry prunts on to glass.

The improvised nature of applied decoration meant that the details were not recorded in the pattern books of the companies. At Stevens and Williams only the outline of the glass was drawn. It is difficult therefore to give precise attributions to a great deal of furnace applied decoration. The problem is further complicated by the emigration of British glassmakers to the United States where they would have continued the same traditions and techniques. One Stevens and Williams vase (Plate 286) in the collections of the Canadian Museum of Civilisation, could have been attributed to a number of factories either side of the Atlantic, if it were not for the signature.

A popular pattern with many factories was the applied acanthus leaf. In the Stuart archive one page illustrates the use of the leaf, either as ornament or doubling as a foot, in combination with threading and crimping (Plate 287). On rare occasions it is possible to find a match for a design (Plate 288).

Within this category of furnace applied decoration one can also place a wide variety of glasses which use the simple technique of picking up colours or glass fragments from the marver and either rolling them into the surface or trapping

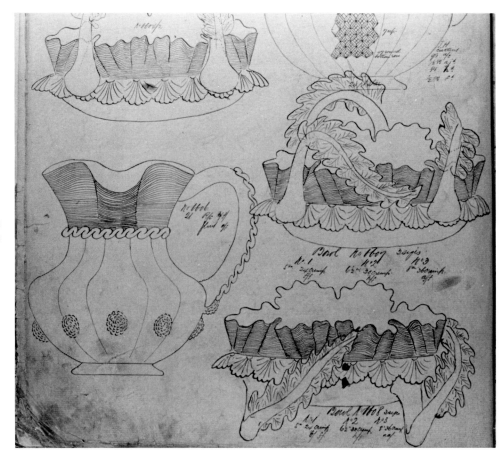

Plate 287. Page from the Stuart and Sons pattern books showing bowls with applied acanthus leaves on threaded and pincered decoration. Stuart Crystal.

Plate 288. A bowl matching one in Plate 287, c.1887. Height 3¾ in. (9.5cm). Private Collection.

Plate 289. Vase in white glass with applied 'Peloton' decoration of multi-coloured strips of glass, possibly English, 1880s. Height 4 ⅜ in. (11 cm).

them between extra layers. In the early part of the century the idea was used on the so-called 'Nailsea' or Wrockwardine jugs and bowls of dark green glass, 'splashed' with white, red and blue fragments. In the latter part of the century factories in Europe and the United States produced a dazzling array of variations.

The 'Peloton' technique involved picking up random strips of coloured glass from the marver (Plate 289). The piece could then be shaped, blown into dip moulds and crimped. One patent for Peloton was taken out on 25 October 1880 by Wilhelm Kralik of the Harrach glassworks in Bohemia.

The effect of tortoiseshell was achieved in a similar manner and was patented in England on 25 October 1880 by F. Pohl and S.A. Wittmann:

> Ornamenting glass in imitation of tortoiseshell. Bulbs of dark and light brown glass are blown, and broken into fragments. A bulb of plain glass is then blown, and its top is cut off from the part which adheres to the blowpipe. Another bulb is rolled while hot in the fragments of brown glass, and, with these adhering to it, is inserted in the cut-off portion, and the two are blown together. The whole is reheated, swung, drawn out, and formed into articles. These are then coated with solution of silver chloride and yellow ochre or other materials for producing a yellow stain, and are afterwards fired.

Other variations were called Spangled glass by the Hobbs, Brockunier company in the United States; Blue Nugget, a type of spangled glass made by Sowerby; and Spatterglass by J.S. Irwin in Pennsylvania. William Webb Boulton of the Boulton and Mills factory patented his version on 25 January 1879:

> 314. Coloured glasses or enamels, powdered or crushed, are spread on an iron slab, and the glass surface to be ornamented is rolled in this powder while in a plastic or semi-molten state, so that the coloured particles adhere and spread a little on the surface. A thin layer of flint glass may be afterwards attached to the ornamented surface. A cracked appearance may be produced on it by plunging in water. Glass so ornamented may be blown, moulded, pressed, cut, &c. as usual. Flower vases, lamp reservoirs, chandelier bodies, &c. may be ornamented in this way, as well as sheets, slabs, or blocks of glass, The coloured particles may be arranged in stripes or other patterns.

The term 'End of Day' glass has become commonplace in the antiques trade for most of the spangled or mottled glasses. The suggestion that they were made at the end of the working day to use up the unwanted glass is erroneous and the large number of patents for the style proves that it was a commercial line with a great number of competitors.

AIR TRAP DECORATION

The idea of trapping air between layers of glass as a form of decoration was patented by Benjamin Richardson in 1857 although as a technique it was known to glassmakers long before then. The commercialisation of the process later in the century saw the usual Victorian development given to any technique whereby every permutation of colour, shape and decoration was applied to it. All of them however, with one exception, used a combination of techniques which Richardson patented and which are discussed in 'The Richardson Dynasty' chapter. The methods involved the glassmaker's regular standby of the dip mould in combination with casing by the cup method or dipping in the pot. In his 1857 patent Benjamin Richardson used a dip mould that is known as a pineapple mould because of the rows of raised diamonds projecting inside the mould (Plate 271, bottom right). A mould of this type would have been used to obtain the honeycomb effect on the outside of the Varnish silvered wine glass cooler in Plate 260. The small gather of glass on the end of the blowing-iron is dropped into the dip mould and pressed firmly down to pick up the impression of the rows of diamonds. By then placing the gather inside a cup of hot glass the outer casing traps the air pockets made by the diamonds. Alternatively the gather can be dipped into the pot of molten glass. Both methods result in rows of small, round, evenly spaced air bubbles trapped as if by magic within the glass.

The commonest objects created by the Richardson glassmakers with this technique, and which can still be found by collectors, were small matchstick holders in the shape of a paperweight but with a hollow to take the matches. They are mainly found in clear glass and occasionally seen with an inner coloured casing, but the technique was taken no further until the 1880s.

From 1881 onwards the picture changed drastically and a flood of new patterns appeared, although the patents for them echoed Richardson's specification almost word for word. Eyecatching names were essential to sell 'novelty' goods

Colour Plate 34. Satin glass with air trap decoration was a favourite with European and English glassmakers. The three vases show the difficulties experienced by collectors in providing correct attributions. On the left, the Stevens and Williams vase, from the mid-1880s, contains an air trap pattern which is almost concealed beneath the layer of red glass, acid etched in a floral pattern, and completed by gilding. On the satin vase on the right the gilding echoes the air trap pattern between the two layers; it is attributed to Thomas Webb and Sons. The vase in the centre has usually been attributed to an unspecified English source mainly due to the mark 'Patent 9159' which appears on the base. The type was christened 'Federzeichnung' by Albert C. Revi in his book Nineteenth Century Glass. *Made by the Loetz factory in Austria in 1888, the vases were given the name 'Octopus'. Heights, left to right: 6¾in. (17cm), 11in. (27.8cm), 5¾in. (14.5cm). Michael Parkington Collection.*

and air trap became known by many different names. Boulton and Mills used 'Nacre de Perle' (1885), Stevens and Williams decided on 'Verre de Soie' (1886), Richardson's suddenly became patriotically Scottish and used 'Tartan' (1886) while Walsh Walsh chose 'Broche' (1886). In the United States trade names ranged from 'Plush', 'Pearl Satin' and 'Mother of Pearl'. Most air trap glasses at this date were given a final treatment with acid to give a delicate sheen to the surface and this was responsible for the generic name 'Satin Glass'.

The air trap patterns now consisted of a multitude of effects from horizontal

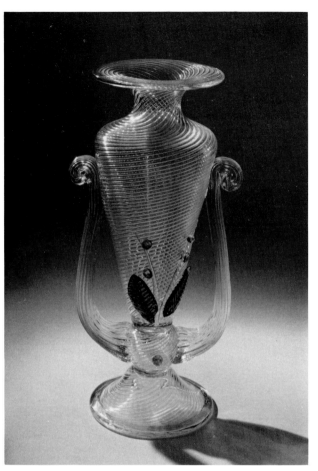

Plate 290. Vase in white glass cased with shaded blue glass with an air trap, diamond pattern, probably by Thomas Webb and Sons, 1880s. Height 8½ in. (21.5cm). Michael Parkington Collection.

Plate 291. Vase with swirling air trap decoration formed by clear glass tubes, with shell handles and applied leaves and berries, probably Stevens and Williams, 1880s. Height 10⅝ in. (27cm). Private Collection.

zig-zags or lattice diamonds to random designs which meandered through the body of the glass (Plate 290). By this date the glass bodies consisted of three or four layers of glass, each of a different colour and each doing a particular job in the overall effect. Some carried the basic body colour while the middle layers were impressed with the air trap patterns. The top layer gave the final colour. Etched cameo designs were added by the firm of Thomas Webb and Sons. Gilding and enamelling completed the exuberant effect (Colour Plate 34).

One particular range of air trap vases seen regularly in England is marked 'Patent 9159' on the base. Because of the mark the glasses have always been called English and attributed to any one of the Midland factories. With the publication in 1989 of two volumes of patterns and glassware from the factory of Loetz the vases can be definitely identified as Continental. The swirling air trap effect was called Octopus and was developed by the Austrian firm in about 1888. Cased amber over white with added gilt and enamel decoration, they were considered one of the company's prize designs and exhibited in many international exhibitions, including the Paris Exhibition of 1900 (Colour Plate 34, centre).

Plate 292. Advertisement by Haden, Mullett and Haden in the Pottery Gazette, *1 September 1925, showing the range of 'Victorian' goods still available at that date.*

The geometric and the random air traps still relied on the pattern within the dip moulds for the final effect. One other method used in England and America to achieve an air trap effect was to blow a gather of glass into a dip mould which was lined with glass tubes. The tubes were marvered into the surface of the glass and twisted to provide a spiral effect (Plate 291). The technique was a speciality at Stevens and Williams where it was cased with the sensuous colour harmonies of heat sensitive glass (Colour Plate 38, top right).

RUBY GLASS

Ruby glass, often referred to as cranberry by collectors, was made in a wide variety of shapes and in an equally wide price range (Colour Plate 35). In the Great Exhibition of 1851 Richardson's and other English firms showed ruby glass of the finest quality. Later in the century the large Stourbridge firms continued to make high quality goods in ruby glass. A jug from the Boulton and Mills factory, identified from the one surviving pattern book, is evidence of the skill expended on coloured glass in the 1880s. At the other end of the scale, the smaller factories concentrated on the cheaper end of the market and produced a huge variety of goods from posy bowls, vases, creams and sugars to the ubiquitous flower stands. Many of these trinkets normally cannot be attributed to any specific factory but a surviving pattern book from Smart Brothers of the Round Oak Glass Works shows the variety that a small company could produce (Colour Plate 36). Another important market for the lesser known firms was the production of lampshades (Colour Plate 37). On a smaller scale again were the backyard 'cribs' which melted cullet in cannon pots measuring up to 36in.

Colour Plate 35. Ruby glass was one of the most popular colours of the 19th century. In his evidence to the Commission of Enquiry into the Glass Excise in 1835, Apsley Pellatt explained that 'the copper red ruby is a very delicate colour, and requires the pot to be open or shut at the command of the manufacturer whenever he requires it; complying with the usual regulations of the Excise would prevent any chance of success'. The obsession of glassmakers prior to the 19th century to create ruby glass was dealt with in the film 'Heart of Glass' by Werner Hertzog. Left to right: Vase with turn-over, crimped rim and applied clear glass decoration, probably Stourbridge, late 19th century, height 5 ¾ in. (14.5cm). Jug with gilt panels, probably Richardson's, late 1840s, height 10 ⅜ in. (26.3cm). Wineglass cooler with pillar moulding, Apsley Pellatt, c.1845-50, height 3 ½ in. (9cm), Michael Parkington Collection. Bowl said to have been shown on the Richardson stand at the Great Exhibition 1851, height 7in. (17.7cm), diameter 11 ¾ in. (29.8cm), Private Collection. Jug with rope twist handle and fine engraved decoration, Boulton and Mills, 1880s, height 9 ½ in. (24.2cm).

(91.4cm) high and 16in. (40.6cm) in diameter, and were fired by coke. Although they were a feature of the Stourbridge district, a somewhat unusual location for them was the area around the village of Fairfield near Bromsgrove. The first crib was set up there in 1867 by James Harrop from Stourbridge and was followed by three more, one in 1880 by William Stevens, another by William Crawford, and the last one in 1895 by Thomas Evans. Products included cruets, marmalade pots, bowls, vases, cream jugs, sugar basins, and communion glasses as well as pipes, cigar holders and walking sticks. George Ernest Fox, who took over the

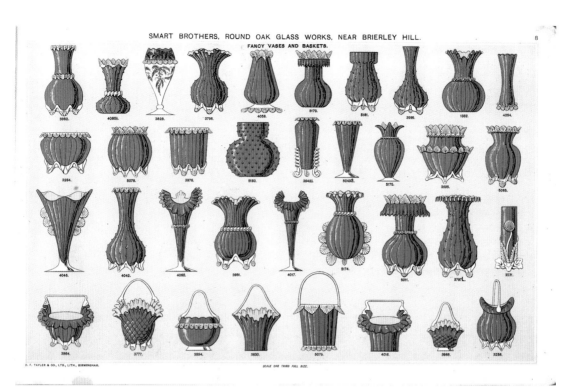

Colour Plate 36. A page from the pattern book of Smart Brothers, Round Oak Glass Works, Brierley Hill, late 19th century. This type of ruby glass, often referred to as cranberry, was made in large quantities, sometimes in backyard cribs using re-melted cullet. Page size 17in. x 11in. (43cm x 28cm). Note states 'Scale one third full size'. The pattern at top left is 2¼in. (5.5cm).

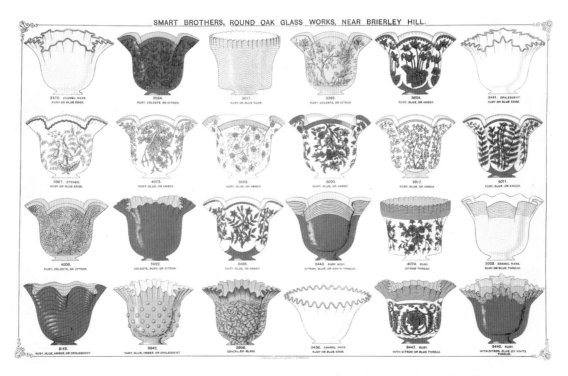

Colour Plate 37. A selection of lampshades from the pattern book of Smart Brothers, Round Oak Glass Works, Brierley Hill, late 19th century. Page size 17in. x 11in. (43cm x 28cm).

Stevens operation, supplied ruby, flint, blue and opal goods to the Stourbridge firm of Haden, Mullett and Haden as late as 1922, the year in which he died (Plate 292). The last Bromsgrove crib closed in 1925.

The ruby colour was obtained by using copper or gold in the batch mixture. There are stories of glasshouse owners throwing a gold sovereign into the molten glass to obtain the ruby colouring but this is technically impossible. The coin would simply melt and sink to the bottom of the pot. However, there seems no doubt that this piece of showmanship took place but it may have been more of a sales gimmick to encourage a potential buyer to place an order. The technical process for imparting the ruby colour required the gold to be dissolved in aqua regia or nitric acid and this solution to be mixed with the raw materials. Gold ruby results in a red that has been described as 'pigeon-blood'. For many articles the depth of colour was too strong and therefore it was cased on to clear glass to lighten the shade. All colours were a valuable commodity and, by casing the colour on to clear glass, the factory could make more items from the batch of colour. A recipe for gold ruby for casing appears in the Webb archives and shows the tiny amount of gold required to achieve the colour:

	lb.	oz.
Sand	188	
Potash	60	
*Lead Carbonate	150	
Regulus antimony	1	8
Tin oxide	1	8
White antimony oxide	1	8
Manganese dioxide	1	8
Red oxide of iron		4
Gold dissolved in 3 pints		
of nitric acid		2 ¾

* From 2 September 1901, red lead was substituted with the result that the glass was 'clearer and better'.

The ingredients had to be mixed separately to ensure a successful melting. The sand and potash were mixed together while the remaining ingredients, except the gold and the lead carbonate or red lead, were mixed in another container. The two mixes were then added to each other.

The lead carbonate or red lead was placed separately into an earthenware container. In a glass vessel the pure virgin yellow gold was added to the three pints of nitric acid and the mixture was heated until all the gold dissolved. After the gold mix cooled, a little water was added and the solution was poured on to the lead carbonate and mixed thoroughly with a wooden paddle. The mix was added to the first mix of potash, sand and other materials and the whole stirred together. The batch was now ready to be loaded into the glasshouse pot which was sealed and heated for eighteen hours. The seal was removed and the glass allowed to cool for about ten minutes, at which point the glassmakers started to gather the glass and make it into solid cylinders, 6in. (15.2cm) long and 1½in. (3.8cm) in diameter. The lumps were stored and could be reheated at any time. Writing about the Bromsgrove glassworks, the late Sir Hugh Chance stated that 'ruby melts took twenty-four hours and the glass was gathered into lumps which were passed down the lear (to "turn" the colour) and when required for ruby "flashing", suitably sized portions of the lumps were picked up on the gathering iron and covered with flint metal.'

HEAT SENSITIVE GLASS

Colour technology reached its peak in the Stourbridge district in the last quarter of the century. Thomas Webb and Sons alone introduced sixty-five separate colours between 1875 and 1898. The complete list of their colours is given in Appendix 7 supplied by Stan Eveson, with recipes for some of the colours. The addition of arsenic, uranium or gold into the batch mixture gave the molten glass the ability to shade from one colour into another when it was reheated at the glory-hole. The glassmaker controlled the precise area of the colour change by only reheating that part of the glass, while it was on the blowing-iron. The ability of the glasses to 'strike' a different colour was quickly exploited in combination with every other technique by English and American glassmakers (Colour Plate 38).

The first patent to be taken out for a heat sensitive glass was registered in America on 24 July 1883 by an expatriate Englishman, Joseph Locke. Locke had started his working life at the Royal Worcester Porcelain factory in England and moved, by way of Guest Brothers etching shop, to work at Hodgetts, Richardson glassworks in Wordsley, at a time when the factory was preparing for the 1878 Paris Exhibition. Armed with a solid background of glassmaking and decorating techniques, Locke moved to the United States in 1882 where he joined Libbey's New England Glass Company. By the following year he had patented Amberina, an amber coloured glass shading to red at the top (Colour Plate 38, top left). In 1886 Locke patented a 'Plated Amberina' which was virtually identical to the 'Peach Glass', brought out by Thomas Webb and Sons in 1885, and enhanced by the addition of gilding and enamelling (Colour Plate 38, second right). The 'Peach Blow' version made by American factories was identical to Locke's and Webb's glass in that they all used a base layer of cream coloured glass which was cased with the heat sensitive layer.

In an article entitled 'The Craze For Peach-Blows' taken from an American newspaper, the *Pottery Gazette* in August 1886 reported that:

> A new craze in glassware has been developed. As might have been expected, it is for anything in 'peach-blow' colour, caused by the public interest aroused in the celebrated vase from the Morgan collection. On the counters and shelves of glassware dealers are beginning to be seen all shades of the 'peach-blow', and it is prophesied that it will spread over nearly every article of ornamental crockery.

The Morgan vase which had inspired the new fashion in the United States was a Chinese ceramic vase, with a peach bloom colour, which had sold for a record

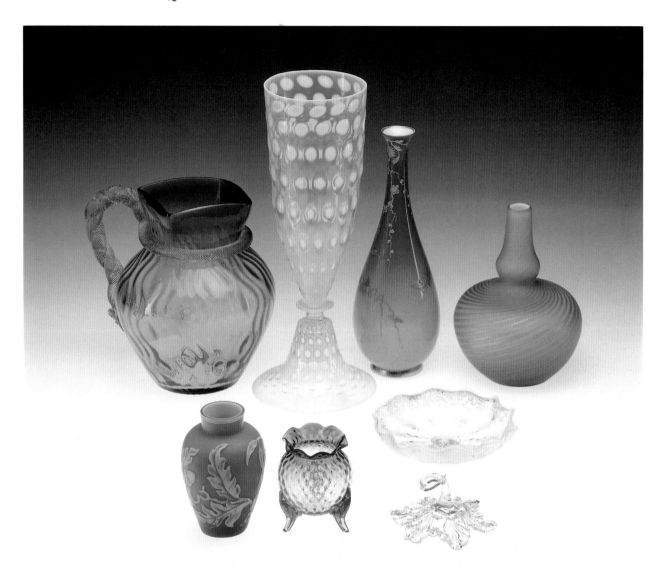

Colour Plate 38. Among the great variety of techniques exploited in the 1880s was the pioneering discovery that the addition of arsenic, uranium or gold to the batch would allow the glass to change colour when reheated. The first patent for heat sensitive glass was taken out by Joseph Locke in America in 1883 and is represented in this group by the 'Amberina' jug.

Back row, left to right. Jug, 'Amberina' glass of yellow shading to red, Libbey Glass Co., Toledo, Ohio, c.1883-4, height 7⅞in. (20cm). Vase with yellow opalescent 'raindrops', probably Richardson's, late 1880s, height 13⅛in. (33.3cm). 'Peachblow' vase, Thomas Webb and Sons, late 1880s, height 10in. (25.5cm), Private Collection. 'Verre de Soie' vase, Stevens and Williams, introduced in 1886, height 7¼in. (18.2cm), Michael Parkington Collection.

Front row, left to right. Cameo vase with shaded background, probably Thomas Webb and Sons, c.1890, height 4¼in. (10.8cm), Michael Parkington Collection. Posy vase, 'Alexandrite' glass shading from amber to ruby to purple, Thomas Webb and Sons, c.1900, height 3¼in. (8.2cm). Tazza, in yellow opalescent glass with an acid etched floral design, Stourbridge, late 19th century, height 4in. (10.3cm), Michael Parkington Collection.

price of $18,000 in a sale of Japanese and Chinese porcelains from the Mary J. Morgan Collection in Baltimore in March of 1886.

No doubt encouraged by the success of the peach-blow glass, Frederick Shirley, of the Mount Washington Glass Company and a rival of Locke, developed the

Colour Plate 39. 'Queen's Burmese Ware' by Thomas Webb and Sons, c.1886-88, decorated in the workshop of Jules Barbe. Left to right. Night-light with Clarke Fairy Light fitting, height 5¾ in. (14.5cm), Hulbert of Dudley Collection. Stand with two flower holders, height 7⅜ in. (18.7cm), Michael Parkington Collection. Vase, height 6⅛ in. (15.5cm), Michael Parkington Collection.

shaded ware known as 'Burmese'. On reheating, the yellow glass shaded to a delicate pink. In June 1886 the formula was patented in England and shortly afterwards Thomas Webb and Sons purchased the license to make it in this country. It is interesting to compare the Webb recipe for Burmese (given in Appendix 7) with Shirley's specification which was given in his original patent:

	lb.
White sand	100
Refined lead oxide	36
Pearl ash (purified potash)	25
Niter	7
Bicarbonate of soda	5
Fluorspar	6
Feldspar	5
Uranium oxide	2
	Pennyweights
Prepared gold	1½

Plate 293. Group of undecorated 'Burmese' glass by Thomas Webb and Sons, late 1880s to early 1890s. Heights: bowl with pale ribs, 3½ in. (9cm); vase with inturned and crimped rim, 4in. (10cm); night-light with Burmese base, 5¼ in. (13.5cm); stick vase, pencilled note on base 'S/R No.2927 Plain' and paper label 'Queens Burmese Ware/Thomas Webb and Sons', 6⅛ in. (15.5cm); bowl with applied collar, 2¼ in. (5.5cm). Private Collection.

Although the Webb recipe contained larger proportions of fluorspar and feldspar which would give a greater opacity, both recipes used virtually identical proportions of uranium oxide to give the yellow colour, and gold to achieve the change to red. Called 'Queen's Burmese Ware' by Webb's, it was made in a variety of shapes including night-lights and a huge array of flower vases and posy holders (Plate 293). It looked especially attractive when decorated with enamelled flowers and fruit (Colour Plate 39).

Variations on shaded wares continued to the end of the century, appearing in the blown wares of Stourbridge and in the pressed glass of Manchester and the North East. On cameo glass stunning effects were achieved by using the heat sensitive layer as background to the floral carving (Colour Plate 38, front left). Thomas Webb introduced a new shaded glass called 'Alexandrite' which needed to be reheated twice, firstly to obtain the red colour change from the amber, and finally to reheat the very top of the glass to get a beautiful violet blue (Colour Plate 38, front centre). Stevens and Williams used heat sensitive glass on some of their spiral air trap vases (Colour Plate 38, top right). 'Shaded Opalescent', 'Lemonescent' and 'Brocade' were some of the names given to shaded glassware which required the presence of bone ash and arsenic to achieve the desired opalescent effect. The glass was blown into a patterned dip mould to give a raised design on the surface. After cooling below red heat the glass was reheated and the raised parts, which reheated first, 'struck' to an opalescent white colour in

Plate 294. Photograph from the Pottery Gazette *November 1897, showing the 'New Opaline Brocade' glass from Messrs John Walsh Walsh, Birmingham.*

contrast to the background which remained clear (Colour Plate 38, second left). One of the first to introduce shaded wares when they advertised their 'Crushed Strawberry' in November 1883, the Birmingham factory of Walsh Walsh introduced their version of opalescent glass, entitled 'New Opaline Brocade', in time for the Christmas market in 1897 (Plate 294).

IRIDESCENT GLASS

Of all the different types of iridescent glassware in the nineteenth century one of the best known and most important was the 'Bronze' glass made by Thomas Webb and Sons from 1878 onwards. The application for the patent stated that:

> the glass articles are exposed, while in the nearly molten state after blowing, and before annealing, to the fumes generated by placing chloride of tin, alone or mixed with the nitrates of barium and strontium, upon a hot plate or spoon. During this process the articles are placed in a muffle or chamber into which the fumes are introduced.

The new glass was first exhibited at the Paris Exhibition of 1878 where it was given its name. Some dispute seems to have arisen between Webb's and the Richardson factory over the new glass. An entry in an unpublished notebook belonging to Benjamin Richardson I seems to indicate that Webb's had complained to Richardson's at the Paris Exhibition about an infringement to their iridescent patent. This may have related to some of the glass shown by Richardson's which may have had an iridescent finish (Plate 93). The note states

Colour Plate 40. Bronze glass vases by Thomas Webb and Sons showing the variations of applied lion masks, crackle, acid etched and enamel infill, plain, and engraved and enamel infill, c.1878-80. Left to right. Vase, height 10¼ in. (26cm), Hulbert of Dudley Collection. Vase with crackled surface, height 4¾ in. (12cm), Michael Parkington Collection. Vase with etched and infill decoration by Guest Brothers, c.1878, height 10½ in. (26.5cm). Plain vase, height 7½ in. (19cm), Michael Parkington Collection. Vase with engraved and infilled hieroglyphics, height 4¾ in. (12cm).

that Richardson's had promised to stop their iridescent experiments after the Paris Exhibition. The letter of complaint suggests that Richardson's forgot their promise and carried on with their products. Some 'Bronze' glass, especially the crackled pieces which Cyril Manley christened 'Brain' glass, is attributed to the Richardson factory but could just as easily be ascribed to Webb's.

In the Webb pattern books the colour is called 'Green Bronze', suggesting that the body colour was always green. By the end of 1878 the factory had developed a crackled version of 'Bronze' which relied on the usual method of dipping the glass into cold water to obtain the crackle, reheating and blowing to the desired shape and then submitting it to the iridescent process. Crackled bronze or 'Scarabeous' appears in the pattern books at Webb's in December 1878, pattern nos. 11272-47, on shapes often decorated with applied lizards, snakes and frogs. 'Bronze Scarabeous' patterns also have flint or clear glass lizards and are

Colour Plate 41. Victorian enamelled glass provides the collector with an excellent choice of styles. In this group the bold, painterly approach of the 1840s contrasts with the more fussy and intricate designs of the 1880s.

Left to right. Bowl of clear glass, cased with white, acid etched and painted with apples and leaves; the background is etched with an overall pattern of small rosettes; possibly the 'Autumnal Cameo' advertised by Boulton and Mills in 1887, height 3½in. (9cm). The Water Lily goblet designed by Richard Redgrave and made by J.F. Christy of Lambeth for Henry Cole's company 'Felix Summerly's Art Manufactures' in 1847; height 7¾in. (19.5cm). Eventually all the Summerly products were stocked in sixteen shops but the venture did not make a profit and allowed Henry Cole's critics to accuse him of being a shopkeeper. Posy vase enamelled with flowers, with a red enamel mark of the letter E and a spider's web (see Appendix 12) probably for Edward Webb of the White House Glass Works, Wordsley, late 19th century, height 4¼in. (11cm). Jug with applied lizard handle, and painted enamel and gilt decoration by Jules Barbe, Thomas Webb and Sons, c.1888, height 12in. (30.5cm). Bowl with machine threaded clear glass painted with sprays of flowers by Oscar Pierre Erard at Stevens and Williams, late 1880s, height 3¼in. (8.5cm). Vase painted with a profusion of English flowers, W.H., B., and J. Richardson, 1847-51, height 17½in. (44.3cm). Jug with sepia enamelled scene of cherubs in a boat, W.H., B., and J. Richardson, 1847-51, height 9½in. (24cm).

Plate 295. Jug with raised enamel willow pattern decoration, signed 'C. Herbert Thompson', c.1895-1900. Height 7¼in. (18.5cm).

sometimes supported on feet shaped as fish. The glass was often enhanced by ornate brass mounts. Other decorative techniques found on 'Bronze' glass include grotesque faces and masks, applied trails and lion masks, etched decoration with infill gilding and engraved hieroglyphics infilled with orange enamel (Colour Plate 40).

VERRE SUR VERRE

'Verre sur verre' was the name given to enamelled glasses which had the background taken down by acid etching leaving a raised area in the exact shape and outline to match the final, enamelled decoration. The enamels were painted to the very edge of the raised section giving the impression of a very thick layer of glass almost in imitation of cameo work. The background could be left frosted or plain or could be further etched with various delicate patterns (Plate 295). The invention was pioneered by Charles Herbert Thompson in Stourbridge in about 1895, a date given in a verbose article in the *Pottery Gazette* of August 1901 which said little else about the colour recipes or firing temperatures. Little is known about Thompson who is shown in a photograph taken in his studio probably about 1900 (Plate 296). The photograph may have been doctored by Thompson himself to give the impression of an alchemist turning base materials into precious objects. A large archive of unsorted papers, acquired by Broadfield House Glass Museum from Thompson's estate, reveals a fascinating yet still slightly mysterious character. He was trained in chemistry, operated the firms of Bullers Ltd. in Tipton and Thompson L'Hospied and Co. Ltd. in Amblecote, owned a ceramic factory in Golfe Juan in France, conducted experiments with enamel colours on porcelain plaques at his home in Stourbridge, designed industrial furnaces and seems to have been involved with the glass firm of Boulton and Mills in Audnam in the early twentieth century.

Thompson's 'verre sur verre' formed part of the products of the firm known as the Crystalline Company, which was created to acquire the patent rights for the invention, by Thompson, of a crystalline tile and to develop it commercially. Made from vitreous materials combined with about fifty per cent kaolin, the new tiles were superior to earthenware examples, it was claimed, because of their lightness, ease of fixing (due to a granulated key on the reverse) and their ability to retain their brilliancy without crazing. The tiles were a great success and were used in banks, railway stations, hotels and hospitals but none, as yet, has been identified *in situ*. The 'verre sur verre' invention formed a logical development of Thompson's work with enamels for ceramics, coloured glazes for pottery, and

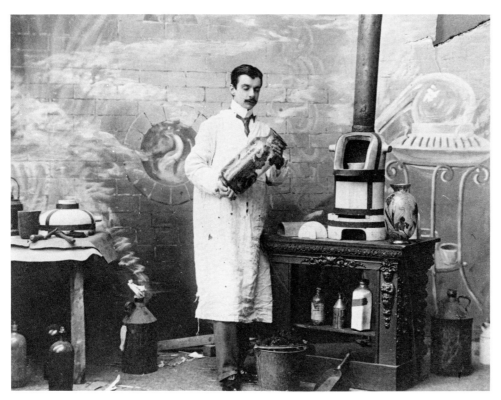

Plate 296. Charles Herbert Thompson in his studio, probably about 1900, from an original photograph discovered amongst papers from his estate.

Colour Plate 42. Enamelled and gilded vase and gilded loving cup by Jules Barbe, late 19th century. The vase, enamelled with swags of roses and signed J. Barbe, has the background taken down by acid etching in a manner similar to Charles Herbert Thompson's verre sur verre. The loving cup is gilded in high relief with a fictitious coat of arms. Heights: vase 10in. (25.4cm), Hulbert of Dudley Collection; loving cup 9¾in. (25cm).

enamels and oxides for the enamelling and decoration of gold, silver, copper and iron. Up to thirty-six different colours could be applied to one piece producing a richness which is suggested by the vases in Plate 296 and proved by the very few known examples. There is a marked similarity between Thompson's vases and pieces by Jules Barbe which have etched backgrounds (Colour Plate 42). A vase seen in a private collection and similar in shape and decoration to the vase held by Thompson was found to be signed by Jules Barbe. Traditionally, in the Stourbridge area, independent decorators rely on the factories and fellow craftsmen to supply their blanks and to carry out work beyond the possibility of

Plate 297. Jules Barbe, from a photograph in the Thomas Webb archives, early 20th century.

their own equipment. When Jules Barbe began to work as a free-lance decorator he would have been in that situation. Working in the same medium and within close proximity to each other, there can be no doubt that Barbe and Thompson knew each other. The question of possible collaborations or assistance between them, however, remains unanswered.

'JULES BARBE
Glass and China Painter, Gilder and Enameller'

The modest word of enamelling stands in the glass industry for one of the most beautiful arts known [Colour Plate 41]...Gilding and enamelling mostly goes together, and it is but little known that M. Jules Barbe [Plate 297], of King William Street, is generally regarded as the most prominent individual exponent of this art in this country.

Having studied this art in France, the home of artistic decoration, he came to Stourbridge in 1879, working exclusively for the Dennis Glass Works until three years ago, when he undertook work for other manufacturers. It is true that gilding and painting was well known in this country when M. Jules Barbe settled down, but for reasons which it is difficult to find out this kind of decorative art was gradually dropped by those manufacturers in whose works it was done, and

M. J. Barbe is now the only representative of it in this district, and of this particular line in this country.

Gilding and enamelling means the painting of designs upon glass or china in gold or colours. All designs are sketched by M. Jules Barbe himself. The gold which, in its dissolved state, looks a brownish paste is put on according to the design by means of brushes, which in the case of painting of monograms, consist sometimes of but a few hairs. The painted glasses are then 'fired' in specially constructed muffles.

After having received two, three or sometimes four firings, they are taken out and burnished, in order to brighten the gold, by the use of brushes made of spun glass, and afterwards with agate, and bloodstone. The gold which after the burning had a dull appearance acquires a wonderful brilliancy. As most of the monograms, crests, coats of arms, and flower decorations are done in raised gold, the results are such as should be seen to be appreciated in all their beauty [Colour Plate 42, right].

Whilst the effects of gold painting are simple and dignified, those secured by enamelling have all the richness of a great painting. Enamels consist of a composition of the nature of glass, and in the firing, which requires very careful attention, mix with the glass and become part of it, giving a brilliant translucency of a large number of varied and most beautiful tints [Colour Plate 42, left].

In M. Jules Barbe's atelier are many samples of his beautiful art. The writer saw a dessert plate, heavily gilded, in Empire style, of exquisite design and artistic execution, and many other works of art decorated either in gold or colours, but it would be impossible to depict their beauty. No catalogue of a picture gallery or an art museum could convey the faintest idea of the treasures stored therein, nor could we describe to the reader the beautiful results of M. Barbe's art; they must be seen to be appreciated.

There is no doubt that among artists of high standing who have applied themselves to decorative art, M. Barbe takes a prominent place, and that in his particular art he is 'facile princeps'.

The anonymous writer who published this account of Barbe's work in *The Black Country and its Industries* in 1905 should be congratulated for his foresight and judgement in featuring the work of a contemporary artist. On this occasion the effusive comments so beloved by writers of the period were well deserved. Family history states that Barbe was born in Paris where he trained as a decorative artist at a time when the 'Union Centrale des Arts Décoratifs' was established to support those arts. Following his wife's death during the siege of Paris in the Franco-Prussian War, Barbe brought his family and twenty-six other French craftsmen to England. Apart from the information that a relative, Paul Tallandier, went to work as an enameller for Coalport, the histories of the other craftsmen are not known. Barbe and his son settled at No. 7 Collis Street, and went to work at Thomas Webb and Sons. Barbe worked exclusively for Webb's until 1901 when he set up as a free-lance decorator. In January of 1906 and 1907 he advertised his trade in the pages of the *Pottery Gazette* as:

Plate 298. Seven glasses decorated with gold and platinum, from a larger collection presented to the British Museum in April 1878 by Paul Raoul de Facheux D'Humy. Heights, left to right: 4 ¼ in. (10.8cm), 2 ⅛ in. (5.4cm), 5 ¼ in. (13.4cm), 7 ⅝ in. (19.5cm), 5 ¼ in. (13.4cm), 5 ½ in. (14.1cm), 5 ¾ in. (14.7cm). By courtesy of the Trustees of the British Museum.

GLASS AND CHINA PAINTER, GILDER
AND ENAMELLER. MATCHINGS.
King William Street,
Dennis Park, STOURBRIDGE.
Speciality of Monograms, Coronets, Crests, Coats of Arms
in Raised Gold, etc. Artistic Works of Art in all Styles.
Enamel, Gold, Platinum, etc.
21 Years at Dennis Glass Works.

A great deal of work was executed for Stuart and Sons whose pattern books are full of Barbe's designs, with his own pattern numbers alongside those of the company. There is some evidence in Stuart's pattern books of a collaboration between Barbe and Shuker, an engraver and cameo artist whose own work is little known. During the First World War Barbe was reduced to painting the name 'Colmans' on glass mustard pots for Thomas Webb's. After the war he retired to Switzerland where he died at the age of seventy-nine. When his name is mentioned in Stourbridge it is in the same company as Fritsche, Woodall and Northwood.

PAUL RAOUL de FACHEUX D'HUMY

Paul R.F. D'Humy remains a mysterious character in the world of glass although he did register at least three patents for glass decoration and improvements to glassmaking equipment and was featured in the *Art Journal* of 1879. In April 1878 D'Humy presented a collection of his glasses to the British Museum (Plate 298).

Plate 298a. Goblet by P.R.F. D'Humy, the glass bowl decorated with gold leaf and set on a silver gilt foot, hallmarked Thomas Johnson, London 1876. Height 8⅜ in. (21.2cm).

Some of the glasses have labels on the bases which give his address as 'Managing Director, Aurora Glass Company Ltd, 21 Litchfield Street, Soho, [London] W.C. Inventor'. In 1881 he appears in the Post Office Directories as the 'Vasa Murrhina Glass Company' with the Litchfield Street address, a gallery at 294 Regent Street and a manufactory at York Place, York Road, Battersea. By 1882 D'Humy had opened another office at 5 and 6 Great Wimbledon Street E.C. In 1883 only the address of the factory is given in the Directories and by 1884 he is not listed at all.

The main form of decoration on the glasses in the British Museum is with the use of platinum, gold and silver, in leaf or dust form, either on the surface or trapped inside the glass, and relates to his patent application of 31 October 1876:

4217. Ornamenting. — Relates to a process of ornamenting glass with metal. Gold or other leaf is applied to the moistened surface of a glass cylinder, and the glass is heated until the metal and glass are united. The coated cylinder is then passed into a closely-fitting cylinder, the ends of which are drawn down, one being closed and the other left open. The two cylinders are united by heat, and elongated to part the metal into strips with intermediate clear spaces, after which the glass is blown to the required shape. The outer cylinder may be dispensed with. The metal may be removed in places by an engraving-tool to produce any desired pattern, after which the glass is blown into shape, or a layer of gold may be placed over a layer of silver, the engraving exposing the silver, or the metal may be applied as an amalgam to the crude glass, or hot glass may be rolled in metal leaf or powdered metal, or the moulds in which the articles are formed may be lined with the leaf. The internal surface of an article is coated with metal by applying the leaf when the article is partially formed, or powdered metal is blown into the crude glass.

On 13 February 1878 further patents were registered for 'Ornamenting glass; Articles with wire or like skeletons; Metallic feet for drinking glasses [Plate 298a]; Treatment of spun glass; Blowing-tubes and Blow-pipes.' On 31 March 1888 another patent described the making of 'lamp globes, shades and chimneys' by winding glass beads, threaded on wire, around metal formers.

In 1879 his products had made sufficient impact for the *Art Journal* to devote an article to him entitled 'Reproduction of The Murrhine Vases of the Ancients'. It complimented him on the successful imitations of ancient glasses decorated in gold and silver and mentioned a 'company for carrying them out under his superintendence', and 'one factory, under the direction of M. D'Humy himself, and an efficient staff of assistants, is now at work'. The article mentions the successful reproduction of Venetian filigree glass vessels and refers to 'the most experienced glass-blowers the continent can supply being engaged to achieve with precision the delicate outlines furnished them to copy'.

———— CHAPTER THIRTEEN ————

Pressed Glass

The most successful example of the mechanisation of glassmaking techniques in the nineteenth century was the press-moulding of glass using an iron mould and a plunger. The technological breakthrough was made in America in the years leading up to 1820. Pressed glass is listed for the first time with other types of glassware in an advertisement in the *Boston Commercial Gazette* on 19 September 1822. Cheap, well-made glass now became available to even the humblest household. By the 1830s the technique spread to Europe and in the early 1840s the French glass firms of Baccarat and Saint Louis were making crisply modelled tablewares in imitation of American pressed lacy patterns.

The patent taken out by Thomas G. Webb of Manchester on 10 November 1870 shows the basic layout of a pressing machine with the mould (e), the plunger (m) and the lever (s) which was pulled down by the operator to force the plunger into the mould containing the hot glass (Plate 299). This form of hand-pressing can still be seen in a number of American factories including the Fenton Art Glass Company and the Viking Glass Company in West Virginia (Plates 300 and 301). The process requires two operators, the first to gather the glass on the iron and let it flow into the mould. The second operator cuts off the gather once the glass is in the mould and then pulls the lever down to press the article. Once the article is removed from the mould the shape can be altered, the surface fire-polished or extra pieces such as handles can be added while the pressed glass body is still hot. In the early days of the process the technique was not sufficiently developed in England to allow the pressing of handles at the same time as the body. Items such as tankards or jugs will have a 'pump' handle where the glass is applied at the top rim and finished off on the lower part of the body. Pressed tumblers were sometimes transformed into rummers by the addition of a stem and foot by traditional hand applied methods. When the stem and foot have become chipped or cracked it is simple enough to grind away the complete stem and foot leaving a pressed tumbler. The same treatment has been given to handmade rummers which have suffered damage but now appear as perfectly good early nineteenth century tumblers.

Some idea of the vast output which could be achieved by pressing is obtained from a letter which was written by Thomas G. Webb of Molineaux, Webb & Co., Manchester, on 29 June 1848, probably to Robinson and Skinner at Warrington. The recipient glassworks were obviously keen on setting up the process or perfecting an existing operation as the letter gives a great deal of detailed information regarding numbers of workmen, wages and numbers of glasses made in each six hour shift.

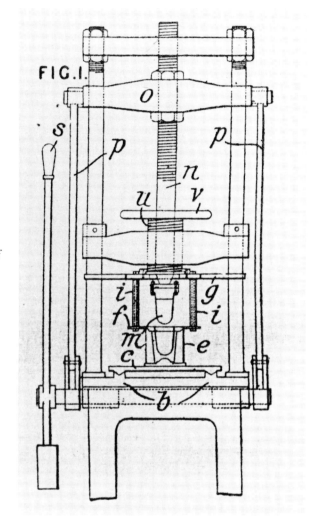

FIG.I.

Plate 299. Design for a pressing machine patented by T.G. Webb of Manchester on 10 November 1870.

Manchester
June 29 1848

Gentlemen

In reply to yours of yesterday we beg to state we have much pleasure in being able to serve you — we desire also to thank you for your kind offer of a reciprocation of such favours — of which at some future time we may avail ourselves.

Our men do not work by time — they all work by piece — making as much as they can in 6 hours. Sometimes more sometimes less according to circumstances.

Eleven moves constitute a weeks work for which we pay as follows — Pressers 21/- to 23/- Melters 21/- to 24/- Gatherers 14/- to 16/- Boys not apprenticed 4/-.

A place consists of presser, melter, gatherer and three boys viz. sticker-up, taker-in and warmer-in.

All work above 11 moves is overwork and paid for at the following rate. Presser 1/9 per move Melter 1/9 per move Gatherer 1/- per move and the 3 boys 4d. each per move.

Such are the general terms — we have one or two pressers and melters at 2/- per move.

The following table will indicate the numbers by which all work is reckoned and

Plates 300 and 301. Pressing glass at the Viking Glass Works, West Virginia, U.S.A., March 1985.

also shows the amount of each article usually made for us in 6 hours.

Articles	No.	No. usually made in 6 Hrs.
Tumblers ¼ pint	300	600-630
" ⅓ pint	240	500-520
" ½ pint	160	450-500
" ⅕ quart	180	500-520
" ⅓ quart	150	430-460
Basins Haddies usual weights say 22oz.	120	290-300, 310 some moulds work much better than others
Sugars of abt. 19oz.	140	300-330
Very light basins and those made from small tumbler moulds	150	290-320
Salts ordinary round of moderate weights say about 8oz.	240	480-500-510

Square Flatted	160	360-365
A few massive ones very		
long in cooling	120	200-240-250
Unmelted (lights)	320	640 700 & 800 as patterns
Dishes 11 & 12 in	40	80
" 10 Round	50	120-130
" 9	80	160
" 8 &	90	180-190
" 7	120	240-260
" 6 Square	160	300-320
" 5	180	390-400-420
Butters — as basins	120 & 140	as basins
Plates — cigars [???]	400	800-820-750 and every number under [???]
" 5 in melted	300	620
" 6 in "	200	400-420-360
" 8 in " abt 17oz	150	350
" " " " 20oz.	120	270
" 9 in " " 24oz.	100	200-250
" 10 in " " 32oz.	80	160-200
Covers to Butters —		
these vary very much.		
Some are finished in		
mould — some	120	300
stuck nobs — and others	160	320 320
with nobs wrought from	and	
a straight piece above	1 mould	
the cover — according	at 140	280 to 300
to trouble & they are		
Mustards — handles	180	390 400 310
" no handles	200	320 350 390
" covers	300 & 320	620 700 750
Pickles light	300	600 620 650
" abt. 7oz.	240	480 500
" heavy and		
similar to		
small dishes	as dishes	
Potting pots 4¼	160	they have not had a
" 4¾	200	first rate go at these yet.

Such are our numbers with which and our wages we find little complaint. That they are not too high is certain when some with diligence can earn 12 and 12½ moves over in 8 turns — which brings a pressers wages to about 42/- and 45/- per week. The men too are not at all averse to them on the whole — only isolated numbers — but a regulation of jobs of which tumblers at 160 is the best quietens all brawlers. I should say dishes from the care required with them is the worst job. That press which makes them receives 2/- per move over for presser and melter. No other save one very upright, honest fellow has 2/- per move over — all 1/9 besides these cases.

In passing a number for a new article we are guided entirely by the amount of trouble and labour required and also weight. We find frequent dissent from them at first — from some of the idle — but it soon dies away and they learn to make sufficient to pay them. We seldom alter a number — if too low, they reap the benefit — if too high we give the maker of the article a good job to equalise with.

Trusting I have been sufficiently elaborate and desiring you will acquaint me if any further information is required or if I have been obscure,

I am

Yours

per pro Molineaux Webb.

The job of the melter was probably to fire-polish the glass after it came out of the mould to reduce any mould lines and he may also have been responsible for altering the shape of the article after it came out of the mould. On a Richardson design for a pressed sugar basin the phrase 'Flanged out is the proper shape' suggests this may have been the case. All of the pieces mentioned in the letter would have been pressed in imitation of cut designs of the period. If the list is taken as a comprehensive record one gets some idea of the limited range that the English factories produced at this date.

It is obvious from the details in the letter that by the late 1840s pressing was well established in England. Although the exact date of the introduction of the process into the country cannot be established with any certainty, it is possible to suggest a likely date. A reference in the Thomas Webb pattern books refers to 'A Salt Presd in No. 62 Mold Wt 14oz cut 1½ Sell 14s'. The pattern, number 778, is dated to early 1842. References made by writers later in the century state that the Thomas Hawkes factory in Dudley operated pressing machines but give no further information. At the very beginning of the century the moulded, lemon squeezer feet of Irish cut glass bowls were a form of pressed glass. The bowls were referred to by Deming Jarves, of the Boston and Sandwich Glassworks in Massachusetts, in his *Reminiscences* published in 1865: 'Fifty years back the writer imported from Holland salts made by being pressed in metallic molds, and from England glass candlesticks, table centre-bowls, plain, with pressed square feet, and rudely made, somewhat after the present mode of moulding glass'. In view of the speed with which English firms copied innovations from Europe there seems no reason to doubt that they applied the same commercial action to pressed glass. A probable date in the early 1830s for the spread of the technique through England would seem plausible. In 1831 Apsley Pellatt took out a patent in two parts, the first for Crystallo Engraving. The second was for a method of assembling moulds which included a drawing of a 'machine for pressing glass by the mode lately introduced from America'. Surprisingly Pellatt did not end up taking the lead in pressed glass manufacture which was readily taken up by the Midlands factories.

Plate 302. Left and centre. Tumbler and matching pickle jar, press-moulded by Thomas Gammon, Birmingham, 1849. Heights: tumbler 4in. (10cm), pickle jar 6in. (15cm). Right. Tumbler, press-moulded and registered by Benjamin Richardson in 1849. Height 4⅛ in. (10.5cm). D. and R. Watts Collection.

MIDLANDS PRESSED GLASS

The few surviving examples from the early years of the invention are invariably of thick glass in crude imitations of cut designs (Plate 302). The Birmingham factories eagerly displayed their achievements in the 1840s, some of which were illustrated in the *Journal of Design* in 1849-50 (Plates 303 and 304). In the Crystal Palace Exhibition, Rice Harris, who seems to have been the first to develop the technique in Birmingham, displayed pressed and moulded tumblers, goblets, wines, sugar basins, butter coolers, salt cellars, honey pots and door knobs while F. & C. Osler showed frosted glass busts of the Queen, Prince Albert, Shakespeare, Milton, Scott and Peel.

Although pressed glass was never produced in the Stourbridge and Dudley area in the vast quantities of the North-East or Manchester in the latter part of the century, it did achieve a measure of success during the middle years of the century. Only one firm, that of Joseph Webb, continued to specialise in pressed wares, the other factories preferring to concentrate on high quality decorative and table glass which made full use of traditional skills.

Richardson's in Wordsley and the Badger Brothers in Dudley pioneered the new skills in the Stourbridge district. A Richardson design from the 1840s suggests a well-developed technique which concentrated on the imitation of cut glass rather than copying the lacy glass of the Americans (Plate 305). The design is the most ambitious of the early patterns, weighing 2½ lb. (just over 1kg) and selling at 1s.8d. Due to the lack of interest in this early period of English pressed glass few glasses have appeared which can help the collector to identify other examples. The weight of the object, given in the Richardson design, should help

335

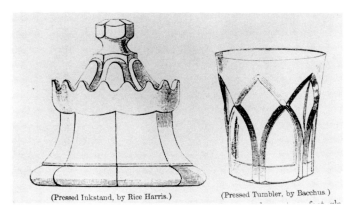

Plate 303. *Pressed inkstand by Rice Harris, and pressed tumbler by Bacchus of Birmingham. Illustrated in the* Journal of Design, *1849-50.*

Plate 304. *'Pressed Glass Fruit Dish or Dessert' by Bacchus and Sons, Birmingham. Illustrated in the* Journal of Design, *1849-50.*

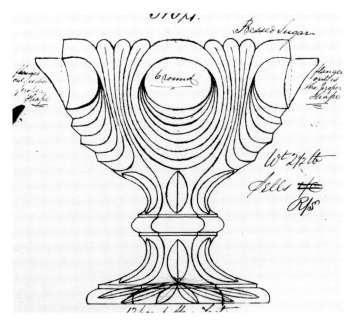

Plate 305. *Design for a 'Pressed Sugar' from the Richardson pattern books, 1840s.*

Plate 306. Pressed sugar basin, probably by Richardson's, 1840s. Height 4in. (10cm). Ann Smith-Hajdamach Collection.

with identification. A sugar bowl which has some of the features of the Richardson design shows the characteristic flow lines which plagued early pressed glass (Plate 306). Although only 4in. (10cm) high it measures ½in. (1.25cm) thick on the rim and weighs 1lb.13oz. (.82kg). Other items from the Richardson factory included tumblers, salt cellars and mustard pots. The earliest surviving pattern of a tumbler dates from January 1845. It is not certain if the firm continued with pressing into the next decade. The Flint Glass Makers' Friendly Society Certificate (see Frontispiece) shows a working glasshouse (in all probability the Richardson factory) with, in the far right background, a simple pressing machine, based on the principles of the machine patented by Thomas Webb in 1870.

Several small saucers with portraits of the young Queen Victoria surrounded by typical American lacy patterns were thought to originate from the Webb Richardson partnership as they bear the initials WR hidden in the design. However, the fact that the partnership ended two years before Victoria's accession and the similarity in style to other American cup plates suggest an American origin. The initials WR would almost certainly have been those of the mould maker and not of the factory.

The sudden increase in pressed glass manufacture in England in the middle of the century owed a great deal to the repeal of the Glass Excise. In the North-East, many firms abandoned traditional glassmaking in favour of pressed glass when the abolition of the tax meant that prices could be kept low in comparison with blown glass. That development is echoed in Stourbridge, at least in the case of Joseph Webb's factory at Coalbournhill which concentrated on pressed glass for most of its life. Joseph Webb is recorded in partnership with his brother Edward in 1850 but by November of that year the partnership was dissolved and Joseph took over the vacated glassworks of J. Stevens, the site of the present Webb Corbett factory. From the outset he began producing pressed glass. A number of patterns registered between 1851 and 1858 show imitation cut designs. Some of Joseph Webb's glass appears in the pattern books of Stevens and Williams from the late 1860s until 1873. The firm continued with pressed glass until 1874, the date of the last registered pressed design. Some time before 1872 Joseph Webb died and the works were run by his executors, Jane Webb, Henry Fitzroy Webb and Joseph Hammond, who extended the range of products at the expense of the pressed range. By 1888 the moulds had been sold to Edward Moore of South Shields.

Once the pressed technique was perfected and the glass factories realised that pressed glass need not be a strict copy of cut glass, the way was open for a flood of new designs and patterns. Rapid strides were made in mould technology which created a highly sophisticated product in comparison with the crude pressings of the 1840s. The bulk of production came from the great factories of Sowerby, Greener, Davidson and Moore at Newcastle and Sunderland, and from Derbyshire, Burtles Tate, Percival Vickers and Molineaux Webb in Manchester.

NORTH-EAST PRESSED GLASS

Sowerby's Ellison Glass Works

Three generations of the Sowerby family created one of the most important pressed glass factories in the nineteenth century. George Sowerby had been connected with glassmaking in Newcastle in the early 1800s. Under the management of his son John, who established the pressed glass works in 1847, the factory thrived and became a highly successful venture. John's partner was Samuel Neville who had served his apprenticeship at the Bacchus factory in Birmingham and must have provided much needed technical ability. When John Sowerby died in 1879 his son John George was already involved in the factory having registered designs for new equipment in 1871 at the age of twenty-one.

The brilliant working knowledge of mould technology shown by J.G. Sowerby gave his company the lead over his competitors. On 15 September 1871 he registered a patent (Plate 307) in which

the outer surfaces of vases and other articles made of pressed glass are ornamented with designs in glass of a different colour to that forming the body of the article. The ornament is formed in a suitable mould B having a counter-balanced false

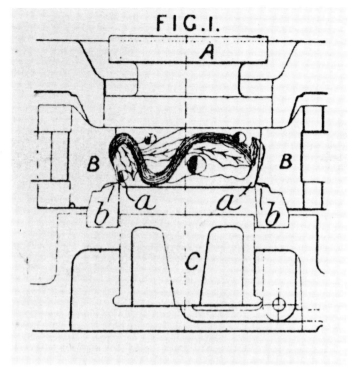

Plate 307. Design submitted by J.G. Sowerby on 15 September 1871 as part of a patent for adding separate coloured glass ornamentation on to pressed glass.

bottom C and a plunger A; the plunger and mould have corresponding bevelled edges a, b, by which all surplus metal is cut off from the casting. Directly the ornament is pressed the section of the mould containing it is fitted in the mould in which the article is to be pressed, this mould being constructed to receive it in the requisite position for ornamenting the article. The fused metal is then run into the mould and pressed to shape, during which operation the ornament becomes incorporated with the surface of the article. The ornament may be made in sections in one or several moulds.

Sowerby continued to improve pressed glass technology with a wide variety of ideas. On 27 November 1874 he patented an 'apparatus for detaching and delivering the moulded articles from presses.' On 29 May 1878 his Ivory glass was registered, which was 'made by adding uranium and cryolite to the ordinary constituents of flint glass, such as a mixture of sand, soda, barium carbonate, nitrate of soda, and manganese [oxide].' Two years later, on 6 February, he developed an idea for ornamenting flat glass sheets. The patent was for

producing in the body of the glass lines of various colours and thicknesses, giving the contours of folds of drapery, and other devices. The gatherer collects some coloured metal on the iron, marvers it, and dips it into the mould around which are spaces containing glass threads of dark colour. These adhere to the metal when it is withdrawn, and the worker then cases it, re-marvers the whole, and blows it out as an ordinary muff or flattens it. By using different tools &c. any desired pattern is formed.

The next decade saw further patents, including an improvement to avoid the 'sucking' action on the withdrawal of the plunger from the mould (12 February 1883), moulds for forming flat jointed articles with a deep-cut pattern on the underside (27 May 1885), the construction of glass articles with handles

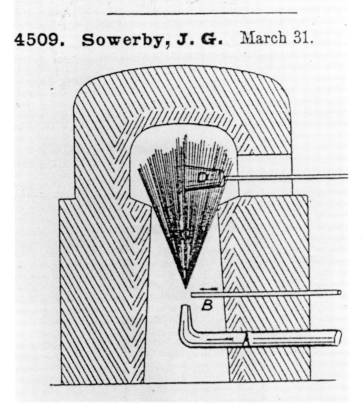

4509. Sowerby, J. G. March 31.

Plate 308. Design submitted by J. G. Sowerby on 31 March 1886 for fire-polishing pressed glass.

formed all in one piece (8 June 1885), a method of fire-polishing (31 March 1886) (Plate 308), moulds for blowing and moulding jugs, gas globes and other hollow-ware (1 March 1890), a means for cutting cylinders, tumblers, or other articles of glassware by electricity (23 December 1890), and a patent for steam pressing to replace hand-operated machines in 1894.

The operation of the Sowerby glassworks was conducted on a massive scale. In 1882 between 700 and 1,000 employees produced 150 tons (152.3 tonnes) of finished goods each week, from seventy-eight pots set in nine furnaces. The glassmakers worked a rota of an eight hour shift throughout the whole twenty-four hours in order to supply the vast world markets enjoyed by the company. In one month in 1883 the sales amounted to a record £48,015. New designs were constantly added to keep ahead of the novelty market and the products were advertised in a series of pattern books of which only two have survived, one for Vitro-porcelain and another for a cross-section of goods in the 1880s.

Vitro-porcelain was the brain child of John George Sowerby who registered the first designs in 1876. The colouring ingredient was cryolite, a compound spar obtained from Greenland, which produced a range of white glass from a transparent effect to a solid white resembling a ceramic body, hence the name (Colour Plate 43). The addition of different oxides to the cryolite offered a wide range of colours which were quickly exploited by Sowerby. Turquoise glass was introduced at the same time as the white and became an extremely popular colour (Plate 309). It was followed in 1878 by the famous Queen's Ivory ware, achieved

Plate 309. Group of Sowerby pressed glass. Purple marbled triangular spill vase marked with the peacock head crest, c.1880. Height 3⅞in. (9.9cm). Turquoise vitro-porcelain castellated spill vase, with peacock head crest and diamond registration for 15 November 1876. Height 3⅞in. (9.9cm). Blanc de Lait basket with peacock head crest and diamond registration for 18 February 1879. Length 6in. (15cm).

by the addition of uranium to the cryolite and comparable in quality to ceramic creamwares (Colour Plate 44). The subtle colour of Ivory ware combined with delicate patterns often based on oriental floral motifs has given it a reputation which it justly deserves and is often reflected in high prices in the salerooms. The speed of the introductions of the new colour ranges combined with original shapes and surface patterns established Sowerby as the leading pressed manufacturers in Britain. When the turquoise and white colours had lost their novelty appeal they were succeeded by a staggering array of new colours. Malachite was the name chosen for the well-known marbled and variegated effect. Developed in 1878 it was made in blue (known as Sorbini), purple, green, brown (known as New Marble glass), black, grey and red (Plate 309). In the past the marbled effect was incorrectly referred to as slag on the misunderstanding that the addition of iron slag waste was responsible for the striations. The Sowerby advertisements make it clear that their Slag glass was a separate colour, black in appearance but made from a bottle green or dark purple glass which did have the addition of slag waste. A new line for 1880 was the charming and pretty Blanc de Lait, reminiscent of the opalescent blue glass of Lalique and often mistaken for it (Plate 309). In 1881 an Aesthetic Green was introduced (Colour Plate 44), followed in 1882 by a bright yellow colour termed Giallo which is now greatly sought after (Colour

Plates 43 and 44). Amber glass was made in two shades, a light version called Gold and a darker shade, made in 1882, called Tortoiseshell. Three types of ruby glass were marketed under the names of Ruby for the standard colour, Rubine for a pinker version, and Rose Opalescent for a shaded heat-reactive effect. In 1883 the New England Glass Company of Cambridge, Massachusetts granted a licence to Sowerby to make pressed amberina glass.

The decision by Sowerby to borrow subject matter from the highly popular children's books illustrated by Walter Crane was one of those strokes of genius which skilfully combined the immediate appeal of the latest fashion and the easy translation of aesthetically pleasing designs into the technology of mass-production. The Sowerby mould makers faithfully copied Crane's designs from his three most successful children's books starting with *An Alphabet of Old Friends* published in 1874. The best known picture from this book is the scene of Old King Cole with his musicians (Colour Plate 43). Crane's next book, *Baby's Own Alphabet,* came out in 1875 and provided J.G. Sowerby with one of his most witty and amusing subjects. In 'Multiplication', schoolboys working at their times tables are plagued by the numbers buzzing around their heads like flies (Plate 310). When *The Baby's Opera, A Book of Old Rhymes with New Dresses* was published in 1877 it provided the Sowerby firm with its greatest selection of source material so far, including Little Jack Horner, Oranges and Lemons, Lavender's Blue, Dance a Baby, Jack and Jill, and Little Bo Peep (Plate 310). Other Crane inspired glass includes a boat-shaped vase with a partly three-dimensional swan at either end, and a cylindrical vase supported by three swans (Colour Plate 43).

John George Sowerby became recognised as a children's book illustrator in his own right with his first publication *Afternoon Tea* which appeared in 1880. Later he worked in collaboration with Walter Crane's elder brother Thomas on a series of books based on the holiday adventures of an English family.

Ironically Walter Crane detested the use of machinery to create art and in all his writings and letters never referred to the Sowerby glasses using his illustrations. In comparison with the tons of imitation cut glass made by other factories in the North-East and Manchester, Sowerby's nursery rhyme vases and posy bowls possess a universal appeal which everyone can identify with and enjoy. They are some of the few Victorian glass pieces which have that rare ability to make one smile. When one considers the delicate and subtle effects of these pieces it is difficult to understand the prejudices which delayed the appreciation of this type of glass for so long.

In the 1880s Sowerby, in common with other pressed firms, reverted to the production of imitation cut glass. Competition from the Manchester factories was exacerbated by foreign imports. In 1891, just eight years after record sales figures, the company's profit was £149.13s.0d. New services were introduced in 1895 to stave off fierce Belgian competition. The company even bought land near Antwerp and built a factory which was never a success and closed in 1907. From the mid-1890s J.G. Sowerby's interest in the works had lessened and he turned more to his book illustrations. When he died on 14 December 1914 his obituary

Plate 310. Group of Sowerby nursery rhyme glass. Turquoise vitro-porcelain spill vase entitled
'Multiplication' from Walter Crane's Baby's Own Alphabet of 1875. Height 4¼in. (10.8cm).
Turquoise vitro-porcelain spill vase in the form of a bellows with figure of Little Jack Horner. Height
5½in. (13.8cm). Queen's Patent Ivory spill vase with figures of Jack and Jill taken from Walter
Crane's The Baby's Opera of 1877. Height 3½in. (9cm). All with peacock head crest, c.1880.
Michael Parkington Collection.

remembered him more for his rowing exploits than for his outstanding
achievements in pressed glass. His company remained active until 1972 and the
works were finally demolished in 1982.

George Davidson and Co., Gateshead

The firm was established in 1867 by George Davidson, a butcher turned
businessman who became Mayor of Gateshead in 1886 and 1887. He bought land
in the area known as the Teams at Gateshead, set up the glassworks with a small
work-force and built up a sizeable trade in glass chimneys. His son Thomas
entered the business in the 1870s and helped to create an efficient organisation
with many innovative ideas admired by other factories. In 1887 the company
employed a work-force of 350 responsible for an output of between 200 and 250
tons (203.2 to 265 tonnes) per month. By 1890 the works had increased to four
furnaces each holding from six to eight pots. The company also employed its own
pot maker. The faster rate of glass production in a pressed factory required the
use of pots with larger capacity than those used in the traditional blown glass
industry. Pot makers were brought in from Stourbridge to build the specialised
pots unavailable from other sources.

The products of the Davidson factory offered a wide selection of patterns and

Plate 311. Group of Davidson pressed glass. Amber glass basket in imitation of cut glass with Registered Number 153858 for 2 August 1890. Height 4⅛ in. (10.5cm). Purple marbled butter dish and cover moulded with corals and seaweed, with the lion and castle mark, c.1880-90. Diameter 7½ in. (19cm). Black spill vase on stippled base with lion and castle mark, c.1880-90. Height 3⅛ in. (8cm).

shapes and are second only to Sowerby's glass. Davidson cornered a substantial part of the Australian market due to his brother Joseph. Between them they operated a barter system whereby George would send glass in return for shipments of food including butter, flour and pork. From 1880 to 1890 the firm marked their glass with the trade mark of a demi-lion rampant rising out of a castle (see Appendix 12). The absence of the mark after 1890 makes it difficult to identify the company's products, although they did use the registered number on later wares (Plate 311). Some pieces, such as the vase in the form of a bugle in marbled glass (Colour Plate 43), are attributed to Davidson's on the basis of the similarities of the concentric rings under the base to other known Davidson items.

Vitro-porcelain was produced in every description and colour (Plate 311). New products were made using old moulds bought from the redundant factories of W.H. Heppell and the lesser known Thomas Gray works at Carrs Hill. Among the imitations of cut glass designs, the Hobnail Suite was introduced in November 1885. A wide range of souvenirs was created for Queen Victoria's Golden Jubilee. The best known speciality of the firm was Pearline, made in two colour ranges of primrose and blue and registered in 1889 (Plates 312 and 313). The opalescent shading was an immediate success and formed a large part of the company's success in the 1890s. The patent specification registered on 14 February 1889 gave the ingredients for the Pearline effect:

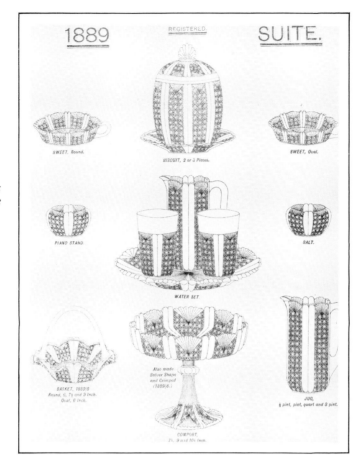

Plate 312. Page of designs of Pearline glass by George Davidson, advertised in the Pottery Gazette in 1889.

Plate 313. Blue Pearline basket by George Davidson and Co., with Registered Number 96945 for 31 March 1888. The mark appears on one of the ribs underneath the handle. Height 6¾ in. (17.2cm).

Articles such as ornamental dishes, vases, jugs, tumblers, etc. are made of clear glass at the base, the glass gradually becoming more opaque towards the top. To a batch of, say, 560lb. [254kg] of sand, 210lb. [95.25kg] of alkali, and 84lb. [38kg] of sodium nitrate, is added 70lb. [31.75kg] of calcium phosphate, 84lb. [38kg] of calcspar, and 35lb. [15.87kg] of arsenic. The proportions of these ingredients may be varied. The article is pressed and moulded in the ordinary manner, and then allowed to cool slightly and re-heated.

A rose coloured version was introduced and is found in the same shapes as the Pearline moulds. On 14 May 1889 T. Davidson patented a method of pressing dishes with one central handle or two smaller ones on either side of the bowl. Company policy after 1889 was to introduce one new line per year and to call it the 1889 suite and so on. In the 1920s the firm introduced the Cloud glass designs which continued to be made into the 1940s. The firm is still in operation and makes industrial glass on the Team Valley Trading Estate.

Henry Greener and Co., Sunderland

The Wear Flint Glass Company which had made the Londonderry service in the 1820s became the pressed glass factory run by James Angus and Henry Greener from 1858. When Angus died in 1869, Greener moved the works to the Millfield site. The factory operated with five furnaces and had the benefit of direct links with the adjacent railway. Like J.G. Sowerby, Henry Greener took an interest in mould technology as well as being aware of the best selling lines in pressed glass. On 15 September 1873 he applied for provisional protection for the following technique:

> Bottles, jugs or decanters, which it is desired to form with a globular body, are cast in two parts, the neck and upper part of the body in one mould and the remainder in another mould. The moulds are formed so as to produce patterns having the appearance of hand-cutting. The two parts having been cast and pressed in the moulds, are fitted together and heated sufficiently to soften the glass; the joint is then rubbed down and a complete union is effected.

In 1874 Greener patented a mould for making glass letters and figures for ornamenting shop windows.

Following close on the heels of the success of Sowerby and Davidson, Greener made vitro-porcelain in puce, blue, green, amber, black, and malachite or marbled glass, often in unusual shapes such as the cup and saucer (Plate 314). Opalescent shaded glass was made sometimes in contravention of other companies' patents. From the wide range of pressed and blown, cut and engraved, and clear and coloured glass, the best known glasses are the commemoratives which were introduced as early as 1869. On 31 July of that year Greener registered the famous 'Gladstone for the Million' design to commemorate the election to power of Gladstone and the Liberal Party. The next commemorative marked the death in November 1869 of George Peabody, the wealthy American philanthropist who did so much to alleviate the housing

Plate 314. Group of Greener pressed glass. Clear glass dish with scalloped corners with the mark of a lion holding an axe, c.1885-1900. Length 11¼ in. (28.5cm). Clear glass sugar basin with the motto 'Peace and Plenty' amid cornucopias, marked with Registered Number 115743 for 14 December 1888. Height 5½ in. (14.2cm). Purple marbled cup and saucer with the mark of a lion holding a star, c.1876-85. Brown opalescent basket with Registered Number 160244 for 3 November 1890. Height 4¼ in. (11cm). Dish Author's Collection.

problems of the poor in England. In 1878 two major designs commemorated the visit to Canada of Princess Louise and her husband, the Marquis of Lorne, the recently appointed Governor-General (Colour Plate 44), and the success of Disraeli who attended the Congress of Berlin and returned with the promise of 'Peace with honour' (Colour Plate 43).

Following the death of Henry Greener in 1882, the factory was taken over by James A. Jobling in 1885 and continued to make high quality glass with the emphasis very much on commemoratives, usually of a patriotic nature. One paperweight in the form of a lion, recorded in a marbled purple and a translucent green glass, was reminiscent of the Derbyshire lion paperweight but had the addition of a shield featuring the Union flag. The factory capitalised on the Jubilee of Queen Victoria in 1887 while two years later it produced a candlestick in the shape of the new Eiffel Tower. The more humble souvenir and commemorative market was also catered for, with one example advertising the diverse operations of a coke merchant (Plate 315).

The firm used two trade marks of an heraldic lion (Appendix 12). The first mark, registered on 29 November 1876, shows a demi-lion rampant facing to the left holding a star in its right paw. After Jobling took over the factory, a new mark

Plate 315. Commemorative plate and two versions of Cleopatra's Needle. The plate was registered by Greener and Co. on 14 June 1894 while the clear glass pomade jar in the shape of the obelisk was registered on 13 October 1877 by G.V. de Luca, a firm of merchants' agents. The white version is unmarked but must date to the same period. The souvenirs of Cleopatra's Needle were made in 1877, the date when the obelisk was to arrive in London from Egypt and be erected on the Embankment. Following an accident aboard the ship carrying the obelisk it sank in the Thames and was not erected until September 1878. Plate 9⅝ in. (24.3cm) diameter; pomade jar 5⅛ in. (13cm) high; Cleopatra's Needle 8½ in. (21.6cm). Pomade jar Author's Collection.

was used in which the star held by the lion was replaced by an axe. After 1883 the products were marked with the registration number. Today the company is still in operation under the control of Corning Glass.

Edward Moore and Co., Tyne Flint Glass Works, South Shields

The quick expansion of the Moore factory from its foundation in 1860 was typical of the success of the pressed glass factories in the 1860s and 1870s. In evidence to the Enquiry into Child Labour in 1865 Moore reported that the company operated two furnaces with a third to be built, and employed a work-force of two hundred men. The susceptibility of the pressed glass trade to depressions and fluctuations in trade was suffered by Moore when they laid off forty men in 1881. To add to their problems one of the chimney stacks fell in. The firm was back in operation by 1882 and the next nine years witnessed a boom period for the company. In 1887 a green colour known as Celadon was introduced together with a distinctive caramel brown. A vivid blue and white marbled glass imitated the Sorbini colour made by Sowerby (Colour Plate 44). In 1888 the firm bought the moulds from the Joseph Webb factory in Stourbridge and by December the

Colour Plate 43. Pressed glass from the Manchester and North-East factories. Left to right. Egyptian sphinx paperweight, matt black glass, Molineaux, Webb & Co., Manchester, registered on 26 July 1875, length 8in. (20.3cm). Sugar bowl with the portrait of Benjamin Disraeli, Earl of Beaconsfield, to commemorate his success at the Congress of Berlin, Henry Greener & Co., marked with a lion holding a star, registered 31 August 1878, height 5½in. (14cm), Michael Parkington Collection. Spill vase in yellow (Giallo) glass, Sowerby, marked with peacock's head crest, registered 14 August 1879, height 3¾in. (9.5cm). Candlestick with spiral leaves and flowers, Sowerby, height 8¼in. (21cm), Michael Parkington Collection. Vase in the shape of a bugle, probably Davidson, 1890s, height 5½in. (14cm). Posy holder in the form of a pike, Molineaux, Webb & Co., with Registered Number 29781 for 14 July 1885, length 10in. (25.4cm). Flower holder in white vitro-porcelain, with the design of Old King Cole, Sowerby, peacock's head crest, c.1880, height 3¼in. (8.2cm).

glasses from those moulds were illustrated in the *Pottery Gazette* (Plates 316 and 317). The re-use of old moulds was a necessary part of financial security but it did result in the continued production of designs regardless of fashion. A glass such as the tumbler, pattern number 1023 to 1029 (Plate 316), made in 1888, was a design that was fifty years old having been copied by Webb from Biedermeier tumblers of the 1830s and 1840s. Pressed glass by the Moore factory does not carry a trade mark and there is some confusion about whether the Webb registration diamonds appear on the later Moore pressings.

The success of the works was brought to a sudden halt on 4 July 1891 when

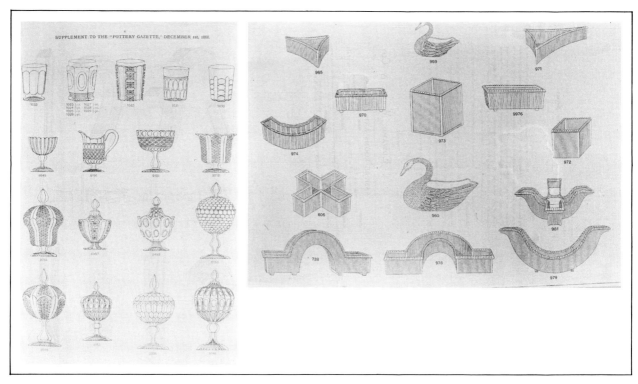

Plates 316 and 317. Two pages of designs for pressed glass by Edward Moore published in the Pottery Gazette *1 December 1888.*

fire swept through the buildings. With indomitable fortitude the operation was in full swing again by May 1892. When Edward Moore died on 4 May 1900, his wife and son persevered with the business until its final closure in 1913. The moulds which Moore had made or had bought from other sources were transferred once more, this time to the Davidson factory.

W.H. Heppell and Company

This factory was situated next to the present Central Station in Newcastle. It was operated for a ten year spell by William Henry Heppell and made some unusual and original designs of coal scuttles, wheelbarrows and colliery coal trucks. An advertisement of 1880 mentioned the opal (opaque white) and marble (opaque brown marble) glass in a vast array of products which ranged from cut and engraved moons, confectionery glass, fancy glass, knobs, lenses, lamps for collieries and street lamps to deck lights, masthead lights and anchor lights. Only the white and the brown marble were made by Heppell's. Glasses which bear its registration diamond but are in other colours, such as green marbled, were made by the Davidson factory which bought the Heppell moulds when the factory closed in 1884. On 6 December 1881 the factory registered an unusual pattern of overlapping conch shells for sugar bowls and cream jugs and covered butter dishes. Another easily recognised pattern, registered on 24 November 1882, was the fish design where the fish's mouth forms the opening of the jug while the upturned tail acts as the handle (Colour Plate 44). On butter dishes the fish became the cover for the shell bowl. Davidson's continued production of the fish

Plate 318. Three pressed figures of Queen Victoria. Black glass bust made by Thomas Kidd of Manchester for the Diamond Jubilee, 1897. Height 3½in. (8.9cm). White glass bust on a pedestal, unmarked, possibly English or Continental, late 19th century. Height 5¼in. (13.5cm). Frosted clear glass full-length figure, unmarked but probably by John Derbyshire, Manchester, c.1874. Height 8¼in. (21.2cm).
Thomas Kidd bust Michael Parkington Collection.

and shell patterns when they acquired the Heppell moulds and advertised their versions in a catalogue of 1885.

Neville Glass Works

After leaving Sowerby's glassworks Samuel Neville established his own factory in Park Road, Gateshead, in 1871. Unfortunately there is no evidence for the range of products although Neville's track record while he was at the Sowerby factory would suggest an important set of designs. Between twenty and thirty mould makers were employed and Neville himself patented some interesting mould techniques. On 20 December 1873 he applied for a provisional patent for a

> rotating table, provided with a graduated dial plate, fitted with a die, or dies. The formed article having been secured to the table, while still hot, melted coloured glass is dropped upon it and is then moulded to an ornamental form by the die or dies. Or the coloured glass is pressed into its required ornamental form and is then fixed to the formed article while both are still hot.

This idea echoed Sowerby's patent of 15 September 1871 (Plate 307).

During the last few months of 1879 the factory had been idle and a fire early in 1880 put a stop to any possibilities of further production. Ironically the moulds

Colour Plate 44. Rare colours and shapes of pressed glass from the North-East factories. Left to right. Oval bowl in yellow (Giallo) glass, Sowerby, marked with peacock's head crest and registration diamond for 12 February 1879, width 8½in. (21.5cm). Round bowl in Queen's Ivory ware, Sowerby, marked with peacock's head crest and registration diamond for 6 June 1879, diameter 9in. (22.7cm). Pin tray in blue marbled glass, Edward Moore and Co., South Shields, 1880s, height 3¼in. (8.2cm). Candlestick in Blanc de Lait with a pale green stain, probably Sowerby, c.1880, height 9¼in. (23.5cm). Two vases supported by swans, probably Sowerby, c.1875, height 6⅞in. (17.5cm). Spoonholder with portraits of the Princess Louise and the Marquis of Lorne to commemorate their state visit to Canada, Henry Greener, marked with a lion holding a star, 1878, height 4⅝in. (11.8cm). Sugar basin in white vitro-porcelain enamelled with flowers, Sowerby, marked with the peacock's head crest and registration diamond for 19 October 1881 and the word PATENT, height 3⅝in. (9.2cm). Tricorn bowl supported by three dolphin feet, in Aesthetic green, Sowerby, marked with the peacock's head crest, early 1880s, height 5in. (12.5cm). Sugar bowl in the form of a fish in marbled glass, W.H. Heppell, with registration diamond for 24 November 1882, height 5¼in. (13.3cm). Michael Parkington Collection.

were bought by Sowerby. Samuel Neville was to die in France in 1883, one of the forgotten pioneers of pressed glass.

MANCHESTER PRESSED GLASS

Although it is often claimed that the Manchester pressed glass factories had surpassed the North-East firms by the end of the century in the overall standard of goods produced, the evidence of the glass itself does little to convince one of that statement. Large amounts of pressed glass were made in Manchester but the bulk of it was in clear glass, consisting of tableware pieces, and not the attractive coloured pieces of which even the smallest North-East firm was capable. Manchester did have a reputation for one speciality, the three-dimensional figures rarely seen in the North-East (Plate 318). The most famous of these figures were made by the Derbyshire factory.

John Derbyshire

This firm is the best known of the Manchester factories and deserves its reputation due to the high quality of goods produced. It was also the only Manchester firm to adopt a trade mark. The firm was set up by three brothers, James, John and Thomas, who operated together until 1873 when John left the partnership and set up on his own at the Regent Road Flint Glass Works in Salford. For a brief period of three years until 1876 a trade mark was used which consisted of an anchor flanked by the initials JD. The year 1874 saw the first production of the classic Derbyshire figurative paperweights. In July the lion paperweight appeared based on the Landseer lions at the foot of Nelson's Column in Trafalgar Square. In September the greyhound was introduced, followed by the figure of Britannia and the Punch and Judy pair in November. In 1876 the firm made its finest piece of pressed glass and probably the finest example of English pressed glass from any factory. The Winged Sphinx displays a grandeur and a majesty few other pieces of pressed glass display (Plate 319). Imitations of vitro-porcelain were made in black or blue glass vases with neo-classical decoration of drapery swags and bunches of fruit. The rest of the items were created using various translucent coloured glasses as well as clear glass which could be frosted (Plate 320). Tableware, including goblets and celery vases, formed the bulk of production. Both the North-East and the Manchester firms engraved some of these tablewares with combinations of names and dates.

Molineaux, Webb and Co.

The firm had a long history of blown and engraved glass and by the middle of the century proved that it could compete with any other English or European factory with its display of cased and coloured glass at the Great Exhibition (Plate 104). The first example of pressed glass was made as early as 1848. A speciality was the frosting of areas of the glass to highlight other patterns such as the popular Greek key motif. Opalescent glass was used for posy holders, one of the more unusual patterns being the pike (Colour Plate 43). The Egyptian sphinx which the firm registered on 26 July 1875 (illustrated in the same plate) may have been the inspiration for the winged version by Derbyshire (Plate 319). The factory continued to work into the early 1920s.

Burtles, Tate and Co.

The company ranked third in importance to Molineaux, Webb and Co. and the Derbyshire factory. First established in 1858 the firm ran two factories by the

Plate 319. Winged Sphinx paperweight in clear glass with a frosted finish, registered by John Derbyshire on 9 March 1876. Height 6in. (15cm), length 10in. (25.2cm). Victoria and Albert Museum.

Plate 320. Three Manchester pressed glass novelties. Piano foot in the shape of a lion's paw, with diamond registration mark for 12 May 1874 and anchor and initial mark of John Derbyshire. 'Glass hand and vase' in vaseline coloured glass, with diamond registration mark for 3 February 1874 and anchor mark of John Derbyshire. Pink opalescent flower holder in the shape of a swan, with Registered Number 20086, by Burtles, Tate and Co. Heights, left to right: 2in. (5cm), 7⅜in. (18.7cm), 5½in (14cm). Swan Michael Parkington Collection.

Plate 321. Plate in clear pressed glass made to commemorate the opening of the Manchester Ship Canal in 1894. The Manchester factory which presumably made this plate has not been identified. Diameter 7in. (17.8cm).

1880s, one in Manchester and one in Bolton. The Bolton works closed in 1887 when a second Manchester glassworks was established in German Street which operated simultaneously with the Poland Street branch. Advertisements of the period credit the firm with flint, coloured, ornamented and fancy glass. From surviving examples it would seem that novelties such as flower vases and posy holders in the form of swans, elephants and even ostriches were the main lines (Plate 320). A shaded colour known as Topaz Opalescent was introduced to compete with Davidson's Pearline. In 1924 the firm was purchased by the last surviving Manchester factory of Butterworth Brothers.

Other Manchester Factories

The four other North-West firms who had a stake in pressed glass manufacture were Percival & Yates (later known as Percival Vickers & Co.), Thomas Kidd and Andrew Ker and Co. of Manchester, and Edward Bolton of the Orford Lane Glass Works in Warrington. Percival Vickers made a large assortment of tableware although the firm had a long history dating back as early as 1846 when it was making cut and engraved glass. Throughout its pressed glass phase it concentrated on general tablewares. The Thomas Kidd factory is well known from its advertisements for 'Penny Glassware' of busts of Queen Victoria (Plate 318), salt-cellars, ashtrays, plates, vases, swans and dogs. Glass furniture consisted of lemon squeezers, piano insulators, drawer knobs and brawn moulds.

The opening of the Manchester Ship Canal in 1894 provided the firms with a ready souvenir market. Few of the souvenirs are marked and one has to conjecture from which factory they came (Plate 321). The same comments apply to the sandblasted tumblers commemorating this event (Plate 344).

Plate 322. Dish in the form of two hands, in clear glass with a satin finish, by John Ford of Edinburgh. The glass is marked on the base with the diamond registration for 25 February 1876 plus 'Patented August 31 1875/298609/Registered 25 February 1876'. Length 6⅛ in. (15.6cm). Michael Parkington Collection.

SCOTTISH PRESSED GLASS

John Ford and Co., Holyrood Flint Glass Works

The products of this factory deserve greater appreciation for they were technical achievements of some style and beauty. Tazzas and candelabra were made with figures of boys and girls acting as supports. Other glasses included jugs with a lake scene, a celery vase decorated with a raised fuschia design and a table service with a scene of a heron holding an eel in its beak. One of the better known Ford pieces is a dish in the shape of a pair of cupped hands which is fully marked on the base with patent numbers and a design registry mark for 25 February 1876 (Plate 322).

In 1990 reproductions of this design, in blue and fawn transparent glass, began to appear in antique fairs. The size of the copies is 7¾ in. (19.7cm) whereas the originals measure 6⅛ or 7½ in. (15.6 or 19.1cm). An example of the slightly larger size is illustrated by Barbara Morris in her book. The modelling on the copies is very close to the originals but with slightly rounded edges lacking the crispness of the originals. Both the originals and the copies have a ring on the underside which acts as a foot. On the original glasses the diameter of the foot ring is 2in. (5.1cm), the thickness of the wall of the foot is ¹⁄₁₆ in. (.16cm) and the rim is left rounded, as it came out of the mould, and not ground down. On

Plate 323. Saucer in clear pressed glass with the name of E.T. Reed Glass Works Newcastle surrounded by a border of bees. North-East, late 19th century. Diameter 4¾in. (12.2cm).

the copies the diameter of the foot is 2½in. (6.4cm), the wall thickness is ¼in. (.63cm), the rim is ground flat with a slightly matt finish, and there are no patent or design registry marks on the underside.

At least one other Scottish factory produced pressed glass in the nineteenth century. Lattimore recorded a trade mark of a thistle on a black glass sugar basin in the shape of a cauldron. The origin of the trade mark is unknown, but one is tempted to make a connection with the little known works of A.M. Allan in Glasgow. Possibly established in the 1870s, they won a medal for pressed table glass at the Cork Exhibition in 1884 but their products remain unidentified.

COLLECTING PRESSED GLASS

Since the appearance of Colin Lattimore's pioneer work *English 19th Century Press-Moulded Glass* in 1979, a great deal of new information about the history of the pressed glass companies and their products has been discovered and published. Barbara Yates discovered a batch of catalogues from Percival Vickers & Co. and published them in *The Journal of The Glass Association* in 1987. Raymond Slack's *English Pressed Glass 1830-1900* has added considerably to our fund of knowledge while *The Identification of English Pressed Glass 1842-1908* by Jenny Thompson lists all the registrations by factory as well as printing the full patent registrations including the registered design numbers up to February 1908. These publications, based on thorough research, provide the collector and the historian with the bulk of the available knowledge and little would seem to remain to be discovered in pressed glass after this amount of attention. However, there are still many avenues for the collector who wishes to specialise in pressed glass but feels that good pieces in an affordable price range are no longer available. A pressed glass saucer with the name of the hitherto unrecorded E.T. Reed Glass Works in Newcastle (Plate 323) is a good example of a rare discovery. Further investigation may determine whether Reed's made this saucer at their own works or whether it was an advertising promotion made for them (see Appendix 10). The Cleopatra's Needle registered as a pomade pot by the retailer G.V. de Luca on 13 October 1877 or the larger version, usually found in white glass, have still not been traced to the company responsible for pressing them (Plate 315). Small hollow busts of Queen Victoria also remain unattributed to a pressed factory, either English, Continental or American (Plate 318). The collecting of pressed glass, therefore, and the research into its history, still retains the possibility of important discoveries.

The diamond shaped registration mark which appears on a great deal of pressed glass gives the day, month and year when the design was registered. The registered number replaced the diamond mark in 1883. Normally copyright protection lasted up to three years. Although not exclusive to pressed glass, the diamond registration appears on that range of objects more than any other because of the relative ease of incorporating the mark into the pattern of the design when it was being cut by the mould maker. On other glass it could be engraved or transfer printed. The code for deciphering the letters and numbers is given in Appendix 11.

CHAPTER FOURTEEN

Cut Glass after 1851 and the Rise of the Brilliant Cut Style

By the time of the Great Exhibition the British glass-buying public had been subjected to cut glass of every description for fifty years. Just as the Bohemians and other European nations had reacted to English cut glass earlier in the century, it was now the turn of the English population to look for a change of style and a new direction.

This inevitable reaction, which equally affected cased and coloured glass after 1851, coincided with John Ruskin's comment, published in his book *The Stones of Venice* in 1853, that 'all cut glass is barbaric'. Ruskin's preference for free-blown glass, with no other decoration to impinge upon the original process, was based on his love of Venetian glass where cutting was virtually unknown. In that context his comment on cut glass was totally biased and grossly generalised. As with so many of his fellow 'tastemakers', his attempts to direct the taste of the population towards his own likes and dislikes were often ignored by the public. The traditional centres of the cut glass industry, such as Stourbridge, paid little or no attention to Ruskin's criticism and, in any case, a large work-force of cutters and polishers could not be disbanded overnight on the single, ill-judged comment of one critic. Although it is true that ornate cut glass went out of fashion in the 1850s and 1860s, cut glass, in more restrained patterns and simpler shapes, continued to be made in large quantities.

Between 1851 and 1860 Stevens and Williams, for example, recorded over 1,000 cut glass designs in their pattern books. The majority of these patterns consisted of flutes, hollows, mitres, prisms and fan scallops on glasses which included sugars and creams, pickle jars, custards and jellies, ice plates, decanters, tumblers and goblets. Almost all of the patterns are given in written descriptions making it difficult to obtain an accurate impression of the appearance of the glassware. Until the 1860s flutes and hollows seemed to be the predominant favourites. The restrained nature of the cut designs, the mundane shapes on to which they were applied and the absence of drawings to help with identification are the three main reasons why cut glass of this date has largely been ignored, and consequently has led to the occasional, erroneous inference that Ruskin's statement dealt a major body blow to the cut glass industry. The lack of research into this period of cut glass, which seems to divulge little of any great merit and would appear to provide few opportunities for major glass historical discoveries, has distorted the true picture and echoes the neglect suffered by British cut glass of the Regency period and the later brilliant style.

English cut glass formed the bulk of glass production in the late Victorian period and the profits from its sale helped to finance the technically complex art glass (Plate 324). The demand for cut glass and the popularity of the large cut

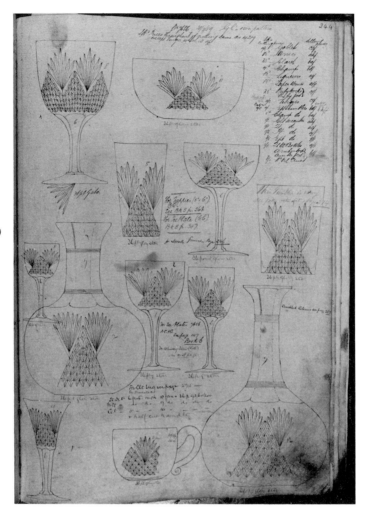

Plate 324. Page showing pattern no. 7656 dated 20 July 1889 for a cut glass service, from the pattern books at Stuart and Sons. Stuart Crystal.

glass service was so great that many of the large companies relied on outside cutters to cope with orders. Occasionally a company would finance free-lance cutters to set up cutting shops which then worked primarily for that company (see Appendix 4). Some cut glass services therefore were not made by one firm but would consist of glasses supplied from different cutting shops but obviously cut to a matching pattern. The intricate designs for cut glass from the 1870s onwards, which included coloured and cased pieces, contain some of the best craftsmanship, skill and ingenuity in the whole field of Victorian glass.

Twenty-five years after Ruskin's attack on it, ornate cut glass was back in fashion in even bolder patterns. The style, known as brilliant cut glass, appeared simultaneously in America and Europe. Brilliant cut glass was introduced in America at the 1876 Philadelphia Centennial Exhibition. Its distinctive style uses the refractive quality of the glass and the full thickness of the blank. The name 'brilliant' refers specifically to the glittering effect which has been described as a mass of diamonds. With its easily recognised curved mitre cuts and the motif of the pin wheel in combination with other geometric patterns, American brilliant cut glass is so distinctive that it cannot be mistaken for English. The very thick

Plate 325. Brilliant cut dish with the characteristic pin wheel motif of American cut glass of the period. Possibly by Libbey and Co., Toledo, Ohio, c.1900. Diameter 8in. (20.5cm).

blanks are always cut much more deeply, giving a reflective brilliance that literally outshines the majority of contemporary English pieces (Plate 325 and Colour Plate 45, front right).

Ironically, it was the large imports of foreign cut glass into the United States that had inspired Americans to promote their own 'rich cut glass' although the cutters and engravers employed by the American factories were often of Bohemian and English origin. In 1907 the *Pottery Gazette* mentioned:

A STOURBRIDGE GLASS CUTTER — Mr. Nehemiah Packwood, who died recently at Sandwich, Mass. of pneumonia, was an expert Stourbridge glass-cutter when he emigrated to the United States in 1868. He was an especially clever designer, and did much to enhance the reputation of the Boston & Sandwich Glass Co. by whom he was employed for some years. In 1888, in partnership with his son and Mr. John Jones, he established a new glass-cutting firm under the name of N. Packwood & Co. Mr. Packwood was 71 at the time of his death. For 39 years the United States glass trade has profited by the labours of this expert Stourbridge glass-cutter, and by the labour of dozens of others. If their labour had been 'protected' here they would not have left us.

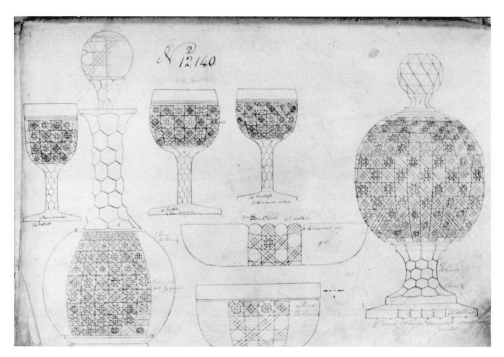

Plate 326. Brilliant cut glass service, pattern no. 12140, c.1880, from the pattern books at Thomas Webb and Sons. Thomas Webb and Sons.

Plate 327. Two wineglasses with brilliant cut cased ruby bowls, probably Stourbridge c.1880. Heights, left to right, 5in. (12.5cm) and 4¾in. (12cm).

It has been generally accepted that brilliant cut glass was a purely American development but it is more accurate to acknowledge the existence of English brilliant cut glass and see it as developing simultaneously with its American counterpart, albeit in different stylistic idioms. Within two years of the introduction of brilliant cut glass in the United States the English factories exhibited glass of equal merit. The Paris Exhibition of 1878 featured sharp, precision cutting from the Richardson factory; the greater part of one service from the exhibition still survives (Colour Plate 11, group of five to right). One very intricately cut bowl by Thomas Webb's, shown by them in the same exhibition, was bought at the time by the Conservatoire des Arts in Paris and is still in their collections. In the pages of the Webb's pattern books a design for a complete service, numbered 12140 and datable to 1880, gives further evidence for the exquisite quality of English richly cut glass at this time (Plate 326). Only one goblet has been found which matches the design (Colour Plate 45, left). Two other ruby cased and richly cut glasses date to the same period (Plate 327). In December 1880 the *Pottery Gazette* featured a note on Stourbridge glass in the United States and stressed that:

> the supreme quality of the celebrated Stourbridge glass has only been made known to the American public through the ceramic department of Messrs. Tiffany & Co. Quite recently this firm accepted the sole agency for this country of the well-known firm of Boulton and Mills and they have devoted a separate apartment in their house to the display of Boulton and Mills' richly cut and engraved full crystal glassware for the table.

At the same time as brilliant cutting was introduced in America, the Stourbridge companies had pioneered cameo and rock crystal glass and it was natural for them to combine some of the skills from those techniques with the brilliant cut style. In the Thomas Webb pattern books the great proportion of the brilliant cut designs reveal a combination of swirling ribs among the standard hobnail and strawberry diamond motifs. The skills of the engraver were also used to produce designs not seen at all in American cut glass. A superb example in the Webb books shows a decanter heavily cut with hobnails and with a handle in the form of a lizard. The pencilled comment states 'engraved over by Fritsche', meaning that the lizard handle was copper wheel engraved and deeply modelled, probably in rock crystal style by William Fritsche (Plate 328).

In the early twentieth century Webb's were supplying Continental firms with cut glass, evidence of the international popularity of the brilliant cut style. One order for jugs came from the Rheinische Glashütten in Germany in 1906 while in 1914 they made an exquisite cut bowl and stand for Carl Fabergé.

At the Stevens and Williams works in Brierley Hill the cutters and polishers created the finest surviving example of English brilliant cut glass. Their masterpiece must be the superb bowl cut with interlacing borders in ogee shapes which is in the works museum (Plate 329). Although the bowl appears at pattern number 11374, dated 28 April 1886 and selling at 354s.9d., the same design and

Colour Plate 45. The correct identification and dating of 19th century cut glass is one of the most difficult areas of glass collecting. The sheer volume of cut glass, much of it in nondescript patterns, makes it impossible to identify every piece. The situation is further complicated by the reproduction of patterns beginning as early as the 1880s and continuing into the 1920s. However, there are many characteristics or hallmarks in cut glass which, once they are recognised, will help place the item in its correct historical niche. This group of cut glasses covers some of the types the collector will find.
Back row, left to right. Wineglass, cased in ruby and cut in the brilliant style, Thomas Webb, c.1880, height 5⅛ in. (13.1cm); this service is illustrated in Plate 326. Pressed glass jug in imitation of cut glass, George Davidson, Gateshead, 1880s, height 6¼ in. (15.9cm); the jug was supplied with a tray and tumblers to match. Celery vase, Webb Richardson factory, c.1830, height 7¾ in. (19.5cm); the design for this unusual shape of celery appears in the Richardson pattern books and is illustrated in Plate 39. Decanter and stopper with brilliant cutting, possibly Stevens and Williams, c.1880s, height 13in. (33cm). Decanter and stopper in yellow/green glass coloured with uranium oxide, Stourbridge, c.1870s, height 12¼ in. (31cm). Vase with turn-over rim in the style of Irish glass of the early 19th century but made about 1930, height 14½ in. (37cm); similar bowls are found in the pages of the Hill Ouston catalogue illustrated in Plate 368. Front row, left to right. Salt cellar, Richardson's, c.1851, height 1¾ in. (4.4cm). Brilliant cut bowl, Canadian 1906-15, marked on the inside of the bowl with a clover leaf enclosing the initials GCC for Gundy, Clapperton Co. who were cutters only and obtained their blanks from American and European glass companies including Baccarat, Val St Lambert and the Libbey Glass Co. of Toledo, Ohio, height 3¾ in. (9.5cm), diameter 7⅞ in. (20cm), Ann Smith-Hajdamach Collection.

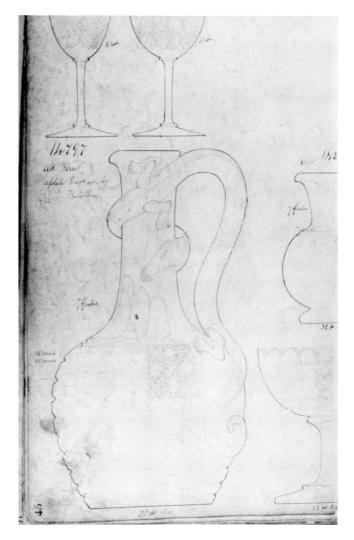

Plate 328. Design for a cut and carved jug by William Fritsche from the Thomas Webb and Sons pattern books, c.1884. Thomas Webb and Sons.

cutting was recorded on a large service at pattern number 5223 dating from 9 March 1878 (Plate 330). This important design plus the pieces from the Webb and the Richardson firms of the same date proves that, by 1878, the three major Stourbridge companies were producing cut glass comparable in quality to their American counterparts. The main difference was in the level of production. The Birmingham companies, including Osler, were also to make significant contributions to brilliant cut glass but the American factories controlled the majority of national and international markets until the early twentieth century.

Throughout the 1880s and 1890s Stevens and Williams continued to make some of the most exquisite cut glass. Some pieces have been identified while others are tantalisingly recorded in the books but have not been found (Plates 331 to 337). Cut patterns from different companies were often very similar and unless one finds precise documentation in a company design book one has to keep an open mind about attributions. Some patterns were peculiar to an individual factory and it is possible to ascribe such glasses to a company even without the existence of an identifying mark. At Stevens and Williams a square basket weave

Plate 329. Brilliant cut shell-shaped bowl with interlacing designs and scalloped top. Stevens and Williams, pattern no. 11374, 28 April 1886. Height 6½in. (16.7cm), diameter 9in. (23cm). Royal Brierley Crystal.

Plate 329A. Inside of Stevens and Williams bowl.

Plate 329B. Detail of Stevens and Williams bowl.

Plate 330. Port glass featuring the same design as the bowl in Plate 329. Stevens and Williams pattern no. 5223, 9 March 1878. Height 5in. (12.7cm).

Plate 331. Brilliant cut basket, pattern no. 7433, 5 May 1882, Stevens and Williams. Height 6⅞in. (17.5cm). Royal Brierley Crystal.

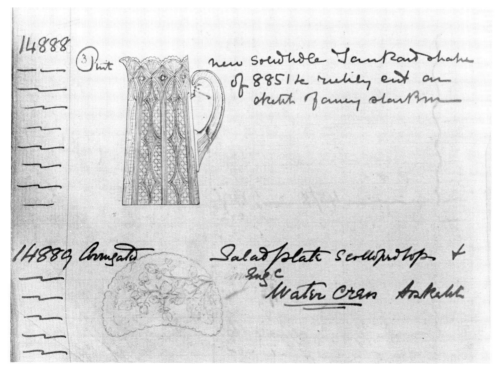

Plate 332. Design for cut glass jug described as 'new solid handle Tankard shape', pattern no. 14888, 20 July 1889, in the Stevens and Williams pattern books. The cutting shop was paid 45s. for the work and the jug sold for 80s. Royal Brierley Crystal.

Plate 334. Tazza, cut festoon decoration with applied rings at the base of the handles. Stevens and Williams, c.1891. Height 7⅛ in. (18.1cm), diameter 9¾ in. (25cm). A full page of festoon cut designs appears at no. 15859 in Book 14, dated approximately 1891.

Plate 333. Cut glass jug, probably Stevens and Williams, late 1880s. Height 8½ in. (21.7cm). The pattern of vertical cuts and fan splits is similar to the 1830s Richardson celery vase illustrated in Plate 39 and Colour Plate 45, although more than fifty years separate the two designs.

Plate 335. Decanter and stopper, cut with pin wheel motif. Stevens and Williams, c.1895. Height 10⅝ in. (27cm).

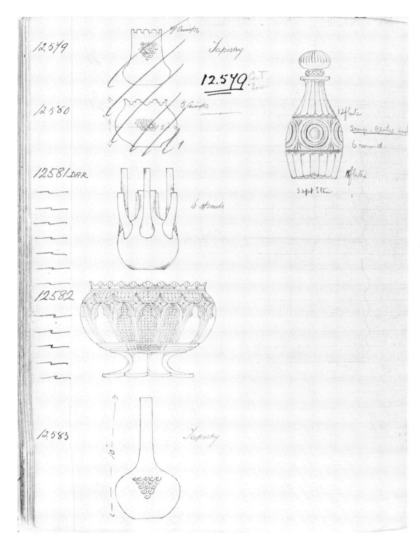

Plate 336. Design for cut glass bowl, pattern no. 12582, in the Stevens and Williams pattern books, 1887. Royal Brierley Crystal.

Plate 337. Design for cut glass bowl and a separate stand, pattern no. 30333, 21 August 1902 in the Stevens and Williams pattern books. A note by the side of the drawing states: 'Bowls weigh 20lbs. Stands weigh 7lbs. Total cutting 240/- shop.' Royal Brierley Crystal.

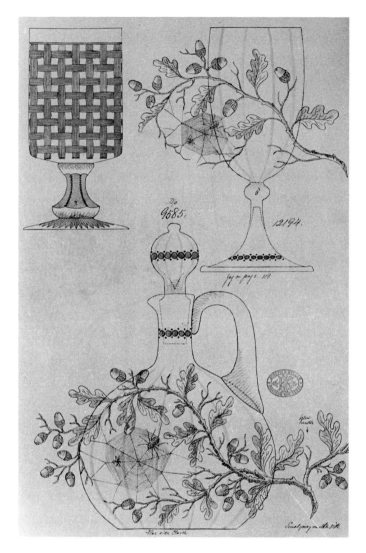

Plate 338. Designs from the Joseph Keller Book of Designs, mid-1880s, showing a goblet in the basket weave pattern which was first recorded in the Stevens and Williams pattern books at no. 10632, 11 November 1885.

effect was developed using a multi-mitre cutting wheel. On 1 December 1885 it was patented under Registered Number 38983. Most, but not all, basket weave pieces will bear this engraved number (Plate 338).

One pattern which was copied by most English factories was the famous American design known as the 'Russian'. Patented on 20 June 1882 by T.G. Hawkes & Co. in Corning, New York State, it was chosen by the Russian Embassy in Washington for a banquet service while the American Embassy in St Petersburg also ordered a service. President Cleveland purchased a six hundred piece service in 1885 for use in the White House. English versions could match the prickliest American pieces but it is more common to find shallow cut versions known in the glass trade as 'cheap Russian' (Plate 339).

In contrast to the glass service, the single large bowl, placed on a separate stand, became a fashionable item in the Edwardian period (Plate 340). The stand would sometimes double as an extra bowl or vase. The bowl shape survived into the 1920s and 1930s, although the cutting became broader and less intricate than the close facet diamond effect of the earlier period. The later bowls were popular

Plate 339. Two Stourbridge wineglasses from the 1890s showing the difference in quality between an expensive brilliant cut glass on the left and the 'cheap Russian' version on the right. The glass on the left is possibly from the Richardson company. Heights, left to right, 4¾in. (12.3cm), 5in. (12.8cm).

Plate 340. Bowl and stand, cut in the Russian pattern by Thomas Webb and Sons, c.1907. Height 11in. (27.9cm). A similar bowl was illustrated in a photograph of Webb cut glass in the Pottery Gazette of 1907.

Plate 341. Vase and square spirit decanter, Stourbridge, early 20th century. Heights: vase 11¾ in. (30cm), decanter 9⅝ in. (24.3cm).

gifts for commemorative occasions and sections of the cut design would be missed out to make room for a suitable inscription. If the bowl did not have a separate stand it would be given an ornate metal mount. Other characteristic shapes of the Edwardian era were the tall vase with panels of cutting incorporating the pin wheel design, and the classic square hobnailed spirit or liquor decanter (Plate 341). The traditional stopper for the decanters was known as a lapidary or lap cut stopper consisting of rows of facets. The lap cutting required great precision and control for there was no marking-up of guidelines as on other cut glass. Coloured glass had been used for cutting in the late nineteenth century (Colour Plate 45, second right) and, as in America, coloured and especially cased glass became even more popular at the turn of the century.

Brilliant cut glass was a symbol of material status with the middle and upper classes. Inevitably pressed glass imitations quickly became available and catered for the cheaper end of the market. Firms such as Davidson's in the North-East produced some excellent designs in a thickly made glass which gave the necessary mirror-like qualities of the originals (Colour Plate 45, second left).

The placing of factory marks on brilliant cut glass created something of a problem for the marking shop, quite simply because few areas of the glass were left uncut. On American and Canadian glass bowls and dishes, for example, the mark is usually on the inside of the base. The marks can be very faint and need to be caught in the right light to be spotted. On wineglasses one should look for the mark on one of the broad flutes on the underside of the bowl. On jugs, some factories placed their mark at the base of the handle.

Unlike engraved, enamelled or cameo glass where the applied skills of the craftsmen are readily visible, much of the preparatory work in the early stages of cutting and polishing is not immediately apparent. In the nineteenth century even the marker-up would judge the qualities of the glass and mark it in a way that the cutter would remove defects such as stones, cords and air bubbles.

In the collecting world of nineteenth century decorative arts, few areas remain where discoveries can still be made. Because of a lack of information on the subject, plus a large measure of prejudice, English brilliant cut glass is a forgotten art. In 1923, when Harry Powell wrote his book *Glass-Making in England,* he began his chapter on cutting with the comment that 'cut glass, as an English craft, has never received adequate and sympathetic treatment'. Over sixty years later that statement still holds good. Long overdue for a reappraisal by British collectors, brilliant cut glass offers the potential for some exciting finds.

CHAPTER FIFTEEN

The History of Sand-blasting

The invention of sand-blasting had taken place by 1870 when an American, Benjamin C. Tilghman, patented a sand-blast machine which was exhibited three years later in the Vienna Exhibition. The patent specified 'a stream of sand or other abrasive powder, usually dry, but sometimes mixed with water, projected with more or less force and velocity to strike and pulverize the surfaces of glass, stone, metal, and other materials upon which it is directed'. The few nineteenth century references to the technique repeat the story that Tilghman's invention was a result of observing the depolishing effect of sandstorms upon the windows of houses on the American prairies. The process was used initially to obscure, decorate and perforate glass but was soon applied to other industrial uses, including removing scale from metal castings and forgings, sharpening the teeth of files, frosting and granulating electroplate, carving on stone, slate and granite, cleaning grime from buildings and paint from ships, and even drawing on lithographic stones.

The early sand-blast machines worked on the principle of a closed iron drum with an opening at the top where the object was blasted. Within the drum a central tube ran vertically from the bottom to the top. Sand was fed from a hopper into the bottom of the drum, where a pipe extracted air from the machine causing the sand to be drawn up the tube and bombard the object held at the top. The vacuum effect also served to extract the dust resulting from the action of the sand upon the glass, while the heavier sand and particles of glass fell to the bottom of

Plate 342. Advertisement for sand-blast equipment from the Pottery Gazette, *1899.*

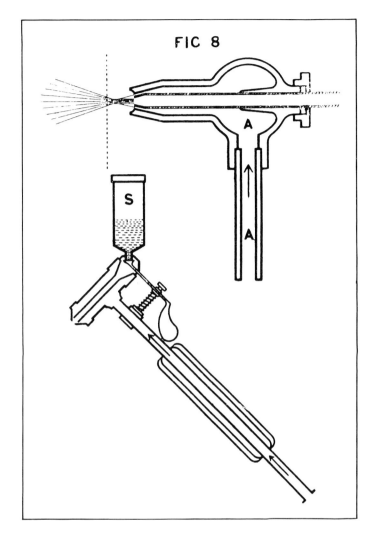

FIC 8

Plate 343. Two versions of the 'sand pencil', 1895. (S = Sand, A = Air.)

the drum to be re-circulated. Several machines could be connected to one exhaust and were normally used for small work such as glasses and bottles (Plate 342), although large sheets of glass could be decorated if they were held by two or three workmen and moved across the opening.

By the 1890s a number of innovations to the equipment had been developed, most of which consisted of better control of the air pressure and of the amount of sand available to the decorators, as well as reducing the escape of sand from the apparatus. These major design improvements form the basis of modern sand-blast equipment in the glass industry.

The main development consisted of an enclosed chamber with a viewing window and two armholes with rubber gloves in the front. The chamber contained the sand-blast dust, allowed it to be recovered, and also gave greater flexibility of decoration. The operator controlled the flow of compressed air by a foot treadle while holding the glass through the rubber gloves, directing the sand on to the glass with a nozzle known as a 'sand pencil' (Plate 343). Mixing the sand with the air blast inside the nozzle itself eliminated much of the excessive wear on the feed pipes and also gave the operator far more control over the quality of his work.

The abrasives used in the process consisted mainly of sand sifted into various sizes, but use was also made of sharp builders' sand, powdered glass, emery, chilled iron-sand, and steel shot. Air pressure could be achieved by steam, by exhaust air, by blasts of air and, more conveniently, by compressed air which is the method used today. The term sand-blast implies a fairly strong air pressure which was certainly possible after the introduction of compressed air or gas in the mid-1890s. The earlier exhaust air systems could only give a working pressure of about 1lb. per square inch (.45kg per 6.45 sq.cm), which could be increased to 20 or 25lb. with the use of steam and very fine sand. Pressure in modern machines ranges from 10 to 15lb. (4.5kg to 6.75kg), up to a maximum of 80lb. per square inch (36.25kg per 6.45 sq.cm).

In glass decoration a protective overlay or stencil allowed the cut-out design and open areas to be sand-blasted while the remainder of the surface was left untouched by the abrasive. The nineteenth century overlay resist was a quick drying mixture of glue, dextrine, glycerine and any powdered colouring matter to give body, very similar to present day resists. This particular combination provided a strong resist to the sand-blast while maintaining a flexibility during application on to the glass. When a design had to be repeated a number of times the simplest and quickest method of producing a stencil was to print the resist from a copper plate and transfer it on to the glass with tissue paper somewhat similar to transfer printing ceramics. Stencils were also made from soft rubber and lead foil. A writer in the *Pottery Gazette* in August 1895 stated that 'for figures and original designs the glass is entirely covered with a sheet of paper dipped in the mixture [i.e. glue, glycerine, etc.] through which, when dry, the design is cut out with a pointed knife; sometimes numerous morsels of the prepared paper are separately attached to the glass'. The modern equivalent are the plastic-backed adhesive papers ideal for creating one-off designs.

The same writer was also aware of the possibilities of sand-blasting cased glass when he wrote that 'the sandblast is in constant use for the decoration, in which the pattern or the field may be left bright and transparent, one being on glass of two or more thicknesses of different colours, to leave the design of one colour on a field of another'. This reference must be to window glass as no nineteenth century cameo vases with sand-blasted decoration are known. The tedious job of painting stencils on to sheet glass by hand was quickly automated so that the stencil was printed on to the glass by rollers, the resist was then covered with a protective drying agent, the glass moved over the sand-blast machines and finally a set of brush rollers removed the resist leaving the decorated glass ready for drying and packing.

Once the stencil had been applied to the glass the speed of decoration was very quick; for example, lampshades could be decorated at between sixty to one hundred an hour. Using a compressed air machine worked by a half horsepower gas engine, the Weights and Measures Offices of the London County Council could mark publicans' half-pint glasses at the rate of 1,200 per hour using only one employee. Even with the less efficient older machines with lower pressure,

*Plate 344. Two pressed tumblers with sand-blast decoration, late 19th century.
Author's Collection. Heights: left 4½in. (11.4cm), right 4¾in. (12.1cm).*

the number of half-pint glasses marked in an hour was still five hundred, and with some machines, which were hand-powered and required two men to operate them, the average number of glasses marked per hour was 650. The average cost of decorating 1,000 glasses varied from 6s. to 2s.11d. depending on the type of machine.

The relative shortage of sand-blasted glass makes it difficult to judge how popular the technique was as a decorative process. In the main, the existing glasses, mostly tumblers and the occasional jug or goblet, are of cheap pressed glass and bear commemorative inscriptions, for example 'A Birthday Gift 1886', or 'Queen Victoria's Jubilee 1837-1897', while events such as the opening of the Manchester Ship Canal in 1894 inspired a number of souvenir glasses (Plates 344 and 345). It is likely that glasses with sand-blasted decoration were made in significant numbers but such objects carried the cheapest form of decoration and if chipped or cracked they would be quickly discarded.

Sand-blast decoration can be recognised by the granular, frosted texture of the designs. The lettered glasses also show the problems with stencil plates where isolated solid portions, as in the centres of numbers 8 or 6 and letters A and B, had to be retained in position with bars or ties (Plate 346). For better work this was overcome by using two or more tinfoil stencils, the first giving the design and the second pierced with holes only, corresponding to the ties.

Today the attitude of the glass decorators to sand-blasting has been completely reversed with the realisation that this technique can produce fine results. All the

Plate 345. Jug and tumbler with sand-blast decoration, late 19th century. Heights: jug 7¼ in. (18.4cm), tumbler 4½ in. (11.4cm).

Plate 346. Two pub glasses, probably early 20th century. Heights: left 4¾ in. (12.1cm), right 4½ in. (11.4cm).

major glass firms involved in decorating glass, especially in the Stourbridge area, rely on sand-blast to the exclusion of acid-etching. In the late 1970s the process was used to create some fine figurative effects on cameo and cased glass by C. David Smith, the chief designer at the Webb Corbett factory.

CHAPTER SIXTEEN

Friggers and Novelties

Friggers, or whimsies as they are called in North America where the English name has less delicate connotations, represent the personal and social aspect of the glass industry. The word 'frigger' has a variety of meanings and an ancient lineage. In Henry Bradley's *A Middle-English Dictionary* the word 'frig' is given as Anglo-Saxon and in *An Anglo-Saxon Dictionary* based on Joseph Bosworth's work, it has two definitions — free and noble, or love, affection and favour. Most English dialects use a form of the word; for example in Yorkshire a 'frigary' was a whim or caprice. Trifles and ornaments were often known as 'friggle-fraggles'. In glass literature the term was first used by Harry Powell in 1923 in *Glass-Making in England* and in 1938 by Arnold Fleming in his *Scottish and Jacobite Glass*. The wide variety of descriptions when placed within a glassmaking context fits in well with the idea of the glassmaker playing about with making small articles for himself in his own time. Throughout the history of glass blowing, the glassmaker has relieved the tedium of production by creating a charming variety of glass novelties (Colour Plate 46).

The term frigger is often used indiscriminately for any glass which is unusual or does not have an obvious use. A true frigger would be a decorative and humorous item, showing off the glassmaker's skill. In this category one would place hats, trumpets and bugles, walking sticks, Jacob's ladders, bellows, pipes, bells and animals of every description with swans and pigs the most popular. Useful objects which are often grouped with friggers but which were made as commercial lines by the factories include fly catchers, linen smoothers, cupping glasses (for blood letting), nipple shields, feeding cups, sugar crushers, hearing trumpets, smoke shades for gas lights, bird feeders and cucumber straighteners (Plate 347). During the nineteenth century they were regarded as essential items for daily use. This category should also contain the well-known gimmel flasks consisting of two separate compartments and decorated in a similar manner to friggers with trails and loops of colour. Somewhere between these two categories would come the novelty glass containers which were used to sell an assortment of sweets and candies. Once the sweets had been enjoyed by the children the containers would be used as toys. Glass pistols were the most popular; one intact example exists at the Castle Museum, York, complete with its contents of 'hundreds and thousands' held in by a cork stopper. They sometimes bear the retailer's name on the side. Railway engines, with sliding metal closures over the cab, and steamships were later variations on the theme. The modern day equivalents for grown-ups are the figurative containers marketed by the Avon cosmetic company containing aftershaves and perfumes.

Some friggers became associated with legends and superstitions. The walking

Plate 347. 19th century utilitarian glassware. Ear trumpet 5 ¼ in. (13.3cm), bird feeder 6 ½ in. (16.5cm), gas bell shade 7 ¼ in. (18.5cm), cupping glass, bottom left, 3 ½ in. (9cm), nipple shield 3 ¾ in. (9.7cm).

stick, for example, was supposed to be hung inside the front door of the house and had to be rubbed and cleaned each day by the housewife to prevent any evil befalling the occupants. The witch's ball served the same function. Made in all sizes and colours, sometimes silvered on the inside, they were hung in a prominent window to repel evil spirits. They are sometimes seen containing a lock of hair to assist the good luck charm. Another novelty, the glass rolling-pin, is traditionally said to have been a token of love brought by the returning sailor to his girl-friend.

Friggers which were definitely put to good use were the bugles and trumpets referred to in many of the reports of glassmakers' processions. Some hearsay stories tell of glassmakers smoking their glass pipes but perhaps this is stretching credibility too far. One of the most popular friggers with nineteenth century glassmakers and one which is rarely mentioned in glass literature is the flip-flop (Colour Plate 46, bottom right). Flip-flops are normally the size of a large wineglass, minus the foot, with a hollow stem and a very thin membrane of glass across the top of the bowl. A gentle blow down the stem to increase the air pressure inside the bowl causes the membrane to vibrate outwards. Their name implies a soft gentle sound but flip-flops give a sharp, ear-piercing crack which frightens not only the blower but also the audience. Falling just within the category of musical instruments they were extremely fragile, hence the scarcity of nineteenth century examples. They were probably made as children's toys, although somewhat dangerous, and required a great deal of control on the part of the glassmaker. In 1893 one writer described them as 'a bottle about the shape but smaller than a mason's mallet, blown so thin at the bottom that the glass vibrates as you blow into it at the neck end, and as a consequence comes back again as you draw back your breath; the noise occasioned by this action produces the noise which resembles the sound by which it is called, viz, "flip-flop". In addition to this action boys used to put this thin part to their lips and sing upon it, when the vibration caused a sound consequent on their breath bearing upon the thin surface; it was then called a "singing glass".'

An engraving of 1711 by Pierce Tempest after Marcel Laroon inscribed 'Buy my fine singing Glasses' shows an itinerant hawker with two glass trumpets and two shorter objects, similar in shape to flip-flops but with a small hole at the flat end. It is difficult to imagine how these open shapes worked but they may be a version of the flip-flop idea. An English writer of 1890 described singing glasses as 'being used 50 years ago by glass lads when going out carol singing at Christmas time', a description which is close to the 1893 one.

Jacob's ladders are as rarely mentioned as flip-flops and if they are mentioned it is with inaccurate information such as. Newman's bold statement in his *Dictionary* that 'Jacob's ladders were made of Nailsea Glass'. Friggers, like so many glasses, were not peculiar to one area, nor was their method of manufacture. The individual spirals of a Jacob's ladder are one of the easiest things to make. The late Colin Gill at the Brierley Hill Glass Centre would delight in revealing the simplicity of the making. The process uses one of the glassmaker's tools, the pincers, which are pressed together almost to closing point but leaving a small amount of spare movement. From a gather of molten glass a small thread is pulled out, still connected to the main gather, and placed on to the widest spacing of the pincers. It is then wound spirally around the handle downwards towards the tips of the pincers. Because the glass is so thin, it cools and sets around the pincers very quickly and is released by pressing in the pincers and taking up the spare movement that was allowed at the beginning.

The majority of friggers which the collector will come across today generally date from the late nineteenth and early twentieth century. Now that the large glass companies no longer use coloured glass there is no opportunity for the glassmakers to rival their ancestors and produce friggers which could be reproductions. However, two types of friggers are still made occasionally in clear glass and could be sold as nineteenth century examples. These are swans and pigs which can be made very quickly by manipulating a solid lump of glass and, because they are made to traditional patterns, it is often impossible to distinguish between old and new.

By the 1870s glass novelties were produced on a regular basis by many glassworks which realised their commercial potential and aimed them at a more sophisticated market which relished the idea of novelties and curiosities. In their display at the 1878 Paris Exhibition Richardson's showed a pair of glass crowns

Plate 348. Glass crowns by Richardson's shown at the Paris Exhibition, 1878. The one on the left sold for 55s., the one on the right for 50s.

(Plate 348) and a miniature bowler hat (Colour Plate 46, top centre). Two flower stands, in the same display, included hanging baskets shaped as half-closed umbrellas which, if they have become separated from their stand over the ensuing years, could be mistaken for friggers. In 1908 Thomas Webb's made little pigs in opalescent glass to give or sell as souvenirs, complete with gift box, at their display at the Franco-British Exhibition in London (Colour Plate 46, centre left).

The best occasions for the glassmakers to exhibit their skills to the public were the processions and picnics which formed a major social event in the life of a glassmaking district. The idea appears as early as 1268 in a Venetian chronicle which lists 'water bottles and scent flasks and other such graceful objects of glass' which were part of a procession celebrating the inauguration of the reign of Doge Lorenzo Tiepolo. The only known illustration of a British trades procession which included glassmakers is a drawing dating from 1831 in the Bristol City Art Gallery (Plate 349). The procession was in celebration of the coronation of William IV. A similar procession, in which the Company of Glassmen 'went on horseback, some with swords, others with crowns and sceptres in their hands made of glass', was held almost a hundred years earlier in Bristol in 1738 to greet the Prince and Princess of Wales. Numerous other written accounts from other parts of the country conjure up the excitement of these events:

> Today, September 28 1823, the workmen employed in several of the glass-houses of Newcastle and Gateshead made a procession through the principal streets, each bearing in his hand a specimen of his art, remarkable either for its curious construction or for its beauty and elegance. The morning was ushered in with the

Plate 349. Detail from the coronation procession for William IV showing the glassmakers' section. Watercolour on paper, published by William Greethead, 1831. Bristol City Art Gallery Collection.

ringing of bells, and notice of the intended procession having been previously circulated, numbers of persons crowded the streets. A little after twelve o'clock it moved forward along the Close amid the cheers of the assembled multitude, the firing of cannon, etc., and preceded by the band of the Tyne Hussars. It was composed of the workmen of the South Shields, the Northumberland, the Wear (Sunderland), the Durham and British (Gateshead), the Stourbridge (Gateshead), and the North Shields Companies, arranged according to the seniority of their respective houses, and each distinguished by appropriate flags. The sky was clear, and the rays of the sun, falling on the glittering utensils and symbols, imparted richness and grandeur to their appearance. The hat of every person present was decorated with a glass feather, whilst a glass star sparkled on the breast, and a chain or collar of variegated glass hung round the neck; some wore glass sashes round the waist. Each man carried in his hand a staff with a cross piece at the top displaying one or more curious or beautiful specimens of art, consisting of decanters, goblets, glasses, jugs, bowls, dishes, etc., the staple articles of the trade in an endless variety of elegant shapes and exquisite workmanship. A glass bugle, which sounded the 'halts' and played several marches, was much admired for its sweetness and correctness of tone. Many of the men wore glass hats, and carried glass swords. When the procession arrived at the Mansion House it halted, while a salute was fired from a fort mounted with glass cannon to the astonishment of the spectators.

In Stourbridge the processions were part of splendid 'monstre-pic-nics' which were more akin to modern fairs and included dancing and singing, archery contests, cricket matches, circus events and exhibitions of glass from all the

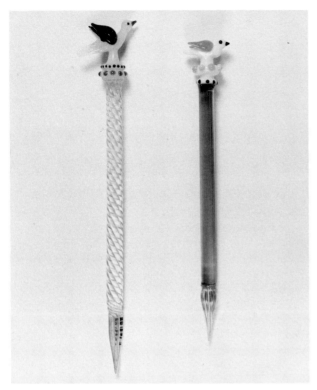

Plate 350. Glass pens, with bird finials, late 19th or early 20th century. Lengths: left 5¾in. (14.7cm), right 5in. (12.5cm).

Plate 351. Three cigar or cheroot holders, the middle one with a cameo scene of Dudley Castle. Late 19th or early 20th century. Lengths: left to right, 3¼in. (8.4cm) Hickman Collection, 4¼in. (11cm), 4in. (10cm.).

factories. Profits went to the glassmakers' and cutters' superannuation and relief funds. The fêtes would be held at one of the larger parks, either Prestwood Park, near Wordsley, or in the grounds of Hagley Hall. A typical fête, of 1859, included the glassmakers procession:

> which started from the Toll Gate, Wordsley soon after nine o'clock. Headed by Moore's Worcestershire Sax Horn Band, came the glassmakers and glass cutters, carrying a variety of beautiful glass ornaments and articles of different descriptions, including vases, decanters, glasses etc., while here and there were articles of a more costly and unique description, such as a pair of blow-bellows beautifully ornamented and gilded, a wheelbarrow, baskets etc. all manufactured from the same brittle material; and not a few wore glass hats of different shapes and designs, of their own manufacture. Prominent amongst the rest of the miscellaneous articles, was a large black rat, distinguished with a tail of considerable length.

Visitors to the 1859 fête were 'initiated into the mysteries of glass-making by Mr. S. Edwards of Stourbridge, who manufactured all kinds of fancy ornaments or anything that was required by the visitor, by means of the lamp and pipe, with surprising facility and evident skill'. Lampworking had become a popular technique during the nineteenth century, often practised by itinerant craftsmen who travelled between the major glassmaking centres and worked free lance at the factories. Three-masted sailing ships with sailors in the rigging are the best known examples of their work. One advertisement which mentions glass ships referred to:

Mr. Johnson, a native of Sweden, and just returned from South America, has had the honour of exhibiting before the King of France and Suite while at Brighton and patronised by distinguished Noblemen and Gentry. Mr. Davis assures the public that they are the only ship builders travelling the Kingdom and they will blow any article wanted while the company are present. Glass Blowing, Spinning, Linking and Modelling.

Birds of paradise with spun glass tails placed in elaborate settings of fountains were a close second in popularity to ships. Spun glass was in use in the eighteenth century; for example, in Milan a glass fibre wig was spun by an Antonio Lerau about 1740. At the Great Exhibition of 1851 multi-coloured ties were in fashion, including one spun in the colours of the St Helens Football Club. Spun glass dresses are also known, complete with spun glass shoes and handbags. In the twentieth century well-known lampworkers such as Billy Swingewood in Stourbridge would make their spun glass by spinning it on to the rim of an old bicycle wheel. Glass pens with bird finials were a favourite with Swingewood and other lampworkers (Plate 350). One range of novelties which never receives mention in glass literature is the glass cheroot or cigar holder, produced in every technique including cased and cut, lampwork, threaded, acid etched and cameo (Plate 351). In the past they have been wrongly identified as posy or flower holders which were probably made but would need to have one end closed to prevent any water soaking on to the clothes.

Lampwork pieces are very rarely signed or labelled but there are at least three stag hunts in existence which are signed with the name Aubin, on the right-hand fence of the tableaux (Plate 352). The style of the cabinet suggests the Regency period, a date confirmed by a poster in the Pilkington Glass Museum advertising Aubin's workshop.

AUBIN
GLASS WORKER IN MINIATURE
To Her Majesty and the Princesses
Respectfully informs the Nobility and Gentry, that he had commenced exhibiting in the above Room,
His experiments of
GLASS-WORKING,
And Spinning of common Window-Glass, into the finer Substance than anything in the World
As he spins from common Window-Glass the Company may bring, One Mile Length of the same in One Minute and Fifteen Seconds, which shall only weigh eight Grains; from that he will prove one Pound Weight of the same sort of Glass will spin upwards on One Thousand Miles!!!
The same he has had the Honour to exhibit repeatedly before THEIR MAJESTIES and the ROYAL FAMILY; likewise on the 3rd of April 1813, he removed his beautiful Apparatus from Oxford to Blenheim House, and had the Honour to display his Works before His Grace the DUKE OF MARLBOROUGH and a select Party, as well as before some of the first Nobility, and received from them the most flattering acknowledgements of their Approbation. Indeed, he presumes from his long experience, and intense application to its Improvement, that he has now brought this Art to the Highest degree of Perfection.
He makes various kinds of Ornaments of all Colours in Glass, before the Company, for Sale.
Open daily from 11 in the Morning till 4. — Saturdays and Sundays excepted.
A variety of Glass Necklaces from 7s. to 11.1s.—Royal 21.2s. each—Feathers, Bandeaus, &c., from 5s to 10s.6d—Baskets of Flowers from 3s. to 11.1s. Pens 1s. to 5s. each.—Glass Anchors, Crosses, Rings, Birds' Nests, Quadrupeds, Smelling Bottles, &c., 1s. to 7s.6d. each
The Figures, Quadrupeds, Birds &c. are all made of different coloured Glass before the Company, whilst the Glass is in a fluid state, without the use of any kind of instrument whatever! and on so deminutive a scale, that Mr. A is in the habit of using Hazel Nuts as packed cases for them; and even
SIX ELEPHANTS are inclosed in ONE HEMPSEED!!!

Plate 352. A stag hunt, lampworked glass set inside a gilt wooden box. Signed 'Aubin' on the fence on the extreme right, early 19th century. 7¼in. high x 15in. wide (18.5cm x 38cm). Private Collection.

Plate 352A. Detail of the stag hunt by Aubin. Mirror panels at the sides and back, with the addition of applied flying crows, enhance the impression both of distance and of the number of huntsmen.

Aubin's full name was Charles David Aubin or St. Aubin. He was born in France in 1778 and, according to family history, fled to England during the French Revolution, although this has yet to be proved. He was known to have staged an exhibition of his work in Shropshire Street, Market Drayton. His son, also a Charles Aubin, became a famous locksmith and exhibited 'The Aubin Lock Trophy' at the Great Exhibition for which he was awarded a Prize Medal. Aubin died in Wolverhampton in 1855.

Plate 353. Joe Lees, master glassblower, making a yard of ale at the Tudor Crystal factory in Stourbridge in the 1970s. Photographs courtesy Mrs. Jane Roberts.

Plate 354. Whatnot (or etagère), cut glass with mirrors and electroplated supports. By F. & C. Osler, Birmingham, c.1882. Height 37¼ in. (94.5cm). Birmingham Museum and Art Gallery.

Within the area of novelty glass one must include the yard of ale. The earliest mention of the predecessor of the yard of ale came in John Evelyn's *Diary* when, on 10 February 1685, he visited Bromley in Kent, made his way to the market place in the midst of soldiers and public and saw 'His Majesty's health being drunk in a flint glasse of a yard long, by the Sheriff, Commander, Officers and cheife Gentlemen'. Later examples were given a flared foot. The stages of making a yard of ale are clearly seen in a series of photographs of Joe Lees working at the Tudor Crystal factory in Stourbridge in the 1970s (Plate 353). It is interesting to note that once the stem and bowl were blown the glass was cracked off the blowing-iron and then held by hand for the re-heating, shearing and final shaping of the rim.

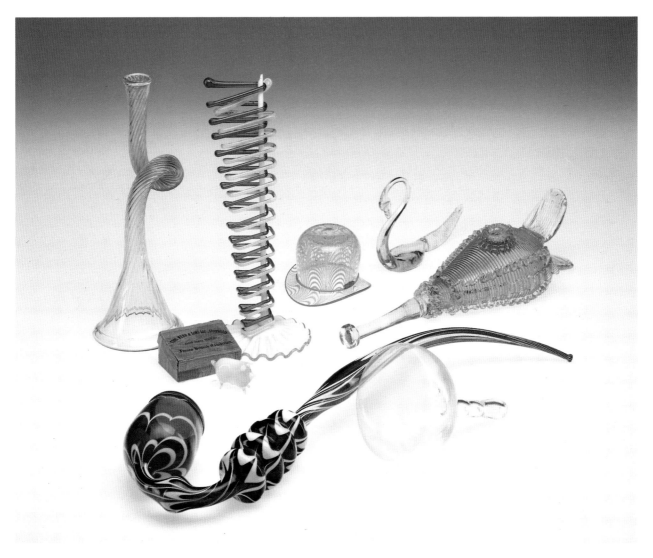

Colour Plate 46. A selection of classic glassmakers' novelties from Stourbridge. Back row, left to right: bugle with wrythen decoration, late 19th century, height 11in. (28cm); pig, complete with its presentation box from the Franco-British Exhibition of 1908, Thomas Webb and Sons, length 2in. (5cm); Jacob's ladder, late 19th century, height 11½ in. (29.2cm); bowler hat, probably by Richardson's, c.1880, height 2¾ in. (7cm); swan, early 20th century, height 4¾ in. (12cm); bellows, late 19th century, length 13in. (33cm).
Front row: pipe, late 19th century, length 20¾ in. (52.7cm); flip-flop, Stuart Crystal, 1980s, length 5¾ in. (14.6cm).

Not within the true spirit of friggers but still in the category of extraordinary glass novelties from the nineteenth century were the spectacular sets of glass furniture produced at Midlands factories. In 1884 the *Pottery Gazette* could not resist commenting upon a

magnificent billiard table, the entire framework of which is made of richly cut crystal glass. It has been manufactured by the executors of the late Joseph Webb of Stourbridge, for a wealthy East Indian merchant. The work is very finely executed, and the effect when lit up by brilliant light, is truly beautiful. This enterprising firm has been very successful lately in obtaining orders from India for crystal glass furniture and they have now another billiard table in hand, in addition to a suite of chairs, settees and sofas.

In Birmingham, the Osler factory transferred its skill of creating enormous glass fountains and candelabra in mid-century to the production of glass furniture at the end of the century. A cut glass whatnot or etagère with electroplated brass supports and mirror shelving, in the Birmingham Museum and Art Gallery, shows the elaborate nature of these constructions which were exported, like the Webb table, to Indian palaces (Plate 354).

CHAPTER SEVENTEEN

Fakes, Forgeries and Reproductions

At first glance the various nineteenth century techniques which were technically difficult to achieve would seem to offer few opportunities for fakes and forgeries. Even if anyone today had the skills to emulate the nineteenth century glassmakers the results would be financially unviable and it would be cheaper to buy the originals. However, there are many areas, even in the highest quality glass, where fake signatures, reproductions or outright fakes can cause difficulties for both newcomer and experienced collector alike.

MARKS AND SIGNATURES

Signatures and factory marks began to appear more often on glassware in the second half of the nineteenth century and these are obviously of great assistance to the collector. The reader is referred to Appendix 12 for detailed information on various signatures and marks. With the large increase in prices for certain types of nineteenth century glass, fake marks and signatures have been added to original items to increase their value. The irony of such fake marks is that they are often put on to very high quality objects which are collectable in their own right.

In one example a superbly engraved rock crystal glass bowl has been given the large signature 'Fritchie' (Plate 355). Genuine signatures by W. Fritsche were wheel engraved in a shallow script complete with initial (see Appendix 12, 29). The depth and regularity of the Fritchie signature, probably done with a flexible drive drill, immediately gives cause for suspicion. The bowl is likely to have been given the fake signature in the Stourbridge area where this Bohemian name was mispronounced and the forger used the phonetic spelling without taking the time to check a genuine signature. The phonetic spelling even appears in the Webb pattern books at number 15037 in 1885, but there can be no doubt that the signature on the bowl is a fake. The bowl was part of a larger English rock crystal service of nineteenth century date, each item monogrammed with the initial G, and is attributed to Frederick Kny rather than to Fritsche. It is interesting to note that another member of the Fritsche family, Hieronimus William Fritsche, travelled via Scotland and Dublin before settling in America where he anglicised his name to Fritchie.

In the field of cameo glass it is impossible for modern engravers to reproduce the quality and feel of pieces from the late nineteenth century. The addition of factory marks or signatures is the only avenue left open to the person who wishes to enhance the value of a piece. Genuine, signed pieces by George Woodall and his brother Tom are easily available for study in the major holdings of glass in museums in America and England and therefore any suspect signatures on cameo

Plate 355. Rock crystal bowl of about 1890 with fake signature 'Fritchie'. Height 2 ¾ in. (7cm), diameter 5 ⅛ in. (13cm). Pacifico Collection.

Plate 355A. Detail of 'Fritchie' signature.

glasses can easily be checked with reputable sources (see Appendix 12, 30). Less easily documented are the clear, engraved glasses which Woodall is said to have worked on but which are difficult to authenticate. The obvious criterion for verifying any glass in this category is the quality of the engraving. Anything less than the quality of his cameo work should be regarded as suspect. An example of this problem has recently been uncovered at the Jones Museum of Ceramics and Glass in Maine, due to the watchfulness of its director, Dorothy-Lee Jones. On display in the museum is a jug, with polished engraving of flowers and leaves

Colour Plate 47. Five examples of 20th century glass made in imitation of 19th century products. Left to right. Burmese-type jug, probably Venetian, 1940s or later, height 5⅜ in. (13.5cm). Bowl in Burmese glass transfer printed with repeat leaf pattern, Fenton Glass Company, West Virginia, c.1970s, height 3½ in. (8.9cm), Hulbert of Dudley Collection. The base has a raised moulded mark with the name of Fenton inside an oval cartouche. The granular texture of the jug and the transfer printed decoration of the bowl do not appear in genuine Burmese examples from the 1880s and 1890s. Amethyst wineglass, made by L. & S. Hingley, Wordsley, early 20th century, height 4⅞ in. (12.4cm). With the rough pontil mark and the capstan stem this glass could easily be mistaken for an early 19th century example, although the ogee shaped bowl and the lack of wear on the foot would give cause for suspicion. Pressed wineglass, marked 'Made in Taiwan', c.1980s, height 4in. (10.1cm), Author's Collection. Without the mark this glass could be mistaken for some of the crude pressed glass of the 1890s. Cut glass tumbler by Richardson's, c.1900, height 3¾ in. (9.5cm). Made as part of a range of reproductions of George III cut glass (see Plate 367), the tumbler has a brilliant silvery quality which is quite distinctive from the sparkle of early 19th century cut glass.

framing the scene of a young girl on a swing, signed with the name George Woodall (Plate 356). Unnoticed until now, on the topside of the foot, is the extremely faint mark for the firm of Thomas Hawkes and Co. in Corning, New York. Investigations by Dorothy-Lee Jones indicate that the engraved jug appears in a photograph taken in 1905 showing H.H. Clinger, a Hawkes salesman, displaying his wares in a hotel room. The circumstances of the addition of the Woodall signature are still under investigation.

Plate 356. Jug engraved with a girl on a swing with a fake signature of George Woodall. The foot bears a faint acid etched mark for the American factory of Thomas Hawkes of Corning. Height 14⅜ in. (36.5cm). Private collection.

Fake Stevens and Williams and Thomas Webb Marks

In the last twenty or thirty years, judging by stories within the antiques trade and from known examples of glass, it appears that acid etched marks from the two companies have been imitated and placed on previously unmarked but genuine items. The fake marks would seem to derive from an unidentified American source and the examples of glass discussed in this section, with the exception of the vase in Plate 363, have all been recorded in the United States.

One fake mark appears on a moss agate vase with ormolu mounts, which normally would be attributed to the French glassmaker Leveille who specialised in this marbled effect (Plate 357). On the shoulder of the vase a circular 'Stevens and Williams/Stourbridge/Art Glass' mark tries to prove that the vase is an English moss agate version. No factory would ever place a mark in such a prominent position. Due to the lower half and base of the vase being covered by

Plate 357. Vase in imitation of moss agate with metal mounts. Probably by Ernest Leveille, it bears a suspicious Stevens and Williams mark. Height 8in. (20.3cm). Jones Museum of Glass and Ceramics, Maine, USA.

the metal mount, the faker, intent on marking it somehow, had no option but to use the shoulder. Ironically, from a financial point of view it may be worth slightly more as a Leveille piece than as a Stevens and Williams example.

A similar Stevens and Williams mark appeared on a millefiori bowl which came up for auction in 1988 in America. The style and technique of the bowl matched the known production of similar millefiori bowls in the 1870s by the Venice and Murano Glass Company in imitation of ancient Roman examples (Colour Plate 24). Without the mark the glass would be attributed to that source. Unfortunately further confusion was added by the attribution of the design to Frederick Carder while he was a young designer at the Stevens and Williams factory prior to his departure to America in 1902. There are no records on either side of the Atlantic to prove or disprove this theory. Carder himself did little to identify items which he may have designed in England and even pieces of Stevens and Williams origin that are in the Carder display at the Rockwell Museum in Corning cannot be proved definitely to be from Carder's own hand. In America, unlike England, the name of Frederick Carder is held in total reverence. Any serious questioning of Carder myths is rarely expressed in public, a situation which makes it ideal for the forger to produce 'Carder/Stevens and Williams' fakes.

The appearance in auction sales in the United States of two cameo vases,

395

Colour Plate 48. Millefiori paperweights and scent bottles. Small scent bottle with millefiori canes including four making up the date 1848 which matches the design known to have been used at the Walsh Walsh factory in Birmingham in the 1920s; height 4in. (10cm), Michael Parkington Collection. Large scent bottle with date canes for 1848; the size and style of the bottle matches the designs from the R.C. Richardson records of reproduction bottles and weights which were supplied through Hill Ouston in 1934, illustrated in Plate 372; height 5½in. (14cm). Paperweight with a portrait of a lady, probably Queen Victoria, mid-19th century; height 1⅞in. (4.8cm), diameter 3⅛in. (8cm); the positioning of the canes has some resemblance to a known weight with the initials IGW thought to stand for the Islington Glass Works of Rice Harris in Birmingham. Paperweight with a tall dome and red, white and blue canes, probably English, mid-19th century, height 3in. (7.5cm), diameter 3¾in. (9.5cm); this type of weight is usually referred to as Stourbridge, but there is no documentary evidence for this speculation.

undoubtedly from the same factory but with two different marks, provides conclusive proof that fake Webb and Stevens and Williams marks have been applied indiscriminately, in America, to genuine examples from those companies. On 18 May 1990 in the sale of art glass at the Bolton salerooms of Skinner Inc. in Boston, Massachussets, Lot 97 was catalogued as a 'Stevens and Williams Heat Reactive Cameo Vase, opal white body overlaid with white over

Plate 358. Group of Stourbridge cameo vases illustrated in the sale of art glass and lamps by Skinner of Boston on 18 May 1990. Lot 97, the heat reactive vase with the fake Stevens and Williams mark, is on the extreme right of the group. All of this group, from Lot 91 on the left to 97, bear the 'Stevens and Williams Art Glass Stourbridge' trade mark. This in itself gives cause for suspicion. In a similar group of Stevens and Williams cameo vases in the Broadfield House Collections, which have known provenances to the factory, none of the pieces is marked.

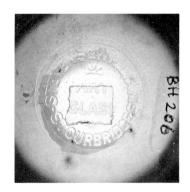

Plate 359. Another view of Lot 97. Height 9¼in. (23.5cm). Michael Parkington Collection.

Plate 360. Detail of fake mark on Lot 97. Diameter ½in. (1.4cm).

Plate 361. Detail of genuine Stevens and Williams mark from a cameo and silver deposit vase.

an amber to blue-green heat reactive layer, the white cameo cut and carved overall with morning glory blossoms, leaves and vines, signed on base with circular "Stevens & Williams Stourbridge Art Glass", ht. 9¼ inches.' (Plate 358). The vase was acquired by Michael Parkington who made it available for documentation (Plate 359). The detail of the mark (Plate 360) shows a number of irregularities when compared with genuine marks from Stevens and Williams (Plate 361). The fake mark lacks the definition of the genuine examples and in places the acid seems to have penetrated underneath the resist layer to make the fake mark difficult to read.

At the same salerooms on 5 October 1990 Lot 101 was an identical vase to Lot 97 in the May auction (Plate 362). The heat reactive colouring was the same while a close comparison of the layout and style of the carving of the flowers and leaves left no doubt that both vases were not only from the same factory but were by the same hand. Both vases were of the identical heights of 9¼ in. (23.5cm). However the Lot 101 vase was stamped with the words 'Thomas Webb & Sons' in a semicircular banner.

A third cameo vase with the identical heat reactive colouring of blue/green to amber but carved with a passion flower and leaves helps to identify the correct factory and provides another example of a fake Webb mark (Plates 363 and 364). The execution of the passion flower is similar to known Stevens and Williams examples, some of which were carved by Joshua Hodgetts. The appearance of the band at the base of the neck is a Stevens and Williams hallmark. This vase therefore confirms the other two vases with the identical heat reactive colouring as Stevens and Williams. However, the faker of the marks has not taken these obvious points into consideration before applying the fake Webb mark.

The final question which remains to be investigated is the source of these forged marks on cameo glass. A clue to the likely culprit or culprits was provided by the provenance of Lot 101 given in the catalogue of the sale which stated 'George Woodall Collection; Beatrice Alice Woodall Collection'. This note refers to the sale of glass held in Kingswinford in 1955 following the death of Woodall's daughter Beatrice Alice who had operated a small antiques business from the shop which had formerly been run as a milliners (Plate 219). In view of the fact that the majority of the cameo glasses which had remained in her possession were acquired by a very small group of dealers and collectors from the United States, it should not prove too difficult a task to trace the history of these examples and consequently the fake marks to their source. This should be done by the pooling of information by all of the interested parties, including the dealers and salerooms who have been asked to sell these glasses and collectors who can trace the previous whereabouts of cameo glasses in their own collections. Such co-operation will reveal not only the full extent of the fake marks and help to clear up the confusion of misleading attributions, but it will remove suspicion from those individuals and companies who deal with cameo glass and are innocent of any fraud, and direct the guilt to the real offenders.

The similarity of the two vases in the American salerooms was first noticed by

Plate 362. Group of Stourbridge cameo vases illustrated in the sale of art glass and lamps by Skinner on 5 October 1990. Lot 101, the heat reactive vase with the fake Webb mark, is on the extreme left. Height 9¼ in. (23.5cm). By having the Lot 97 vase from the earlier sale to handle and compare with this photograph there is no doubt that the two vases are by the same factory and by the same hand.

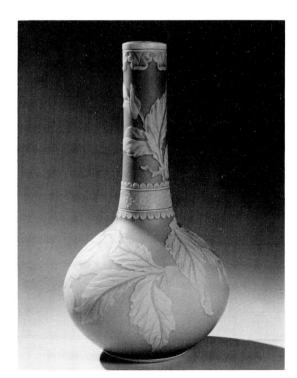

Plate 363. Heat sensitive vase, shading from the base from blue to green to amber, carved with a passion flower and leaves. The vase, measuring 9in. (22.8cm) is from the Stevens and Williams factory but has been given a fake Webb mark. The band around the neck, a characteristic of the Stevens and Williams cameo carvers, can be compared to the band on the vase in the centre of the group in Plate 358, which, disregarding its possible fake Stevens and Williams mark, is from the Stevens and Williams factory.

Plate 364. Detail of fake 'Thomas Webb and Sons Cameo' mark on the vase in Plate 363. Diameter ½ in. (1.3cm).

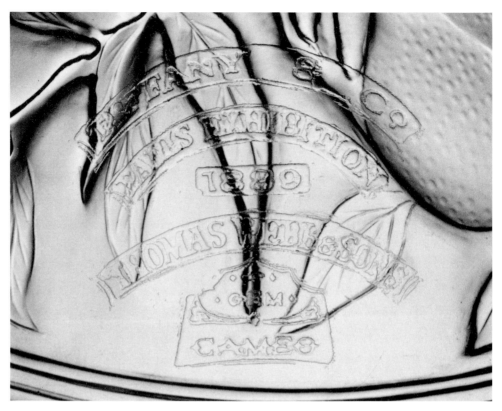

Plate 365. Detail of Tiffany mark; the origin is uncertain. Photograph courtesy Corning Museum of Glass.

Michael Parkington who also brought the discrepancy of the marks to my attention. I am indebted to him for giving me access to the Lot 97 vase which is now in his collection. I am also grateful to Louise Luther and Skinner Inc. who generously provided the two photographs originally used in their sale catalogues (Plates 358 and 362) and for their eager co-operation in the efforts to identify the source of the fake marks.

In recent years a number of glasses, usually cameo but occasionally in rock crystal or with copper wheel engraving, have appeared which bear an acid etched mark which reads 'Tiffany and Co./Paris Exhibition/1889/Thomas Webb & Sons' sometimes with the additional words 'Gem Cameo' (Plate 365). According to Jane Shadel Spillman at the Corning Museum of Glass, the marks vary in size and in the order of the wording. It has been suggested by dealers themselves that these marks are fake. Neither the Tiffany archives in New York nor the Webb papers in Amblecote have shed any light on the Tiffany/Webb group or the mark in question. In view of the lack of conclusive evidence the possibility must be accepted that genuine pieces are circulating with forged marks. Any marked piece which raises cause for concern should be judged on its merits and compared to pieces with known provenances. A further slant to the puzzle appears on a cameo vase illustrated on page 375 of *English Cameo Glass*. The mark reads 'Davis Collamore & Co., Paris Exhibition 1889, Thomas Webb and Sons, Gem Cameo'.

Faced with this obstacle course, the advice to collectors should be to buy glass for its intrinsic qualities and artistry in decoration. The mark, if genuine, will be an added bonus; if fake it will at least be a tantalising curiosity. Constant handling of a wide range of glass and a knowledge of the history of glassmaking are the two main tools available to the collector. Armed with these skills one reduces the possibilities of buying dubious items even though one cannot completely eliminate that possibility. It is a fact that many items produced in glassworks were never recorded officially. They may have been made as one-offs or perhaps in small runs, sometimes to use up a pot of coloured glass that had gone wrong, or as trials which were taken 'over the wall' or 'spirited away' from the factory instead of being broken. Within this group are the Edward VIII commemoratives which should, theoretically, have never appeared in public once the abdication was announced. The possibilities are numerous but although they add uncertainty they do give glass collecting an element of excitement.

BURMESE

The two main sources of twentieth century Burmese glass are the United States and Italy. The American production is well documented and recorded, unlike the Italian which is a matter of supposition.

Following its invention in America by Frederick Shirley in 1885 it seems natural that Burmese should hold a special fascination for the American glassmaker and collector alike and that production should be revived in the twentieth century. According to Janie Chester Young, in the New Bedford Glass Museum catalogue *The Queen's Choice* which examines one hundred years of Burmese, the original Mount Washington company was reorganised as firstly The Pairpoint Corporation and later as Gundersen-Pairpoint. The new company revived production of Burmese in 1932, 1952 and 1956. Recorded pieces from the 1930s production include a cylindrical vase with a crimped rim (diameter 9½ in. — 24cm), possibly a Jack in the Pulpit Vase (height 9½ in. — 24cm) and a 6in. (15cm) vase with nine crimps on the rim and enamelled and gilt in Royal Flemish style with a coat of arms. The 1932 pieces should be discernible by their heavy pedantic shapes and darker colours. The company also produced a spectacular dinner and dessert service for twelve people. The Pairpoint factory closed in 1956 but on 4 July a small group of Burmese pieces was made when Robert Bryden inspired Manny Amaral and 'Gilly' Gulbranson to make a final celebration of the technique. Janie Chester Young also comments on later Pairpoint glass:

> At his reincarnated Pairpoint Glass Company of Sagamore (Massachusetts), Robert Bryden again made Burmese three times between 1970 and 1978. Typical Bryden pieces are often miniature, small-scaled reproductions of Mount Washington shapes or whimsies [friggers] that approximate the 19th century in all but colour and thickness. Twenty-first century Burmese collectors should have no trouble discerning his pieces, thanks to Bryden's restraint. One unusual Bryden

creation is the covered pokal [goblet] and candlestick blown in 1978. By juxtaposing Burmese colour and a basically Rhenish style, Bryden creates an entirely new and striking effect.

The other contemporary American firm to make Burmese is the Fenton Glass Company of Marietta, West Virginia. The Fenton policy in recent years has been to make a restricted range of Burmese only once a year. Normally these limited editions are snapped up months ahead by collectors. The 1985 production included an epergne or centre stand with a single crimped trumpet surrounded by three Jack in the Pulpit style holders set in a wavy crimped bowl. The item was available in the factory retail outlet at $100. Undecorated Fenton Burmese can be identified by the greater thickness of the body compared with nineteenth century examples. Decoration, when applied, consists of transfer prints (Colour Plate 47, second left). Genuine nineteenth century examples would be totally hand enamelled. All Fenton Burmese bears a raised mark of the name in script set in an oval, although this can easily be ground out by the faker.

Judging by twentieth century examples in American and English museums the glassmakers of Murano seem to have been responsible for making Burmese reproductions from the 1940s onwards. Some of the vases with elaborately crimped tops were given applied decoration of cherries and leaves, sometimes with applied feet and a raspberry prunt on the underside. More recent reproductions have been closer in design to the original Mount Washington designs especially in the characteristic way of applying the foot (Colour Plate 47, left). The colour of this jug is markedly different from that produced by Mount Washington or Webb's and it has the granular texture of sugar mice. Some pieces have also been seen with a clear casing. Although the cased items should be easy to differentiate, the more restrained and derivative pieces such as the jug could pose problems for the inexperienced collector.

When placed under a short wave ultraviolet light the Fenton Burmese will fluoresce very brightly whereas there is hardly any reaction from the fake Italian specimens where the content of uranium oxide is much lower or even totally eliminated. Genuine English and American Burmese items will fluoresce in a middle range of the two extremes shown by the fakes.

The Fenton company also produces a range of Victorian replicas of which collectors, especially in America, should be aware. Items include red baskets with crimped rims, mottled coloured decoration rolled into the surface and frosted handles; pressed items in a vibrant red marbled effect; and hobnail jugs based on clear nineteenth century types (Plate 366). The Fenton versions are in a heat-sensitive amethyst glass where the upper sections of the hobnails have turned to a white opalescent colour on reheating. The matching coloured handles have the shell moulding which was introduced in the 1860s and the crimped rims are pushed in to form a pouring lip. In 1985 the price of a jug was $37.50.

CUT GLASS

Reproductions of cut glass began to appear at the very end of the nineteenth

Plate 366. Jug with moulded hobnail decoration and shell handle. Probably late 19th century. Height 8⅝ in. (22cm).

century and were still in production by the 1930s. At the time these pieces were made there was no intent to deceive; it is the later re-labelling which causes confusion. Glass, like other decorative arts, was made in reproduction styles to fit in with the taste and fashion for the Georgian style. Firms such as H.G. Richardson which had produced some of the best Regency cut glass at the beginning of the nineteenth century turned their hand to imitations by 1900. One advertisement from Richardson's proudly boasts their 'Reproduction of Old Cut Glass (period George III Reign)' (Plate 367). The design of the six items shown and the cut patterns on them can easily fool the inexperienced eye. Even the crispness of the cut edges, which at this time could still be polished by the traditional methods using a brush wheel with putty powder followed by cork wheels for final buffing, would suggest an early nineteenth century date.

Fortunately for the collector there is one aspect which gives the game away and that is the colour of the metal itself. A tumbler which matches a pattern shown in the Richardson advertisement (Colour Plate 47, right) reveals a 'white', sparkling, brilliant quality which would never be found on a genuine early nineteenth century example. The tumbler was illustrated in an article about the company's products in the *Pottery Gazette* in 1900. It is difficult to explain the difference between the two types but regular handling of modern cut glass and genuine early nineteenth century pieces will gradually bring an ability to distinguish the differences.

The introduction of acid polishing from about 1900 onwards resulted in cut glass losing the crisp edges and traces of the stone cutting wheels which were left

Plate 367. Richardson photograph of about 1900 showing their George III cut glass reproductions.

by the more sensitive brush method of polishing. Acid polishing removes more of the glass and the edges will appear softened and slightly rounded. Some modern cut glass is over polished and has less crispness than some of the excellent French pressed glassware such as Crystal D'Arques. Although acid polishing, because of its speed and cheapness, did take over gradually, many glassworks would have retained the facility for brush polishing and therefore the collector must judge cut glass on a number of criteria.

The accurate identification of cut glass is hazardous but is further complicated by such terms as Anglo-Irish or Old Waterford. The myth of the blue tint of Waterford is still heard today even though this long-held theory was disproved as long ago as 1920 by Dudley Westropp, the first accurate commentator on Irish glass. After the end of the First World War interest increased in Irish glass following the publication of Westropp's book. Once prices began to rise in the salerooms fakes began to appear. Some individuals such as Mrs Graydon Stannus confused collectors by making deliberate fakes or 'enhancing' original glasses with new cutting or engraving. The vogue for reproductions produced further specimens which now regularly appear in fairs and salerooms.

In the late 1920s and early 1930s the Birmingham and London retailers Hill Ouston published a number of catalogues filled with designs for 'Reproduction Antique Glassware' including the classic Irish shapes of the turnover edge and the canoe-shaped bowl (Plates 368 and 369). As with so many fakes it is the feet of the bowls which provide the clue to their age. Although Irish glass bowls and urns from 1800 or so do exist with square feet the proportions are usually more

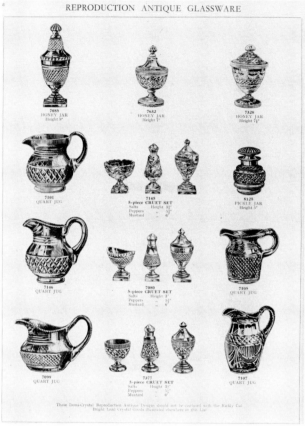

Plate 368. Reproduction cut glass from the 1934 catalogue issued by the Birmingham and London retailers, Hill Ouston.

Plate 369. Reproduction cut glass from the 1934 Hill Ouston catalogue.

restrained, whereas the feet on the 1930s versions are much thicker and larger and, like the turnover rim, totally out of proportion (Colour Plate 45). Because of the extra thickness of glass in the later examples, the whiteness of brilliance, referred to earlier, is much more pronounced.

Recent investigations in the United States have uncovered a major fraud in American cut glass. Ian Berke, a knowledgeable collector from California, has revealed that new blanks have been cut with rare old patterns and passed off as genuine American cut glass from the 'Brilliant' period. The following named patterns should be treated with caution: Aberdeen, Alhambra, Arabesque, Arabian, Assyrian, Aztec, Byzantine, Calve (triple mitre), Chrysanthemum, Cluster, Columbia, Comet, Concentric Circle, Coronation, Croesus, Delphos, Drape, DuBarry, Genoa, Grand Prize, Grecian, Imperial, Isabella, Kensington, Marcella, Nautilus, Panel, Queens, Rex, Shell, Theodora, Trellis (Lattice and Rosette), Waldorf (Quatrefoil and Rosette), Wedding Ring, and Wheat. Ian Berke has reported that new cut glass will fluoresce purple-pink using a black light (short wave ultraviolet light).

RUMMERS AND GOBLETS

Drinking glasses of all ages have always been popular with collectors. The

Plate 370. Reproduction wines and rummers from the 1934 Hill Ouston catalogue.

Plate 371. Reproduction coloured suites and finger bowls, Hill Ouston catalogue 1934.

nineteenth century produced a vast array of shapes and decoration which gives the collector a marvellous opportunity to amass an impressive collection. An examination of late nineteenth and early twentieth century pattern books from various glass companies suggests that many more wineglasses are later reproductions than has been thought. Firms such as Walsh Walsh and Stevens and Williams supplied glass directly to retailers including Hill Ouston. One page of designs from Hill Ouston's 1934 catalogue reveals the extent of the imitations including eighteenth century wineglasses (Plate 370). The four rummers at the bottom of the page can easily deceive but collectors can get a clue to dating by looking at the proportions of the feet in comparison with the rest of the glass. A glass with a foot that is much smaller than the diameter of the bowl will normally be a later reproduction. The colour of the 'metal' will also be brighter. Wear and tear on the foot is normally a sign of age and genuineness but there is one story from a Stourbridge firm in the 1930s which tells of the company employing a retired glassmaker to sit on the front doorstep and grind the feet of wineglasses to give them the required amount of age.

A number of coloured glass suites are featured in the Hill Ouston catalogue (Plate 371). Produced in up to five colour ranges of Bristol blue, amethyst, amber, emerald green and crystal, the designs of the decanters and the jugs are easily recognised as later copies. However, the various glasses which are described as goblets, champagne, claret and port would be extremely difficult to identify. One amethyst goblet from the same period was identified by an ex-traveller of the company as a product of the Stourbridge firm of L. & S. Hingley (Colour Plate 47, third left). With items which are exact replicas, such as the Hill Ouston lipped finger bowl, there are no tell-tale features which can be used for dating and therefore it would be difficult to argue against a nineteenth century label and price tag to match.

PAPERWEIGHTS AND SCENT BOTTLES

The introduction of the ingenious and pretty ornaments from Bohemia has induced some of our glass manufacturers to turn their attention to the production of similar objects. We have seen a large number of home manufacture, which for beauty and variety of colour, are equal to the best imported; and in design are superior to them. Mr. Bacchus an eminent glass manufacturer of Birmingham, has produced some that deserve special notice for their novelty and elegance.

(*Art Union,* November 1848)

At the 1849 Exhibition in Birmingham Bacchus & Co. displayed 'letter weights' listed at no. 91 in the catalogue. Bacchus paperweights are referred to in the *Journal of Design and Manufacture* Volume 1, in 1849, while the *Art Journal* (formerly the *Art Union*) in 1849 mentioned the paperweights made by Rice Harris at the Islington Glass Works, also in Birmingham. With these scant references providing no direct evidence for colour combinations of the canes or the profiles of the weights it is not surprising that attributions and datings have been conjured up from nowhere. A few weights contain a cane with the letters IGW which have been taken to stand for the Islington Glass Works but other weights, without any basis in fact, have been attributed to Stourbridge or to the Whitefriars glassworks in London. Stourbridge firms were using coloured canes in their glassware and there is no reason to think that they did not try their hand at paperweight manufacture. Until a thorough and detailed survey is carried out of so-called English weights one must tread carefully through this minefield where each collector and dealer will express different views.

The rise of paperweight collecting in the first twenty years of this century was the signal for the Birmingham and Stourbridge firms to increase the supply, even of dated weights, to meet the new demand. The Walsh Walsh firm in Birmingham made many of the fake weights. Fortunately an existing letter from Mr M. Parkes, a manager at the works, gives some vital clues to distinguish the imitations. Each number of the date was set in a separate cane. The blue numbers, set against white opal, were inserted among the millefiori canes in the second outer ring. The pontil mark was not ground out and the base was abraded to show signs of wear. The letter states that 'All the experts fell over each other

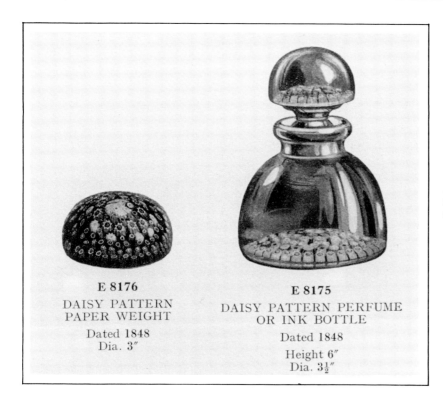

E 8176
DAISY PATTERN
PAPER WEIGHT

Dated 1848
Dia. 3″

E 8175
DAISY PATTERN PERFUME
OR INK BOTTLE

Dated 1848

Height 6″
Dia. 3½″

Plate 372. Millefiori paperweight and bottle with fake 1848 date canes. Hill Ouston catalogue, 1934.

to buy the genuine millefleur paperweights' and it finishes with the proud boast that 'the old British craftsman could equal and very often surpass your Bigaglias, Saint Louis etc...' The company also supplied millefiori stoppers for decanters (Colour Plate 48).

In the Hill Ouston catalogue one page contains illustrations of a 'Daisy Pattern Paper Weight' and a 'Perfume or Ink Bottle' to match (Plate 372). Both are 'dated 1848' and, like the Walsh example, a separate cane was used for each number of the date (Colour Plate 48). A pattern book of the early twentieth century presumably from the Richardson factory, from a collection of documents inscribed R.C. Richardson, shows a virtually identical bottle and two weights, in two sizes. A note by the side of the weights gives the colour combinations of some of the canes: 'centre white ruby outside, amber white outside, blue white outside, pale amber white outside, white blue green, ruby white outside and white blue outside'. The added note 'flattd' suggests that at least some of these weights would have their bases ground flat. Both items were still advertised in the 1936 Hill Ouston catalogue; the weight sold at 19s. and the bottle at 55s. The prefix E denoted items of English manufacture.

PRESSED GLASS

Stories exist in the antiques trade about recent reproductions of pressed glass. The former George Davidson factory in Gateshead, Newcastle upon Tyne, is said to have made some glasses from original moulds in their factory but so far the results, if they do exist, have not been recorded. Some pressed glass is coming into England from the East, such as the small stemmed glass in amethyst (Colour

Plate 47, second right), which bears the raised mark 'Made in Taiwan'. Without the mark the glass could just possibly be accepted as a crude pressing from the very end of the nineteenth century. Reproductions of the cupped hands plate by John Ford & Co. are discussed in the chapter on Pressed Glass.

The English pressed glass collector therefore has little to worry about, unlike his American counterpart. The reproduction of pressed glass in America has been widespread and the range of objects imitated is so large that a separate book would be required to cover it adequately. The American glass historian Ruth Webb Lee did some sterling work in identifying some of these reproductions. Her discoveries were published in an excellent series of articles in the *American Collector* in the January, March, April and May editions in 1940. In an effort to stop the flow of reproductions made by using old moulds, the Heisey Collector's Club bought the entire collection of moulds from the Heisey factory when it closed in the 1980s.

CUP PLATES

Pressed glass cup plates were an American phenomenon of the nineteenth century when it was fashionable to drink tea from the saucer rather than the cup. The glass saucers were introduced as a smart way to hold the cup rather than setting it directly on the table. A number of American factories continue to make cup plates and these are well documented by American collectors. In England, where this information is not so easily available, some of the new patterns have been mistaken for nineteenth century pieces. The best example of this confusion is a saucer and a larger plate showing a Cardinal bird, a well-known American species, sitting on a branch inside a border of holly leaves. The pieces have the minute initials AW placed in the border. Theories have been put forward to match these and other initials to the names of English mould makers. In reality the initials AW are those of Alvin A. White, an extraordinary artist who engraves the moulds for the cup plates made today by the Pairpoint Glassworks on Cape Cod.

MARY GREGORY

'Mary Gregory' must be among the ten best known names in the field of glass collecting. In her book on nineteenth century art glass Ruth Webb Lee mentions the existence of a lady called Mary Alice Gregory who worked as a decorator for the Boston and Sandwich Glass Company in the 1870s and 1880s. Apparently she lived in Sandwich, Massachusetts, where she died in 1908. Her speciality subject in glass enamelling was said to be the figures of boys and girls, usually in white enamel, that we all know today as 'Mary Gregory'. That theory is now being questioned by glass researchers in America and it is suggested that Mary Gregory may have specialised more in snow scenes.

Whatever the final outcome of the new research, it is correct to say that most of the jugs and vases bearing this decoration came from the Bohemian factories and outside decorators in the late nineteenth and early twentieth century and

Plate 373. Genuine 'Mary Gregory' jug with enamelled decoration. Bohemian, c.1900. Height 7¼in. (18.4cm).

Plate 374. Bubbly glass from the Hill Ouston catalogue, 1934.

were exported in large numbers to Europe and America (Plate 373). Modern reproductions of 'Mary Gregory' have been appearing on the market in the last few years. The full range of the new versions can usually be seen at the large annual giftware trade show known as the 'Spring Fair' held at the National Exhibition Centre near Birmingham in February. Seen in this context one can recognise the glossy and shiny new look of the glass and the enamelling but, given some 'enhanced' wear and tear to soften the newness, it might be more difficult to identify the same pieces if they appeared separately amongst an assortment of other antiques and bric-à-brac.

BUBBLY GLASS

There is a current notion that glass which appears imperfect in some way or contains air bubbles has automatically to be either 'very old' or 'ancient'. In fact the presence of air bubbles and imperfections in the glass was anathema to all glassmakers from whichever country until the latter part of the nineteenth century. Much time and effort was spent in experimenting with the use of chemicals, added to the molten glass, to remove unwanted air bubbles. The historicising influence amongst designers and glassmakers in the 1880s led to the use of streaked and bubbled glassware perhaps best seen in the 'Clutha' range designed by Christopher Dresser for the Glasgow firm of James Couper. The Thomas Webb firm made a similar range known as 'Old Roman' which has not been identified. The slight irregularities in shape combined with the air bubbles were designed to give the suggestion of Roman glass. The originals would have been in clear or coloured glass and if they did contain the odd slight imperfection it was by accident rather than choice.

By the 1930s Hill Ouston were carrying a range of 'Bubbly Glassware' in two colours, amber and willow green (Plate 374). These pieces have been seen in sales and antiques shops and can be distinguished by their large size, from 10in. to 13½in. (25.5cm to 35cm) and by the large air bubbles and rough surface of the glass. The strident colours cannot be confused with the subtle tones of early nineteenth century coloured glass. The shapes too are not those used by nineteenth century glassmakers except for the jug No. E5428 which one could imagine carrying a 'Nailsea' label.

Appendix 1

GLASSMAKERS IN ENGLAND, SCOTLAND AND IRELAND
PAYING DUTY IN THE YEAR ENDED 5TH JANUARY 1833

Taken from the Thirteenth Report of the Commissioners of Enquiry 1835

The figures include costs for the total number and expenses of the officers employed in the collection of the duty. Where one name appears a number of times with separate payments it indicates that the person operated more than one glass house or cone, even though these may have been on the same site.

ENGLAND									
Collection	No.	Name	Where situate	Amount of Duty			Total		
				£	s	d	£	s	d
Bristol	1	Henry Ricketts and Co.	Bristol	4,714	8	6			
	2	John Nicholas and Co.	Do	2,653	13	6¾			
	3	Henry Ricketts and Co.	Do	3,677	2	0			
	4	Thomas Powell and Co	Do	3,523	3	9			
	5	Couthupe and Co.	Nailseaheath	18,792	1	8			
	6	Couthupe and Co.	Do	20,398	2	4	53,758	11	9¾
Durham	7	Isaac Cookson	South Shields	9,764	14	0			
	8	Isaac Cookson	Do	11,848	4	0			
	9	Isaac Cookson	Do	12,704	8	0			
	10	Isaac Cookson	Do	13,602	0	0			
	11	Isaac Cookson	Do	3,797	6	9			
	12	Isaac Cookson	Do	1,464	14	3			
	13	Isaac Cookson	Do	3,615	0	0			
	14	Richard Shortridge	Do	14,946	4	6			
	15	Richard Shortridge	Do	7,432	9	4¼			
	16	Charles Atwood	Southwick	17,680	8	6			
	17	Addison Fenwick and Co.	Sunderland	9,507	4	6			
	18	Addison Fenwick and Co.	Do	3,478	13	0			
	19	Walker Featherstonhaugh	Ayres Quay	3,603	5	0			
	20	Walker Featherstonhaugh	Deptford	5,095	4	8			
	21	Walker Featherstonhaugh	Do	2,544	4	4			
	22	William Booth and Co.	Do	4,351	5	3			
	23	John Hubbard	Do	3,919	14	1			
	24	John Hubbard	Do	3,841	3	11	133,196	4	1¼
Leeds	25	William Usherwood	Worsbro' Dale	1,421	2	11½			
	26	John Bower	Hunslet	1,547	14	0			
	27	John Bower	Do	2,222	8	9			
	28	John Bower	Do	2,866	10	0			
	29	John Bower	Do	10,106	5	0			
	30	Noah Turner	Thornhill Lees	989	16	0	19,153	16	8½
Lichfield	31	Hannah Shakespear & Co.	Birmingham	5,207	10	6			
	32	John Biddle	Do	4,337	7	3			
	33	Rice Harris and Co.	Do	7,259	8	0			
	34	George Bacchus and Co.	Do	11,015	11	0			
	35	William Gammon and Co.	Do	6,939	6	6	34,759	3	3

ENGLAND										
Collection	No.	Name	Where situate	Amount of Duty			Total			
				£	s	d	£	s	d	
Liverpool	36	Abraham Akers and Co.	Newton	2,421	16	6				
	37	Thomas Cockburn and Co.	Thattoheath	15,924	0	0				
	38	W.A.A. West and Co.	Do	14,394	19	6				
	39	John William Bell	Ravenhead	5,035	14	3				
	40	Peter Greenall and Co.	St. Helens	19,227	12	0				
	41	Thomas Moore and Co.	Kendrick's Cross	3,158	1	0				
	42	James Holt and Co.	Liverpool	2,031	4	3				
	43	Thomas Choll and Co.	Old Swan	17,845	16	0				
	44	William Foster and Co.	Vauxhall Road	2,690	2	0	82,729	5	6	
Manchester	45	Thomas Molineux	Manchester	5,199	19	6				
	46	Daniel Watson and Co.	Do	188	12	6				
	47	William Robinson	Do	2,426	9	6				
	48	William Maginnes and Co.	Do	402	15	6				
	49	Frederick Fareham	Do	6	18	3	8,224	15	3	
Newcastle	50	Charles Atwood	Gateshead	20,241	18	0				
	51	Joseph Price	Do	6,808	7	0				
	52	Joseph Price	Do	1,446	14	3				
	53	George Sowerby	Do	6,705	19	6				
	54	George Stevenson	Carr Hill	568	16	6				
	55	Joseph Price	Newcastle	4,894	14	3				
	56	Isaac Cookson and Co.	Do	2,072	0	0				
	57	Isaac Cookson and Co.	Do	2,637	12	0				
	58	Joseph Lamb and Co.	Do	5,688	2	6				
	59	Joseph Lamb and Co.	Lemington	9,091	19	0				
	60	Joseph Lamb and Co.	Do	11,366	15	6				
	61	Joseph Lamb and Co.	Do	3,796	5	6				
	62	John Carr and Co.	Hartley Pans	2,953	11	4¼				
	63	John Carr and Co.	Do	3,527	0	7¾				
	64	John Cookson and Co.	Bell Quay	3,919	13	3¼				
	65	John Cookson and Co.	Do	3,878	6	8¾				
	66	Thomas Ridley and Co.	St. Peter's	3,160	10	0				
	67	William Richardson and Co.	Do	17,230	4	9				
	68	William Richardson and Co.	Do	16,708	7	9				
	69	Sir M.W. Ridley and Co.	Newcastle	2,839	10	0				
	70	Sir M.W. Ridley and Co.	Do	18,275	15	0				
	71	Sir M.W. Ridley and Co.	Do	19,124	14	6				
	72	Robert Todd and Co.	Do	4,046	14	0	170,983	12	0	
Northwich	73	John Clare	Warrington	24,482	17	0				
	74	John B. Falkner and Co.	Do	2,090	17	7¼				
	75	John B. Falkner and Co.	Do	7,832	6	0				
	76	John Alderson and Co.	Do	4,300	10	3				
	77	Thomas Robinson and Co.	Do	2,015	5	9	40,721	16	7¼	
Salop	78	John Biddle and Co.	Moss	459	4	0				
	79	John Biddle and Co.	Do	5,116	10	0	5,575	14	0	
Sheffield	80	Close and Clark	Rotherham	2,346	15	3				
	81	Thomas May	Catcliffe	868	12	9	3,215	8	0	

ENGLAND					
Collection	No.	Name	Where situate	Amount of Duty £ s d	Total £ s d
Stafford	82	John Davenport	Langport	4,211 8 3	4,211 8 3
Stourbridge	83	William Chance	Spon Lane [Birmingham]	24,302 0 9	
	84	William Chance	Do Do	4,044 19 0	
	85	William Chance	Do Do	25,635 1 9	
	86	Joseph Guest and Co.	Dudley	4,008 12 9	
	87	Thomas Hawkes	Do	5,593 1 6	
	88	Joseph Stevens and Co.	Hollyhall	2,938 14 3	
	89	Thomas Badger and Co.	Dudley	4,870 7 3	
	90	Thomas Davis and Co.	Dickson's Green	3,460 14 3	
	91	Joseph Silvers and Co.	Moore Lane	2,438 11 6	
	92	Edward Westwood and Co.	Do	1,380 15 0	
	93	William S. Wheely	Brettle Lane	3,667 8 6	
	94	Michael Grazebrook	Andmain	2,218 5 3	
	95	Thomas Littlewood	Holton End	3,645 4 0	
	96	Richard B. Usell	Wordsley	1,758 2 3	
	97	Thomas Hill	Coalburn Brook	1,645 14 0	
	98	Thomas Webb and Co.	Wordsley	5,745 6 0	
	99	John H. Pidcock and Co.	Platts	2,637 12 0	
	100	Philip Rufford	Stourbridge Heath	2,756 10 0	
	101	Sarah Eusell	Wordsley	2,254 7 9	105,001 7 9
York	102	Jepson and Co.	Mear	1,196 13 0	
	103	Charles Priestly	York	2,233 16 6	3,430 9 6
London, within the Limits of the Chief Office	104	Apsley Pellatt	Holland Street Blackfriars	7,852 9 9	
	105	William Christie	Stangate	3,523 13 3	
	106	William Holmes	Ashentree Ct., Whitefriars	3,746 6 0	15,122 9 0
				Total, England	680,084 1 8¾

In No. 94 'Andmain' refers to Audnam, in No. 95 'Holton End' probably means Holloway End and in Nos. 96 and 101 the surnames Usell and Eusell respectively were in fact Ensell. Although the owners were given as Ensell the works were operated by the Richardson brothers.

SCOTLAND					
Collection	No.	Name	Where situate	Amount of Duty £ s d	Total £ s d
Ayr	1	Kerr, Dunlop, and Co.	Cartsdike	3,800 12 4½	3,800 12 4½
Edinburgh	2	Edinburgh & Leith Glass) Company)	Leith	4,592 1 9	
	3	Edinburgh & Leith Glass) Company)	Do	2,936 17 0	7,528 18 9

SCOTLAND					
Collection	No.	Name	Where situate	Amount of Duty	Total
				£ s d	£ s d
Glasgow	4	Allan Fullarton	Dumbarton	12,318 12 0	
	5	Allan Fullarton	Do	826 8 9	
	6	William Geddes	Anderston	4,980 17 0	
	7	John Geddes	Finnerston	3,058 3 0	
	8	Geddes, Kidston and Co.	Anderston	4,530 0 3	25,714 1 0
Haddington	9	William Baillie and Co.	Portobello	6,476 3 1½	6,476 3 1½
Stirling	10	John Sandeman	Alloa	1,971 19 3	1,971 19 3
				Total, Scotland	45,491 14 6

IRELAND					
Collection	No.	Name	Where situate	Amount of Duty	Total
				£ s d	£ s d
Cork	1	Jeffrey O'Connell	Cork	1,958 17 9	
	2	Richard and E. Ronayne	Do	2,917 4 6	4,876 2 3
Dublin	3	Andrew Crean	Dublin	2,491 3 9	
	4	Charles Mulvany	Do	3,476 16 0	
	5	George Forbes	Do	546 17 6	
	6	Costello and Co.	North Wall	3,390 17 9	9,905 15 0
Dundalk	7	Isaac M'Cane	Newry	1,269 10 9	1,269 10 9
Lisburn	8	John M'Connell	Belfast	1,651 11 6	
	9	John Kane	Do	1,694 11 9	3,346 3 3
Waterford	10	Galehill and Co.	Waterford	3,002 7 9½	3,002 7 9½
				Total, Ireland	22,399 19 0½
			Totals Collected	(England	680,084 1 8¾
				(Scotland	45,491 14 6
				(Ireland	22,399 19 0½
				Total United Kingdom	747,975 15 3¼

Appendix 2

REPORTS TO THE COMMISSIONERS ON THE EVIDENCE ON
THE EMPLOYMENT OF CHILDREN. DUDLEY 1842.

No. 258. April 30. Mr. Thomas Irwin, aged 57, Glass-cutter:

Employs six men and four apprentices; the two who are bound are above 18 years of age, the other two agree to be bound, and have been with him three years. There are several of the same trade in the place, but none of them employ above a dozen boys at the outside. Considers his business an unhealthy one, and all the medical men know it. Thinks the first process of cutting glass is not unhealthy, provided they are not in the same shop where the glass is finished, and to effect this requires a material, a sort of putty made of lead and pewter, and this gets under their nails and often causes the hands to contract; they also breathe it, and it causes rheumatic pains. The chief thing as a preservative is to have plenty of ventilation at the top of the shop, and for those who use the putty to be more careful as to cleanliness, particularly under the nails. Has often seen boys eat their victuals without washing their hands, to their certain injury. Frequently his boys come to work at 12 years of age; thinks they should not come sooner; they ought to be kept at school. Thinks they ought not to come to his sort of work after they are 12 years of age; if a boy of 15, habituated to the air of the country fields, were to come to this work for the first time, it would probably much injure him in a short time.

No. 259. April 30. Henry Ellis, aged 14:

Works at glass-cutting; works for Mr. Irwin; is paid by the week; gets 5s. a-week regularly — not by the piece; gives it to his father. Does not feel sick ever with the work. Has the headache sometimes. Has worked at it about four years; likes it pretty well. Comes at six in the morning till six at night, with half an hour for breakfast and an hour for dinner; goes home to tea. Breaks his work sometimes, and gets beaten a bit; does not feel the beating quite half an hour; it is not much to signify. Can read and write, learnt at a day-school, and then went to a night-school after his work. Take 25 from 100 there remained 75; 10 farthings are 2½d.; there are four feet in a yard — no, three; and 36 inches in a yard. There were twelve apostles. Knows about Jonah; he was in the whale's belly three days and three nights, because he did not go to the place where the Lord sent him.

(Signed)   Henry Ellis.

Pretty well grown: not unhealthy but pale. A smiling, happy expression; clean, and in a proper working dress.

No. 260. April 30. Richard Pickering, aged 16.

Works at glass-cutting; has worked at it five years; gets 5s. a-week regularly; does not work piece-work. Feels the headache, but very seldom; feels sick sometimes, and has the stomachache nearly every week; thinks it's the putty; sometimes has a handkerchief round his mouth while at work, but this don't do, he must breathe, and it makes him too hot; very seldom vomits. The work is not hard, only it's disagreeable, because it makes you feel ill. Seldom hears the men complain; has heard one complain very often, who has been at work this week — been ill — not drunk. One man has been ill these six or seven weeks now; thinks it's with the work. Can read, not write; learnt to read at the Sunday-school of the Independent Dissenters, who never teach writing on Sundays, but two nights in the week instead. Is not bound apprentice yet, but means to be. His master treats him kindly. He's a good-natured master, and works hard himself too.

Pretty well grown; not strong; pale, clean, and in a proper working dress.

No. 261. April 30. Mr. Richard Timmins, aged 46, Glass-cutter.

Employs from three to eight men, according to the demand for work. Has three apprentices bound; they do not live with him; he pays them about 4s. at the age of 14, and advances 6d. a-week every year till they are 20 years of age, and then advances a shilling a-week, and sometimes more if he had the boys as early as from nine to eleven. His business is no doubt injurious to health, but thinks very much of this might be avoided if the boys could get more exercise in the open air, and if the shop had a contrivance to separate it from the shop of the putty department, or at all events to contrive that the particles of putty dust should be driven out by some specific ventilation, as by a current of air from below, with some corresponding opening above. If he were to build for himself he would so construct the shops. Rents his workshops, as do four other small glass-cutting establishments, of a mill owner, who also lets them off a sufficient quantity of steam-power for each.

Appendix 3

EXTRACT FROM 1849 EXHIBITION CATALOGUE AT BINGLEY HALL, BIRMINGHAM

TABLE, No. 44.
Specimens of Glass.
Manufactured by W.H., B., & J. Richardson, Wordsley, near Stourbridge.
All painted articles are done in Vitrified Enamel Colours.

1. Vase painted, 6 Grecian figures shaded in colours.
2. Ditto painted, 4 coloured figures sacrifice to Apollo.
3. Vase printed, Pet Fawn, tinted in colours.
4. Nine inch Vase, printed Grecian figure in red and painted border.
5. Nine inch Vase, printed Grecian figure, in black.
6. Twelve inch Vase, printed season, and tinted in colour.
7. Twelve and a half inch Vase, Grecian Flute Player, red and black border.
8. Fourteen inch Vase, Three Grecian Figures, painted in black.
9. Four lipped Vase, painted, Grecian Female playing Crotals.

10. Vase, blue ground, painted, Atalante and Hippomede.
11. Antique Vase, painted, Christ and the Woman.
12. Flower Vase, with enamelled snake entwined.
13. Small vase, enamelled and gilt, and coloured flowers.
14. Small vase, ditto ditto
15. Portland Vase, painted, Fawn Figures.
16. Portland Vase, blue ground, and black shaded figures.
17. Piano candlestick, painted Three Groups of Flowers, and gilt.
18. Sweetmeat, or Saucer, painted, strawberry and gold leaves.
19. Small Portland Vase, printed figures.
20. Large Antique Vase, Morning and Thetis commanding the Neraids, after Flaxman.
21. Small Vase, printed, Queen Elizabeth.
22. Small Vase, printed, St. Mary's Abbey, Yorkshire.
23. Quart Jug, painted, the Arab Water Carriers in colours.
24. Goblet to match.
25. Ditto ditto
26. White Jug, painted black, shaded, Grecian Figures.
27. Quart Jug, painted, Rebecca at the Well.
28. Goblet to match.
29. Shell Dish, painted, Bunch of Grapes.
30. Shell Dish, painted, Peach.
31. Cream, frosted and painted, Milk Maids, in black. [See Colour Plate 10]
32. Antique Tazza, Red Figure and border.
33. Soda Goblet, painted, Bubbles Bursting.
34. Jug, painted, Water Lily.
35. Antique Jug, painted Water Lily.
36. Two handled Vase, painted, Bull Rushes, and gilt handles.
37. Two handled four-lipped Vase, painted Water Iris.
38. Flower Glass, covered lavender and cut sprig.
39. Soda Tumbler, covered blue and white, cut off.
40. Crysolite Toilette, gilt.
41. Ruby Goblet, engraved, cupids gathering grapes, &c.
42. Ruby Finger Cup, cut pillars, ruby and flint alternately.
43. Ruby Caraff and Tumbler, cut and engraved, cupids and venus, &c.
44. Squat Champagne Ruby, engraved, vine and cut star, foot.
45. Ruby Taper Decanter, cut, hollows, &c.
46. Blue engraved Claret Jug and fluted pillars.
47. Green covered Decanter, cut, honeysuckle and fluted neck.

48. Victoria Decanter, cut hollows, and hollow diamond neck.
49. Antique Venetian Jug.
50. Green covered Champagne, engraved, vine, border, &c.
51. Three lipped Decanter, cut hollows, pillars, &c.
52. Goblet, cut prisms and diamonds, &c.
53. Rich engraved Decanter.
54. Decanter, cut diamonds, &c.
55. Decanter, cut hollows, &c.
56. Decanter, green band, engraved, vine and gilt, 'Sherry'. [See Plate 77]
57. Claret Decanter, engraved, three Grecian figures, &c.
58. Antique Claret Decanter, engraved, six Grecian figures.
59. Antique Claret Decanter, engraved, oak leaves.
60. Antique Jug, engraved, Grecian figures and cut.
61. Goblet to match.
62. Antique Jug, engraved, cupids in three panels of flowers.
63. Antique Jug, engraved, flowers in panels.
64. Jug, engraved, vine, serpent and birds.
65. Antique Goblet, engraved, vine, border, &c.
66. Thistle Wine, fluted bowl and stem.
67. Button stem Wine, six flutes and cut between buttons.
68. Egg bowl Wine, six flutes and cut stem.
69. Wine, engraved, pheasant.
70. Egg bowl Wine, straw stem, engraved, vine.
71. Venetian stem Wine, fluted stem, &c., engraved, vine, border and diamonds.
72. Threaded stem Wine, engraved, The Royal Arms.
73. Lily Wine, engraved.
74. Gilt tendril stem Wine. [See Plate 76]
75. Enamelled Wine, blue and gold.
76. Rich Sugar, cut, six panels of strawberry diamonds, &c.
77. Rich Butter, complete, cut pillars and strawberry diamonds.
78. Rich Butter, cut prisms and strawberry diamonds, &c.
79. Rich Butter, complete, cut, sloping leafage.
80. Loo Dish, richly cut.
81. Richly cut Centre and Stand, prisms and scolloped and cut.
82. Decanter, cut prisms, &c., to match.
83. Specimen of Glass, lapidary, cut diamonds, &c.
84. Plain egg-shape Specimen.
85. Large crystal Ink, cut flat diamonds.
86. Pine Salt and Stand, cut flat diamonds, crystal.

87. Lamp, Grecian figures and Holy Family at bottom.
88. Ruby Pane, engraved, deer.
89. Ruby Pane, printed, The Holy Family.
90. Large Pane, painted, group of flowers in colours.
91. Pane, painted, The Holy Family.
92. Camphine Oil Lamp, gilt stem and painted flowers.
93. Globe, two Grecian subjects in fawn shaded.
94. Globe, two Grecian subjects in black, shaded figures.
95. Vase, black key border and black shaded figures.
96. Vase, printed, season and gilt oak leaves.
97. Vase, red ground and black Grecian figure.
98. Crysolite Vase, three black Grecian figures.
99. Blue Vase, fluted all down and gilt. [See Colour Plate 10]
100. Claret, painted, Christ and the Woman of Samaria, in black.
101. Claret Jug, ground, gilt, scaled handle, and painted flowers.
102. Jug, printed sowers and gleaners, in colours and gilt.
103. Summerly Jug, painted travellers, in black.
104. Small Antique Jug, black key border, two Grecian figures.
105. Blue cut-off Jug, cut body and under handle.
106. Cream and Sugar, gilt Grecian honeysuckle.
107. Cornelian Butter, frosted and painted strawberry and gilt.
108. Vase, blue ground and Grecian figure.
109. Vase,   ditto   ditto.
110. Small blue Sugar.
111. Smoke colour covered Finger Cup, cut and engraved.
112. Green and white covered Finger Cup, cut sprigs.
113. Portland Cream, fawn figures.
114. Small leaf Dish, gilt fibres, &c.
115. Ditto   ditto   ditto.
116. Tall Venetian Stem Goblet, engraved.
117. Tall flint Goblet, richly gilt and cut stem.
118. Topaz Goblet, richly cut.
119. Goblet, painted Water Lily.
120. Claret Jug, yellow ground, and painted flowers and gilt handle.
121. Flower Vase, two Grecian coloured figures and red borders.
122. Bread Dish, painted ears of wheat, &c.
123. Flint-frosted Ice Dish, leaf.
124. Wine, painted, ivy border and gilt.
125. Wine, gilt inside and vine border outside.
126. Mahogany colour, glass Salt, cut flat diamonds. [See Colour Plate 10 and Plate 61]
127. Turquoise Dessert Knife.
128. Oriental Blue ditto.
129. White opal ditto.
130. Large Centre and Stand, richly cut diamonds and hollows.
131. Rich cut Dish.
132. Decanter, cut diamonds, and pillars.
133. Decanter, cut hollows, and small diamonds.
134. Decanter, cut diamonds, and hollows.
135. Jug, cut, bold pillars and diamonds.
136. Jug — engraved Lotus.
137. Goblet to match.
138. Wine, six fluted stem, and hollow diamond bowl.
139. Wine, hollow stem and diamond flutes on bowl.
140. Topaz Spoon, cut handle.
141. Pyramid Decanter, fluted all down, enamelled blue and engraved.

Appendix 4

MEMO. OF AGREEMENT MADE 28 JULY 1859 BETWEEN RICHARD MILLS GLASS MANUFACTURER OF WORDSLEY & THOMAS MORGAN MASTER GLASS-CUTTER OF BRETTELL LANE

(From Stafford Record Office D 695/1/21/1.)

The said Richard Mills for the consideration herein after mentioned, does hereby undertake and agree to build and erect, upon a Plot of Land situate at Buck-Pool near Wordsley, a Glass-Cutting Shop with Warehouse, Engine House, Engine, Boiler etc. etc. with all the necessary shafts, pullies, lathe and plant usual and necessary for Fifteen Glass-Cutters. The said Cutting

Shop to be completed and in efficient working order on or before the 28 day of December next ensuing: The said Thomas Morgan does hereby, for himself, his hrs., exors, adminsr or asigns, covenant and agree to and with the said Richard Mills that he the said Thomas Morgan will enter upon and take possession of the said Cutting-Shop (to be erected for his use and benefit) upon a *Lease* for twenty one years as soon as the same Cutting-Shop shall be completed and in efficient working order and will pay or cause to be paid unto the said Richard Mills the nett yearly rental of Forty Pounds, payable quarterly, the said Thomas Morgan doing all the necessary repairs to the satisfaction of the said Richard Mills — and it is here mutually agreed that the terms and provisoes of the said Lease here after to be Executed shall be the same as those contained in a Lease now in force between the said Richard Mills and Parrish and Co. of Wordsley and both parties hereby further agree that they will perfect, complete and sign the said Lease when required so to do.

In presence of George Mills, Richard Mills, Thomas Morgan.

With this document is a Specification from Hugh and James Wright and Co., Steam Engine Manufactory, Dudley Foundry, Dudley dated 4 August 1858 to Mr. G. Mills of Wordsley for a 6 H.P. High Pressure Horizontal Steam Engine with a cylindrical boiler and equipment which consisted of:

31 feet of shafting turned to $2^7/_{16}$ dia. in 2 lengths
1 Coupling Bar
4 Carriages fitted with Bottom Brasses Iron Caps and Bolts
2 Wall Boxes
1 Driving Pulley 2ft 9 Diam 6in. face Bored and Keyed on Shafting
14 Speed Pulleys 4 speeds each 9-12-15-18 Dias, Bored Turned and Keyed on Shafting
   delivered and fixed at Wordsley for sum of £115
£57-10 paid in cash on delivery of fly wheel and boilers and
£57-10 on completion.
N.B. All excavations, masonry and timber work to be supplied by you.
N.B. 1st Bill paid Sept 13th 1859.

A surviving receipt, dated 15 September 1859, for the sum of £60 'on account of work done at Cutting shop at Buck Pool' is signed W. Northwood. Another bill dated 27 October 1859 reads 'Bt. of Mr. Northwood for bricklayer, carpenter £7-5-0d.' This W. Northwood may be the William Northwood who was the eldest son of Frederick and Maria Northwood, and brother of John Northwood I.

Appendix 5

MAP OF WORDSLEY AND AMBLECOTE SHOWING THE POSITIONS OF PRESENT DAY GLASSWORKS AND SITES OF HISTORIC INTEREST

The term 'Stourbridge' is normally used when referring to glass from the districts of Wordsley,

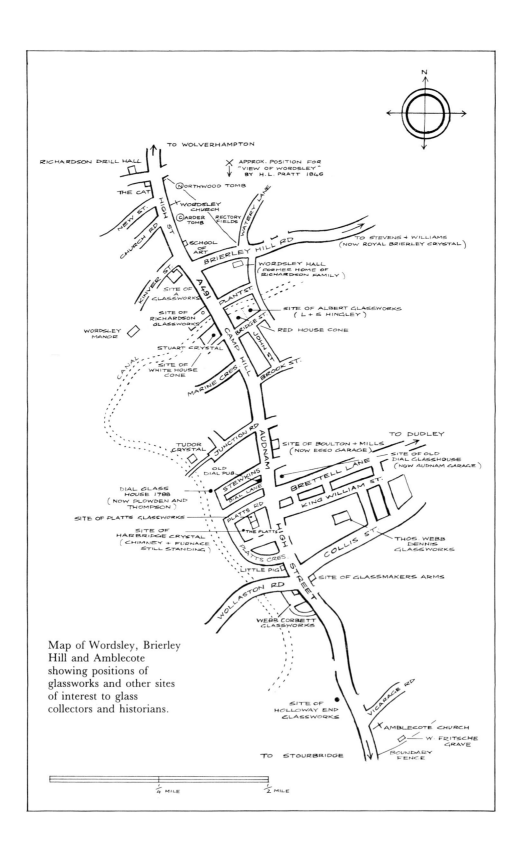

Map of Wordsley, Brierley
Hill and Amblecote
showing positions of
glassworks and other sites
of interest to glass
collectors and historians.

Brierley Hill and Amblecote, but it should be pointed out that most of the glassworks in the nineteenth century were situated outside the boundaries of the town of Stourbridge. The use of the term 'Stourbridge glass' seems to have arisen in the last century when the glass companies used the facilities in Stourbridge, especially for banking and transport. Invoices and letterheads gave the postal address as Stourbridge.

In 1846 Hilton L. Pratt painted a view of Wordsley (Plate 369) from the hill behind Wordsley Church looking due south towards Stourbridge, almost the same view as taken by the photographer in about 1900 (Plate 1). The size of this close knit community becomes apparent when one knows that the distance from Wordsley Church to Amblecote Church is approximately one and a quarter miles (2km). The distance from the end of Brierley Hill Road to the Stevens and Williams glassworks is one and a half miles (2.5km). During the time between the painting in 1846 and the photograph in 1900 most of the greatest contributions to glass were made within this tiny area or very close to it.

The map shows some of the historic sites including the Northwood family tomb in Wordsley churchyard. Nearby, in the same churchyard, is the grave of Stanley Carder, the son of Frederick Carder, who died at the age of seven in 1899, three years before Frederick Carder left for the States. At either end of the tomb are two terracotta panels with a figure of an angel carved by Frederick Carder, signed and dated 1901. Four terracotta panels by Frederick Carder are located on the front of the former Wordsley School of Art, near the High Street entrance to the church. It is currently planned to dismantle the Wordsley School of Art and re-erect the facade on the site of Stuart Crystal.

Plate 377. View of Wordsley by Hilton L. Pratt, signed and dated 1846. Oil on canvas, 25 ¾ in. x 47in. (65.5cm x 119.5cm). The cone on the extreme left is the Red House glass cone which still stands on the site of the present Stuart Crystal factory.

423

Appendix 6

STOURBRIDGE ENGRAVERS OF THE NINETEENTH CENTURY

I am indebted to Ian Wolfenden for permission to publish his compilation of Stourbridge engravers and decorators.

1. Notes from Littlebury's Worcestershire Directory 1873

Littlebury's had appeared earlier as the *Postal and Commercial Directory and Gazetteer of the County of Worcester*. The lists for Stourbridge include Wollaston and Amblecote, but not Wordsley.

a) John Hubert   glass engraver and ornamental painter, Collis St., Dennis Park.
    [misspelling of Herbert]
b) Alfred James Nash   glass engraver, Raglan Villa, Victoria St.
c) Joseph Parsons   glass engraver, Hollies, Love Lane.

A separate section headed 'Trades: Glass' has the following: Hubert and Nash and

d) Edwin Hatton   Mount St. Hatton advertises on page 9: 'Dealer in All Kinds of Flint Glass, Mount St. and the Market Hall, Stourbridge. Engraving on glass done to pattern at the shortest notice.'

2. Notes from Mark and Moody's Stourbridge Almanack and Directory from 1885

This began in 1885 and was published annually. The Directory from 1887 gives a list of inhabitants paying a rental of £15 per annum or upwards and from 1895 a similar list with a rental of £20 or upwards. The notes are based on a complete search from 1885 to 1901, with further checks at 1905 and 1910.

a) Henry Cooper   glass engraver, Wordsley 1886. N.B. there is a tombstone in Wordsley Parish Church for Henry Cooper of Belle Vue d. 5 November 1889 aged 82. Cf. address of Samuel Cooper.
b) Samuel Cooper   glass engraver, Wordsley 1886. The name occurs twice more, once for a glass cutters' foreman, Belle Vue, Wordsley, 1888, and once for the years 1890-1891, Belle Vue, with no occupation given.
c) Clay Brothers   glass engravers, The Platts, 1890-1901. They are recorded at Amblecote in the Stourbridge lists for 1905 and 1910.
d) William Fritsche   25 Collis St. 1902-1907. This house was pulled down to make way for the '1908 Institute' which still stands on the site. Also note entries for the Red Lion Inn, Brettell Lane — William Fritsche 1886-1887 and W. Fritsche 1888-1892. The Red Lion entries are in the Stourbridge section of the Directory; in the Wordsley section appears — Licensed Victualler, Brettell Lane, W. Fritsche 1887-1892 and W. Fritsche 1886. W. Fritsche appears for 1902-1906 at Swiss Cottage, Collis St. In 1893 the Red Lion is noted without a specific proprietor but a Sidney Scriven does occur as a Licensed Victualler in Brettell Lane.
e) E. Grice   glass decorator, 17 Church St. 1888-1905. Not in the Stourbridge lists for 1910.
f) Guest Brothers   glass engravers, Wordsley 1886-1887; glass decorators, Wordsley 1888-1892; glass engravers, Brettell Lane 1893; glass engravers and factors, 1894-1901; they are further entered for Wordsley in 1905 and 1910.

g) Thos. Guest	glass decorator, Wollaston 1887-1889; Wood St., Wollaston 1890-1891 (no occupation given); Coalbournbrook 1892 (no occupation given); glass decorator, White House glassworks, Wordsley 1893-1898.
h) J.T. Hambrey	glass cutter and decorator, George St. Wordsley 1889-1905; in 1910 'Hambrey, Glass Manufacturer, George St. Wordsley'.
i) E.H. Hands	glass engraver, Wordsley 1886.
j) John Hill	glass engraver, Dennis Park 1886-1889.
k) Jabez Hingley	glass engraver, Dennis Park 1886-1889; Vale St., Dennis Park 1890-1901 (no occupation given). In Littlebury's 1873 Directory L. and J. Hingley were given as glass engravers, Dennis Park. The Stourbridge Almanack has L. and J. Hingley glass manufacturers, King William St. 1895.
l) T. King	glass engraver, Duncombe St., Wollaston 1887-1900.
m) F.E. Kny	glass engraver, Platts glassworks 1889-1892; then Kny Bros. glass engravers, Platts glassworks 1893-1910; Fred. E. Kny Buckpool House, Wordsley 1891-1899; F.E. Kny Camp House, Wordsley 1900-1906; in the following year, after F.E. Kny's death Camp House is in the name of Mrs Kny.
n) W. Kny	27 John St. 1900-1902; 6 Brook St. 1903-1906; Bromley Lane 1907. Son of F.E. Kny.
o) F. Kretschmann	glass engraver, Duncombe St., Wollaston 1886-1892.
p) Thomas Morgan	glass engraver etc. Buckpool, Wordsley 1887.
q) W.H. Morgan	glass cutter and decorator (Wordsley list) 1888-1889; glass cutter 1890-1892 at least.
r) J. Northwood I	John and Joseph Northwood glass engravers 1886-1889, also entitled glass ornamenters and engravers. Not checked beyond 1901. Also in 1905 and 1910 when they are at Barnett St., Wordsley.
s) Frank Scheibner	glass engraver, Queen St., Wordsley 1888-1889.
t) Walter Smith	glass engraver, New St., Wordsley.
u) J. Sutton	glass engraver, Coalbournbrook 1887-1888.
v) J.W Sutton	glass engraver, Coalbournbrook, Amblecote 1902-1905. Also in 1906 and 1907.
w) Frederick Webb	glass engraver, Wordsley 1886; Alwen St., Wordsley 1887-1901. In the Wordsley list until 1907.
x) David Wood	glass engraver, Wollaston 1886-1889; a David Wood, with no occupation noted, is given for Duncombe St., Wollaston at least from 1892-1898.
y) Thomas Woodall [brother of George Woodall]	glass engraver, Wordsley 1886; New St., Wordsley 1887-1893; glass decorator New St. 1894-1901. In the Wordsley list until 1907. N.B. a music teacher of this name at 28 New St. 1910 [almost certainly the same person]. Tombstone of a Thomas Woodall at Wordsley Parish Church, d. 2 June 1926 aged 76.

Also note B. Fenn at Rectory St., Wordsley in 1890 in the Almanack. This may be the engraver. There is a tombstone to a Benjamin Fenn at Wordsley Parish Church, d. 27 January 1896 aged 41.

Appendix 7

THOMAS WEBB GLASS

The following information has been kindly supplied by Mr Stan Eveson who joined the firm of Thomas Webb in 1929 and eventually became the Works and Technical Director of the company. Since his retirement in 1978 Mr Eveson has researched the Webb archive of pattern books and brought to light a wealth of information about the products of the company in the nineteenth and twentieth centuries. I am indebted to him for generously allowing me to reproduce the fruits of his research in these pages.

*   *   *

A very detailed examination of existing records has made it possible to provide information which can be useful to collectors when estimating dates of manufacture. In particular, it will enable a collector to determine the earliest possible year for some specific articles and, in certain instances, the latest possible date. These criteria can be listed under seven headings and with explanatory remarks.

1. TRADE MARKS

Records indicate that Thomas Webb's acid etched trade marks were introduced in the 1880s but, because of the laborious process involved, were confined to a relatively few specialised items in Cameo and Burmese. It was not until 1906 that most first quality pieces of all kinds bore the Webb trade mark applied by a new process involving the use of an engraved copper plate, an acid paste and a paper transfer. In 1966 sand-blasted trade marks, which had a much more distinct outline, were introduced.

Collectors almost invariably look for a Webb trade mark underneath an article but should note that it can sometimes be found on the base of the handle of a jug or claret decanter and, in rare instances, on the cut flute where the stem of a wineglass joins the bowl.

There are no references to trade marks in the sketch books or price books. Information has been obtained from many sources but there may have been additional trade marks which are not included in the drawings shown here. The dates are open to correction if more information becomes obtainable.

c.1906 to c.1935	c.1936 to c.1949	c.1950 to JULY 1966	AUG 1966 to AUG 1980	FROM SEPTEMBER 1980
'ACID BADGED'	'ACID BADGED'	'ACID BADGED'	'SANDBLASTED'	'SANDBLASTED'
Webb	*MADE Webb IN ENGLAND*	*Webb ENGLAND*	THOS WEBB ENGLAND	THOMAS WEBB ENGLAND

2. ENGRAVERS' SIGNATURES

Carefully preserved sketch books and price books have made it possible to publish a list of 'master' engravers who are specifically mentioned. Information from other sources has been added which may also be of value to collectors fortunate enough to possess signed glassware and wishing to know more about the engravers and dates of manufacture.

Many connoisseurs are particularly interested in the signature of George Woodall. Factory records seem to indicate that articles bearing joint signatures of George and his brother Thomas can be dated between 1889 and 1899. The signature 'G. Woodall' appears to have been used from 1886 to 1891 whereas some articles in the 1891-99 period were signed 'G. Woodall' and others 'Geo. Woodall'. From the turn of the century the signature 'Geo. Woodall' appears to have been used exclusively. George Woodall was still undertaking cameo work for Thomas Webb & Sons Ltd. for several years after he retired from the factory.

Sequence in which names of engravers appear in Thomas Webb sketch books and price books

1840-55 Thomas Webb's Glass Works, The Platts

T. WOOD	First mention	1845
J. RICHARDS	" "	1845

1855-1980 Dennis Glass Works

LEWIS	" "	1862	Referred to in sketch book as 'Lewis Edinboro'. Probably John A. Lewis of 73 George Street, Edinburgh.
E. PAZALT	" "	1864	
HOCKEY	" "	1864	
T. WOOD	" "	1864	Possibly the T. Wood who engraved for Thomas Webb at the Platt Glass Works.
HANKEY	" "	1864	Possibly a mis-spelling of Hanke.
DAGNIAR	" "	1864	Probably a descendant of the Dagnia family of Italian glass makers brought to England from Altare by Sir Robert Mansell in 1630.
F.E. KNY	" "	1865	Frederick Engelbert Kny, who signed his work 'F.E.K.', was a Bohemian who came to Dennis Glass works c.1860. The last mention of Kny's name in the sketch books or the price books was in 1896.
BARNES	" "	1866	
BOIIM	" "	1866	Presumably the Bohemian engraver August Bohm, who travelled extensively in England and America.

CARTWRIGHT	"	"	1869
MILLER	"	"	1871
W. FRITSCHE	"	"	1871

William Fritsche, a Bohemian engraver, came to Dennis Glass Works in 1868 at the age of fifteen. He died in 1924.

BAAZLAR	"	"	1878
T. & G. WOODALL	"	"	1881

The brothers George (1850-1925) and Thomas (1849-1926) came to Dennis Glass Works in 1874.

F. WEBB	"	"	1881

The last mention of F. Webb's name was in 1888.

SUTTON	"	"	1884
HORNE	"	"	1887
F. KRETSCHMANN	"	"	1888
J.T. FEREDAY	"	"	1912

John Thomas Fereday (1854-1942) came to Dennis Glass Works c.1880 and retired in 1922.

J. MAY	"	"	1913
J. LLOYD	"	"	1928

J. Lloyd came to Dennis Glass Works in 1927 and was in charge of the Engraving and Intaglio Department until he left in 1929.

J. PALME	"	"	1930

Franz Joseph Palme, a Bohemian, came to Dennis Glass Works in 1882 and continued to work there as an engraver until c.1930.

G.H. POPE	"	"	1936

G.H. Pope came to Dennis Glass Works in 1929 and was head of the Engraving and Intaglio Department for over thirty years.

H.J. BOAM	"	"	1937

H.J. Boam was a descendant of the Bohemian engraver August Bohm. He signed his work H.J. Boam.

C.P. KIMBERLEY	"	"	1953

Cyril Kimberley came to Dennis Glass Works c.1930 and retired in 1978. Returned to Webb's in 1979 to engrave the rock crystal goblet illustrated in Plate 112.

The Thomas Webb sketch books and price books do not appear to contain the names of the following members of staff, who were also engravers of note:

DANIEL PEARCE	(1817-1907)	Came to Dennis Glass Works in 1884
LIONEL PEARCE	(1852-1926)	Son of Daniel Pearce, who came to Dennis Glass Works in 1884. He retired in 1920.
JAMES O'FALLON	(of Irish descent)	James O'Fallon, an expert in the carving of fruit and flowers, was Art Director at Dennis Glass Works for many years. He left the company in the early 1920s after more than forty years' service.

3. NINETEENTH CENTURY THOMAS WEBB COLOURED GLASSES

A list of dates when specific types of coloured glasses were introduced will enable collectors to avoid the error of estimating dates of manufacture which are earlier than the year of introduction.

Sequence in which various glasses were introduced into the Thomas Webb range of glassware

1840-55 Thomas Webb's Glass Works, The Platts			OLIVE GREEN	1883
			RED (SANGUIS DRACONIS — DRAGON'S BLOOD)	1884
GREEN	1840		CANARIENSIS	"
RUBY	1842		OPALESCENT PINK	"
AMBER	1844		OPALESCENT AVENTURINE	"
OPAL	"		PEACH	1885
TURQUOISE	"		GOLDEN AMBER	"
CANARY	"		FLESH COLOUR	"
BLUE	"		CARNATION	"
AMETHYST	"		PLUM	1886
PUCE	1847		BURMESE	"
CHRYSOPRASE	1848		BURMESE YELLOW	"
POMONA GREEN	1850		TRICOLORE	"
ALABASTER BLUE	1854		AZURE	"
ALABASTER WHITE	"		BURMESE WHITE	1887
			LILAC	"
1855-98 Dennis Glass Works			AURORA	"
			SYRIAN GREEN	"
OPAL	1857		BLUE BURMESE	"
POMONA GREEN	"		BURMESE LILAC	1888
RUBY	1860		LAVENDER	"
ALABASTER WHITE	"		SUGAR COLOUR	"
BLACK	1874		SALMON	"
YELLOW	1876		BROWN MOSS AGATE	"
LEMON	"		GREEN MOSS AGATE	"
PINK	1877		AMBER MOSS AGATE	"
OPALESCENT WHITE	"		POPPY RED MOSS AGATE	"
AMBER	"		OPALESCENT YELLOW	1889
BRONZE	1878		OPALESCENT RUBY	"
BLUE	1879		OPALESCENT GREEN	"
SMOKE	"		LEMON OPALESCENT	1890
CHOCOLATE	"		CONVOLVULUS	"
BROWN	1880		RUSSET GREEN	1891
PEACOCK BLUE	1881		GOLDEN RUSSET	"
CLARET	"		CHESTNUT COLOUR	1894
OPALESCENT BLUE	"		CHRYSOPRASE	"
TOPAZ	1882		PURPLE	"
ROSE	"		BERYLINE	"
IVORY	"		AZURINE	1895
POPPY RED	"		SUNRISE	"
SILVER (PHEASANT)	1883		EAU DE NIL	1896
AMHERST	"		CARMINE	"
GOLD (PHEASANT)	"		ORIENTAL	1897
BLUE (PHEASANT)	"		AQUAMARINE	1898

Recipes for colour batches for melting in covered pots.

	Opaque blue		Alabaster		Chrysoprase		Lemon	
	lb	oz	lb	oz	lb	oz	lb	oz
Sand	120		120		120		120	
Potash	56		56		56		56	
Red lead	8		8		8		8	
Limespar	3		3		3		3	
Plaster of Paris	2	8	2	8	2	8	2	8
Barytes	3		3		3		3	
Black copper oxide	1				5			
Uranium oxide					2		2	8

	Turquoise		Lemon		Opal		Ivory		Yellow Ivory	
	lb	oz	lb	oz	lb	oz	lb	oz	lb	oz
Sand	125		125		120		125		22	
Potash	40		40		40		40		7	
Red lead	100		100		200		100		17	8
Uranium oxide				7½			1	4		10
Arsenious oxide	2		3	4	5		5	4		8
Bone dust	20		20		20		10		1	12
Brass pin dust	2	8					1			
Saltpetre	5		5		5		10		1	12
Manganese dioxide								8		2½

	Tricolour		Carmine		Convolvulus		Oriental	
	lb	oz	lb	oz	lb	oz	lb	oz
Sand	37	8	37	8	37	8	37	8
Litharge	44		44		44		44	
Potash	12	8	12	8	12	8	12	8
Sodium nitrate	2	8	2	8	2	8	2	8
Bone dust	1	8	1	8	1	8	1	8
Manganese dioxide		5		1½		6		3
Regulus antimony		5		10		6		5
White antimony oxide		5		10		6		5
White tin oxide		5		10		6		5
Uranium oxide		5		8				14
Ground slate		4						5
	Pennyweights		Pennyweights		Pennyweights		Pennyweights	
Gold dissolved in nitric acid	5		2		3½		4½	
			Grains		Grains		Grains	
Selenium			1		2		2	

	Rich golden amber		Royal purple		Black		Old bronzing green		Ordinary blue	
	lb	oz	lb	oz	lb	oz	lb	oz	lb	oz
Lead crystal batch	50		50		224		100		112	
Ironstone	2			1	7		2			
Uranium oxide	1	8								
Cobalt oxide				⅛		6				
Manganese dioxide		8		8		16	1			
Bone dust						12				
Brass pin dust								2		1

	Casing blue		Dark casing green		Casing purple		Olive green		Amber	
	lb	oz	lb	oz	lb	oz	lb	oz	lb	oz
Lead crystal batch	150		150		150		112		28	
Lead crystal cullet									28	
Cobalt oxide		1								
Black copper oxide				4						
Red oxide of iron				8						
Uranium oxide				8						
Manganese dioxide						12	1			8
Arsenious oxide						8				6
Ironstone							4		5	
Brass pin dust							1			

	Purple		Chrysoprase green		Lemonescent		Eau de Nil	
	lb	oz	lb	oz	lb	oz	lb	oz
Lead crystal batch	112		112		112		112	
Cobalt oxide		½						
Manganese dioxide	1	8						
Ironstone		8						
Uranium oxide			3	4	3¼		5	
Arsenious oxide			2	12	2	12		
Brass pin dust				4			1¼	

	Aqua marine green		Emerald green		Lavender		Rich topaz		Light blue	
	lb	oz	lb	oz	lb	oz	lb	oz	lb	oz
Lead crystal batch	112		112		100		112		80	
Uranium oxide		1½		6				3		
Brass pin dust		1½		3						
Ironstone				6		2				
Manganese dioxide						8		4		
Cobalt oxide						¼				1½

431

	Burmese	Burmese opalescent green	Lemon	Opal for coating on brown	Russet
	lb oz	lb oz	lb oz	lb oz	lb oz
Sand	500	37 8	125	125	19
Litharge	140	10 8			
Potash	130	9 12	40	40	
Fluorspar	73				
Felspar	70				
Soda ash	35	2 12			
Sodium nitrate	30	2 4			
Uranium oxide	8	6	7 ½		4 ½
Ironstone	3				
Brass pin dust		7 ½			
Red lead			100	100	21
Saltpetre			5	5	7
Arsenious oxide			3 4	5	
Bone dust			20	15	
Silver chloride					½
Manganese dioxide					2 ½
Regulus antimony					12
Ground slate					3
White tin oxide					5
	Pennyweights				Pennyweights
Gold dissolved in nitric acid	7 ½				¾

4. OPTICAL SURFACE EFFECTS

Many such effects have been applied to 'Thomas Webb' hand-made glassware by the use of iron or brass 'pattern' (dip) moulds into which hot glass was blown or dipped prior to fashioning the shape of an article. Rough thumb-nail sketches of these effects, when applied, for example, in the making of tumblers, show the varied and extensive range of patterns, but it should be noted that such patterns can become very distorted when applied to a great variety of shapes. Dates of introduction of the moulds into production will prevent collectors from ascribing too early a date of manufacture to the relevant glassware.

SEQUENCE IN WHICH VARIOUS MOULDS WERE INTRODUCED INTO THE THOMAS WEBB RANGE OF GLASSWARE				
1840-1855 (THOMAS WEBB'S GLASS WORKS, THE PLATTS)				
PILLAR (6,8, 10 & 12) (sometimes round twisted)	RIB (8 & 12) (sometimes round twisted)	FESTOON (6 Round)	DIAMOND	LARGE DIAMOND
1843	1844	1844	1847	1850

THOMAS WEBBS	1855-1980 (DENNIS GLASS WORKS)			
PEARL 1879	**HONEYCOMB** 1886	**WATER WAVE** 1886	**ARABESQUE** Also called Scale 1886	**SQUARE** 1889
TWISTED RIB (HAND TWISTED DURING BLOWING PROCESS) (ALSO MADE UNTWISTED WITH 16 VERTICAL RIBS) 1890	**FOUR FEET** 1893	**GOTHIC** 1896	**CASCADE** 1900	**FIRCONE** 1903
BALL MOULD OR 'OLD ENGLISH' 1903	DOUBLE HAND TWISTED PILLAR 1904	**PINEAPPLE** 1905	**LATTICE** 1905	**MIRROR** 1905
CELLINI 1906·	**MOIRE** 1907	**WAVE** 1908	**RIBBONETTE** 1910	**SHELL** 1911
CORDUROY 1911	**SPIRAL** 1913	**LILY** 1930	**TULIP** 1930	**PEA** 1933

5. THOMAS WEBB 'BURMESE' GLASS

Much has been written about this very attractive opaque glass which contains Uranium and Gold and which was greatly enhanced when painted (and sometimes gilded) by the renowned Jules Barbe and his assistants. Close examination of the Barbe record books has now made it possible to provide additional information in the form of a list of design descriptions, together with relevant dates of introduction.

Sequence of floral decorations painted on 'Burmese' glassware

Jules Barbe Pattern No.	Type of Decoration	Date of Introduction	Jules Barbe Pattern No.	Type of Decoration	Date of Introduction
2363	Hawthorn	1886	2486	Ivy and Berries	"
2465	Ivy	"	2575	Chrysanthemum	1887
2475	Virginia Creeper	1886	2576	Japanese Berries	"

433

Jules Barbe Pattern No.	Type of Decoration	Date of Introduction	Jules Barbe Pattern No.	Type of Decoration	Date of Introduction
2618	Heather	1887	3115	Fuschia	"
2649	Clematis	"	3123	Periwinkle	"
2654	Nasturtium	"	3141	Mistletoe	"
2681	Pansy and Violet	"	3142	Holly	1887
2735	Dog Rose	"	3170	Maidenhair Fern	"
2736	Convolvulus	"	3171	Blackberry	"
2787	Japanese Creeper	"	3211	Forget-me-not	"
2821	Bramble	"	3215	Oak (on Lilac Burmese)	1887
2830	Honeysuckle	"	3229	Grasses (" " ")	1888
2832½	Barberry	"	3244	Forget-me-not (" " ")	"
2853	Daisies	"	3253	Barberry (" " ")	"
3099	Passion Flower	"	3264	Clematis (" " ")	"
3104	Holly and Mistletoe	"	3314	Fir (" " ")	"
3105	Iris	"			

6. PATTERN/DESIGN NUMBERS

Some collectors have obtained information relating to the actual pattern or design number of a particular nineteenth century article and for such fortunate connoisseurs a list showing the relationship between pattern/design numbers and dates of introduction will be of assistance. The list excludes special numbers allocated to Woodall and Barbe ware and also to articles with silver or E.P.N.S. mounts.

	Year		Year
1- 369	1840	7100- 7394	1866
370- 749	1841	7395- 7689	1867
750- 1129	1842	7690- 7984	1868
1130- 1499	1843	7985- 8279	1869
1500- 1879	1844	8280- 8574	1870
1880- 2249	1845	8575- 8869	1871
2250- 2629	1846	8870- 9164	1872
2630- 2999	1847	9165- 9459	1873
3000- 3629	1848	9640- 9754	1874
3630- 3749	1849	9755-10054	1875
3750- 4099	1850	10055-10349	1876
4100- 4249	1851	10350-10749	1877
4250- 4499	1852	10750-11299	1878
4500- 4619	1853	11300-12032	1879
4620- 4799	1854	12033-12765	1880
4800- 4999	1855	12766-13499	1881
5000- 5199	1856	13500-13934	1882
5200- 5399	1857	13935-14412	1883
5400- 5599	1858	14413-14943	1884
5600- 5749	1859	14944-15424	1885
5750- 5999	1860	15425-15849	1886
6000- 6219	1861	15850-16599	1887
6220- 6439	1862	16600-17196	1888
6440- 6659	1863	17197-17929	1889
6660- 6879	1864	17930-18635	1890
6880- 7099	1865	18636-19413	1891

	Year		Year
19414-19944	1892	26120-26920	1902
19945-20000		26921-27584	1903
A1- A809	1893	27585-28386	1904
A810-A1000		28387-29340	1905
B1- B486	1894	29341-30179	1906
B487-B1150		30180-31176	1907
22000-22064	1895	31177-32102	1908
(Numbers 20001 to 21999 inclusive were not used)		32103-33059	1909
22065-22697	1896	33060-33929	1910
22698-23720	1897	33930-34629	1911
23721-24355	1898	34630-35309	1912
24356-24861	1899	35310-36219	1913
24862-25534	1900	36220-36993	1914
25535-26119	1901		

7. INTERESTING EXAMPLES OF GLASSWARE IN THOMAS WEBB RECORDS

It seems natural, when one has the privilege of examining the sketch/price books, that certain items have a particular appeal and thumb-nail drawings are made for future reference. Here (excluding Cameo and Burmese etc.) are a number of such items which were of general interest.

INTERESTING EXAMPLES OF GLASSWARE RECORDED IN THOMAS WEBB SKETCH BOOKS				
Vase with 'Raspberry Prunts.' Design No. 5544 1858	Threaded Wine Service Design No. 9535 1874	Vase with Air Bubbles in base (i.e. 'blebbed' Base) Design No. 9839 1875	Glass Slipper. Design No. 10050 1876	Coloured Vase with white festoons. Design No. 10078 1876
Vase with Lizard. Design No. 11895 1879	Vase with applied leaves and flowers. Design No. 13964 1883	Vase with elephant heads. Design No. 14514 1884	Jug with Warrior handle. Design No. 14581 1884	Vase covered with frills. Design No. 15075 1885
Tankard with 'Claw' handle. Design No. 16881 1888	'Melon' Decanter. Design No. A200 1893	Posy 'rings' (Straight and curved). Design No. A234 1893	Decanter with 'Pinched Strips'. Design No. B18 1894	Sweet dish mounted on elephant. Design No. 2576C 1901

435

'Open Trellis' Vase with coloured lining. Design No 25929 1901	Vase with twisted 'teardrops'. Design No. 26113 1901	Vase with inverted 'teardrops'. Design No. 26757 1902	'Rustic' flower holder. Design No. 27351 1903	Posy bowl with 'Cats Eyes' teardrops. Design No. 27414 1903
'Swan Lake'. Design No. ◊ 271 1903	'Notched' or 'Jewelled' Vase. Design No. 28161. 1904	Bowl with twisted (coloured) 'ribs'. Design No. 29843 1906	Vase with three coloured teardrops. Design No. 30736 1907	Wine service with cut square feet. Design No. 31231 1908
Vase with hexagonal top. Design No. 34644½ 1912	'Flower Stand' with metal fittings. Design No. ◊ 1683 1912	Large 'Trumpet' vase. Design No 1604A 1912	Centre Vase with prunts and 'pinched strips' Design No 37920 1916	Threaded Centre Vase with 'strips'. Design No. 37922 1916

In November 1990 glassmaking at Thomas Webb stopped following the bankruptcy of the Coloroll group who had acquired Webb and Edinburgh Crystal a few years earlier. The receivers of Coloroll Tableware Ltd had attempted for many months, without success, to find a buyer for the works. On Thursday 24 January 1991 the remaining glassmaking furnaces, equipment, polishing plant, tools and pots were sold, bringing an end to 150 years of glassmaking.

Appendix 8

DOCUMENTS RELATING TO JOHN NORTHWOOD I (1836-1902)

MARRIAGE OF JOHN NORTHWOOD I

Marriage Register at Snow Hill Church, Wolverhampton.
John Northwood married at Snow Hill Congregational Church 5 February 1859 to Elizabeth Duggan. Both were twenty-three years old. He was described as Glass Ornamenter of Wordsley; she lived in Goss Street, Wolverhampton. The fathers were Frederick Northwood and Samuel Duggan.

DEATH OF MR. JOHN NORTHWOOD

No one in this district who is at all interested in art, and in the application of art to the beautifying of our local manufactures; no one associated with the glass trade, which has for long been the pride of Stourbridge and neighbourhood, and no one who, apart from these things, had the slightest acquaintance with the late Mr. John Northwood, of Wall Heath, will fail to share with us the sense of regret and loss with which we pen this brief tribute to his memory. Mr. Northwood has been for so many years honourably associated with our interesting and beautiful industry that he has become the 'grand old man' of the glass trade; and the traditions of his achievements in the industry, superadded to his striking figure and attractive personality, unite to make the gap left by his removal keenly and deeply felt. Not only 'in his own country' is Mr. Northwood honoured, but the fame of his work has spread far and wide. As a clever workman, as a resourceful artist, as a successful copyist of great masterpieces and a creator of new and charming works of art, his name will be handed down to future generations. Born at Wordsley, in the heart of the glassmaking district, some sixty-five years ago, he, in common with most boys at that period, commenced work at an early age. His first employment was at the works of Mr. Benjamin Richardson, Glasshouse Bridge, where he learnt the etching and enamelling processes. He soon gave evidence of a taste for art which prophesied his future successes, and, as opportunity afforded, he attended the Stourbridge School of Art, and became a student in that delightful branch of education in which he was after to become a master. Aided by his art studies, he attained to a proficiency in his trade which encouraged him in after years to enter into partnership in the glass decorating business with his brother, Mr. Joseph Northwood, now of Wolverhampton. The brothers erected a works at Barnett Street, Wordsley, and for many years the business was successfully carried on. Mr. Northwood had now opportunities for exercising his inventive genius, and he initiated many improvements in the art of glass decoration, such as etching by machinery, and the application of white acid. But the achievement which has brought him lasting fame was his introduction of the famous cameo ware. The first completed specimen of this was a flint vase, which has been presented by Sir Benjamin Stone to the Birmingham Art Gallery. Other and more famous works of a similar class are the matchless copy of the Portland or Barberini Vase, from the original in the British Museum; the Milton Vase, and the Dennis Vase. We regret that space will not allow us to enter into detailed description of these beautiful works; but many of our readers had the privilege of a personal inspection of the two first-named when some six years ago they were loaned by their owner, Mr. Philip Pargeter, for exhibition in the Town Hall, Brierley Hill. The third was made for Messrs. Thomas Webb and Sons, Dennis Glass Works and now forms a conspicuous feature in an American collection. Nearly 21 years ago, Mr. Northwood became associated with the works of Messrs. Stevens and Williams, glass manufacturers, Brierley Hill, as manager. Up to this time his art knowledge had been applied almost exclusively to the decoration of glass; he now found exercise for it in all the departments, and the result of his efforts was a great elevation in the style of the goods produced at these important works. With the collaboration of Mr. J. Silvers Williams, the present chief of the firm, many new methods of manufacture and decoration have been introduced. The association of Mr. Northwood with the employees has always been of the most pleasant, and his some-what sudden death has shrouded the establishment in unaffected gloom.

It is about twelve months since there came a premonition of the end in failing sight, and in May of last year it was found necessary that Mr. Northwood should undergo an operation for cataract. Dr. Loyd Owen successfully operated on the eye, but the patient's general health seemed shattered, and throughout the year he was alternately better and worse. Complications weakened his formerly robust frame, and when, after attending on the works on Saturday last, he was forced to take to his bed, there was little hope of his recovery. Dr. Pearson attended him, but he gradually sank, and passed quietly away at 6.30 on Thursday morning. The body will be interred on Monday in the family vault at Wordsley Church; the procession, which will include representatives from the works, will start from The Cedars, Wall Heath, at three o'clock. In the passing of Mr. Northwood the district has lost a great and talented son, who will be mourned not only by his own family, but by a wide circle of friends.

(From the Palfrey Collection in the Worcs. Record Office; cutting possibly from the *County Express*).

THE LAST WILL AND TESTAMENT OF JOHN NORTHWOOD I

This is the last Will and Testament of me John Northwood of Wall Heath in the parish of Kingswinford in the county of Stafford Glass Manufacturer I appoint my son Harry Northwood of Indiana Pensylvania in the United States of North America Glass Manufacturer and David Campbell of Kidderminster in the County of Worcester Designer (hereinafter called my Trustees) to be the Executors and Trustees of this my will and who and the survivor of them and the Executors and

Plate 375. Photograph of Harry Northwood, the son of John and Elizabeth Northwood, taken about 1905. From the collection of Harry's granddaughter, Miss Elizabeth N. Robb of Wheeling, West Virginia.

administrators of such survivor are intended to be hereinafter included in the description of my Trustees and I direct payment by them of all my just debts Funeral Probate and Testamentary expenses and subject thereto I give and devise all my Real and personal Estate of which I shall be possessed at the time of my decease unto my wife Elizabeth Northwood for and during her life and from and after her decease I devise and bequeath all my Real Estate of every tenure and all my Personal Estate and Effects whatsoever and wheresoever not otherwise disposed of by this my Will or any Codicil hereto Unto and to the use of my Trustees their heirs executors and administrators respectively according to the nature thereof Upon the trusts and with and subject to the powers and provisions hereinafter declared and contained concerning the same (that is to say) Upon trust that my Trustees shall sell call in collect and convert into money the said Real and

Personal Estate and premises at such time or times and in such manner as they shall think fit and so that they shall have the fullest power and discretion to postpone the sale calling in or conversion of the whole or any part or parts of the said premises during such period as they shall think proper without being responsible for loss In trust for all or any my children or child (except my son John Northwood the younger of North Street Brierley Hill in the County of Stafford Glass Works Manager whom I have otherwise provided for in my lifetime) who shall be living at my decease and being a son or sons attain the age of twenty one years or die under that age leaving issue or being a Daughter or Daughters attain that age or marry and any children of mine (except as foresaid) who may have died in my lifetime (whether before or after the date of this my Will) leaving issue living at my death if more than one in equal shares as Tenants in Common and so that the share hereby expressed to be given to any such deceased Child as aforesaid shall vest in his or her representatives as part of his or her personal Estate in the same manner as the same would have done if he or she had survived me and died immediately after me having attained a vested Interest and I declare that on the distribution of my trust property the sum of One hundred pounds each already advanced by me to my four Daughters who are now married namely Amy Glaze the Wife of Albert Glaze, Eva Campbell the wife of David Campbell, Ina Attwood the Wife of Charles Attwood and Winifred Meredith the Wife of Will Meredith shall be accounted for by them and the sum of Two hundred pounds already advanced by me to my Daughter Mabel Bradley who is now married and is the Wife of John Bradley shall be accounted for by her and the sum of Three hundred pounds already advanced by me to my son Fred Northwood shall be accounted for by him And lastly I hereby revoke and make void all former or other Wills and Testamentary Writings by me at any time heretofore made and declare this only to be my last Will and Testament In Witness whereof I the said John Northwood the Testator have hereunto set my hand on the twenty fifth day of October One thousand eight hundred and ninety eight
Signed and acknowledged by the above
named John Northwood the Testator as his
last Will and Testament in the presence of

                         John Northwood
us both being present at his request and in the
presence of each other have hereunto
subscribed our names as witnesses
W.O.C. Addison Solicitor Brierley Hill
Abraham Harris Brierley Hill his clerk

On the fifteenth day of March 1902 Probate of this Will was granted at Lichfield to Harry Northwood the Son and David Campbell the Executors.

[John Northwood I left a total of £5,622.14.4; other wills of 1902 left sums in hundreds. Information supplied by Ray Notley.]

DETAILS FROM THE NORTHWOOD FAMILY TOMB, WORDSLEY CHURCHYARD

John Northwood
son of Frederick and Maria Northwood
Who Died at Wall Heath
Feby 2 1902
aged 65 years
Also of Elizabeth Northwood
His Wife
Who Died Jan 7 1908
Aged 70 years
also
Minnie Northwood
Who Died 1868 aged 3½ years
Ada and John
Who Died in Infancy
Children of John and Elizabeth Northwood
William Northwood
Died March 18 1937
aged 79 years
William Northwood
Eldest son of
Frederick and Maria Northwood
Who Died April 1 1867
aged 39 years
also
Sarah Northwood
His Wife
Who Died Sep 22 1899
aged 76 years

Frederick Northwood
Who Died Feby 13 1881
aged 75 years
also
Maria Northwood
His Wife
Who Died June 19 1864
aged 60 years
Also of their Daughters
Elizabeth who died Aug 21 1836
aged 1 year
Maria who died June 26 1848
aged 19 years
Eliza who died Oct 5 1856
aged 24 years
Mary Ann who died Oct 13 1856
aged 22 years
Joseph Northwood
son of Frederick and Maria Northwood
Who Died Nov 15 1915
aged 76 years
Interred at Bispham, Lancs.

CHILDREN OF
FREDERICK AND MARIA NORTHWOOD

	BORN	DIED
William	1828	1867
Maria	1829	1848
Eliza	1832	1856
Mary Ann	1834	1856
Elizabeth	1835	1836
John	1836	1902
Joseph	1839	1915

Plate 376. The Northwood family tomb at Holy Trinity Church, Wordsley. The inscription for John Northwood and his wife is on the left half of the tomb, which is surmounted by a stone version of the Portland vase.

EXTRACT FROM *THE POTTERY GAZETTE* **1 DECEMBER 1915**

MR. JOSEPH NORTHWOOD, who has died at Bispham, near Blackpool, was for a long period engaged in the glass and china trades. A native of Wordsley, near Stourbridge, he was trained at the glass works of his uncle, Mr. Benjamin Richardson, and at the age of 21 years he commenced business with his brother, John, as glass decorators. After a partnership of 20 years duration, deceased went into business as a glass and china merchant in Victoria St., Wolverhampton, and this he carried on for 27 years. He had resided at Bispham for about 10 years.

Appendix 9

JOSHUA HODGETTS (1857-1933)
(Notes by his grandson, Mr Stuart Rayner Gittins, compiled in February 1976)

My grandfather died on 12 May 1933 aged seventy-five years. At this time I was fourteen years old. As Mr Hodgetts had lived with my father and mother I am able to give some details of his working life in so far as they were known to me or were told to me by him.

He was born in 1857 at The Cot, Cot Lane, Kingswinford. His father, William Hodgetts, is given as a coal miner in his birth certificate. I have heard my grandfather say that the family had lived in the Kingswinford area for many hundreds of years. He told me on many occasions that he started work at the age of eight years at the Heath Glass House and when I asked him what he did, he replied 'carrying glass'.

His mother died when he was still in his infancy and his father remarried not long afterwards. This caused an absolute estrangement between father and son which was final. I have often wondered why as a young child he should have commenced work at the Heath which, in addition to a long working day, would entail a very long journey backwards and forwards. There were many other glasshouses in the near vicinity of Kingswinford and I have the feeling that there were some particular reasons, perhaps of a family nature — many long established families in those days had family ramifications. Some time afterwards his uncle, who considered that by starting work so early in life he had not been given sufficient educational opportunities, took him under his care and he was sent to relatives in Newcastle-upon-Tyne where he went to school and studied art and design.

Although I never specifically heard him say so, it would appear almost certain that he was also working in the glassworks in that area. He returned to the Midlands when he was about eighteen years old and probably about this time would have become known to John Northwood. His admiration for Northwood was unbounded and he never referred to him by any other term than as 'The Great'. Joshua was a man with a very keen sense of humour and it was a practice of his to confer a nickname on practically everyone with whom he came into frequent contact. Some were very descriptive, as I can well remember. Although a man of dignified appearance and manner, he always preserved a sense of humour and play that was quite childlike. Simple things and the observation of nature was a joy to him to his very last hours. In his old age he would sit in the garden for hours watching the birds — he loved birds.

About 1879 he married Ann Maria Whitehouse, also of Kingswinford, who came from a family of Whitesmiths and Millers, and they had eight children, seven of whom survived, one being drowned in a skating accident. Of these children two, in due course, served an apprenticeship to the glass trade, both at Moor Lane [Stevens and Williams] where their father was then working (having started there in about 1888 and continuing until 1930). The two children who entered the glass trade were very different. The elder, Rupert, although a very competent workman, never really had an affinity for the job. He would have been much more suited as a schoolmaster. I do not think he ever really enjoyed his work to any extent. He was the son who inherited his father's sense of humour. Rupert continued at Stevens and Williams until the Second World War and, after a spell at the R.A.F. Maintenance Unit at Hartlebury, resumed work at Stevens and Williams until his death in the early 1950s.

The younger son, Frederick Joshua Hodgetts, on the other hand, had tremendous enthusiasm for glass decorating and was, in my opinion, a man of no less potential than his father who himself secretly recognised this but, with the jealous temperament of the artist, was often reluctant to admit it. In addition to being an intaglio worker, Frederick Joshua was as good a glass cutter as any. Unfortunately he was born in a different age from his father. Joshua was able to produce his art for the delight of patrons of tremendous wealth in Victorian times. Frederick Joshua spent most of his working life in the post-war period in which wealthy aristocrats, like the crowned heads of Europe, had virtually ceased to exist. Really fine work was no longer wanted.

To return to Joshua. He made the acquaintance in the 1920s of George Veitch who lived at Holbeache House, Wall Heath. This again seems to point to a connection back to the Walkers who owned the Heath Glass Works as Mr Veitch was connected with the firm of Gladstone and Walker who made bricks. This firm eventually failed and caused much distress in the district. Mr Veitch was a retired banker who had spent most of his life in China and this opened up an entirely new field of art to Joshua. They would spend many (very convivial) evenings together — Mr Veitch had connections with the Dewar firm of distillers — planning the decoration of glass with Chinese motifs. A particular favourite with my grandfather was one of Chinese fighting cocks. Ancient Chinese silk prints, which Mr Veitch had collected during his lifetime in the East, were the inspiration of many of these. The large unfinished cameo vase that was acquired by the Corning Museum in New York a few years ago has this motif, as has the shield-shaped piece of cameo in the possession of the Dudley Metropolitan Collection [at Broadfield House Glass Museum].

In the year 1930 the glass industry felt the depression like all other branches of industry and there was something of a decline in the demand for intaglio. My grandfather said that there were no longer sufficient men who had the skill to do it justice as the female labour that was then a large part of the

work-force were only able to execute simple and ineffective design work. Joshua was then seventy-three but in the best of health and with his faculties quite unimpaired. The shock when he was told he must retire was heavy indeed. The Directors of Stevens and Williams Ltd., in recognition of his long and valuable service, were pleased to grant him a pension of £1 per week on condition that he did not engage in his trade to the detriment of the Company. Although it was true that this was the first instance of a pension ever having been given to a member of the production personnel, he did not consider it an adequate recognition of so many years' service and the prohibition of further work seemed to him unjust. His obligation was not, however, of long standing as shortly afterwards (about six months as I recall, and certainly not more than twelve) he received a notification that as the Company was so hard pressed they found themselves unable to continue to afford the £1 a week payment. At least he was independent again and he found that there was a terrific demand for his work from members of the aristocracy. Lord Ebbisham, a well-known City figure and former Lord Mayor of London, insisted that all his glassware should be done by Joshua Hodgetts and no one else.

Dealers in quality glassware in Birmingham also demanded as much of his work as he could produce — unfortunately, as he was reduced to working entirely on a treadle lathe, he could by no means satisfy all the orders that came his way.

The provision of blanks was another problem and he had at one time to have recourse to glass imported from Val Lambert of Belgium — this grieved him but was unavoidable. These last few years of his life probably saw Joshua Hodgetts at his most versatile as he was executing orders in accordance with the personal wishes of his clients. For a Mr Booth of Solihull, who was a leading figure in the Masonic world, he produced many pieces with Masonic symbols. It is a fair guess to say that any piece of glass bearing these symbols is his work of that last period.

So he continued until he was taken ill in May 1933 and died after a very short illness. At the time of his death the last consignment was on the water, bound to His Britannic Majesty's Chargé d'Affaires, Santa Domingo — a complete set of table glass.

E.T. REED (1821-1888)
FLINT GLASS MANUFACTURER OF NEWCASTLE UPON TYNE
SOME BIOGRAPHICAL DETAILS

Following the acquisition of the E.T. Reed saucer (Plate 323) by Broadfield House Glass Museum in 1989 and the publication of a photograph of it in the Summer 1990 issue of *The Glass Cone,* the newsletter of The Glass Association, Alan Leach, the organiser of the North East branch of The Glass Association, began to research into the history of this hitherto unknown factory. With his kind permission it is possible to reprint his findings which reveal the amount of information that the discovery of a single glass can unearth.

* * *

James Reed, the father of E.T. Reed, came to Newcastle from Ovingham, about ten miles up the River Tyne, shortly before 1820. Here he met Elizabeth Taylor, daughter of William Taylor, a whitesmith, and married her on 31 May 1820. Edward Taylor Reed, their first child, was born in Newcastle in 1821, and baptised at St Andrew's Parish Church on 29 April.

A second child, William Leech Reed, was baptised in December 1822; the middle name was James' mother's maiden name. Tragically, Elizabeth lost two further children in childbirth, before she herself died on 14 November 1828, aged only thirty. She was buried in the plot her parents had reserved for themselves in the grounds of St Andrew's Church in Newcastle. Both of her parents died within a few years of her.

Edward was apprenticed to his father, who in 1827 was in partnership as a flour dealer with a Mr Mason, with premises in King Street. By 1838 James was on his own, now in Newgate Street. He was a flour and provision dealer (both wholesale and retail), with other premises in Dog Bank.

It is in Newgate Street that the 1841 Census finds the family, but by 1844 James had moved to Chimney Mills on Claremont Terrace. (This mill, built in 1782 to a design by John Smeaton, was a five-wand mill, and still stands. Its windshaft and cap were removed in 1951 and it is now a suite of offices.) He was still there in 1851, but after that we hear no more of James.

Edward, however, remained in Newgate Street, where in 1844 he was a glass dealer. This seems to have been a very brief initial flirtation with glass for the next year he married Faithfull Bone, from Berwick, and in 1847 was living with her parents in Brandling Place.

Edward was a 'merchant' on the marriage certificate, while his father was a 'miller' and his father-in-law, John Bone, was a 'cartman'. In 1847 Edward was both a floor cloth manufacturer and a flour merchant. In 1850 he is recorded as a corn and flour dealer and miller, with his business premises still in Newgate Street. Here he remained in business, though by 1851 he had moved house to the Five-Wand Mill (also known as 'Gibbon's Mill') in Gateshead. This was one of several mills on Windmill Hill and was located immediately opposite the Borough Arms, a pub which still stands. The only five-wand mill in Gateshead, it was fine and well-founded, and also worked by steam when the wind failed. Edward was still there in June 1859, according to the Election Poll books for that year, but by the time the mill burned down in September 1859 he had moved back to Newcastle.

He was now at 33 Forth Banks — indeed *Kelly's Directory* records him there in 1858 — near the Northumberland Glass Company's works. He continued as a miller with premises in Newcastle, in Bigg Market and Newgate Street, and in Gateshead High Street. His brother, William Leech Reed, worked from here as a cart proprietor, probably organising the transport of Edward's flour to its various locations. It is interesting to note that the Wright Brothers, who by 1847 had set up a flint glasshouse at nearby Regent Street, were living in Forth Banks. Edward would have known William Wright, the leading partner, well. Later the address became 13 Forth Street and the works were known as the Newcastle Glass Works. Nevertheless Edward remained a flour dealer through most of the sixties, living in Forth Banks, with business premises first in nearby Skinnerburn, then at Stockbridge.

On William Wright's death in 1867, Edward took over his flint glass works, though without abandoning his flour business. The 1871 Census finds him in Forth Banks described as a Flint Glass Manufacturer, employing forty men, thirty-two boys and twelve women. William Wright had taken out three patents in 1856-7, one of which was for moulding articles such as jugs in two pieces. Obviously he was capable of producing some pressed ware, though neither he nor Edward, during his ownership, ever advertised the fact. In 1873 the Forth Street works changed hands again. It went briefly to the partnership of Heppell, Garbutt & Co., but by 1875 W.H. Heppell was in full control. In the eighties Heppell was to produce some of the finest machine pressed glass to come out of the North East. No doubt this was due to his family's business which involved making moulds for the pressed glass industry.

Edward Reed now moved to premises in Forth Banks and seems to have relinquished his interests in flour dealing at the same time. He may well have been using the Northumberland Glass Company's factory, with his adjacent building providing storage. Three times during the seventies Edward tried to have plans passed to convert premises adjacent to the Northumberland site to warehousing. Finally passed in May 1878, these elaborate plans are still held in the Tyne and Wear Archives and show a capacious four-storey building with a fine frontage. It was clearly intended only as a warehouse for there was no manufacturing area. It is not clear whether it was ever built, however, for the 1896 map does not show a building which reflects the proposed plans. Perhaps he could not afford it due to the economic depression at the time.

When he moved the business to Forth Street, Edward began moving house to better and better properties. First he went to Rye Hill, then Park Road, and finally, by 1879, to Leazes Terrace. This fine block of houses, built by the architect Thomas Oliver, still stands, near Leazes Park and St James's Park, the latter now the home of Newcastle United Football Club. Edward lived at No. 24, one of four houses on the north face of the block. It is interesting to note that next door to him, at No. 23, in 1881, was living James Augustus Jobling. He was listed as an oil and grease merchant but actually had many irons in the fire. During the early 1880s Jobling was supplying the Sunderland pressed glass firm of Henry Greener with glass-making chemicals. He then took over the firm, being its main creditor, in 1885. It is quite likely that he was dealing with Edward too. The 1881 Census has Edward here, though he is described as having 'no occupation'. However, directories tell us that he was still in business. He was a glass manufacturer until 1884. During the eighties many glass businesses folded (as Greener's would have done without Jobling), due to

a combination of labour troubles and cheap imports.

From 1881 Edward was additionally described as a mineral merchant — perhaps another link-up with Jobling. He could probably see the economic writing on the wall and was diversifying out of the glass business. His premises were still in Forth Banks. He also seems to be listed as a beer retailer at 99 Westgate Road, although this is probably his brother William's son, who was named after him. Edward T. Reed seems to have retired from business altogether by 1887, when *Bulmer's Directory* finds him in Darn Crook, adjacent to St Andrew's Church, where he was baptised. He died in the following year, while living at Elswick Row, and was buried on 19 May 1888 in Jesmond Old Cemetery, in unconsecrated ground, in an unmarked grave.

We know of only one piece of glass bearing the name of E.T. Reed, the small plate in Broadfield House Glass Museum. It is crisply pressed with the words 'E.T. REED GLASS WORKS' stamped on the underside. Nine bees, in high relief, buzz around the rim. We cannot be sure that the plate was produced at Reed's works, though we know it could have been. Equally, it may have been produced for Edward, to help promote his business, by W.H. Heppell; alternatively, William Heppell may have had the mould made for Edward to use. The symbols on the plate appear to have no reasoning behind them. The works was never called the Crown Works, as suggested by the rebus of the crown within the shield, and even Edward's other business, of flour milling, did not involve bees. They may have been intended merely to symbolise Industry, with the crown representing Empire.

We have nothing else which bears E.T. Reed's name, but I have in my collection a pressed glass lemon squeezer, of unremarkable design, but which has written around the rim, in upper case letters similar to those used on the plate:-

W. HANDYSIDES NEWCASTLE
FOR FRUIT AND FLOWERS

In 1858 William Handyside took over a business his father had started in 1849, and by 1877, according to a contemporary advertisement, had an extensive business. Being in the grocery trade, Edward will have known him, so it may have been he who made that most appropriate advertising 'free gift'. But the plate is certainly unique. And it has been useful too, for without that picture in *The Glass Cone* I would never have been prompted to find out about a small, but obviously significant, flint glass works in my home town. It has been a pleasure rescuing Edward Taylor Reed from undeserved oblivion.

Alan Leach.

Since Alan Leach wrote this article about E.T. Reed, another glass collector and member of The Glass Association, J.D. Edgley, has identified a similar saucer in his collection, with an identical border and central crown but with the words 'BATTY & CO./TRADE MARK/PAVEMENT FINSBURY'. Batty and Co. were pickle and sauce manufacturers of 123 Finsbury Pavement who registered several designs between 1884 and 1907. All of the designs were for bottles and as yet there is no indication of the actual glass manufacturer. Unfortunately, for the time being, the appearance of this second saucer does little to identify the likely maker. However, the date of the Batty saucer can be fixed to 1874 or later since trade marks did not arise until the 1874 Act. If E.T. Reed made it, it would have been in his second factory in Forth Street. Another possible source for the saucer could be W.H. Heppell.

Of the three patents taken out by William Wright, referred to by Alan Leach, two are related directly to glassmaking and are recorded in the Patent Abridgements. The first was for a Provisional Patent on 14 June 1856 for 'Moulding bottles &c. — Decanters, cruets, water jugs, cream jugs, &c. are moulded by a plunger which forms the body and neck, the former being open at the bottom. The bottom of the vessel is moulded in a separate piece, and is united to the body while both parts are still pliable.' His patent of 9 June 1857 was for an annealing mechanism which consisted of two tiers of cast iron annealing trays which rotated almost like the tracks of an army tank. The top tier carried the articles; once they were removed the tray moved on to the bottom tier and was carried by the mechanism back to the opening of the annealing tunnel to be refilled with newly made glass. The patent did away with the need to carry the annealing trays back to the entrance of the lehr by hand.

Appendix 11

DESIGN REGISTRATION MARKS

From 1842 manufacturers were able to register their designs at the Patent Office Design Registry. Until 1883 they could mark their objects with a diamond registration mark which contained a code in letters and numbers for the day, month, year and parcel number of the date of registration. Glass objects were registered under Class III. After 1883 a system of registered numbers was used.

The diamond registration mark and the registered number appear mainly on pressed glass as it was simple enough to cut the mark into the mould. However, blown glass was also sometimes marked, either by engraving or by transfer print.

By deciphering the code on the diamond mark, or using the registered number, it is possible to identify the manufacturer from the official records held by the Public Record Office. A complete copy of the written records relating to glass designs up to 1908 has been printed in *The Identification of English Pressed Glass 1842-1908* by Jenny Thompson. Anyone wishing to refer to the illustrations and drawings that were submitted as part of the copyright registration must still visit the Public Record Office.

1. 1842-1867

Years		Months	
1842 — X	1855 — E	January	— C
1843 — H	1856 — L	February	— G
1844 — C	1857 — K	March	— W
1845 — A	1858 — B	April	— H
1846 — I	1859 — M	May	— E
1847 — F	1860 — Z	June	— M
1848 — U	1861 — R	July	— I
1849 — S	1862 — O	August	— R
1850 — V	1863 — G	September	— D
1851 — P	1864 — N	October	— B
1852 — D	1865 — W	November	— K
1853 — Y	1866 — Q	December	— A
1854 — J	1867 — T		

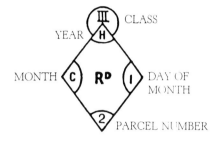

1 January 1843

'R' may be found as the month mark for 1-19 September 1857, and 'K' for December 1860.

2. 1868-1883

Years		Months	
1868 — X	1876 — V	January	— C
1869 — H	1877 — P	February	— G
1870 — C	1878 — D	March	— W
1871 — A	1879 — Y	April	— H
1872 — I	1880 — J	May	— E
1873 — F	1881 — E	June	— M
1874 — U	1882 — L	July	— I
1875 — S	1883 — K	August	— R
		September	— D
		October	— B
		November	— K
		December	— A

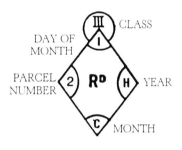

1 January 1869

For 1-6 March 1878, 'G' was used for the month and 'W' for the year.

3. Registered Numbers from 1884-1908

A new method of registration began in 1884 which used a numerical series and listed all classes irrespective of material. Details of the first registration number for glass in January of each year from 1884 to 1908 are given below.

1884 — 675	1893 — 205280	1902 — 385541
1885 — 19937	1894 — 224765	1903 — 403012
1886 — 40484	1895 — 247064	1904 — 424157
1887 — 64590	1896 — 268508	1905 — 447615
1888 — 90649	1897 — 291360	1906 — 471617
1889 — 116710	1898 — 311691	1907 — 493532
1890 — 141333	1899 — 331808	1908 — 518475
1891 — 163914	1900 — 351372	
1892 — 185803	1901 — 368272	

Appendix 12

MARKS AND SIGNATURES

Nineteenth century glass does not benefit from the abundance of marks which appear on ceramics but some of the marks which the glass collector will find are illustrated here. They are taken mainly from objects illustrated in the main text, and unless otherwise stated, are reproduced approximately actual size.

Pressed Glass Marks

1. Peacock's head crest used by Sowerby from 1875 to about 1930. From a turquoise vitro-porcelain pin tray c.1876. Height ⅜ in. (1cm).
2. Lion rampant inside a castle, used by George Davidson, Gateshead, from about 1880 to 1890. From an imitation cut tumbler in the same set as the jug in Colour Plate 45. Diameter ½ in. (1.2cm).
3. Lion holding a star, used by Henry Greener, Sunderland, 1875 to 1885. From a purple marbled cup and saucer in the Michael Parkington Collection. Height ⅜ in. (1cm).
4. Lion holding an axe, used by Henry Greener from about 1885 until 1900. From the lobed dish in Plate 314. Height ½ in. (1.2cm).
5. Initials J D either side of an anchor, and a diamond registration mark, used by John Derbyshire, Salford, from 1873 to 1876. From the piano support in the shape of a lion's foot in Plate 320. Overall height of both marks 1⅜ in. (3.5cm).

1

2

3

4

5

Richardson Marks

The five Richardson marks illustrated here are invariably found on glass which is pre-1851. The firm does not appear to have used a trade mark in the second half of the nineteenth century. In the twentieth century two marks were used, both acid etched, one which reads 'Richardson British' surrounding a Union flag, and another with the words 'Rich Cameo' on the Cameo-Fleur range of acid etched cameo vases, made in the late 1920s, which are also found with a Webb mark.

6. Transfer-printed mark on the decanter bottle decorated with the name Gin in Colour Plate 10. Width 1⅜in. (3.5cm).

7. Transfer-printed mark on a spill vase in white glass, transfer-printed with a coloured view of Castle Howard, Yorkshire. The spelling of the word 'Colors' was peculiar to the Richardson factory. Width 1in. (2.5cm). Hickman Collection.

8. A very complete transfer-printed mark including the diamond registration and the title of the subject, found on the vase with a blue background in Plate 72. The mark can be seen on the original transfer sheet in Plate 71. Width 1⅜in. (3.5cm), height 1¾in. (4.3cm).

9. The significance of the enamelled 'P' numbers found on some Richardson glasses is not apparent. In the surviving pattern books some designs are given a 'P' number in addition to their regular pattern number. This example is from the base of a white trefoil lip jug with fine gilding around the shoulder. Diameter ½in. (1.2cm). Broadfield House Collections.

10. Ornate gilt mark with the monogram FS for Felix Summerly, the name of Richard Redgrave the designer and the factory name of Richardson, from the sherry decanter in Plate 77. Width 1⅜in. (3.4cm), height 1in. (2.6cm).

6

7

8

9   10

Thomas Webb Marks

11. Etched mark on an ivory glass vase (illustrated in 11A, left) in the Broadfield House Collections. Width 1¼ in. (3cm).
11A. Two ivory glass vases by Thomas Webb and Sons, 1880s. Height 6½ in. (16.4cm) and 5¾ in. (14.6cm).
12. Etched mark on an ivory glass (illustrated in 11A, right) in the Broadfield House Collections. Diameter ¾ in. (2cm).
13. Etched mark on an ivory glass vase, with gilded and enamelled fish, in the Broadfield House Collections. Diameter ½ in. (1.3cm).

11

11A

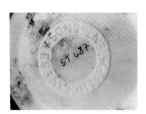

12

13

Stevens and Williams Marks

14. In this example the lettering of the circular mark and the word PATENT are etched in relief. From the chipped background cameo vase in Colour Plate 18. Width of PATENT ⅞ in. (2.1cm), diameter of mark ¾ in. (1.9cm).

15. Faint acid etched mark with the fleur-de-lis between the initials S W on a slender green alabaster vase with white alabaster foot, late 19th century, in the Broadfield House Collections. Height ⅝ in. (1.7cm).

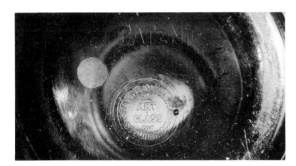

14   15

Other Nineteenth Century Glass Marks

16. Transfer-printed mark on a white vase in the Broadfield House Collections. The identical mark appears on the Bacchus vase in Colour Plate 13. Width 1¼ in. (3.2cm).

17. Red enamelled mark which is thought to represent Edward Webb of the White House Glass Works, Wordsley. On the pale cream enamelled vase in Colour Plate 41. Height ⅜ in. (1cm).

18. Black enamelled mark probably for Molineaux, Webb & Co., Manchester, on the vase in Plate 105. Scratched in diamond point is the undeciphered price code 'o/r above L(?)72/14 each'. As pieces for sale would not normally carry a price code one possible explanation of this diamond point mark is that the piece was intended as a reference example to be kept in the works. Width ¾ in. (2cm).

19. Acid etched mark 'Rd.' in a circle, found on the opalescent vase in Plate 256. Diameter ⅝ in. (1.5cm).

20. Raised letters 'E. VARNISH & CO. PATENT LONDON' on the metal plug used to seal the honeycomb moulded wineglass rinser in Plate 260. Diameter ⅞ in. (2.3cm).

21. Wheel engraved mark on the foot of both oil lamps in Plate 250. Width ½ in. (1.2cm).

16   17   21

                                        19   20

                          18

European and American Marks

22. Black enamelled mark 'Pat. 9159' on a Loetz 'Octopus' vase in the Broadfield House Collections. On some pieces the word 'Patent' is written in full. Width ⅜ in. (1cm).

23. Unidentified mark of 'W. PATENT L.', enamelled in black, on a bluish opalescent vase on three rustic feet, with applied clear glass beads over painted areas of apples and leaves, probably American, late 19th century. Broadfield House Collections. Width ⅞ in. (2.3cm).

24. An example of the black enamelled Propeller mark which is often attributed, without proof, to Thomas Webb and Sons. This version is on a two-handled oval vase in cream coloured glass enamelled with an exotic bird in a panel surrounded by flowers. The ground down rim and the style of the enamelling point to a Continental, probably Bohemian, origin. The mark has also been found on heat sensitive glass shading from pale cream to blue, with enamelled and gilded decoration, which would normally be attributed to Stourbridge. These heat sensitive pieces perhaps should be regarded as Continental. Private Collection. Height 1in. (2.5cm).

25. Tiffany mark on the metal foot of a cameo vase with added gilding and enamelling with all the characteristics of the Webb factory. This mark would appear to be the first recorded example on a metal fitting on a glass vase and is thought to be genuine. The metal fitting complements the high quality cameo carving and gilding. The mark in Plate 365 is very close in detail. Photograph courtesy Mallett's.

22

23

24

25

Signatures

26. Diamond point signature of W.J. Muckley from the goblet in Plate 83. Length ¾ in. (2cm).
27. Enamelled signature of Jules Barbe from the vase enamelled with swags of roses in Colour Plate 42. Length ⅜ in. (1cm).
28. Enamelled signature of Oscar Pierre Erard from a ruby bowl enamelled and gilded with panels of oriental figures surrounded by peonies and leaves, in the Broadfield House Collections. Length ¾ in. (2cm).
29. Wheel engraved signature of William Fritsche from the two-handled bowl in Colour Plate 15. Length ½ in. (1.2cm).
30. Carved signature of George Woodall from the plaque known as 'The Armenian Girl' in the Broadfield House Collections. Length ¾ in. (1.9cm).

26

27

28

29

30

Bibliography

Contemporary Documents

Dodds, George. *Days in the Factories,* Charles Knight & Co., London, 1843.

Jarves, Deming. *Reminiscences of Glass Making,* Eastburn's Press, Boston, 1854.

Jones, Owen. *Grammar of Ornament,* 1856 and 1865.
Examples of Chinese Ornament, S. & T. Gilbert, London, 1867.

Pellatt, Apsley. *Memoir on the Origin, Progress and Improvement of Glass Manufacture including an Account of the Patent Crystallo Ceramie,* B.J. Holdsworth, 1821.
Curiosities of Glassmaking, David Bogue, 1849.

Pugin, A.W.N., *Floriated Ornament,* 1849.

Thirteenth Report of the Commissioners of Inquiry into The Excise Establishment and into the Management and Collection of the Excise Revenue: Glass, London, 1835.

Pattern and design books of Thomas Webb and Sons (placed on loan with Dudley Library); Stevens and Williams (at Royal Brierley Crystal); Stuart and Sons (at Stuart Crystal); John Ford (at Huntly House Museum, Edinburgh); Richardsons, Boulton and Mills, Smart Brothers and Joseph Keller (at Broadfield House Glass Museum).

Archive material at Staffordshire County Record Office, Worcester County Record Office, Wakefield Libraries, Birmingham Reference Library, Dudley Reference Library and Broadfield House Glass Museum.

Periodicals

Art Union 1839-1848.

Art Journal 1849-1912.

Journal of Design and Manufactures 1849-1851.

Pottery Gazette and Glass Trades Review, 1877 to present day (now called *Tableware International*).

Nineteenth Century International Exhibition Catalogues

Great Exhibition of the Industry of All Nations, London 1851.

Dublin International Exhibition, 1853.

Universal Exhibition, Paris 1855.

International Exhibition, London, 1862.

Universal Exhibition, Paris 1867.

International Exhibition, London 1871.

Universal Exhibition, Vienna, 1873.

Universal Exhibition, Paris 1878.

Universal Exhibition, Paris 1889.

Twentieth Century Books and Articles

Anon. *The Black Country and its Industries,* Mark and Moody, Stourbridge, 1905.

Allwood, John. *The Great Exhibitions,* Studio Vista, 1977.

Amic, Yolande. *L'Opaline Française au XIXe Siècle,* Libraire Grund, Paris, 1952.

Angus-Butterworth, L.M. *British Table and Ornamental Glass,* London, 1956.

Arwas, Victor. *Glass; Art Nouveau to Art Deco,* Academy Editions, 1987.

Aslin, Elizabeth. *The Aesthetic Movement,* Ferndale Editions, 1981.

Baker, J. *Glassmaking on Wearside,* Tyne and Wear County Council, 1979.

Barnsby, G.J. *Social Conditions in the Black Country in the 19th century,* Integrated Publishing Services, Wolverhampton, 1969.

Baumgärtner, Sabine. *Porträtgläser,* F. Bruckmann, Munich, 1981.

Beard, Geoffrey. *Nineteenth Century Cameo Glass,* Newport, Mon., 1956.

'The Documentation and Variety of Stourbridge Glass', *The Glass Circle* Paper No. 135, March 1964.

Boggess, Bill and Louise. *American Brilliant Cut Glass,* Crown, 1977.

Bonython, Elizabeth. *King Cole; A Picture Portrait of Sir Henry Cole, KCB 1808-1882,* H.M.S.O., 1982.

Boydell, Mary. 'The Pugh Glasshouse in Dublin', *The Glass Circle,* Vol. 2, 1975, pp.37-48.

Bradbury, Frederick. *A History of Old Sheffield Plate,* Northend, 1983.

Briggs, Asa. *Victorian Things,* Penguin Books, 1990.

Brooks, John. *The Arthur Negus Guide to British Glass,* Hamlyn, 1981.

Glass Tumblers 1700-1900, J. Brooks, 1987.

Brown, C.M. 'The glass industry in the eighteen-thirties', *Journal of Society of Glass Technology,* Vol. 21, No. 4, August 1980, pp.184-9.

'The Changing Location of the West Midlands
    Glass Industry during the Nineteenth
    Century', *West Midland Studies,*
    Wolverhampton Polytechnic, Winter 1978,
    Vol II, pp.11-8.

Brown, Ronald. 'The Davenports and their Glass', *The Journal of The Glass Association,* Vol. 1, 1985, pp.31-40.

Buckley, Francis. 'Notes on the Glasshouses of Stourbridge 1700-1830', *Transactions,* Society of Glass Technology, 1927, 11, pp.106ff.

'The Birmingham Glass Trade 1740-1930',
    Trs., S.G.T., 1927, 11, pp.374-86.

'Glasshouses of Dudley and Worcester', *Trs.,*
    S.G.T., 1927, 11, pp.287-93.

Buckridge, Martin. 'The Early History of the Redhouse Glassworks, Wordsley, Staffordshire', *The Journal of The Glass Association,* Vol. 1, 1985, pp.17-30.

Chance, Sir Hugh. 'The Bromsgrove Glasshouses', *Transactions,* Worcestershire Archaeological Society, Vol. 36, 1954.

Charleston, Robert J. *English Glass and the glass used in England, c.400-1940,* George Allen and Unwin, 1984.

'The Glass Engraver F. Zach: 17th or 19th Century?', *Apollo,* February 1964, pp.133-6.

'Wheel-engraving and Cutting; Some Early Equipment', *Journal of Glass Studies,* 1964, VI, pp.83-100.

'Wheel-engraving and Cutting: Some Early Equipment, II, Water Power and Cutting', *Journal of Glass Studies,* 1965, VII, pp.41-54.

'A Glassmaker's Bankruptcy Sale', *The Glass Circle,* Vol. 2, pp.4-16.

'Decoration of Glass, Part 5: Acid-Etching', *The Glass Circle,* Vol. 3, pp.31-9.

'Some English Glass-Engravers: late 18th-early 19th century', *The Glass Circle,* Vol. 4, 1982, pp.4-19.

Churchill, Arthur. *History in Glass,* London, 1937.

Cottle, Simon. *Sowerby; Gateshead Glass,* Tyne and Wear Museum Service, 1986.

Crompton, Sidney. *English Glass,* London and Melbourne, 1967.

Davis, Derek. *English and Irish Antique Glass,* London, 1964.

Dodsworth, Roger. *Glass and Glassmaking,* Shire Publications, No. 83, 1982.

'The Manchester Glass Industry', *The Glass Circle,* Vol. 4, 1982, pp.64-83.

Douglas, R.W. and Frank, S. *A History of Glassmaking,* G.T. Foulis & Co., 1972.

Dunlop, Paul H. *The Jokelson Collection of Antique Cameo Incrustation,* Papier Presse, Phoenix, Arizona, 1991.

Elville, E.M. *English and Irish Cut Glass 1750-1950,* Country Life, 1953.

Paperweights and other Glass Curiosities, Country Life, 1954.

Essick, Robert and La Belle, Jenijoy (ed.). *Flaxman's Illustrations to Homer,* Dover, 1977.

Eveson, S.R. 'Reflections: Sixty Years with the Crystal Glass Industry, Part 4. Glass Technology', *The Journal of The Society of Glass Technology,* Vol. 31, No. 4, August 1990, pp.139-48.

Flavell, Ray and Smale, Claude. *Studio Glassmaking,* Van Nostrand Reinhold Co., 1974.

Frost, John. 'The Glass Carafe: 18th-19th century', *The Glass Circle,* Vol. 5, 1986, pp.86-99.

Gardner, Paul V. *The Glass of Frederick Carder,* Corning Museum of Glass, 1971.
  Frederick Carder: Portrait of a Glassmaker, Corning Museum of Glass, 1985.
Gibbs-Smith, C.H. *The Great Exhibition of 1851,* H.M.S.O., 1981.
Godfrey, Audrey and Launert, Edmund. 'A Glass Puzzle Solved: the glass cheroot holder', *Antique Collector,* July 1982, pp.61-2.
Good, Harold M. 'Georgian Glass with Cork Connections in Early Canada', *The Glass Club Bulletin,* No. 160, Winter 1989/90, pp.4-7.
Gray, Cherry and Richard. 'The Prince's Glasses: Some Warrington Cut Glass 1806-1811', *The Journal of The Glass Association,* Vol. 2, 1987, pp.11-8.
Greenslade, M.W. and Jenkins, J.G. 'A History of Amblecote & The Staffordshire Glass Industry', extracts from the *Victoria County History of Staffordshire,* reprint Staffordshire County Council for Dudley Metropolitan Borough Council, 1989.
Grover, Ray and Lee. *English Cameo Glass,* Crown, 1980.
Guttery, D.R. *From Broad Glass to Cut Crystal,* Leonard Hill, 1956.
Haden, H.J. 'The Stourbridge Glass Collection', *The Connoisseur Year Book,* 1956, pp.111-6.
  The Stourbridge Glass Industry in the 19th Century, Black Country Society, 1971.
  Notes on the Stourbridge Glass Trade, Dudley Libraries, 1977.
  'The Etymology of a Glass "Frigger"', *The Glass Cone,* No. 15, Autumn 1987.
Hajdamach, C.R. 'Glass' in *The Arts of Britain,* edited by Edwin Mullins, Phaidon, 1983.
  'Glass' in *Is It Genuine?,* edited by John Bly, Mitchell Beazley, 1986.
  'The Richardsons of Wordsley', *Ceramics,* May/June 1986.
  'English Glass, An Exciting Decade', *Antique Dealer and Collectors Guide,* June 1986.
  'A Finer Substance Than Anything', *Antique Dealer and Collectors Guide,* November 1986.
  'Two Bohemian Engravers Rediscovered', *The Journal of The Glass Association,* Vol. 2, 1987, pp.41-54.
  'Natural Elegance', *Antique Dealer and Collectors Guide,* August 1988.
  '19th Century Wineglasses', *Antique Collecting,* Vol. 23, No. 9, February 1989.
  'Threaded Glassware', *Antique Collecting,* Vol. 24, No. 9, February 1990.
Holford, Katy. *Enamelled Glass in France and England in the Period c.1850 to 1914.* Unpublished B.A. thesis 1988, North Staffordshire Polytechnic.
Hollister, Paul. 'The Glazing of the Crystal Palace', *Journal of Glass Studies,* Vol. XVI, 1974.
  Glass Paperweights of the New York Historical Society, Clarkson N. Potter, New York, 1974.
  'Muranese Millefiori Revival of the Nineteenth Century', *Journal of Glass Studies,* Vol. 25, 1983, pp.201-6.
  'Paris in the Spring, 1878', *The Glass Club Bulletin,* No. 143, Spring 1984, pp.11-14.
Hopkins, Eric. 'An Anatomy of Strikes in the Stourbridge Glass Industry 1850-1914', *Midland History,* Vol II, No.I, 1973, pp.21-31.
Ingold, Gerard. *Saint Louis from 1586 to Today,* Denoel, 1986.
Jervis, Simon. *High Victorian Design,* Boydell Press, 1983.
Jokelson, Paul. *Sulphides: The Art of Cameo Incrustations,* Nelson, 1968.
Jones, Olive R. and Smith, E. Ann. *Glass of the British Military,* Parks Canada, 1985.
Klein, Dan and Lloyd, Ward. *The History of Glass,* Orbis, 1984.
Larmour, Paul. *Celtic Ornament,* Eason and Son, 1981.
Lattimore, Colin, R. *English 19th Century Press-Moulded Glass,* Barrie and Jenkins, 1979.
Lee, Ruth Webb. 'Reproduction Glass', *American Collector,* January 1940, p.15.
  'New Arrivals in Glass', *American Collector,* March 1940, pp.15 and 20.
  'More Blown-Glass Reproductions', *American Collector,* April 1940, pp.15 and 20.
  'Thousand-Eye Reproductions', *American Collector,* May 1940, p.18.
  Victorian Glass, Lee Publications, Massachusetts, 1944.
  Nineteenth Century Art Glass, M. Barrows & Co., New York, 1952.
Locke, Joseph H. and Jane T. *Locke Art Glass; A Guide for Collectors,* Dover, 1987.
MacCarthy, Fiona. *A History of British Design 1830-1970,* George Allen and Unwin, 1979.
Manley, Cyril. *Decorative Victorian Glass,* Ward Lock, 1981.
Matcham, Jonathan and Dreiser, Peter. *The Technique of Glass Engraving,* Batsford, 1982.
Matheson, Jean. 'Henry Cole and Victorian Taste', *Antique Dealer and Collectors Guide,* April, 1983.

Matsumura, Takao. *The Labour Aristocracy Revisited: The Victorian Flint Glass Makers 1850-80,* Manchester University Press, 1983.

Mentasti, Rosa Barovier. *Il Vetro Veneziano,* Electa, Milan, 1982.

Moody, Brian. 'The Windmills: a notable family of glassmakers', *The Glass Circle,* Vol. 6, 1989, pp.46-53.

Morris, Barbara. *Victorian Table Glass and Ornaments,* Barrie and Jenkins, 1978.
'The Bathgate Bowl', *The Glass Circle,* Vol. 2, 1975 pp.17-25.
'Flaxman's illustrations to Homer as a design source for glass decoration in the 1870s', *The Burlington Magazine,* May 1987, pp.318-21.

Murray, Sheilagh. *The Peacock and the Lions: The Story of Pressed Glass of the North East of England,* Oriel Press, Stocksfield, 1982.

Newman, Harold. *An Illustrated Dictionary of Glass,* Thames and Hudson, 1977.

Norie, John. *Caddy Spoons: An Illustrated Guide,* John Murray, 1990.

Northwood, John II. *John Northwood: His Contribution to The Stourbridge Flint Glass Industry 1850-1902,* Mark and Moody, 1958.

Notley, R. *Pressed Flint Glass,* Shire Publications, No. 162, 1986.

O'Looney, Betty. *Victorian Glass,* H.M.S.O., 1972.

Parry, Stephen. *Rummers and Goblets,* Polyptoton, 1987.

Pazaurek, Gustav E. *Gläser der Empire- und Biedermeierzeit,* Von Klinkhardt & Biermann, Leipzig, 1923.

Polak, Ada. *Glass, its Makers and its Public,* Weidenfeld and Nicolson 1975.

Powell, Harry J. *Glass-Making in England,* Cambridge University Press, 1923.

Rakow, Juliette K. and Dr. Leonard S. 'The Glass Replicas of the Portland Vase', *Journal of Glass Studies,* Vol. 24, 1982, pp. 49-56.
'The Cameo Glass of Joseph Locke', *The Glass Club Bulletin,* No. 138, Fall 1982, pp.3-7.
'Franz Paul Zach, Nineteenth Century Bohemian Master Glass Engraver', *Journal of Glass Studies,* Vol. 25, 1983, pp.195-200.
'Joseph Locke and his three careers in England and America', *The Glass Circle,* Vol. 6, 1989, pp.54-67.
'Bohemian Cased Engraved Glass, English Cased Cameo Glass and Related Paperweights', unpublished article.
'Stuart and Sons' Cameo and English Rock-Crystal-Cut Glass', *Antiques,* February, 1991; pp.382-7.

Revi, Albert Christian. *Nineteenth Century Glass,* Thomas Nelson, 1967 (revised edition).

Rose, J.A.H. 'The Apsley Pellatts', *The Glass Circle,* Vol. 3, 1979, pp.4-15.

Ross, Catherine. 'The Excise Tax and Cut Glass in England and Ireland, 1800-1830', *Journal of Glass Studies,* Vol. 24, 1982, pp.57-64.
'The North of England Bottlemakers' Strike of 1882-1883', *The Journal of The Glass Association,* Vol. 1, 1985 pp.41-50.
'Death and the Glassmaker', *The Glass Cone,* No. 21, Spring 1989.

Sandilands, D.N. 'The Birth of Birmingham's Glass Industry', *Journal of the Society of Glass Technology,* Vol. V, 1931. XX, pp.227-31.
'The Last Fifty Years of the Excise Duty on Glass', *Journal of S.G.T.,* Vol. V, 1931, XXI, pp.231-245.
'The Spon Lane Works', *Journal of S.G.T.,* Vol V, 1931. XXII pp.245-51.

Shuman, John A., III. *The Collector's Encyclopaedia of American Art Glass,* Collector's Books, 1988.

Sinclaire, Estelle F. 'American Fine Glass: The Birmingham Connection', *The Glass Club Bulletin,* No. 145, Winter 1985, pp.3-7.

Slack, Raymond. *English Pressed Glass 1830-1900,* Barrie and Jenkins, 1987.

Smith, John P. *Osler's Crystal for Royalty and Rajahs,* Mallett at Bourdon House Ltd., 1991.

Spiegel, Walter. *Glas des Historismus,* Klinkhardt & Biermann, 1980.

Spillman, Jane Shadel. *Cut and Engraved Glass of Corning 1868-1940,* Corning Museum, 1977.
American and European Pressed Glass in the Corning Museum of Glass, Corning Museum, 1981.
Glass From World's Fairs, Corning Museum, 1986.

Stevens, Gerald. *Canadian Glass c.1825-1925,* Ryerson Press, Toronto, 1967.

Tait, Hugh. *The Golden Age of Venetian Glass,* Trustees of the British Museum, 1979.

Thomas, Margaret. *The Nailsea Glassworks,* H.G. and M.A. Thomas, 1987.

Thompson, Jenny. *The Identification of English Pressed Glass 1842-1908,* Jenny Thompson, 1989.

Trubridge, P.C. 'The English Ale Glasses, 1685-1830', *The Glass Circle,* Vol. 1, 1972, pp.46-57.
    'The English Ale Glasses, 1685-1830', *The Glass Circle,* Vol. 2, 1975, pp.26-36.
    'The English Ale Glasses, Group 4. Ale/Beer Glasses in the 19th century', *The Glass Circle,* Vol. 3, 1979, pp.87-96.

Vincent, Keith. *Nailsea Glass,* David and Charles, 1975.

Vose, Ruth Hurst. *Glass,* Collins, 1980.

Wakefield, Hugh. *Nineteenth Century British Glass,* Faber and Faber (second edition 1982).

Warren, Phelps. *Irish Glass,* Faber and Faber, 1970.
    'Apsley Pellatt's Table Glass, 1840-1864', *Journal of Glass Studies,* Vol. 26, 1984, pp.120-35.

Webber, Norman. *Collecting Glass,* David and Charles, 1972.

Weeden, Cyril. 'The Ricketts Family and the Phoenix Glasshouse, Bristol', *The Glass Circle,* Vol. 4, 1982, pp.84-101.

Westropp, M.S. Dudley. Irish Glass. London, 1920. Revised edition by Mary Boydell published by Allen Figgis, Dublin, 1978.

Williams-Thomas, R.S. *The Crystal Years,* Stevens and Williams 1983.

Wills, Geoffrey. *Glass,* Orbis, 1972.
    Victorian Glass, G. Bell & Sons, 1976.

Witt, Cleo, Weeden, Cyril and Schwind, Arlene Palmer. *Bristol Glass,* Redcliffe Press, 1984.

Wolfenden, Ian. 'Victorian Decanters. Part 1: The Early Victorian Period, c.1835-1865', *Antique Collecting,* Vol. 14, No. 7 , December 1979, pp.20-3.
    'Victorian Decanters. Part 2: The Later Victorian Period, c.1865-c.1900', *Antique Collecting,* Vol.14, No.8, January 1980, pp.24-7.
    'English Rock Crystal Glass, 1878-1925', *The Glass Circle,* Vol. 4, 1982, pp.20-45.
    'Victorian Stemmed Drinking Glasses', *Antique Collecting,* Vol. 20, No. 5, October 1985, pp.68-71.
    'The "W.H.R." Drawings for Cut Glass and the Origins of the Broad Flute Style of Cutting', *The Journal of the Glass Association,* Vol. 2, 1987, pp.19-28.

Woodward, H.W. *Art, Feat and Mystery—The Story of Thomas Webb and Sons, Glassmakers,* Mark and Moody, 1978.
    The Story of Edinburgh Crystal, Dema Glass, 1984.

Yates, Barbara. 'The Glassware of Percival Vickers & Co. Ltd., Jersey Street, Manchester, 1844-1914', *The Journal of The Glass Association,* Vol. 2, 1987 pp.29-40.

EXHIBITION CATALOGUES

The International Exhibition of 1862. Victoria and Albert Museum, 1962.

Bohemian Glass. Victoria and Albert Museum, 1965.

Christopher Dresser. The Fine Art Society, 3 to 27 October 1972.

Danish Glass 1814-1914: The Peter F. Heering Collection. Victoria and Albert Museum, 1974.

English Rock Crystal Glass 1878-1925. Dudley Art Gallery, 1976.

John Henning 1771-1851 '. . .a very ingenious Modeler', Paisley Museum and Art Galleries, 1977.

Christopher Dresser 1834-1904. Camden Arts Centre, London 3 October to 25 November 1979 and Dorman Museum, Middlesborough 8 December to 19 January 1980.

Cameo Glass: Masterpieces from 2000 Years of Glassmaking, Corning Museum of Glass, 1982.

The Queen's Choice, Burmese 1885-1985. New Bedford Glass Museum, Massachusetts, 17 August to 29 December 1985.

Champagne Antiques. Exhibition by Brian Beet and Jeanette Hayhurst, 3b Burlington Gardens, London, November 1985.

Truth, Beauty and Design. Victorian, Edwardian and Later Decorative Art. Fischer Fine Art, London 15 May to 27 June 1986.

In Pursuit of Beauty: Americans and the Aesthetic Movement. Published in conjunction with the exhibition 'In Pursuit of Beauty' held at the Metropolitan Museum of Art, New York, from 23 October 1986 to 11 January 1987. Metropolitan Museum of Art, 1986.

Index

Page references in bold type refer to illustrations and captions. Page references in italics refer to appendices.